TRANSITION TOWARDS SUSTAINABLE MOBILITY

T0330523

Transport and Mobility Series

Series Editors: Professor Brian Graham, Professor of Human Geography, University of Ulster, UK and Richard Knowles, Professor of Transport Geography, University of Salford, UK, on behalf of the Royal Geographical Society (with the Institute of British Geographers) Transport Geography Research Group (TGRG).

The inception of this series marks a major resurgence of geographical research into transport and mobility. Reflecting the dynamic relationships between socio-spatial behaviour and change, it acts as a forum for cutting-edge research into transport and mobility, and for innovative and decisive debates on the formulation and repercussions of transport policy making.

Also in the series

Integrating Seaports and Trade Corridors
Edited by Peter Hall, Robert J. McCalla, Claude Comtois and Brian Slack
ISBN 978 1 4094 0400 2

International Business Travel in the Global Economy
Edited by Jonathan V. Beaverstock, Ben Derudder, James Faulconbridge and Frank Witlox
ISBN 978 0 7546 7942 4

Ports in Proximity
Competition and Coordination among Adjacent Seaports
Edited by Theo Notteboom, César Ducruet and Peter de Langen
ISBN 978 0 7546 7688 1

Railways, Urban Development and Town Planning in Britain: 1948–2008
Russell Haywood
ISBN 978 0 7546 7392 7

Transit Oriented Development
Making it Happen
Edited by Carey Curtis, John L. Renne and Luca Bertolini
ISBN 978 0 7546 7315 6

Transition towards Sustainable Mobility
The Role of Instruments, Individuals and Institutions

Edited by

HARRY GEERLINGS
Erasmus University Rotterdam, The Netherlands

YORAM SHIFTAN
Israel Institute of Technology, Israel

DOMINIC STEAD
Delft University of Technology, The Netherlands

Routledge
Taylor & Francis Group

LONDON AND NEW YORK

First published 2012 by Ashgate Publishing

2 Park Square, Milton Park, Abingdon, Oxon OX14 4RN
711 Third Avenue, New York, NY 10017, USA

Routledge is an imprint of the Taylor & Francis Group, an informa business

First issued in paperback 2016

British Library Cataloguing in Publication Data
Transition towards sustainable mobility : the role of
   instruments, individuals and institutions. -- (Transport
   and mobility series)
   1. Transportation--Environmental aspects.
   2. Transportation and state. 3. Transportation--
   Technological innovations.
   I. Series II. Geerlings, H. III. Shiftan, Yoram. IV. Stead,
   Dominic.
   388-dc22

Library of Congress Cataloging-in-Publication Data
Transition towards sustainable mobility : the role of instruments, individuals and institutions / [edited] by Harry Geerlings, Yoram Shiftan and Dominic Stead.
      p. cm. -- (Transport and mobility)
   Includes bibliographical references and index.
   ISBN 978-1-4094-2469-7 (hbk.)
   1. Transportation--Environmental aspects. 2. Transportation and state--Environmental aspects. 3. Sustainable development. I. Geerlings, H.
II. Shiftan, Yoram. III. Stead, Dominic.
   HE147.65.T698 2011
   388'.049--dc23
                                                                    2011030393

ISBN 978-1-4094-2469-7 (hbk)
ISBN 978-1-138-25241-7 (pbk)

Contents

List of Figures

List of Tables

List of Boxed Text

Biographical Notes on the Contributors

Jan Anne Annema is Assistant Professor at Delft University of Technology in the Transport and Logistics Section. He teaches transport policy and transport economics, and conducts research in the field of transport policy with an emphasis on pricing and environmental policies. Until 2009 he worked at the Netherlands Institute for Transport Policy Analysis. From 1988 to 2006 he worked in the National Institute of Public Health and the Environment. Jan Anne Annema holds a PhD in Transport Policy from Delft University of Technology and a first degree in Chemistry from Utrecht University. He is a member of the research school TRAIL (TRAnsport, Infrastructure and Logistics).

Theo Arentze is Associate Professor in the Urban Planning Group of Eindhoven University of Technology. He received a PhD in Decision Support Systems for Urban Planning from Eindhoven University of Technology in 1999. His research interests include activity-based modelling, discrete choice modelling, agent-based modelling, knowledge discovery, learning-based systems and decision support systems for applications in transportation research, urban planning and consumer research. He is a member of the editorial board of several international peer-reviewed journals, the Eric Pas Award Jury, and the programme committees for several journals, conferences and research foundations in transportation, planning, geography and consumer research.

Olu Ashiru is a transport planner with over 10 years' professional experience in accessibility modelling, transportation planning, policy development and software engineering. He is a consultant at Halcrow Group Limited, a Director of Takedo International, and a part-time PhD student at the Centre for Transport Studies, Imperial College London. His PhD focuses on the development and application of advanced measures of accessibility.

Flor Avelino is Researcher and Advisor at the Dutch Research Institute for Transitions (DRIFT, Erasmus University of Rotterdam), where she has been since 2005. She completed in 2011 her PhD-thesis on the role of power and empowerment in sustainability transitions, focusing on the interface between transport and land-use planning. Flor has worked as a transition advisor for several governmental organizations, and has been actively involved in various sustainable mobility projects. She is currently setting up a new research project on transitions to sustainable communities and regions, focusing on bottom-up innovation, social movements and social entrepreneurs.

David Banister is Professor of Transport Studies at the University of Oxford and Director of the Transport Studies Unit. He is also currently Director of the Environmental Change Institute in the School of Geography and the Environment at the University of Oxford. Until 2006, he was Professor of Transport Planning at University College London.

Thomas D. Beamish studied innovation processes in the commercial construction/ real estate industry; social and organizational response to environmental change and disaster; and how and why community movements mobilize and respond as they do to risky developments. Dr. Beamish has published articles in journals such as Social Problems, Annual Review of Sociology, Research in the Sociology of Organizations, and Organizations and Environment, as well as chapters in edited volumes. He also authored the book, *Silent Spill: The Organization of an Industrial Crisis* (MIT Press), in 2002.

Luca Bertolini is Professor of Urban and Regional Planning in the Department of Geography, Planning and International Development Studies at the University of Amsterdam. His research and teaching focus on the integration of transport and land-use planning, the contribution of planning to achieving a transition to sustainable urban mobility, concepts for coping with uncertainty and complexity in planning, methods for supporting the option-generation phase of the planning process, and ways of enhancing theory-practice interaction.

Suzanne van den Bosch received her PhD degree in September 2010 at the Dutch Research Institute for Transitions (DRIFT), which forms part of the Faculty of Social Sciences of the Erasmus University Rotterdam. Suzanne has a first degree in Industrial Design Engineering from Delft University of Technology and a Master's degree in Innovation Management. She has worked as an independent advisor at SUSI Sustainable Innovation and as a consultant on Sustainable Product Innovation and Corporate Social Responsibility at BECO. Suzanne currently works as an advisor in processes of societal change at Viatore, focusing on the transition to sustainable health care.

Nanny Bressers is a Researcher in the Department of Public Administration at Erasmus University Rotterdam, where she has been appointed since 2007. In 2011 she received her PhD from this university. She has a background in international relations and the influence of NGOs. Her PhD thesis focuses on the impact of knowledge and innovation development programmes. Between 2007 and 2009 she was a member of the Transumo research project team on Transition Monitoring.

Marco te Brömmelstroet is Assistant Professor in Urban Planning at the University of Amsterdam. In March 2010, he defended his PhD thesis *Making Planning Support Systems Matter*. His teaching and research interests focus on issues of land use and transport planning, and mainly deal with the use of knowledge (provided by computer models and instruments) in integrated strategy making. He has a first degree in urban planning, a Master's degree in Environmental and Infrastructure Planning from the University of Groningen and a Master's degree in Geographical Information Management and Applications from the University of Utrecht.

Jan Brůha is a Researcher at the Kolin Institute of Technology, Czech Republic, He obtained his PhD in Econometrics at the Faculty of Statistics and Computer Science of the University of Economics in Prague (2005). His research interests include econometrics, statistics, and applications of computational and simulation methods in the social sciences.

Hana Brůhová-Foltýnová is a Researcher at the Kolin Institute Technology, Czech Republic. She obtained her PhD in Economic Policy at the Faculty of Economics and Administration of the Masaryk University in Brno (2006) and a Master's degree in Finance from the same Faculty, and in Environmental Humanities from the Faculty of Social Sciences of the Masaryk University. Her research is concerned with the economic aspects of sustainable development with an emphasis on transportation issues, particularly the economic and environmental impacts of transport regulation. She is a member of several international and national research teams working on a research and policy-orientated projects.

Caspar Chorus is Associate Professor in the Faculty of Technology, Policy and Management at Delft University of Technology. His research aims to understand mobility-related decision-making (of travellers and policymakers alike). His dissertation *Traveler Response to Information* has won a number of awards, including IATBR's Eric Pas prize. Most of Caspar's current research is centered on a four-year research project 'Regret-Based Models of Mobility' which is sponsored by the Netherlands Organization for Scientific Research in the form of a personal VENI grant. Caspar is co-Editor-in-Chief of the open-access journal *European Journal of Transport and Infrastructure Research*, and serves on TRB's Travel Survey Methods and Travel Behaviour and Values committees.

Dick Ettema is Associate Professor at Utrecht University. His current research interests include the influence of ICT and social networks on travel and activity patterns, developments in leisure travel, households' longer-term mobility decisions, and the relationship between travel behaviour and well-being. He is a member of the TRB Committee on Travel Behaviour and Values, Chair of the WCTR Special Interest Group on ICT and Travel and of the TRB Subcommittee on Time Use and Activity Patterns and Director of Education of the Netherlands Graduate School of Urban and Regional Research (NETHUR).

Harry Geerlings is Professor of Governance and Sustainable Mobility in the Department of Public Administration at Erasmus University Rotterdam. He is a member of Erasmus Smart Port Rotterdam, a new initiative between the Port community and the Erasmus University Rotterdam. Most of this research is related to the interaction between transport, environment and spatial planning. He holds a PhD in economics from the Vrije Universiteit Amsterdam. He is a staff member of the TRAIL PhD school (TRAnsport, Infrastructure and Logistics).

Teije Gorris has been working as a Consultant in the field of Mobility and Logistics at the Dutch Research Institute TNO since February 2010. Teije has a first degree in traffic and transport engineering from Breda University of Applied Sciences, and a Master's degree in urban geography from Utrecht University. More recently, he completed the postgraduate course Transition Management at Erasmus University Rotterdam. Before starting work at TNO, Teije was Programme Secretary at Transumo, the Dutch knowledge programme on sustainable mobility.

Ryken Grattet is Professor of Sociology at the University of California, Davis. His research concerns law and public policy, focusing specifically on how law is reinterpreted and remade in localized contexts. His articles have appeared in the *Law & Society Review*, the *American Sociological Review*, *American Behavioral Scientist*, *Criminology*, the *Journal of Criminal Law and Criminology*, *Social Forces*, and *Social Problems*. He is the author of *Making Hate a Crime: From Social Movement to Law Enforcement* (with Valerie Jenness, Russell Sage Foundation Press, 2001) and *Parole Violations and Revocations in California* (with Joan Petersilia and Jeffrey Lin, National Institute of Justice, 2008).

Robin Hickman is Senior Lecturer at the Bartlett School of Planning, University College London, and visiting research associate at the Transport Studies Unit, University of Oxford. He is a specialist on transport and climate change issues, and integrated transport and urban planning strategies. Prior to his current position, he was an Associate Director at Halcrow Group Limited, London.

Nicole Huijts is a Researcher in the Faculty of Technology, Policy and Management at Delft University of Technology. She has a Master's degree from Eindhoven University of Technology. After studying the public acceptance of carbon capture and storage for her Master's thesis, she began a PhD on the public acceptance of hydrogen technologies in transport. The main focus of the research is on modelling the causal factors that influence the acceptance of hydrogen refuelling stations near residential areas, with a focus on the psychological factors. Nicole Huijts is a member of the research school TRAIL (TRAnsport, Infrastructure and Logistics).

René Kemp is a Professorial Fellow at UNU-MERIT and Professor of Innovation and Sustainable Development at ICIS (International Centre for Integrated Assessment and Sustainable Development), Maastricht University. He is an expert on eco-innovation and sustainability transitions. He has held research positions at TNO, DRIFT, and the University of Twente. He is a member of the Editorial Board of the new journal *Environmental Innovation and Societal Transitions*, editor of the Springer book series *Sustainability and Innovation* (since 2004), a member of the Scientific Board of ARTEC, University of Bremen, and advisory editor of *Research Policy*.

Alissa Kendall is Assistant Professor at the University of California Davis in the Department of Civil and Environmental Engineering. She holds a joint PhD from the University of Michigan School of Natural Resources and Environment and Department of Civil and Environmental Engineering. Her main research interest is the application of life-cycle assessment methods to transportation infrastructure, transportation energy systems, and agricultural systems for food and fuel production. Her current research emphasizes the development of life-cycle assessment methods for long-lived and complex systems.

Jasper Lohuis is a Researcher at I&O Research, focusing on research into public welfare policies. Jasper has a degree in Public Administration from Technology University Twente. Before starting work at I&O Research, Lohuis was a researcher in the Department of Public Administration at Erasmus University Rotterdam and was involved in the Transumo-A15 project, dealing with transition management in the Rotterdam port area.

Jonathan London is Assistant Professor in the Department of Human and Community Development and Director of the Center for Regional Change at UC Davis. He is an educator, researcher, and community-builder with experience in participatory research, rural community development, and community-engaged planning. Jonathan holds a first degree in Environmental Studies from Brown University, a Master's in City and Regional Planning and a PhD in Environmental Science Policy and Management from University of California, Berkeley. His research is related to conflicts and collaboration in natural resource and environmental management.

Eric Molin is Associate Professor in the Faculty of Technology, Policy and Management at Delft University of Technology. He is interested in behavioural modelling in transport, mainly in the context of multi-modal transport systems and new transport technology. Eric is programme leader of a research consortium on the Synchronization of Networks that is funded by the Dutch national research council. He co-chairs the TRB subcommittee on Stated Response Methods and is a staff member of the TRAIL research school (TRAnsport, Infrastructure and Logistics). Eric received his PhD degree from Eindhoven University of Technology.

Deb Niemeier is Professor of Civil and Environmental Engineering at the University of California, Davis. Her research interests include transportation-air quality modelling, energy consumption and land use interactions, sustainability, and the project development process for major infrastructure projects. Working with an interdisciplinary research group of graduate students, post-doctoral researchers, and faculty collaborators, she has published more than 100 journal articles and book chapters. She currently serves as the Editor-in-Chief for Transportation Research Part A.

Bonno Pel is a PhD candidate in the Department of Public Administration, Erasmus University of Rotterdam. He has a background in transportation planning and socio-political philosophy. His forthcoming PhD thesis concerns innovation cycles, intersecting translation sequences and system synchronization in the Dutch traffic management field. This research into 'system innovation in the making' was part of the research programme of the 'Knowledge network on System Innovations and Transitions' (KSI).

Carolyn de la Peña is Professor of American Studies, Director of the University of California, Davis Humanities Institute and co-editor of the journal *Boom: A Journal of California*. She also chairs the system-wide network of Humanities Center Directors and co-coordinates the Multi-Campus Research Initiative 'Studies of Food and the Body' for the University of California. She is the author of two books (*The Body Electric: How Strange Machines Built The Modern American*, 2003 and *Empty Pleasures: The Story of Artificial Sweeteners from Saccharin to Splenda*, 2010), one co-edited volume *Re-Wiring the Nation: The Place of Technology in American Studies* (2007), and numerous articles on the history of our relationship with technologies and objects in the United States.

Odette van de Riet is Programme Manager at KiM Netherlands, an independent research institute within the Dutch Ministry of Infrastructure and the Environment. Between 2005 and 2008, she was Assistant Professor at Delft University of Technology, where her main topic of interest was policy analysis in multi-actor policy settings. From 1992 to 2005, Odette was Programme Manager at RAND Europe, the European office of the policy analysis institute RAND Corporation. Odette holds a PhD in policy analysis from Delft University of Technology and a first degree in Policy Sciences and Civil Engineering from Twente University.

Anaïs Rocci is a Research Manager at 6T-Bureau de recherche. She holds a PhD from the Sorbonne University Paris V-René Descartes. Her PhD, conducted at INRETS (The French National Institute for Transport and Safety Research), dealt with the limiting factors of behavioural change and the potential for change. Her current research focuses on the role of information as a factor of change, and the implementation of mobility management tools such as individualized marketing.

Yoram Shiftan is Associate Professor of Civil and Environmental Engineering and the Head of the Transportation and Geo-Information Department in the Technion, the Israeli Institute of Technology. He teaches and conducts research on travel behaviour with a focus on activity-based modelling and response to policies, the complex relationships between transport, the environment and land use, and transport economics. Yoram is the editor of *Transport Policy*, Secretary/Treasurer of the International Association of Travel Behaviour Research (IATBR), member of the TRB Committee on Travel Behaviour and Values, co-Chair of the Network on European Communications and Transport Activities Research Cluster on Environment and Policy, and member of the World Conference Transportation Research (WCTR) Scientific Committee.

Dominic Stead is Associate Professor at Delft University of Technology. Much of his research and teaching is comparative in nature and focused on issues concerning territorial governance. He has experience of a wide range of research projects related to spatial planning and transport policy, including EU-funded ESPON, INTERREG and Framework Programme projects. He has published widely in international books and journals. He is currently a member of the editorial boards of the *European Journal of Transport and Infrastructure Research* and *Planning Practice and Research*.

Yusak O. Susilo is Assistant Professor in the Department of Transport Science and the Centre for Transport Studies at KTH Royal Institute of Technology, Stockholm. He was previously senior lecturer in transport and spatial planning in the Centre of Transport and Society (CTS) at the University of the West of England, Bristol. His main research interest is in understanding the way individuals choose their daily travel patterns and the interaction of such patterns with changes in activity location, urban form, socio-demographic factors and transport policies. He received his PhD degree from the Department of Urban Management, Kyoto University, Japan.

Julie Sze is Associate Professor in American Studies at the University of California, Davis, and Founding Director of the Environmental Justice Project affiliated to the John Muir Institute of the Environment.

Harry Timmermans is Professor of Urban Planning at Eindhoven University of Technology. His main research interests concern the study of human judgement and choice processes, the mathematical modelling of urban systems, spatial interaction and choice patterns, and the development of decision support and expert systems for application in urban planning. He has published several books and many articles in journals in the fields of Marketing, Urban Planning, Architecture and Urban Design, Geography, Environmental Psychology, Transportation Research, Urban and Regional Economics, Urban Sociology, Leisure Sciences and Computer Science.

Diana Vonk Noordegraaf is a Researcher in the Faculty of Technology, Policy and Management at Delft University of Technology. She also holds a part-time position as a transport consultant at the Netherlands Organization for Applied Scientific Research (TNO). The main focus of her PhD research is on the implementation of advanced road pricing policies. Diana holds a Master's degree in Systems Engineering, Policy Analysis and Management with a specialization in transport (Delft University of Technology). She is a member of the research school TRAIL (TRAnsport, Infrastructure and Logistics).

Bert van Wee is Professor of Transport Policy and Head of the Section Transport and Logistics at Delft University of Technology, Faculty of Technology, Policy and Management. His main interests are in the long-term developments in transport, the environment, safety and accessibility, and in policy analyses. He is Editor-in-Chief of the *European Journal of Transport and Infrastructure Research* and is a member of the Editorial Board of Transport Reviews and Transport Policy. He is a staff member of the research school TRAIL (TRAnsport, Infrastructure and Logistics) and has several academic positions in the Netherlands related to research coordination, education, and advising policy makers and interest groups.

Marcus Wigan is Principal of Oxford Systematics, a consulting organization in transport and information systems policy and practice. He is Professor Emeritus at Edinburgh Napier University, a Professorial Fellow at the University of Melbourne, and Visiting Professor at Imperial College London. He has researched and published across a wide range of transport and policy areas, with a special interest in ethics, privacy and surveillance issues. He is an Emeritus Member of the Freight Transportation Data, Motorcycle, and Bicycle Transportation Committees of the TRB. Professor Wigan received his DPhil in nuclear physics from Oxford University.

Issa Zananiri is currently working in the transportation team of Netivei Ayalon, where he is developing the new Tel-Aviv metropolitan activity-based model. Issa previously worked for NTA, the company responsible for developing the Tel-Aviv light rail system. He also worked under the supervision of Professor Yoram Shiftan from the Technion, where he was involved in developing and estimating models of policy evaluation.

Preface

Transportation has many positive characteristics both for the individual user and for society as a whole. This explains why the transport sector, for several decades, has experienced unprecedented growth. At the same time, transportation has undesired side effects. The almost unlimited demand for transportation cannot be facilitated on an equal basis by the construction of new infrastructure, a situation which leads to congestion. At the same time, there are serious concerns related to emissions (at the regional, national and the global level), safety, health issues, and resource management. These concerns are encompassed in the concept of sustainability that advocates a balance between social, economic and environmental imperatives (people, profit, and planet).

Governments and other stakeholders are generally aware that policy measures are needed to find a balance between accessibility and sustainability. This is an enormous challenge, and the question arises: how can this be materialised? The challenge is often presented as the need for a *sustainable transport system.* Evolving within the framework of policy making is a new approach called *transition management.* Transition management is an innovative approach to overcome barriers and can be considered as a management strategy to help public decision makers and private actors deal with questions regarding *how* and *to what extent* complex societal transformation processes can be guided in a certain desirable direction, in this case a more sustainable transport system.

This book presents a selection of chapters on the theme of transition management and sustainable mobility. Many of the contributions were first presented at a workshop held at Erasmus University in Rotterdam in May 2008 and brought together about 40 scholars, from various disciplines and countries, each with an interest in sustainable mobility. The aim of the workshop was to discuss the relationships between policy instruments, individual behaviour, institutional practices and the transitions toward sustainable mobility. The event was generously supported by funds from the Network on European Communications and Transport Activity Research (NECTAR), the Transumo A15 project (described in more detail by Bressers et al. in Chapter 6) and the Erasmus University Rotterdam.

While there is a rich literature on sustainable mobility, there are few specific works that deal with the *transition process* that is required to achieve a more sustainable transport system. This is the niche that this book seeks to fill. Reflecting the dynamic relationships between socio-technical behaviour and change, it is a timely contribution to a highly relevant topic with important implications for transport policy-making. This volume focuses on making transitions happen, looking at the various aspects and factors that are involved in this process.

We hope the book will be of benefit to researchers, practitioners (from the public and private sectors) and students engaged in transport and environment research and practice, and that it will help to meet the challenge of achieving the transition to a more sustainable transport sector.

Harry Geerlings, Yoram Shiftan and Dominic Stead,
Rotterdam, Tel Aviv and Delft

Chapter 1

The Complex Challenge of Transitions Towards Sustainable Mobility – An Introduction

Harry Geerlings, Yoram Shiftan and Dominic Stead

Introduction

In many research studies and publications on transport, the need to achieve a more sustainable transport system is frequently highlighted. This is not an easy task, not least because society has been confronted with a huge growth in transport demand over many decades, which has led to faster and longer distance travel, the dominance of the car, and many unexpected and undesired side effects. This situation is apparent in most parts of the world.

Sustainable mobility requires an alternative approach that leads to a rethinking of the present situation and meets the urgent need to make a transition to this desired state. Transition management is the process that tries to address this challenge. It requires clear and innovative thinking about the role transport can (and should) play in modern societies, which is addressed in this first chapter. Three main issues are discussed. First, attention is given to the meaning of transportation and the functions it performs. Its unprecedented growth is explained from a historic perspective. Second, the concept of sustainability and sustainable transport is discussed. Third, the complexity of governance in relation to transitions and transition management is considered.

The Meaning of Transportation in Modern Societies

Mobility is one of the most fundamental and important characteristics of modern societies, as it satisfies the basic need of going from one location to another. Mobility fulfils this need for passengers, goods, and information. The transport sector can be considered as an important economic sector and an important component of people's welfare. In many developed countries, transportation accounts for between 6 and 12 per cent of GDP.

The history and development of the transport sector is strongly linked with innovation. The first means of transport were walking and swimming, but the domestication of animals then made it possible to haul heavier loads, and to travel at a higher speed and for a longer duration. Early inventions such as the wheel helped to make animal transport more efficient through the introduction of vehicles. A real trend break took place during the Industrial Revolution in the 19th century, when a number of inventions fundamentally changed the character of transportation. The invention of the steam engine, closely followed by its application in rail transport, made land transport independent of human or animal power. Both speed and capacity increased rapidly. The development of the combustion engine and the automobile at the beginning of the 20th century created a second revolution, as it meant that road transport became viable. After World War II, the automobile and the airlines took higher shares of transport, restricting rail and water to freight and short-haul passenger transport. In the 1960s international air travel became much more accessible with the commercialization of the jet engine.

New transport technologies have been so vital, beyond the transport sector alone, that economic historians have termed whole periods of economic development after various transport developments (e.g. the 'age of canals' in the first half of the 19th century or the 'railway and coal era' which refers to the expansion of rail transport that ended with the Great Depression in the 1930s). The oil and automobile alliance was the symbol of 'the age of the automobile'. Moreover, the car is one of the main contributory factors to a period of expansion unprecedented in the economic history of mankind. The transport sector is the only economic sector that has shown such continuous growth for more than a century now.

Efficient transport systems can provide economic and social opportunities and benefits that result in positive multiplier effects, such as better accessibility to markets, employment, and additional investments. This is an important explanation for the success of the transport sector. In the European Union, the transport industry accounts for about 7 per cent of European GDP and for around 5 per cent of employment in Europe, with more than 10 million jobs in the transport-related sectors of the economy (service, equipment, infrastructure), mostly in the road sector (CEC 2006). At the microeconomic level (where transportation is important for specific parts of the economy or individuals), transportation is linked to producers, consumers, and production costs. The importance of specific transport activities and infrastructure can thus be assessed for each sector of the economy. For example, transportation accounts on average for between 10 per cent and 15 per cent of household expenditures, while it accounts for around 4 per cent of the costs of each unit of output in manufacturing. This illustrates the significance of a flourishing transport sector, and a number of policies have been formulated to maintain or expand the transport potential. Some countries have become strongly dependent on transport; China's emerging economy for example is based on the import of resources and the export of consumer goods. However, regions can show a strong dependency on transport, such as the port areas in Shanghai, Singapore, and Rotterdam. The opportunities offered by transport are always not always equally shared: the 'average American' travels about 27,000 km per year, while in Africa it can take three days' walk to reach a post for basic healthcare (Schäfer et al. 2009).

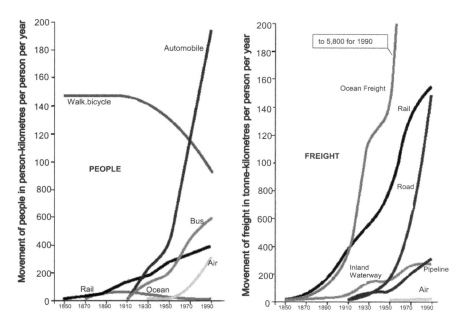

Figure 1.1   Changes the in use of various transport modes over time

At the same time we see that the areas with a strong car dependency are daily confronted by a serious congestion problem. The spectacular growth of transport is reflected in Figure 1.1.

The Urgent Need for Sustainable Transport

Transport is associated with many positive connotations: it enables individuals to fulfil their needs in terms of opportunities for employment, education, recreation, and so on. However, the impacts of transportation are not just positive: the benefits of transport come at a high price. Sometimes transport can have unforeseen or unintended consequences. No mode of motorized transport is completely environmentally-friendly. Some modes of transport, notably rail and inland waterways, have lower impacts than others, such as road and air. An analysis of transport developments and their impact on the environment must therefore distinguish between different modes of transport (traffic volume), the substitution effect of a modal shift and individual behaviour.

The negative external effects of motorized transport are quite substantial in significant ways. In terms of timescales, some are instantaneous (e.g. noise), some are pervasive (e.g. hydrocarbons), some are permanent (e.g. visual intrusion), and others are cumulative (e.g. CO_2). Spatially, there is a clear distinction between those adverse effects that have a direct impact at the place where they are generated (e.g. emissions of lead) and those which are transported through the air on a continental or even a global scale (CO_2). Some of the impacts are associated with direct physical effects and can be easily measured (SO_2); others, particularly those affecting public heath and the quality of urban life, are more subtle, and less susceptible to objective measurement. Some of the impacts result from transport vehicle operation, but some are simply a consequence of infrastructure location or design (visual intrusion), or of land and natural resources used for the construction of infrastructure (Geerlings 1999).

The reduction of CO_2 emissions, an important cause of global warming, is a priority, and there is increasing pressure on governments and industries to come forward with initiatives to reduce these emissions. This is highly relevant for the transport sector. The combustion of fossil fuels has a serious effect on the climate change problem, as nearly a quarter of the world's energy-related CO_2 emissions (IEA 2009) originates from transport activities. Moreover, the share of transportation is still increasing, while other sectors are reducing their CO_2 footprint. Assuming that the current trends continue, transport-related CO_2 emissions are expected to increase by 57 per cent worldwide between 2005 and 2030, mainly as a result of rapid motorization in developing countries. The question arises whether we can maintain the present rate of growth. At present, transportation already accounts for more than half of global liquid fossil fuel consumption, and after 2020, the availability of fossil fuels will become a concern as it is expected that while the demand will continue to increase, we are now at the peak of production.

Besides climate change, there are other impacts that we have to acknowledge. We see, for instance, that transportation is responsible for around 80 per cent of developing cities' local air pollution, and for more than 1.3 million fatal traffic accidents worldwide, most of which occur in developing countries (WHO 2009). In Europe 40,000 people are killed in traffic accidents per year. Furthermore, the chronic traffic congestion caused by excessive motorization leads to lower productivity and reduced levels of accessibility in many of the world's urban areas. The costs of such congestion are enormous. In the European Union, the total costs of road congestion have been estimated at around €120 billion or some 2 per cent of GDP. Congestion costs in European aviation are at least €2.4 billion, and railway costs amount to about €0.15 billion (EC 2006).

The concern for the negative external effects is reflected in the notion of sustainable mobility. Sustainability refers to a development that enhances the human and natural environments now and over the long term. In this perspective, a *sustainable* transport system would make a positive contribution to the environmental, social, and economic sustainability of the communities they serve.

This concern for the negative external effects of transportation and the need to address this issue in policy making has been apparent to policy makers for a long time. For example, the 2001 White Paper on European transport policy stated that 'numerous measures and policy instruments are needed to set the process in motion that will lead to a sustainable transport system', and noted that 'it will take time to achieve this ultimate objective, and the measures set out in this document amount only to a first stage, mapping out a more long term strategy' (CEC 2001: 18).

The objective of a sustainable transport policy is that the transport systems should meet society's economic, social and environmental needs. Effective transportation systems are essential for people's prosperity, having significant impacts on economic growth, social development and the environment. The challenge is to translate this into specific goals and actions that will lead to a competitive, secure, safe, and environmentally-friendly mobility. Stronger international competition with emerging countries such as China, India and Brazil, together with concerns about economic growth, has made the task of ensuring sustainable mobility even more challenging.

The concept of sustainability and sustainable transport provides guidance for long-term, strategic decision-making. Traditional transport planning aims to improve mobility, especially for vehicles, and may fail to adequately consider wider impacts. However, the real purpose of transport is access to work, education, goods and services, friends and family. There are proven techniques to improve access, while simultaneously reducing environmental and social impacts, and managing traffic congestion. Communities that are successfully improving the sustainability of their transport networks are doing so as part of a wider programme of creating more vibrant, liveable, sustainable cities.

The Complexity of Governance Structure and the Need for Transitions

The transport sector is a complex system that depends on multiple actors and factors, including the pattern of human settlements and consumption, the organization of production, and the availability of infrastructure. This means that decision-making in the transport sector is often a complex issue. Any intervention to make the transport system more sustainable must be based on a long-term vision concerning the goals of sustainable mobility for people and goods, not least because policies of a structural character take a long time to be successfully implemented.

We see new agenda concerning the role governments should play in creating the right conditions for effective policy making, including the domain of transport. Nowadays, the real aim in transportation is to improve accessibility, while simultaneously achieving a reduction of the societal and environmental impacts. Policy makers, industry and academics are confronted on a daily basis with the dilemma of the (short-term) demand for mobility of citizens and, at the same time, the pressure to fulfil the (long-term) sustainability needs. These are evidently conflicting interests, and reconciling them requires effective and legitimate public policy, service delivery and decision-making. The issue of decision making in complex situations has been tackled in recent studies on public policy making, where it is called the governance of complex systems (see for example Teisman et al. 2009). Representatives of this school of thinking state that policy makers are increasingly confronted with complex and fragmented governance systems which consist of many different actors and interests. This fragmentation has multiple forms and implications. The fragmentation is present in multi-level governance systems because public authorities have different responsibilities and jurisdictions. But there is also fragmentation between the public and the private domain, between the worlds of science and policy, between formal politics and citizen movements, and between interest groups and administrators. This leads to a fragmentation of interests, between disciplines, and of policy domains. Thus there is an increased need to have integrated solutions for a wide variety of problems related to sustainable transport and spatial development. This is particularly relevant when dealing with the challenge of sustainable mobility, where multiple levels, interests and individual behaviour play a decisive role. This is reflected in the subtitle of this book: the role of instruments, individuals and institutions. The governance of complex systems approach provides important support for identifying and formulating the responsibilities of the government and translating them into operational policies.

The new-government approach is built on two different social scientific orientations. The first is the policy orientation. This orientation originates from the increasing interest about the context in which policy and steering are affected. Recently, this approach has been extended by interesting notions which are derived from insights provided by the theory of evolution. In general, Darwinians point out the similarity between the course of natural variation and selection processes and the way in which changes in organizations occur. This functional way of explaining is justified by the phenomenon of the selection process which hampers socially-optimal outcomes. This development in the science of public administration shows a remarkable resemblance to technological dynamics, where evolutionary theory borrows perceptions from the field of biology (Geerlings 1999).

The second orientation originates from the study of organizational and social sciences, in which considerable attention is paid to the institutional environment of policy and steering processes. This source of inspiration is interesting because a connection is made with the theory on transition management. Transitions can be understood as a specific type of social change, which is characterized by non-linearity, a long time frame and structural changes. This fundamental change might include interrelated changes in behaviour, technology, governance, production and consumption and perceptions (Geerlings 1999). Transition theory can be divided into two main sub-fields:

1. Transition Dynamics: this domain aims to develop fundamental knowledge on the dynamics of transition processes, including past, ongoing, and future transitions; and
2. Transition Management: this field aims to develop fundamental knowledge and practical knowledge to influence and direct transitions towards sustainability.

This book focuses on the latter approach. Transition management in the transport sector can be considered as an additional mode of governance besides the governance of complex systems approach, as it refers to the insights provided by the governance of complex systems for achieving sustainable transportation which aims to enable, facilitate and guide transitions to sustainability. The underlying assumption is that full control and management of transitions is not possible. At the same time, transition management claims that it is possible to influence the direction and pace of transitions in subtle ways by a series of interventions at different levels using different instruments (Van den Bosch 2010). The transition management approach does not start by focusing on a solution but is instead explorative and process-orientated. The concept of sustainability is used as a normative frame to develop a future orientation. In this respect, the application of transition management is not an easy task. The following three observations need be taken into account when considering the achievement of transitions in the transport sector:

1. The achievement of sustainable transport is a collective aim that requires restrictions, incentives and enforcement to encourage and promote more sustainable actions. Changes in individual behaviour are of great importance.
2. The relations between governance, the markets and society are complex, and the mechanisms are sometime difficult to predict or to manage. Cooperation between government and trade and industry is of vital importance because of the contribution of trade and industry to innovation processes.
3. The sustainability challenge in modern societies has a wider impact than just transportation. The notion of sustainable development, based on the existing views originating from ecological and economic theory, is not sufficient. Instead, the notion of sustainable development can be better understood as a path of investigation for risk-minimization where it concerns the sustainability-related characteristics.

This book deals with all three of these elements, and examines them in different contexts and at different scales.

Outline of the Book

Transitions in transportation, in the context of sustainability and spatial planning policies, are central elements in this book. The relevant elements of transition management (theoretical and practical) are presented from four different perspectives, reflected in the four parts of the book. The book begins with an introduction of the challenge to come to a sustainable transport system, and the role of Transition Management in this. Part I focuses on the phenomenon of transition management, which is currently of great interest in policy-making.

The first three chapters in Part I deal with the theoretical notions behind the concept and the origins of the theory. The first two chapters by Geerlings et al. (Chapter 2) and Avelino et al. (Chapter 3) focus on the translation from theoretical notions into practical implementation. Meanwhile, Pel (in Chapter 4) focuses on the evolution of transition processes. The second half of Part I is structured around the challenges of transition management in the transport sector in specific cases. Gorris and van de Bosch (Chapter 5) study the application of transition management theory to a case in the Netherlands. Bressers et al. (Chapter 6) evaluate different case studies in which theory is applied to practice in order to evaluate the challenges and relevance of the theory of transition management.

In Part II the focus is on transport energy use and emissions. The issue of the acceptability of policies is also central to the contributions. Niemeier et al. (Chapter 7) specifically look at the interactions between science, the policy process, and public interests, and at how these relationships influence the creation, implementation, and enforcement of local land use policies that target climate changes. Huijts et al. (Chapter 8) examine the issues surrounding the public acceptance of hydrogen as a transport fuel. Susilo and Stead (Chapter 9) show trends in individual country's CO_2 emissions in the Netherlands and the UK, and discuss the acceptability of different policy options to reduce individual country's CO_2 emissions. Hickman et al. (Chapter 10) examine issues of transport and global warming in the UK, and consider a range of options for carbon reduction.

Part III deals with the importance and role of information in transport policy. Wigan (Chapter 11) discusses three elements that are required for public policy to be credible and efficient: evidence based policy, contestable evidence policy, and accessible information. He then discusses the role they play in the transition to sustainable transport. Rocci (Chapter 12) examines individuals' mobility practices related to environmental values in order to grasp the potential for change. She specifically focuses on the role of information in changing mobility behaviour towards more multimodal and sustainable practices. Her results show that information plays a significant role in change. Te Brömmelstroet and Bertolini (Chapter 13) propose a new participatory development approach for planning support systems to implement and integrate land-use and transport planning.

Finally, Part IV is concerned with the issue of policy evaluation. Shiftan and Zananiri (Chapter 14) discuss the evaluation of such policies taking into account travellers' response to such policies, and how they affect their design and efficiency. Brůhová-Foltýnová and Brůha (Chapter 15) use a global sensitivity analysis to evaluate the regulation of environmental external costs of transport. Their model integrates estimates of environmental external costs, and estimates of the behaviour of households and that of public transport agencies. Ettema et al. (Chapter 16) develop a land-use transport interaction (LUTI) model, taking into account the influence of temporal and monetary constraints on activity participation, travel, consumption of goods, residential location, and work status. Finally, Vonk Noordegraaf et al. (Chapter 17) discuss the adoption of road pricing policies and the factors that influence the policy actors' decision to adopt road pricing.

The book ends with an Epilogue by the editors (Chapter 18), in which theoretical and practical lessons are discussed, general conclusions are drawn, and new directions for future research are identified.

PART I
Concepts and Challenges

Chapter 2

Transition Management:
A New Opportunity for Introducing
More Sustainable Transport Policies?

Harry Geerlings, Jasper Lohuis and Yoram Shiftan

Introduction

Transportation has many positive characteristics. This applies for the individual user, as well for as society as a whole. This explains why the transport sector, for decades now, has experienced unprecedented growth. This is the case for the transportation of passengers, freight, and (more recently) the transportation of information. At the same time, we see that the success of transportation has undesired negative side effects. The almost unlimited demand for transportation can not be fully satisfied by the construction of new infrastructure, so this inevitably leads to congestion. Other concerns are related to emissions (on both the regional level and the global level), safety, and resource management. Governments and other stakeholders are generally aware that policy measures are needed to find a balance between accessibility and sustainability. This is an enormous challenge, and the question arises how this can be achieved.

In this chapter the dilemmas and difficulties for a new strategy for effective policy making in the transport sector are presented. The chapter is divided into five parts. First, the main trends in transportation are outlined. Second, the concept of sustainable transportation is examined. Third, attention is given to the policy development and the need to come to more effective policy making. Fourth, the principles of successful sustainable transport policies are identified. The authors outline the need for governments to develop new, integrated policy principles, and discuss the rationale for backcasting approaches. The chapter also advocates the application of new guiding principles for policy initiatives. Taken together, these contribute to the implementation of transition management in the transport sector.

Trends in Transportation

Over the last four decades, the transport sector has been characterized by unprecedented growth. This growth can be observed in both passenger and freight transport, and it is a trend that is occurring all over the world. In general, the growth in passenger and goods transport has been faster than the economic growth. In emerging economies in the Far East, such as China and Vietnam, car ownership is doubling every year. Projections up to 2020 indicate a further growth in transport, particularly in freight transport and concentrated in Asia: freight and passenger transport is predicted to increase in by 52 per cent and 35 per cent, respectively, between 2000 and 2020 (EUROSTAT 2007).

Transport plays a crucial role in modern societies, and that the growth of transportation is a reflection of economic dynamics. Well functioning transportation systems facilitate the process of globalization and ongoing economic growth; they are a motor for economic processes. In direct terms, the manufacturing of transport modes, the construction and maintenance of infrastructure and related service industries represent about 10 per cent of the employment in the EU-27. Transport plays an important role in shaping the form and function of a region. Transport fulfils an important stimulus for social activities, such as the internationalization of student exchange programmes or the migration of workers. This all underlines the meaning of transport for a well-functioning society.

The success of the transport sector also has a negative impact in several respects. We see that the transport sector is increasingly associated with negative feelings. There are concerns about the environmental impacts of transportation, such as adversely affecting air quality. Initially the attention was on the impacts of emissions (such as SO_2, HC and NO_2) on health and safety, but at present a new concern has been added to the political agenda: climate change (CO_2). The growth of the transport sector has not been followed or been accompanied at the same speed by an expansion of the required infrastructure, which leads to increasing congestion. The availability of resources is at stake and we see an increasing demand for bio fuels (for instance in the US), which is causing an increase in the price of food in Mexico (the 'tortilla crises' that took place in 2007). And this is all taking place in a context where there is an unbalanced growth in transport modes towards faster, more flexible and more energy-consuming modalities (a shift from the use of bus and train via the car towards air transport).

The Demand for Sustainable Transport

The concern for the environmental burden caused by human action has been studied for many years and is reflected in numerous reports and policy documents. The discussion has gained new momentum by the introduction of the concept of sustainable development in the 1980s.

One of the first references to the term sustainable development appeared in UNCED's 1980 World Conservation Strategy. Later, in 1987, the World Commission for Environment and Development (WCED) described the concept of sustainable development more extensively in their report 'Our Common Future' (the Brundtland Report). In this report, sustainable development is defined as:

> development that meets the needs of the present without compromising the ability of future generations to meet their own needs.

It is interpreted by Geerlings et al. (2009) as 'a process of change in which the exploitation of resources, the direction of investment, the orientation of technical development, and institutional change are all in harmony and enhance both current and future potential to meet human needs and aspirations'.

As a result the thinking about sustainable development in relation to technological development also received considerable attention. On the international level, the discussion then received a new impetus from the Rio de Janeiro Summit organized by UNCED in 1992, where the action plan Agenda 21 (UNCE 1992) was adopted in which Sustainable Development was chosen as the leading principle for future development.

There is, however, as yet no universally accepted definition of sustainability, sustainable development, or sustainable transport. The Brundtland report interprets sustainable development as a process of change in which the exploitation of resources, the direction of investments, the orientation of technical development, and institutional change are all in harmony, and enhance both current and future potential to meet human needs and aspirations. In the WCED report on sustainable development, three interrelated systems are identified: the ecological system (the exploitation of resources); the economic system (investments and technological development); and the social-cultural system (institutional change). These systems are interrelated and these interrelations can be expressed as functions. Two of these are the production and the regeneration function.

Sustainable development distinguishes several, sometimes seemingly opposing, goals, which hence makes it a very difficult task to find synergy between these different goals. Three interrelated systems within sustainable development include the ecological system ('planet'), the economic system ('profit'), and the socio-cultural system ('people'). Especially in matters where finding the right balance between ecological and economic aspects is concerned, development in harmony with sustainability will be more difficult to put into operation. Sustainability is sometimes defined narrowly. Some studies of sustainability focus on long-term resource depletion and air pollution problems, on the grounds that they represent the greatest risk and are prone to being neglected by conventional planning (TRB 1997).

Table 2.1   Sustainability issues

Economic (profit)	Environmental (planet)	Social (people)
Affordability	Pollution prevention	Equity
Resource efficiency	Climate protection	Human health
Cost internalization	Biodiversity	Education
Trade and business activity	Precautionary action	Community
Employment	Avoidance of irreversibility	Quality of life
Productivity	Habitat preservation	Public Participation
Tax burden	Aesthetics	

Given the serious impact of transportation, there is growing interest in the concepts of sustainability and sustainable transport. Transport systems exist to provide social and economic connections, and people tend to quickly take up the opportunities offered by increased mobility. But sustainability is increasingly being defined more broadly to include the range of issues listed in Table 2.1.

It is also important to stress that the concept of sustainable mobility is not a static situation that can be described in the sustainability issues as presented above. The concept of sustainability has to be achieved over time, and is part of a process (temporal aspects) which also manifest on a spatial scale (spatial aspects). The concept of sustainability is being translated and applied in many different sectors, such as agriculture, production processes, and energy conservation. It is also being applied in the transport sector. Sustainable transport, according to a report by the Transportation Research Board (TRB 2008), is a transport system which:

1. allows the basic access and development needs of the people to be met safely and consistent with human and ecosystem health, and promotes equity within and between successive generations;
2. is affordable, operates fairly and efficiently, offers a choice of transport mode and supports a competitive economy, as well as balanced regional development; and
3. limits emissions and waste, and uses resources at the level of generation or development, while minimizing the impact on the use of land and the generation of noise.

Overall, according to the World Bank (1996), sustainable transportation should consider all the following three angles which aim:

(i) to ensure continuous capability to support an improved standard of living corresponding to economic and financial sustainability,

(ii) to generate optimum possible improvement in the general quality of life that relates to the concept of environmental and ecological sustainability, and

(iii) to produce equitably benefits shared by all sections of the community which term social sustainability.

But in the development of the transportation sector and all its external effects, this optimum situation rarely occurs. There is, for instance, a tension between improving accessibility and the increase of emissions, or between economic growth and increasing congestion. It is expected that the environmental interest will increase in importance, and will have implications for the transport sector (see also Lohuis et al. 2008).

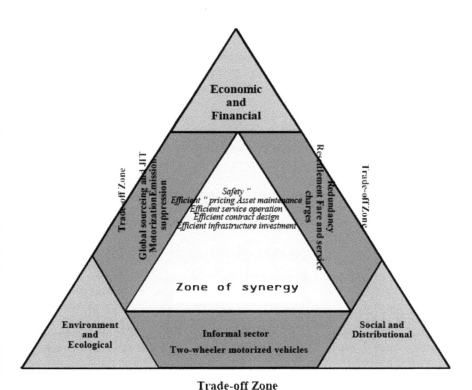

Figure 2.1   The three dimensions of sustainability

The Traditional Policy Reflex

Traditional transport planning aims to improve mobility, especially for vehicles, but may fail to adequately consider the wider or long-term impacts. Initially, just after World War II there were high hopes concerning the potential of mankind to construct a new and better society (the welfare state). The ideology of a welfare state was generally accepted, however differently interpreted, in both the capitalist and the communist system.[1] There was also a new spirit within political science, where governments were encouraged to claim a central role in society to provide guidance for these new prospects. Therefore, a new policy steering paradigm was developed. This paradigm, what we nowadays consider to be the 'classical steering paradigm' in political science, identifies the relationship between the policy maker and the public as the central object of study. In this concept, the public is subordinate and regarded as one homogeneous object of steering. Consequently, this approach is also called the 'one-actor approach' and/or 'thematic policy making'.

The basic assumption in this approach is that governing organizations and policy makers want to reach their objectives. The government should play a central role in defining objectives which reflect the collective interest, and has to provide the necessary resources (including regulation). In this 'top-down' approach, the effectiveness of policy making depends on to what extent the (pre-stated) objectives of the governing organization are reached. Consequently the effectiveness of instruments has become an important topic for study.

Box 2.1   Transport policy-making in Europe

The 1957 Treaty of Rome, which marked the foundation of the European Economic Community (EEC) stated that the aims of the EEC would be *'to take care of the continuous improvement of the living and working conditions of its* population' and that at the same time the EEC would strive for the *'harmonious development of her economies'*. Looking back, it can be concluded that, in the early days of EU policy-making, the policies were based on a sectoral approach, in which transport was strongly valued as a driving force for economic prosperity. The free movement of people and goods was strongly enhanced as a stimulus for the creation of a single European market (one of the pillars of the Treaty of Rome). Traditionally, governments address these problems by classical steering instruments based on the principles of direct regulation (the stick), indirect regulation (the carrot) and self-regulation (the sermon). These policies were also mainly effect oriented: good examples are the introduction of road pricing, fuel taxation, and the construction of new infrastructures.

---

1   This hope was strengthened by the results of the Conference of Bretton Woods (1944), which led to the establishment of the World Bank, the Marshall Plan (1945), the founding of the United Nations (1945), and the founding of the predecessor of the OECD, the Organisation of European Economic Cooperation (1948).

After all the expectations raised by new management tools and the government policies developed in the 1950s, 1960s and 1970s, the results actually achieved were quite disappointing. The failures of government policies were reflected in new types of problems, such as the economic recession, unemployment, and environmental problems. It appeared that the execution of each policy has its own dynamics. Consequently, policies were less effective than expected, the benefits of policies were addressed to the wrong group, procedures and legislation took more time than was expected. There are various explanations for the failure of government policies. Firstly, the problems confronting society became increasingly complex. Secondly, an increasing number of actors became involved in the decision process. Thirdly, there was an increasing interdependence between (related) policy areas.

As a result a debate took place on the role of the central rationale and central directing role of government in society. The conclusion was that the classical steering paradigm was not capable of implementing effective policies of central governments. The opinion became accepted that these failures have led to a strong decline in the legitimacy of governments and governmental agencies, on both the international and the national level; hierarchically-organized governments create bureaucracies, are less efficient, and are mainly focused on their own interests. At the same time, new factors became apparent.

Presently we observe, partly because of the need to address new and very complicated policy challenges such as global warming and to transform transportation into real <u>sustainable</u> transportation, that is now time for new policy paradigm that focuses on a transition management. This important and structural change requires a redefinition of European institutions, and will affect the balance between transport policy, environmental policy and spatial policy. The Cardiff Agreement, initiated at the EU-Council meeting in Cardiff in 1998, aimed to integrate environmental concerns into transport policy. Since then the idea of sustainability has been implemented in the EU-treaty, and, at the Stockholm Summer in 2001, the European Union's Sustainable Development Strategy was published. The White Paper on European Transport states that '*a modern transport system must be sustainable from an economic and social, as well as an environmental viewpoint*'.

The Need for New Policy Concepts

The Relevance of Policy Integration

There are increasing demands for policy integration from a number of areas, due to the complexity of problems that arise in the wider context of transportation. At the beginning of the 21st century, two OECD reports referred to policy coordination for a thorough analysis (see Stead and Geerlings 2005). The first of these reports focuses on policies to enhance sustainable development, and includes analysis and advice on how governments can develop integrated approaches to decision-making (OECD 2001a). The second discusses the critical issues for sustainable development, and talks about the need for greater policy coherence and the better integration of economic, environmental and social goals in different policies. It identifies three distinct organizational approaches for the integration of sustainable development into policy (OECD 2001b).

Within the literature concerning the theory on policy integration various concepts can be found (for a more detailed review, see Geerlings and Stead 2003). These include *coherent policy-making*, *cross-cutting policy-making*, *policy coordination* and *holistic government*, also known as *joined-up policy* or *joined-up government*. Whilst some authors see policy coordination as more or less the same as integrated policymaking, others regard them as quite separate and distinct. The OECD (1996), for example, observes that policy integration is quite distinct and more sophisticated than policy coordination in two ways:

1. the level of interaction; and
2. the output.

Stead et al. (2004) distinguish between a number of distinct terms and suggest a hierarchy:

- policy cooperation, at the lowest level, which simply implies dialogue and information;
- policy coordination, policy coherence, and policy consistency – all quite similar, implying cooperation plus transparency and some attempt to avoid policy conflicts (but not necessarily the use of similar goals);
- policy integration and joined-up policy – includes dialogue and information (as in policy cooperation), transparency, and avoidance of policy conflicts (as in policy coordination, policy coherence, and policy consistency), but also includes joint working, attempts to create synergies between policies (win-win situations), and the use of the same goals to formulate policy.

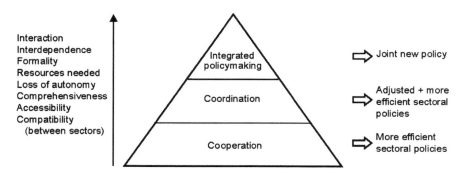

Figure 2.2   Different levels of policy cooperation and integration

Other related concepts in the organizational literature that have potential relevance concerning policy integration include *inter-organizational coordination, inter-organizational collaboration, inter-governmental management* and *network management*. These related concepts primarily concern cooperation between organizations, rather than cooperation between departments within one organization, but are nevertheless also relevant since inter-organizational policymaking and intra-organizational policymaking are to a considerable extent similar when it comes to integrating issues that are cross-sectoral. After all, within one organization, different sectoral departments often operate as different organizations with their own specific professional styles, approaches, needs, agendas, and modes of operation.

The interest in policy integration also has links with various recent policy documents on *governance*, such as the European White Paper on European Governance (CEC 2001a[2]), although the document contains no specific details about the process of policy integration. The need for cooperation and new instruments is also reflected in present policymaking in the EU and in the member States of the EU. In this chapter we concentrate on the integration of transport, land use planning and environmental policies.

A number of interesting trends in policymaking can be observed since the early 1980s. At first, the emphasis was on a *sectoral approach* (focusing on different policy domains), particularly on economic growth, agricultural policies, and transport policies. In the second half of the 1980s, *harmonization* of various policies became important. In this respect, harmonization means that different policy initiatives were judged on whether the initiatives did not contradict to each other. Attention was given to new policy initiatives, the development

---

2   The White Paper on European Governance makes recommendations in three areas: (i) with regard to participation in and the openness of policymaking and decision making; (ii) with respect to the coherence and effectiveness of policies; and (iii) with respect to the division of powers between European Institutions.

of policy instruments, and the development of research initiatives that would support this broadening of the policy area. From the mid-1990s, it became clear that harmonization was not enough. For instance, it became evident that the structural funds for the southern European countries had led to the construction of new infrastructure, while at the same time the environmental policies had to be strengthened because of damage to the natural landscape. As a result, the dominant paradigm changed from harmonization to *coordination* (longer-term policies and preventative policies for example). This development is reflected in policy papers and research programmes.[3] It was later recognized that a reinvention of policy making was also needed as a consequence of the proposed expansion of the European Community. From the environmental perspective, CO_2 emissions became more of a policy priority, whilst in the field of urban planning, congestion in urban areas became a new policy priority. As a result of these new challenges there was more need for further policy coordination; namely, the awareness amongst politicians that policies had to be directed towards *sectoral integration.* This change in policy priorities was also reflected in the policy documents and research priorities (see Geerlings and Stead 2003; and Stead et al. 2004).

From Forecasting to Backcasting

The concept of Sustainable Transport refers to the need to find a new balance between accessibility and sustainability over time. The growth of Sustainable Transport has not yet been extensively studied, but as transport can be considered as a derived effect from economic growth, we can learn from the economic sciences. Economic growth has been studied for many years. It was Kondriatieff (1926) and, elaborating on Kondriatieff's work, Schumpeter (1939) who explicitly linked economic development and technological change. Kondriatieff focused attention on the interaction between economic and technological development in a long-term perspective. He argued that capitalist economies went from boom to bust in a long cycle or wave of about 55 years. Schumpeter expanded the idea. He developed the proposition that important innovations occur at the beginning of an economic recovery, and maintained that, particularly in times of economic crisis firms are willing to take risks and open new channels for trade.

In addition to the opinion that technology develops as a process of major technological changes and technological breakthroughs, there are other scientists who state that the process of innovation is a much more discontinuous process of small (incremental) improvements. In their opinions the development of technologies is more a process of 'adoption' and an 'innovation permanence'.

---

3   See, for example, *Energy for a New Century* (CEC 1990); *Towards Sustainable Mobility* (CEC 1992); *The Green Paper on the Urban Environment* (CEC 1990).

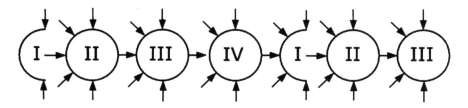

Figure 2.3   The process of cumulative synthesis

Representatives of the view that technological changes are gradual are Ruttan (1959) and especially Rosenberg (1982). These authors criticize the simple linear model, inspired by Schumpeter, which has been widely used by economists and historians. They consider technological innovations as a continuing process of small changes which could accelerate, as is shown in Figure 2.3.

In the traditional Schumpetarian model, technological development will follow a linear pattern, dependent upon the innovative attitude of the potential adopters. According to Rosenberg's model, there is a place for all kinds of feedback and further developments. We can speak of a process of co-evolution of old and new technologies in which the environment plays an important role. A major integration, but also scientific breakthrough in the thinking on innovation theory took place in the work of Nelson and Winter (1977) and Dosi (1988). These authors, among many others have, when elaborating on the Schumpetarian theory, focused on the role that the social-cultural and institutional factors play in the processes of innovation and the diffusion of technology.

Nelson and Winter observe that technological change depends on variation and selection processes aimed at solving technologically defined problems. To understand this phenomenon, they introduce the concept of a technological regime: the 'direction of progress' of technological change. According to Dosi, a technological trajectory contains the changes in technology which take place in the framework of a technological regime or paradigm. A technological paradigm or regime is defined by Dosi as a model or pattern of solutions of selected technological problems, based on selected principles derived from the natural sciences, and on selected material technologies. In this approach, there is the growing recognition that history counts. Past technological achievements influence future developments via the specificity of knowledge that they entail, the development of specific infrastructure, and the emergence of various kinds of increasing returns.

In a way, technological developments can be considered as a process of variation and selection. This process is interlocked and has specific feedbacks. This phenomena is called path-dependency or locked-in development. Path-dependency (and the irreversibility's of diffusion patterns) also implies a fundamental role for 'routines' and 'trajectories'. Routines differ from trajectories because routines are related to the process of decision making and learning. They are in many cases persistent and hard to change, partly because not all relevant variables can be included in the decision-making process. Social systems also consist of routines. Trajectories, on the other hand, concern the process of technological development. The general message behind the academic notions described above, is a general feeling that it is possible to initiate and maintain a process of change, albeit under difficult and sometimes unpredictable circumstances.

From the early 1990s, we observe an increasing interest in technology development in transportation. Technological development in the transport sector can be explained as a process of small incremental changes. According to Montroll (1978), evolution is the result of a sequence of replacements. Often, new technologies create new 'niches' that lead to products and services hitherto unavailable. More frequently, successful innovations can pre-empt an established niche by providing improved technical and economic performance, or by promoting the social acceptability of existing services through new ways of fulfilling them. Circumstantial evidence shows that many pervasive systems have evolved through both of these evolutionary paths. They replaced older technologies, and then created new and additional market segments that did not exist before. This process is illustrated by Seiffert and Walzer (1989) who show that the technological development of a basic innovation changes over time due to the dominant heuristic as shown in Figure 2.4.

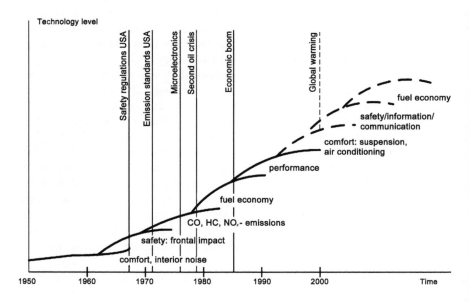

Figure 2.4   Dominant heuristics in the technological development of the car 1950–2010

A very important change took place as a result of a programme initiated by the the Dutch Ministry of Environment and Spatial Planning (VROM). This is the research programme Sustainable Technological Development (DTO 1992). This programme aims to determine the characteristics of technological developments that have to exist in order to contribute to sustainable development. In the DTO study it is assumed that technology provides social functions (such as transportation), but that technology itself develops in close association with cultural and structural factors. Against this background, it is argued that the analysis of sustainability-orientated technologies must include:

a. an analysis of the cultural and structural pre-conditions within which the technology concerned must function; and
b. an analysis of the cultural and structural ex-ante conditions that have to be fulfilled so that specific techniques or systems can function.

Subsequently, the programme is marked by a unique approach. It is established that a great deal can be achieved by the implementation of (improved) 'end-of-pipe technologies' and process-integrated technologies. But the real challenge for sustainable development is to be found in fundamental change. However, it will take many decades for the development of these technologies. This time-perspective demands a phased approach. This is no longer concerned with improving the existing technology, but tackles the challenge of finding new technological combinations and concepts by which the proposed improvement of the environmental efficiency can be achieved. One can think of an improvement of efficiency by a factor of four to 100. The achievement of this aim demands a quantum leap, as well as a new approach to assess the technological potential. This new approach, in which technical, scientific, communicative, and innovative factors are integrated, is indicated by the term backcasting.

Within the framework of technology development, forecasting aims to extrapolate developments into the future, as well as to explore the achievements that can be achieved with technology. Backcasting, on the other hand, has a reverse reasoning:

1. the direction the process must take is determined, starting from a coherent image of the requirements that the specific technology has to meet in the future; and
2. the needs of society are translated into 'criteria for sustainability' for the year 2040. In order to explore a direction within this searching process, a number of processes which are likely to be successful from a techno-economic point of view are subsequently developed.

This approach was used by Geerlings (1999) as the starting point for his work where he presented the concept of generating a 'Window of Technological Opportunity'. In this approach he developed an ex-ante methodology to direct technological innovations in a (more) sustainable direction. He presents seven steps that are important elements in the process of policy making, so it will lead to the expected outcome.

The Application of New Leading Principles in Transportation

Finally *new principles* of policy making for the transport sector that need to be introduced should be based on a set of priorities which are in balance with the importance to facilitate transportation, but which also specifies enhance criteria from the point of view of sustainable development. The priority is prevention, modal shift, optimization, and facilitation.

The pyramid shown in Figure 2.5 (known as a priority ladder) presents options and types of transport that could help policies to save transportation problems. The fact that transport growth can not be followed at the same speed by the expansion of the required infrastructure shows that coping with the increased demand of transport by infrastructure construction (bottom of the pyramid) does not comply with the sustainability perspectives. In fact, it often leads to more congestion. On the other hand, integrating transport and spatial planning may result in a more sustainable outcome with, for example, reduced travel demand and increased also of non-motorized transport.

The preferred measure are those that combine specific spatial characteristics and situations leading to a symbiosis of the production processes that take place (in business management this approach is called 'industrial ecology').

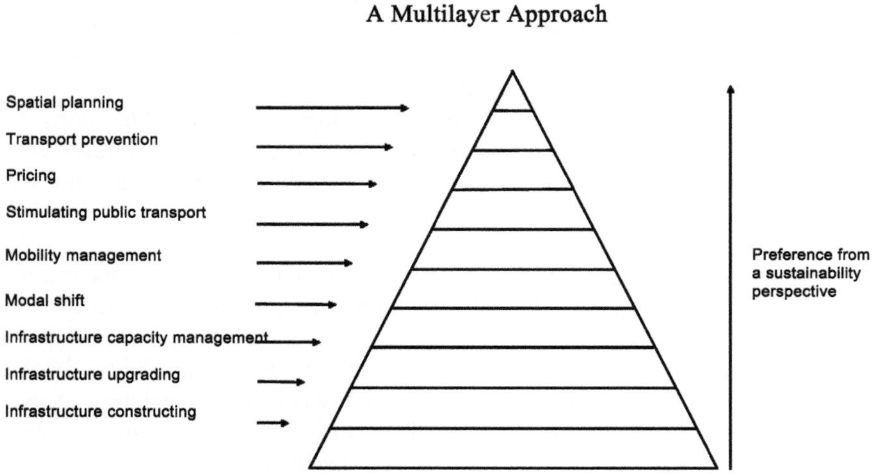

A Multilayer Approach

Spatial planning
Transport prevention
Pricing
Stimulating public transport
Mobility management
Modal shift
Infrastructure capacity management
Infrastructure upgrading
Infrastructure constructing

Preference from a sustainability perspective

Figure 2.5   Priority pyramid

Spatial planning may work best if it is supported by the implementation of both public transport improvement and transport prevention. But it is clear that this will not always be possible. It is obvious that the prevention of unnecessary transportation by intelligent logistic planning is a much more preferable solution compared with the construction of new infrastructure.

The Emerging Concept of Transition Management

As already explained in the previous section, within the framework of public policy making, 'forecasting' aims to extrapolate developments towards the future as well as to explore the achievements that can be achieved with technology. *Backcasting*, on the other hand, has a reverse reasoning: the direction the process must take is determined starting from a coherent image of the requirements that the specific technology has to meet in the future. The previous subsection also clearly illustrates that at the same time there is a shift from a strong techno-centric perspective towards a (more) process-orientated approach to technology dynamics.

From this perspective, technology dynamics can best be described as a highly complex and dynamic process characterized by a multi-actor setting, a strong interrelationship with other technological domains, and non-linearity. Furthermore, several authors have referred to the role that government could play in the development of technological innovations (in relation to sustainability).

The new approach of *transition management* seems to evolve in a natural way from the existing process-orientated perspectives on technology dynamics and system innovation. Transition management is a management strategy for public decision makers and private actors that deals with the question how and to what extent complex societal transformation processes can be directed in a certain desirable direction (Rotmans et al. 2001).

The theoretical concept of transitions refers to a transformation process in which society changes in a fundamental way over a generation or more. Transitions can best be understood as gradual transformation processes as a result of simultaneous developments in different societal domains and the combined action of macro-, meso- and micro-level developments (Rotmans 2003). An important hypothesis in transition theory is that fundamental change only breaks through if developments at the macro-, meso- and micro-level reinforce each other, and if developments within different domains come together at a particular scale level. A transition then is the result of a mixture of long-term, slow developments and short-term, fast developments. This is illustrated in Figure 2.6, where the classical linear approach and the evolutionary way of thinking are combined and integrated in the concept of transition management.

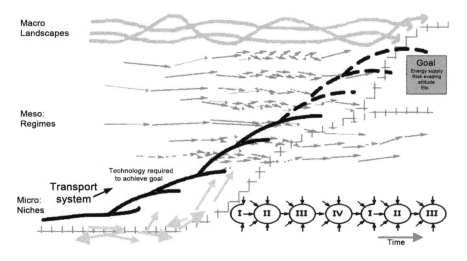

Figure 2.6   Transition management in an overall setting

It is generally accepted that the physical infrastructure is considered as a relatively stable environment where change is difficult to achieve (e.g. cities, road infrastructures). Transition management also considers the institutional environment as an inert system, whereas the socio-technical landscape has to deal with often slow-changing factors like cultural values, political coalitions, and long-term economic developments induce incremental innovation. As such, transition management is an evolutionary steering tool based on mutual learning and adaptation.

In what are 'transition arenas', heterogeneous multi-actor, multi-level, and multi-domain groups of individuals are challenged to form shared long-term visions with respect to the desirable transition. This latter example illustrates that transition management focuses strongly on micro-level interactions which induce fundamental societal change and on the process-orientated approach to technology dynamics.

The Meaning of Transition Management for Sustainable Transportation

The concept of transition management is being applied in various sectors, such as the energy sector, agriculture and water management. The transportation sector is considered as another suitable sector in this regard. The situation in relation to transport is becoming more and more challenging. The continuous growth of transport in all parts of the world has created problems such as the emission of CO_2, noise, congestion, and a strong dependency on energy supply. It seems quite clear that sustainable solutions need to be found for these transportation problems, and that technology in relation to transition management might be a promising approach: a significant environmental amelioration can be gained from the implementation of new technologies. These prospects are in line with the revaluation of the role of technology in society that is presently taking place. We observe a certain fascination with technology, which is seen as key to a number of different problems (e.g. introducing filters, alternative fuels). From this perspective, technological innovations are considered to be the motor for economic welfare. This opinion is expressed particularly in the transport sector. Indeed, it is indisputable that technological development has made possible the more efficient use of energy, materials and capital that, in turn, has led to higher productivity and, as a direct effect, more transportation in the world.

Rotmans (2003) states that a significant improvement of the factors contributing to transport problem is simply not attainable with present technological insights and policy structures. Measures to tackle these problems often lack widespread support or fail to bring true solutions. In his opinion, the transport system seems to be locked-in, and is not developing in a sustainable direction. He thinks that this is caused by lack of a sustainability objectives, and innovation on the system level. In this context, Rotmans calls for change in thinking, leading to new perspectives, with far-reaching measures and integrated solutions based on the new theory of transition management.

Some authors (Rotmans 2003; Grin et al. 2010) present the concept of transition management as an innovative approach to overcome barriers from the past. They advocate solutions for the system as a whole, instead for parts of the system (see Figure 2.4). Therefore, top-down governance needs to be partly abandoned in favour of user demands and market-developments. In this way, a transition path is not chosen, but rather created in the attempt to traverse. In this way possible breakthrough solutions have to be generated instead of designed, with technology playing a role.

The above-mentioned approach of transition management sounds ambitious, but the practical implications still remain rather unspecific. Past transport policies are described as ineffective, but a thorough analysis has not been made, and appealing alternatives are lacking. Specific expertise in the technological aspects of the transport sector is needed in order to understand its underlying processes and mechanisms. However, the impression has been created that transition management is a methodology that consists of a toolbox applicable in every sector, in every situation, and at any moment. In its case studies, the approach is rather descriptive, not analytical and hardly ex-ante orientated (applicable). In advocating a 'radical' approach and ideas, the different scholars do not acknowledge the achievements achieved in the past.

Transition management stems from the existing process-orientated perspectives on system innovation. Transition management can be considered as a management strategy for public decision makers and private actors, and deals with the question how, and to what extent, complex societal transformation processes can be directed in a certain desirable direction. As transition management is still in its initial phase and has not yet generated sound concepts, it is time for future contributors to be more specific about their approach. Until that time the practical merits of transition management to implement a change to a (more) sustainable transport sector remains an open question.

Over the last 10 years, there has been an increasing call for greater integration in European policies and related research programmes. This has come at a time when decision making is facing increasing complexity as a result of various developments. Within the academic literature concerning the theory of policy integration various concepts and instruments are being studied. These experiences have led to a new paradigm for policy-making where three patterns of governance can be determined:

1. governance by negotiation;
2. governance by hierarchy; and
3. governance by facilitated coordination.

All three paradigms can adequately be used in understanding policy integration in practice.

Synthesis and Conclusions

In the field of transport, there is a general awareness that new approaches are needed to find a balance between accessibility and sustainability. The need for a more sustainable transport sector is relevant on different levels such as local, regional, continental and global, but the spatial-temporal characteristics of the impacts differ very strongly.

History has a lot to offer when it comes to the better understanding of transport developments and the trends in the sector. A transition towards Sustainable Transport has become the latest challenge in this development. The authors of this chapter stress the need for governments to come up with new and integrated policy principles; they (re)introduce the concept of backcasting instead of forecasting; and the theory of transition management is introduced. In the same context, they advocate the application of new guiding policy principles before policy initiatives are taken. And, finally, it is illustrated that all these different approaches should be implemented in an integrated approach.

From a long-term perspective it appears that Kondratieff cycles, as a model of the discontinuous nature of economic development, couple the dynamics of both the discontinuous introduction and the diffusion rates of innovations with strong discontinuities in long-term economic development. Since the early 1980s, there has not only been increased attention for the impact of technological innovation in society, but there is also increasing concern for the environment. On the one hand technology was welcomed as part of the solution but, on the other hand, technology itself was considered as the origin of the problem.

Traditional policies are not able to cope with the new challenges, and that is why another approach is needed, which combines the specific concepts of paradigm shift and path-dependency as helpful tools to reach more sustainability-orientated development within the transport sector. The challenge is to develop a pro-active and ex-ante methodology that addresses the economic (people), environmental (planet), and social objectives (people) in one coherent strategy.

At the same time, it is necessary to recognize the need for cooperation and interaction between the government and private firms to fulfil the changing needs of society. The methodology to develop a sound sustainable transport policy should be based on developing targets for the longer term.

This ambition is embodied in the new approach named transition management. From a theoretical perspective this approach is challenging as it attempts to combine different notions: the macro and the micro-level, the system approach and phenomenological studies, the techno-centric perspective and the process-orientated approaches and the interest of producers, as well as that of governments and consumers. In theory, the concept of transition management creates a common basis for understanding the complexities related to this challenge. When the necessary conditions are fulfilled, this concept can contribute to a process of transition that might lead to a more sustainable transport system.

Chapter 3

Transition Management as New Policy Making for Sustainable Mobility

Flor Avelino, Nanny Bressers and René Kemp

Introduction

In the following chapters, the reader will encounter various case-studies of 'transition management' programmes and projects in the Dutch mobility sector. As such, we have been asked by the editors to write an introductory chapter on 'transition management' in relation to mobility. This is not an easy task, for 'transition management' can be described as many things: as a governance model for sustainable development, as a specific policy discourse, and as a field of academic research. More importantly, these different dimensions of 'transition management' are all intertwined. The transition management approach as it exists today has been 'co-produced' by researchers, policy-makers, and other practitioners (Kemp and Rotmans 2009; Loorbach 2007). This chapter aims to provide an overview of how transition management developed, how it emerged in the Dutch policy arena, and finally, how this is manifested in Dutch mobility policy and various research programmes and innovation projects that deal with sustainable mobility. The research objective of this chapter is to present the reader with background knowledge of transition management, in order to be able to comprehend the following chapters. More specifically, this chapter can be seen as background reading for Chapter 4 (Pel), Chapter 5 (Gorris and van den Bosch) and Chapter 6 (Bressers et al.), which all discuss the application of transition management within the Dutch mobility sector. Moreover, this chapter can also be read as a case-study in itself: a case-study on how researchers, policy-makers, and other practitioners together develop a policy approach to deal with sustainable development, and how this policy context affects several research programmes and innovation projects in the mobility sector.

The purpose of this chapter is not to test empirical or theoretical hypotheses, nor to discuss the many academic discussions on transition management in relation to other policy approaches to sustainable development. Also, this chapter explicitly does not aim to either celebrate or criticize transition management. Rather, our aim is to provide an overview of transition management, its concepts, it background, and the mobility context in which it is applied. We will therefore not discuss transition management's successes or failures. For more in-depth academic discussions about transition management and its pros and cons, we refer to several books and articles in the growing field of transition studies (Loorbach and Rotmans 2010; Van der Bosch 2010; Voss et al. 2009; Kemp and Rotmans 2009; Meadowcroft 2009; Avelino 2009; Shove and Walker 2007, 2008; Kemp and Rotmans 2008; Loorbach 2007; Smith and Kern 2007, 2008; Smith and Stirling 2008; Hendriks 2007; Berkhout et al. 2004).

The chapter is structured as follows. In the first section we introduce the theoretical basis of transition management and its related management principles and instruments, as discussed in the academic literature. We start with the basics of transition management, continue with the more abstract and theoretical aspects of transition management, and then proceed gradually toward the more concrete and practice-orientated instruments and principles which transition management researchers have developed over the course of time. Due to the interactive development of transition management, the reader will encounter a complex theory and model, in which many different aspects play an equally vital role. In the second section we describe the rise of transition concepts in the Dutch policy arena, how these concepts 'landed' in various research and development programmes, and how these applications are being monitored, evaluated, and studied. Finally, the third section discusses how transition management emerged within Dutch *mobility* policy, and how these concepts subsequently manifested themselves in various policy documents, research programmes, and innovation projects that deal with mobility. In our conclusion, we provide a concise summary in which we depict the overall policy context of transition management in relation to sustainable mobility.

Transition Management – An Introduction

Transition management is presented as a new mode of governance that aims to resolve persistent problems in societal systems, including a policy model to influence long term societal change (Rotmans et al. 2001; Rotmans 2005, 2003; Loorbach 2007; Kemp et al. 2007a, 2007b; Loorbach and Rotmans 2006; Kemp and Loorbach 2005). Transition management aims to foster learning about system innovations, and to bring together many actors (technologists, designers, governments, business, and citizens) to work on sustainability transitions, taking on board sociological critique that ecological modernization is often too much supply and technology orientated and that it neglects issues of lifestyle and values (Spaargaren 2003 and Shove 2004). Transition management is a model for working towards systemic change and innovation (Weterings et al. 1997; Elzen et al. 2004; Tukker et al. 2009).

No standard definition of transition managements exists. It is a governance approach which *makes the future more clearly manifest in current decisions*, by adopting longer time frames, exploring alternative trajectories, and opening avenues for system innovation (as well as system improvement), which seeks to *transform established practices in critical societal* subsystems within which unsustainable practices are deeply embedded, *develop interactive processes* where networks of actors implicated in a particular production/consumption nexus can come together, develop shared problem definitions, appreciate differing perspectives, and, above all, develop practical activities; *link technological and social innovation; engage in 'learning-by-doing'; tailor support for technologies to the different phases of the innovation cycle; and encourage a diversity of innovations ('variation') and competition* among different approaches (selection) to fulfill societal needs (Meadowcroft 2009: 325–6).

Transition management differs from classical management or innovation management in that it is not so much concerned with achieving predefined results, but rather with orienting development towards sustainability goals, while acknowledging that the exact outcomes of this development are unknown. Transition management seeks to help societies to transform themselves in a gradual, reflexive way through guided processes of variation and selection, the outcomes of which are stepping stones for further change (Kemp et al. 2007). Therein governance arrangements themselves become objects of change (Loorbach 2007).

The basic premise of transition management in both theory and practice, is that sustainable development requires transitions: non-linear processes of social change in which a societal system is structurally transformed (Rotmans 2003). 'Transition studies' apply theories and methods from various disciplines to study the history, dynamics and governance of 'transitions' and 'system innovations' (Rotmans et al. 2001; Rotmans 2005, 2003; Kemp and Rotmans 2002; Geels 2005; Grin 2005; Loorbach 2007). Drawing on complex system theory, the primary object of transition studies concerns societal systems (e.g. sectors or regions), which are viewed as 'complex adaptive systems'. In order to describe processes of change in these complex societal systems, different levels in time and (functional) aggregation are distinguished, resulting in the 'multi-phase', 'multi-level' and 'multi-pattern' frameworks applied in transition analysis (Rotmans 2005; Rotmans and Loorbach 2009). This complex system perspective, and the multi-level and multi-phase frameworks in transition studies, form the theoretical basis of transition management.

Transition Studies and the Theoretical Basis of Transition Management

The systemic perspective of transition studies requires a certain holistic view that acknowledges the interaction between human and non-human aspects. Cultural change interacts with technical change through social processes in a sociotechnical and economic landscape, in which policy is not an exogenous force but part and parcel of the change process it seeks to manage. As societal systems are complex (e.g. interactions at the micro-level have unintended effects at the macro-level) and open (i.e. adaptive to the systems' surroundings), these systems have certain dynamics of their own which no actor or group of actors can control.

The discussion on steering is placed within a multi-level framework, in which a distinction is made between *landscapes*, *regimes* and *niches*. The landscape refers to the surrounding of a societal system under study, where one sees trends with a relatively slow progress and/or developments with a high autonomous character (the macro-level). The regime is defined as the most 'dominant' configuration of actors, structures, and practices; the regime dominates the functioning of the societal system and defends the status quo (the meso-level). Niches on the other hand are defined as specific settings in which non-conformism and innovation can develop (the micro-level). These niches are also part of the societal system, but able to deviate from the dominant structures, practices and actors within that system. As the regime dominates the societal system, a necessary condition for a transition to occur is that this regime is either transformed or replaced by a new regime, and that niches challenge the regime and/or form such a new regime (Rotmans 2003).

A transition occurs when a societal system moves from one dynamic state of equilibrium to another, through a sequence of alternating phases of relatively fast and slow dynamics, which form a non-linear pattern (Rotmans 2003). Such non-linear change occurs through particular interactions between the macro-, meso- and micro-levels. A visual representation of multilevel interaction is given in Figure 3.1, indicating three processes: 1) the creation of novelties at the micro-level against the backdrop of existing (well-developed) regimes, 2) the evolution of the novelties, exercising counter influence on regimes and landscape, 3) the macro landscape which is gradually transformed as part of the process.

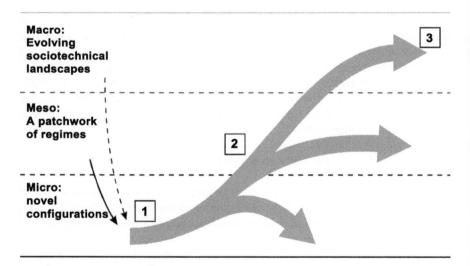

[1] Novelty, shaped by existing regime
[2] Evolves, is taken up, may modify regime
[3] Landscape is transformed

Figure 3.1   The multilevel model of innovation and transformation

Enabling 'niches', and transforming 'regimes' in interaction with a changing landscape, is an essential aspect of transition management. In each of the distinguished phases of a transition – predevelopment, take-off, acceleration, and stabilization (Rotmans 2003) – the challenges and possibilities for transition management are different. The complexity of societal systems prescribes that the way in which actors can influence interaction processes, differs for every level of aggregation and for every phase in time. As such, transition management requires an understanding of the 'internal dynamics' of a societal system, awareness of its multi-level interactions, and insight in its non-linear phase alternation through time. Transition management is not directly focused on a solution, but rather explorative and design-orientated. An essence of transition management is that it focuses on the content of societal issues as well as the process, by organizing an interactive and selective, participatory stakeholder-process aimed at learning and experimenting. Transition management starts off from the premise that full control and management of societal problems is not possible, but that we can 'manage' these problems in terms of adjusting, adapting, and influencing the societal system by organizing a joint searching and learning process, focused on long-term sustainable solutions (Rotmans 2005; Loorbach 2007).

According to Loorbach (2007: 105), long-term processes rely on 'coincidence, informal networks, intellectual capacities, and creativity, rather than on government-based planning; 'long-term goal setting is not the domain of policy, but rather that of opinion leaders, individuals with strategic capabilities and powerful actors from business, policy, science or society and culture'. As such, the more practice-orientated ambition of transition management is to bring such opinion leaders together, and enable them to integrate 'long-term governance activities into the realm of policy-making' (Loorbach 2007: 104). The transition management literature offers management principles and instruments to help organize such a process.

Until this point we have discussed the many things that transition management *is*. The reader may have wondered what transition management *is not*. To tackle just a few often heard confusions we can say that transition management is *not an instrument* but a framework for policy, it is *not a model for innovation management* and it is explicitly distinguished from Porter's model of five forces of competitive advantage (Porter 1980). The approach of transition management was born in a collaborative project of Dutch researchers and policy makers for the 4th national environmental policy plan in 2000.[1] Transition management was, therefore, developed in close interaction with practice. This resulted in a complex approach, developed both for theory-building as for practical societal change processes. In order to make it more applicable in practice, transition management researchers have worked on several more concrete principles and instruments (Rotmans 2003; Loorbach 2007).

---

1 This is discussed in more detail later in this chapter.

Principles and Instruments of Transition Management

First, a distinction can be made between the strategic, the tactical and the operational levels of management. Second, basic *management principles* and *instruments* are distinguished (Loorbach 2007: 81 and 114). Aside from a transition arena, transition pathways, a transition agenda, and transition experiments, these instruments also include participative process tools such as integrated system analysis and scenario exercises (Loorbach 2007; Sondeijker 2009; Van der Bosch 2010). Third, these levels, instruments, and principles are captured in a 'cyclical process model as a basis for operational management of multi-level governance', including the following set of activities: i) problem structuring, establishment of the transition arena and envisioning; ii) developing coalitions and transition agendas (transition images and related transition paths); iii) establishing and carrying out transition experiments and mobilizing the resulting transition networks; iv) monitoring, evaluating and learning lessons from the transition experiments and, based on these, adjust vision, agenda and coalitions (Loorbach 2002 and Rotmans 2003, in Loorbach 2007: 115).

The term 'cycle' suggests a sequence of activities, but according to Loorbach there is no fixed sequence in transition management activities, they are carried out 'partially and completely in sequence, in parallel and in random sequence' (Loorbach 2007: 115). While the problem structuring and envisioning occurs at the strategic level (long-term focus on system level), coalitions and transition agendas are developed at the tactical level (mid-term focus on regime level), and at the operational level (short-term focus on niche-level) actors are mobilized and transition experiments are implemented. Monitoring, evaluating, learning, and adapting concern an ongoing activity at all the levels of transition management (Loorbach 2007: 116–25).

As for its relation with traditional policy, transition management does not necessarily intend to replace mainstream policy; the two processes can initially 'co-exist'. TM can be used as a 'meta-level instrument to transitionize[2] a regular policy context' (Loorbach 2007: 272), for example by starting with a 'strategic transition arena on a small scale to explore alternative visions in an area where innovation and innovative visions are scarce' (ibid: 291). This is also referred to as the 'two-track approach'. With time and patience the transition movement may spread out and have a transformational influence on mainstream policy. While this type of 'transitioning' aims primarily at (government) policy, it also affects ongoing projects at operational levels, as one 'transitioning strategy' is to 'build on existing projects and experiments to *transitionize* these and by broadening and scaling-up and (re)defining visions' (ibid: 291–2: emphasis added).

---

2   'To transitionize' is a direct translation from the Dutch verb 'transitioneren', which has been invented in the context of transition management. The concept of transitionizing has been elaborated by Van der Bosch (2010).

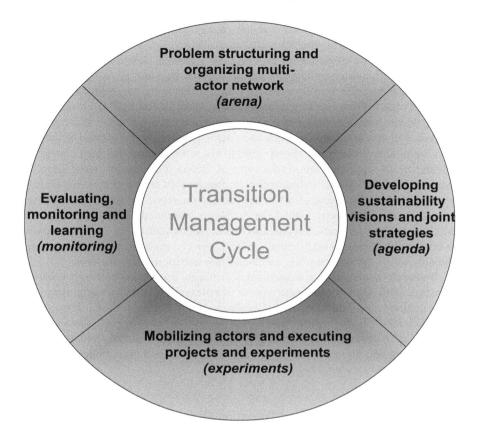

Figure 3.2   The transition management-cycle

Transition Management as an Evolutionary Governance Approach[3]

Transition management can be viewed as 'evolutionary governance' or 'co-evolutionary steering', as it is concerned with the functioning of a variation-selection-retention process: creating variety informed by visions of sustainability, shaping new paths, and reflexively adapting existing institutional frameworks and regimes (Kemp and Loorbach 2006). It is a model for escaping lock-in and moving towards solutions offering multiple benefits, not just for users but also for society as a whole. It is not a megalomaniac attempt to control the future, but an attempt to insert normative considerations into evolutionary processes in a reflexive manner, i.e. with attention for system-wide effects which are evaluated from a normative point of view (c.f. Voss and Kemp 2006). Learning, maintaining variety (through

---

3   This section draws heavily on Kemp (2009).

portfolio management), and institutional change are therefore important policy aims (Kemp et al. 2007a, 2007b).

The reliance on evolutionary processes of variation, selection, and retention is deliberate. Evolutionary change, on the basis of trial and error, is believed to bring greater benefits than revolutionary design. Planning based on anticipatory rationality has been shown to produce many undesirable results (March and Olsen 1995). Some element of planning is required to inject collective goals in the market process, which is orientated towards short-term economic gains instead of longer-term optimality (Kemp and Soete 1992). These considerations lead transition researchers to argue that we need a form of 'directed evolution', combining an element of planning with evolutionary mechanisms of trial and error. Evolution must be guided by ideas of what constitutes progress. To avoid modernistic mistakes, one might start with acute problems (Lindblom 1959; Meadowcroft 2005) in defining progress, but one also needs visions such as the vision of 'cradle to cradle' (McDonough and Braungart 2002), or visions of low-carbon mobility, chain mobility, mobility leasing, and intelligent transport infrastructures.

Research on transition management is primarily positioned in the governance literature, with reference to concepts such as reflexivity, networks, social learning, participation, co-production, etc. (Loorbach 2007; Rotmans 2005; Kemp and Loorbach 2005), including attention for the interaction between policy-makers and researchers (Kemp and Rotmans 2009). The next section describes how transition management and the cooperation between researchers and practitioners emerged in the Dutch policy context.

The Origins and Application of Transition Management

In recent years, the transition management approach has gained a great deal of attention from policy-makers, managers, and other practitioners in the Netherlands. It has been applied in various policy contexts, and to various programmes and projects (Loorbach 2007). In this section we first describe the rise of transition concepts in the Netherlands – as a particular interaction between researchers and policy-makers – and we subsequently discuss how transition management landed in various innovation programs and how these applications are being monitored, evaluated, and studied.

The Origins of Transition Management: A Short Historical Overview

In 2000 the first ideas on transition management were formulated in the project 'Transitions and transition management', as a preparation for the Fourth National Environmental Policy Plan (NEPP4). The first concepts and principles of transition management were created during this project. The idea of orienting innovation policy towards long-term change was not new as it was also a key feature of the DTO programme (Sustainable Technological Development) (1993: 7). By 1999 the DTO no longer existed, but the ideas that were born in the programme lived on. They were discussed in the working group KETI,[4] which consisted of policy officials discussing issues of knowledge and technological innovation. In 1999 KETI discussed several ideas on integrated long-term innovation policies for sustainable development. During a KETI-workshop with scientists, the notion of 'transitions' came up as a potential policy concept, together with the notion of 'system innovation'. The creation of new knowledge and new technology was seen as necessary for achieving policy goals related to sustainable development. It was believed that the improvement of existing systems of production was not enough for reaching (environmental) policy goals, and that existing functions had to be fulfilled in radically novel ways (i.e. 'system innovation'). The shift from the existing system towards a new system was conceptualized as a 'transition'.

This line of thinking was well-established among innovation researchers in the Netherlands. A group of researchers had been investigating possibilities for transitional change under the labels of system innovation and technological regime shifts.[5] Although the term 'transition' was frequently used, it was not yet theoretically defined. In 2000 this changed, when VROM (the Ministry of Housing, Land-use Planning and Environment) funded two projects to define and investigate the notion of transition: the project 'Transitions: can 3 people change the world?' (te Riele et al. 2000) and the project 'Transitions and Transition Management' (Rotmans et al. 2000). The latter project was specifically instituted to provide inputs for the fourth National Environmental Policy Plan (NEPP4), and involved an active interaction between policy makers and researchers. Details of the interactions are described by Kemp and Rotmans (2009). The project helped to make transition management an official concept for policy, following support by the Energy Council (AER) and Environment Council (VROMraad). The Ministry of Economic Affairs started using it to change its relation with business and to have a more active agenda for energy innovation, aligned with climate policy and business creation goals.

In 2001 the concepts of 'transition' and 'transition management' were presented in the 4th Dutch National Environmental Policy Plan (NEPP4). Therein, four transitions were identified as necessary: 1) to sustainable energy, 2) to sustainable use of biodiversity and natural resources, 3) to sustainable agriculture, and 4) to sustainable mobility. 'Transition management' was presented as a strategy to deal with environmental degradation by stimulating sustainable development as a

---

4   KETI is an abbreviation for 'Kennis en Technologische Innovaties', translated as 'Knowledge and Technological Innovations'.

5   These researchers were Johan Schot, Rob Weterings and René Kemp using terms such as technological regime shifts and system innovation. At the time the only project to use the transition concept as a theoretical organizer was the PhD project of Frank Geels on technological transitions which started in 1998. The project was part of the NWO research project 'Technological Regime Shifts to Environmental Sustainability' of MERIT and the University of Twente, of which René Kemp was the project leader.

specific aim of policy making. Several Dutch ministries mentioned the strategy, under which the Ministry of Economic Affairs (EZ), the Ministry of Housing, Land-use Planning and Environmental Management (VROM) and the Ministry of Transport, Public Works and Water Management (V&W).

Transition Management and Dutch Knowledge and Innovation Policy

At the end of 2003, the Dutch government decided to grant subsidies out of natural gas revenues to 37 cooperation alliances and consortia, dedicated to work on fundamental research to create new products, arrangements and concepts to 'strengthen the Dutch knowledge economy in its innovative and societal needs'.[6] This subsidy structure (referred to as the 'BSIK-regulation'[7]), was intended to prevent the 'Dutch disease', a phenomena in which increasing revenues from natural sources decrease competitiveness in the manufacturing sector, and therefore causes economic downfall in the sector. This can be seen as one of the main reasons of the government to spend these revenues on investments in the Dutch knowledge infrastructure. Next to that, in a knowledge-orientated society such as the Netherlands, the development of innovative concepts and new ideas is viewed as crucial for its international competitiveness. Considering the diversity of the selected projects, the term 'innovation' is to be interpreted broadly. Both *product* innovation and *process* innovation, as well as *scientific* innovation, were part of the BSIK-subsidy programme. The alliances and consortia resulting from these subsidies covered various topics, from health care and biotechnological innovations to construction, from ICT to nano-technology, from agriculture to mobility.

The core idea was that not just the government pays for the development of the innovations, but also the consortia partners. As a general rule, BSIK subsidizes 50 per cent of the total project cost, while the other 50 per cent is brought in by consortia partners.[8] This is not just for financial purposes, but also in order to actually involve businesses, governmental agencies, and knowledge institutions in innovation, and to create support in society for the developed ideas and knowledge. When viewed from a BSIK-perspective the 37 consortia are 'projects', however, when viewed individually they are programmes with their own projects. In some of these programmes and projects, transition management concepts have been (partially) applied.[9]

---

6   www.senter.nl/bsik/algemeen.

7   BSIK is an abbreviation for Besluit Subsidies Investeringen Kennisinfrastructuur, literally translated as 'Decision Subsidies Investments Knowledge Infrastructure'.

8   There are other divisions, however, where the consortium pays more than 50 per cent. The maximum amount of subsidy is never more than 50 per cent of the total project costs.

9   This was not in the original plans of the subsidiser; hence it is not an obligation for the programmes. The ideas of TM, however, have proven rather applicable for two of

In the majority of cases, this application of transition management in practice does not occur 'according' to the prescriptive TM-model as described above. The TM-literature frequently emphasizes that any tendency to institutionalize or control a transition process should be avoided, as it removes its innovative potential. However, in practice, many of such hierarchical institutional constructs are already in place, and completely replacing them by a TM-approach is often impossible or deemed undesirable. In those cases the challenge becomes to explore to what extent transition management can be used to improve or change existing policies, or to organize a complementary trajectory that deals with a more innovative and long-term perspective (the 'two track' or 'transitioning' approach as mentioned earlier). In fact, this occurred in several BSIK programmes. The application of transition management may therefore become more institutionalized or fixed than theory prescribes. This way the room for reflection and learning, as advocated by transition management, decreases. Aside from external demands of control and accountability, resulting in more institutionalized types of transition management, internally we can also find the need for fixation or control. This will elaborated later in the chapter, where we discuss the application of TM within a specific BSIK programme.

The BSIK programmes were initially set up according to a classical programme and project management model, albeit with an explicit focus on innovation. Only *later on* transition management was partially applied through as so-called 'transitioning' of ongoing initiatives, both at the level of programmes and projects. Six BSIK-programmes in particular were interested in applying transition concepts. Via presentations, workshops and literature they initially became acquainted with transition management, and usually one or two people from the programme management picked up on it and started applying it in their programme. Moreover, various people involved in the projects had worked with transition management previously, and therefore gradually introduced the concept in a bottom-up manner via the concrete projects they were working on. Because of this top-down and bottom-up influx of transition management-ideas, it soon became one of the theoretical frameworks used in these six BSIK programmes.

Monitoring and Evaluating the Application of Transition Management

As mentioned before, the transition management model as it exists today has not been merely developed by researchers: it has been 'co-produced' by researchers, policy-makers, and other practitioners (Kemp and Rotmans 2009; Loorbach 2007). Researchers are not just describing and analysing transition management practices or developing instruments, they are also involved in monitoring 'transition management projects' by evaluating process- and content-criteria, and by offering suggestions for improvement.

---

the five subparts of the group of 37 consortia; 'sustainable system innovation' and 'spatial planning'.

To strengthen the transition management development occurring in the BSIK programmes, and to connect the different initiatives in the programmes with each other, a project was set up to connect the different transition management efforts within BSIK. One of the TM-instruments mentioned earlier – 'monitoring' – became the prime focus of this joint project. The six programmes were evaluated regarding their 'transition potential' and the activities they undertook to strengthen this transition potential. Aside from that, the aim was to foster cooperation and mutual learning between the programmes. Transition monitoring is a form of monitoring that goes beyond testing the achievement of pre-set programme objectives, and instead recognizes the complex, multi-actor environment in which these programmes operate (Bressers and Diepenmaat 2009a, 2009b).

This environment leads to a setting where multiple objectives co-exist and where the more or less abstract objectives of the programmes ('stimulating transitions' and 'contributing to long-term sustainability objectives') can be monitored. Transition monitoring therefore does not measure the amount of dissertations published or the amount of newspaper articles produced, for instance. Instead, it measures the relative success of a programmeprogram in influencing a transition and positioning itself in that transition. It is not orientated towards statistical information about what has been achieved, but rather at harvesting lessons about the process of transformative change through the application of a standard framework. Methods that are common for transition monitoring include (in-depth) interviews, surveys, and participatory observation (Bressers and Diepenmaat 2009a, 2009b). Typical questions revolve around respondents' future images, current urgent problems, and the role that the programmes under research play in these processes. Transition monitoring is constructivist in nature, and focused on improvement and advice.

Most forms of monitoring measure transition potential at a certain point in time. Because transition monitoring is an ongoing process that can stretch over a period of years, experiences from the earlier period of the monitoring provide lessons for current and future monitoring, and can therefore contribute to change in monitoring approach along the way. Because of this a form of learning-while-evaluating, where experiences along the way of the monitoring process have an impact on the monitoring yet to be carried out, a type of 'learning monitoring' comes into existence (Guba and Lincoln 1989: 11). The monitored objectives are not limited to the pre-set programme objectives, but can also include programme objectives that were developed along the way. As with many learning organizations, the BSIK programmes started with only limited knowledge about the content of the total runtime of their programme, and they learned new lessons and insights along the way. Rather than ignoring these, they generally applied them directly in the programme, in order to maximize profit from them for the rest of their programme's runtime. These newly developed goals also became part of the transition monitoring.

Transition Management in Dutch Mobility Policy

As stated before, 'the transition to sustainable mobility' was one of the four 'necessary transitions' mentioned in the 4th Dutch National Environmental Policy Plan in 2001. Subsequently, 'transition-to-sustainable-mobility' emerged as a combination of words that has been increasingly used throughout the Netherlands. Besides the research community around transition studies and transition management, a variety of policy-makers, business-representatives, and NGO-representatives referred to this 'transition to sustainable mobility' in both written and spoken word. One can distinguish between four main settings in which the concept of transition (management) appeared in relation to sustainable mobility: 1) national mobility policy, 2) transition research on sustainable mobility, 3) the Dutch 'energy transition', and 4) the innovation programme Transumo (Avelino and Kemp 2009; Avelino, forthcoming). In this subsection we briefly discuss how the concept of transition (management) appears in these four settings. The aim is to give an overview of how transition management concepts emerged in Dutch mobility policy, the efforts made by researchers and practitioners to apply these concepts to the mobility sector, and how these concepts subsequently appeared in various policy documents, research programmes, and innovation projects – in order to determine its salience and the way in which it was used. We will demonstrate that the application of transition management may not always go by the book or according to ideal types.

The Ministry of Transport and Dutch Mobility Policy

Details of the use of transition management by the Ministry of Transport, Public Works and Water Management are described by Nooteboom (2006), who states that the support for transition management was weak within the Department for Transport of the Ministry. Instead of creating a transition platform, an 'innovation board' ('Innovatieberaad') was established in 2001 by a handful of civil servants. It was an informal network, with no budget and little decision-making power. In the first three years they focused their attention on organizing an EU conference for which they developed a set of 'roads to sustainable mobility'. The network was widened to include representatives of the ANWB (a Dutch organization representing the interests of road users and tourists), Toyota, Shell, and an environmental NGO. The mind map representing these 'roads to sustainable mobility' was perceived by the members of the innovation board as a breakthrough (Nooteboom 2006: 124). The innovation board allowed for informal discussions and mutual learning. The members were careful not to cause tension with the Ministry, Shell, or the automotive industry. Only the members of the innovation board, and sometimes their superiors, could see the significance behind the scenes of the innovation board (Nooteboom 2006: 125).

The 'transition to sustainable mobility' was mentioned in the cabinet's Mobility Policy Document ('Nota Mobiliteit', hereafter referred to as the Policy Document). This Policy Document was developed, presented, discussed, adapted, and formalized between 2004 and 2006, in cooperation between the Ministry for Transport and Water (V&W) and the Ministry of Housing, Land-use Planning and Environmental Management (VROM). The 'transition to sustainable mobility' is mentioned and 'transition management' as an innovation strategy for the long term, which the cabinet chooses in order to 'achieve sustainable mobility ... with a long-term time horizon and – related to that – innovation programmes ... for the short-term'. The use of 'transition terminology' increased in the period 2004–2005, but the final version of the Policy Document (2006) stopped mentioning both 'transition' and 'sustainability' altogether (Avelino and Kemp 2009). This demonstrates that there is an interest in transition management at the policy level, but that this does not guarantee the appliance of transition management in the actual implementation of mobility policy. The application of transition management in Dutch mobility policy is in fact fragile and partial.

Transition Research on Sustainable Mobility

The transition research perspective has been applied to the transition from sailing boats to steam ships (Geels 2002) and the building of highways in the Netherlands (Geels 2004, 2007). An attempt to apply transition management ideas to contemporary mobility *policy* was made by transition researchers Kemp and Rotmans (Kemp and Rotmans in, Elzen et al. 2004). The authors criticize Dutch policies on sustainable mobility for being too much orientated on technological fixes. The authors also criticized policy on new transport technologies (e.g. hybrid or electric cars) for being fragmented (being scattered over various stimulation programmes), and opportunistic. It was argued that experiments are carried out more or less *ad hoc*, without a coherent future vision and without sustainability considerations (Kemp and Rotmans 2004: 154).[10] Transition management was proposed as a new mode of governance to orient policy and societal interactions in the field of mobility more towards transitional change. It was argued that policy should be aiming for long-term solutions that are attractive from a user and societal sustainability point of view, including the following suggestions:

1. *Customized mobility*: individualized public transport and combining cars with other forms of transport (i.e. chain mobility); cars would be used more selectively and owned less.

---

10   An exception is the programme 'wegen naar de toekomst' (roads to the future).

2. *Mobility management*: the management of traffic streams through highway entry control, road pricing, cars automatically following each other at short distance using sensors and safety control ('platooning'), information services, electronic zone access management systems using transponders (devices that transmits a predetermined message in response to a predefined received signal) to control access to city centres, parking policy, possibly the use of tradable mobility credits where people get mobility rights which they can either use or sell.
3. *Cleaner cars*: low-emission internal combustion cars, electric vehicles (hybrid vehicles of full electric vehicles powered by batteries or fuel cells), urban cars, long-distance energy efficient cars with gas turbines.
4. *Underground transport*: this may take various forms including the radical option of vacuum pipes for transporting capsules.
5. *Teleworking*: working from home or a local 'telecentre', using modern computer communication, and teleconferencing, reducing the need for commuting but, as a rebound effect, possibly leading to increased travel outside work.
6. *Spatial planning limiting the need for transport*: compact cities, the (re)location of office buildings close to (public) transport nodes.
7. *Regulation* that strongly favours and encourages customized mobility and discourages car-use in specific zones.

In terms of policy and governance, the authors recommended that long-term goals and sustainability visions should be articulated for the mobility sector (e.g. customized mobility, mobility management, and underground transport); that there should be *social experiments with promising technologies and creation of niches for promising technologies*; that *programmes for system innovation* should be set up (e.g. programmes for chain mobility and for electric mobility, not just in terms of technology but also in terms of creating partnerships); that these programmes should be based on promising options, be limited in time, be continuously assessed and eliminated when found unnecessary or undesirable; and that the institutionalization of a long-term innovation agenda should not be merely developed by transport engineers, car lobbyists, or public transport companies, but rather involve innovative outsiders in the policy formulation process (Kemp and Rotmans 2004: 158–61). It was argued that such a process could be best organized through the set up of a transition arena (Dirven et al. 2002), a network of innovators willing to explore new mobility arrangements that could contribute to a transition, and the set up of a strategic 'transition council' with independent experts.[11]

---

11   More recently, transition research has been focused on car transport, in the book project *Automobility in Transition?*, a collaborative project of Dutch transition researchers and UK transport experts. The various chapters in the book examine the issue of stability and change in automobility from a transition point of view, discussing the difficulties of

The Dutch Energy Transition

The 'Platform for Sustainable Mobility' is one of the six innovation platforms in the Dutch 'energy transition', which is the official name for the new approach by the Dutch government to realize a sustainable energy system (Min EZ 2001, 2002, 2003, 2004). This energy transition is overseen and coordinated by the 'Interdepartmental Program Directorate of the Energy Transition' (consisting of six ministries) and a 'Taskforce Energy Transition' (composed of top-representatives from business, government, research organizations, banking, and NGOs). The Platform for Sustainable Mobility was created in 2005, to define transition paths and experiments towards sustainable mobility. In the 'Implementation Agenda' of the Policy Document on Mobility (published in September 2005, as discussed in the previous section) this Platform for Sustainable Mobility is mentioned as *an example of the application of transition management*. The platform itself is composed of representatives from government, one environmental NGO, the ANWB (Dutch organization representing the interests of road users and tourists), and business representatives (including Shell, BP Netherlands, Peugeot Netherlands, and DaimlerChrysler). On the website of the energy transition, the purpose of the Platform for Sustainable Mobility is described as follows:

> Transport is crucially important for our society, now and in the future. However, the current generation of motor fuels produces excessive emissions of CO_2 and other hazardous substances, and we depend on the oil-producing countries for these fuels. *During the transition to a sustainable energy supply*, the Platform therefore *aims to ensure affordable and independent mobility as well as sustainability* (emphasis added).[12]

It is interesting to see that in this description of its purpose, the Platform for Sustainable Mobility does not speak about 'the transition to sustainable mobility', but rather about 'the transition to a sustainable energy supply' (Avelino and Kemp 2009). Next to that, the text also states that the Platform aims to ensure 'affordable and independent mobility' *as well as* 'sustainability' as two separate things, rather than mentioning 'sustainable mobility' as one goal. The Platform does however distinguish 'four transition paths leading to sustainable mobility', consisting of:

1. hybridizing the fleet,
2. using bio-fuels,

---

changing mobility in a car-dependent world. As for policy, the book generally argues for the combined use of niche policies for alternative mobility and regime-changing policies through which car use is discouraged (Geels et al., forthcoming).

12   www.senternovem.nl/energietransitie/.

3. driving on hydrogen (including natural and biogas vehicles as precursor), and
4. intelligent transport systems.

The example of the Platform for Sustainable Mobility demonstrates the different uses of the idea of 'sustainable mobility'. The sharp division drawn between 'affordable and independent mobility' and 'sustainability' corresponds with differentiation and fragmentation in the mobility sector, which is also reflected on by Pel (Chapter 3). Transition management, on the one hand, aims for increased integration, but, on the other hand, acknowledges aspects of societal fragmentation (see Chapter 3). The example of the energy transition demonstrates the different ideas on sustainable mobility in the Netherlands, and the attempt to overcome these differences through the appliance of transition management.

The Transition Programme Transumo

As mentioned before, several BSIK-programs have (partially) applied transition management to their research programmes. One of these 37 BSIK-projects concerns the organization Transumo, a research programme on sustainable mobility. Transumo is an abbreviation for 'TRANsition to SUstainable MObility' and was founded in 2004. More than 150 organizations from the public, private and 'knowledge' sectors collaborate in applied research within well over 30 innovation projects related to transport and traffic. On its website, Transumo describes its mission as follows:

> to accelerate/encourage the transition to sustainable mobility. This will be achieved
> by initiating, and establishing for the long term, a transition process that leads to
> the replacement of the current, supply driven, mono-disciplinary technology and
> knowledge infrastructure, with a demand driven, multidisciplinary and trans-
> disciplinary, participative knowledge infrastructure.[13]

The Transumo-organization is part of the broader national BSIK-programme (as described earlier) to improve the 'knowledge infrastructure' by encouraging and subsidizing research programmes that specifically aim for applied, multidisciplinary science at the interface between knowledge and practice. On its website, Transumo describes this as 'the transition to the new knowledge infrastructure' which is supposed to lead to 'advances that help to strengthen the competitiveness of the Dutch transport sector ("Profit") and to preserve and improve spatial and ecological ("Planet"), and social ("People") aspects of mobility'. In the National Policy Document on Mobility (version 2005), Transumo is described as follows:

---

13   http://www.transumo.nl/Nl/Organisatie/Missie.aspx.

(...) a knowledge consortium of companies and research organisation that aims for innovations that lead to a more sustainable traffic and transport system: a better product for lower societal costs, meaning less traffic jams, less traffic accidents and less environmental hazard. Transumo is geared at personal mobility, freight transport and logistics, traffic management and infrastructure. Under each theme projects are carried out in so called experimental gardens in which diverging mobility challenges are combined (...) The aim of Transumo is to construct a knowledge network in the coming four years that can eventually lead to sustainable mobility and to a better position of the Netherlands on the international knowledge market. The Ministry for Transport and Water is involved with the content through clusters and projects, and operates as the representative on behalf of the central government (2005: 44).

Transumo serves as an example of the application of transition management in practice. As mentioned earlier, attempts to apply transition management often result in institutionalized and controlled forms. To a certain extent this was also the case in Transumo. The innovation projects and contributions to (the transition to) sustainable mobility had to be placed in pre-set formats, sheets, and other measurement devices, in order satisfy the desire for accountability and control on the part of the subsidizer.

Transumo provided a 'format' in which project proposals and reports have to be delivered,[14] in which project- leaders were required to report whether and how their project 'contributed to the transition to sustainable mobility', and how transition management was applied. Besides these formal reporting requirements, Transumo organized various workshops and sessions on how to 'learn' and deal with the challenges of 'the transition to sustainable mobility' and the application of 'transition management'. During these workshops managers and participants from different projects presented their concrete challenges and dilemmas to each other, and 'transition researchers' were invited to help structure the discussion and offer suggestions on how to move on (as will be elaborated in following chapters).

Also within the programme actions were undertaken that appeared more institutionalized than transition management would prescribe. One of the major problems Transumo saw for itself was 'the lack of vision'. To tackle this problem a vision group was set up, which would develop 'the Transumo vision', thereby institutionalizing the trajectory. Meanwhile, in both programme, projects, and at the level of individual stakeholders, the more concrete future images began to be considered to be 'the right image'. The 'quest for integration' as described in Chapter 3 (by Pel) appears to be visible in Transumo. Due to the aim of developing an integrated vision on sustainable mobility, together with stakeholders from all

14   The purpose of these reports is described as 'essential input for the obligatory monitoring of projects' and 'formal accountability' to the programme management concerning financial investments.

heritages, the idea may rise that one has developed *the* vision, thereby falling into the same trap as other stakeholders before.

On the other hand, the case of Transumo demonstrates that transition management, as an abstract theoretical notion, can find a place in a more practice-orientated research environment. The idea of the transition arena, transition monitoring, and other key instruments and principles of transition management were applied, and helped the programme in its ongoing development. Just like the application in policy, it is not always carried out as prescribed 'by the book', but it does enrich classical project and programme management.

Conclusion

Transition management is presented as a new mode of governance for sustainable development, aimed at resolving persistent problems in societal systems, including ideas on long term societal change. These processes of societal change, transitions, exist in a complex, multi-actor and multi-level setting with diverging time scales and actor interests. In these complex societal systems change is not a simple matter of planning and management. Transition management aims to offer tools and concepts to influence actors and interaction processes in order to increase the likelihood of an intended transition. Transition management starts off from the premise that full control and management of societal problems is not possible, but that we can 'manage' these problems in terms of adjusting, adapting and influencing the societal system by organizing a joint searching and learning process, focused on long-term sustainable solutions (Rotmans 2005; Loorbach 2007).

The model of transition management has been both appraised and criticized,[15] and received much attention in academic debates (Voss, Smith and Grin (eds) 2009; Shove and Walker 2007, 2008; Smith and Kern 2007, 2008; Smith and Stirling 2008; Hendriks 2009). The transition management approach has also gained a great deal of attention from policy-makers, managers, and other practitioners in the Netherlands. It has been applied in various policy contexts, and to various programmes and projects (Loorbach 2007). As we described above, in 2001 the concepts of transition and transition management were presented in the 4th Dutch National Environmental Policy Plan (NEPP4). Therein, four transitions were identified as necessary, one of which concerned the 'transition to sustainable mobility'.

Despite of these developments, there has been relatively little support for transition management within the ministry of Transport, Public Works and Water Management (Nooteboom 2006). In this chapter we demonstrated that even

---

15 The criticisms primarily pertain to the way in which transition management has been applied in some contexts; too low involvement of civil society (Hendriks 2009), too much influence of incumbents (Smith and Kern 2007; Kern and Howlett 2009) and too little attention for everyday politics of it (Shove and Walker 2008, 2007; Smith and Stirling 2007; Meadowcroft 2009).

though concepts such as 'transition' and 'sustainable' were initially addressed and discussed as an explicit aim of mobility policy, these ideas did not survive the last round of policy deliberations resulting in the 'Officially adopted Policy Document' in 2006. However, despite of the relatively weak support for transition management *within* the Department for Transport, the idea of 'a transition to sustainable mobility' has emerged and spread throughout the Netherlands, amongst a variety of policy-makers, business-representatives, and NGO-representatives. This attention for a transition to sustainable mobility was primarily manifested in the context of 'the Dutch energy transition' (in the form of the Platform for Sustainable Mobility), and in the context of the innovation programme Transumo.

Because several chapters in this book revolve around Transumo, our chapter has given additional attention to the policy context in which this Transumo programme emerged. Transumo was one out of several research innovation consortia funded by the government dedicated to do fundamental and applied research for innovation to strengthen the Dutch knowledge economy in its desire to be innovative and socially relevant. In several of these programmes and projects (such as Transumo), transition management was partly applied. Often, this application of transition management to practice did not occur 'according' to the prescriptive transition management-model as described in the literature. Therein the challenge became to explore to what extent transition management can be used to improve or change an ongoing process, or to organize a complementary trajectory that deals with a more innovative and long-terms perspective (the 'two track' or 'transitioning' approach as described before).

The chapter by Gorris and van den Bosch (Chapter 5) discusses the Transumo programme in more detail, including the way the organization is set up and operating, and then focuses on one of Transumo's projects; *Rush Hour Avoidance*, exploring the concept of 'transitioning'. The chapter by Bressers et al. (Chapter 6) also focuses on a project, by analysing *the A15-project*. It will explore the application of transition management in terms of the so-called 'two-track approach', discuss the challenges of combining a short-term and long-term orientation, and identify concrete transition management tools to deal with these challenges. The chapter by Pel (Chapter 4) will offer a critical reflection on fragmentation and integration in the mobility sector, and the role that transition management can play in this.

Our aim so far has been to describe the origins of transition management and to depict the policy context in which the Transumo-projects have been set up. In the mean time, critical academic debates on transition management (as referred to earlier) inspire the further development of transition management, as transition researchers reassess and refine their models and concepts based on these debates (Grin et al. 2010; Loorbach and Rotmans 2010; Avelino, forthcoming). Processes of change as well as the system of governance are expected to evolve with experience. Transition management is not something static or finalized, but rather a governance model in development, which is continuously adapted and extended on the basis of explorative and design-orientated research, including experience with its application in practice.

Chapter 4

Reflection on Transition Management: Mobility Policy between Integration and Differentiation

Bonno Pel

Introduction: Mobility Policy between Integration and Differentiation

In the developed countries there is widespread concern about mobility problems, and both societal actors and mobility researchers are seeking solution strategies towards 'sustainable mobility'. Despite considerable efforts to reduce the adverse effects of mobility however, some problems prove to be very persistent. As suppressed problems keep resurfacing, researchers and policy makers have come to understand that isolated measures are insufficient, and that sustainable mobility requires an 'integrated' approach.

This chapter seeks to make a critical contribution to this integration debate. The many integration ambitions are not rejected *a priori*, however; rather, they are examined in terms of their implicit assumptions. Such a critical approach will be shown to have practical value: it enhances our understanding of recurring problems in mobility policy. Well known is the phenomenon of partial solutions that fail to deliver the results hoped for, or even backfire – sometimes despite deliberate integration attempts. But however unfortunate, the apparent hiccups in integration attempts should not be mistaken for incidental 'barriers on the road'. This would underestimate the complexity ensuing from societal differentiation. The integration ambition is deceptively self-evident. Turning analysis on its head and taking societal *differentiation* as a starting point, the integration ambition will be presented as a fundamental challenge for governance. In a differentiated society, societal actors are necessarily non-comprehensive in their solution strategies, and different notions of sustainable mobility coexist. This 'reality check' may seem to only complicate matters, but it also allows for integration strategies better equipped to deal with differentiation. Transition management (TM) will be discussed as a prominent attempt in this direction.

This chapter begins by briefly reviewing some systemic analyses of mobility problems that underly the calls for an integrated approach to sustainable mobility. The chapter then specifies these analyses by highlighting some specific examples from the traffic management 'subsystem'. Next, the 'integration debate' and the mirror 'view from differentiation' are discussed. TM is treated as an evolutionary approach to integration. It deliberately confronts the differentiation challenge, instructively drawing the attention to the phenomenon of 'pseudo-solutions'. In its attempts to reconcile integration ambitions with differentiated conditions, transition management is not without tensions. Critical Systems Thinking helps us come to grips with these tensions. It helps to disclose the various ways in which actors reduce complexity, thus opening up the space for reflection, discussion and deliberation. The chapter concludes that Critical Systems Thinking sensitizes integration strategies at the risk of arriving at 'pseudo-solutions', thus harnessing integration strategies against societal complexity.

Sustainability and the Self-propagating Dynamics of the Mobility System

A wide range of social problems seem to call for a transition towards sustainable mobility. Congestion, emissions, noise, and safety are prominent social problems in highly developed countries. All of these have been the subject of mitigation policies, but to no avail, it would seem. Apart from these manifest problems, there are also less obvious, indirect mobility effects that can be considered problematic. Adams (2005) poses the counterfactual situation in which the congestion and pollution problems are dealt with, and a 'perpetuum mobile' mobility system is achieved. He suggests that the sky is not the limit. Unfettered mobility growth will only exacerbate the indirect social mobility effects: the 'hyper-mobile' society will need increasing amounts of space, especially for parking. It will pose increasing difficulties for those not able to drive a car, and it will be more dangerous. And, on closer inspection, a great manifold of indirect effects can be discerned: obesity, because of the marginalization of non-motorized transport; 'McCulture' homogenization, alienation and loss of social ties; and the intensification of surveillance.

For a long time, sustainable transport has been approached by means of an incremental strategy of easing constraints (Cohen 2006: 24). Typically, such strategy addresses issues such as fuel efficiency and urban congestion. It disregards the effects on 'sedentary lifestyles', however (idem: 30). This latter category, corresponding with Adams' 'indirect mobility problems', is the third dimension of Cohen's 'systems view of automobile dependence'. And indeed, a systems view on the mobility system seems indispensable for the understanding of current mobility problematics (see also Meyer and Miller (2001)). The variety of mobility problems could then be addressed coherently. Similarly, the difficulty to address them all at once becomes more understandable by observing it as a typical property of a composed system. Mobility system evolution is not determined by 'the mobility sector'; it emerges from the interactions between many societal sectors that together form a mobility system. The mobility system is co-determined by many sectors: the spatio-temporal organization of work and leisure, for instance, is alone the result of many sectoral policies combined.

In several renowned systemic analyses, current mobility systems are characterized as systems of automobile dependence (Newman and Kenworthy 1999; Dupuy 1999; Urry 2004). This specifies 'systemness', emphasizing the structural nature of mobility problems. This systems view diverges from the common focus on mobility externalities that suggests policies to combat them. 'Car dependency' points to an underlying systemic condition that tends to be immune to externality-mitigating solutions: modern societies are essentially dependent on cars, and are locked in an unsustainable path dependency. The problem, however, is not only that society has come to depend on cars. What is more, the diagnosis emphasizes that this dependency has an inherent tendency to increase. In the words of Urry:

> Automobility can be conceptualized as a self-organizing autopoietic, nonlinear system that spreads world-wide, and includes cars, car-drivers, roads, petroleum supplies and many novel objects, technologies and signs. The system generates the preconditions for its own self-expansion (Urry 2004: 27).

As an autopoietic system, the system creates the preconditions for its own self-expansion. This hypothesis presupposes a mechanism of reproduction that needs to be explained. In fact, the claim can be substantiated in many ways. Car dependency theory has brought forward the following accounts. A basic explanation is the operation of the landuse-transport cycle. Car mobility has facilitated urban sprawl, a land-use pattern that gives strong incentives for car use, rather than public transport or bicycle transport (Wegener and Fürst 1999; Newman and Kenworthy 1999). Dupuy (1999) emphasizes the network effects of car mobility, the incentive for individuals to join the system. Finally, Urry himself gives the following substantiation of his own claim:

> It is through automobility's restructurings of time and space that it generates the need for ever more cars to deal with what they both presuppose and call into existence (Urry 2004: 3).

Clearly, there are different accounts of self-reproduction, indicating theoretical inconclusiveness about the specific mechanisms which account for it. And indeed, the very composite character of the mobility system should warn against simplistic explanations; self-reproduction is unlikely to rely on a single mechanism. But without entering the theoretical intricacies of *specifying* the self-reproducing dynamic, and considering the evidence that there is such a dynamic, it will be accepted as a basis for further analysis. Against its inherent expansion, and the mobility system's tendency to turn into an automobility-dominated system, incremental strategies are bound to fail. Apart from the multi-faceted collection of mobility 'externalities', there is this meta-problem of self-propagation. The next section describes how this manifests concretely in mobility policy paradoxes, with examples from the traffic management field.

Self-propagation and Accommodation: Traffic Management

Many problems and aspects of the mobility system can be considered unsustainable in their own right. But, as suggested by the systemic analyses in the previous section, the main difficulty is posed by the meta-problem of self-propagating system dynamics. In more concrete terms, the structural problem is the social structure that continues to favour the car over more sustainable alternatives. Compared with the flexibility and possibilities of the car, other travel modes tend to fall short. On strong accounts of this systemic and also structuralist analysis, system feedbacks tend to overpower system improvement: modal shift policies amount to 'flogging a dead horse', and sustainable mobility seems to be fundamentally out of reach. Incremental system improvements and reformist tinkering are just not sufficient, as they fail to tackle the system on the appropriate *structural* level.

A good example of system improvement is traffic management. Traffic management is concerned with guiding vehicles over the infrastructure. This guidance takes many forms: as well as the static arrangements of road signs, traffic lights and road designs, there are the dynamic traffic management (DTM) arrangements that are responsive to actual conditions. Traffic management essentially serves the two goals of ensuring traffic safety and efficient traffic flow. The latter goal in particular makes clear how traffic management can be considered the typically accommodative subsystem of the mobility system: it prevents the persistent mobility from 'getting out of hand', and has an efficiency rationale. It seems to be an ideal field of empirical investigation into the relation between accommodating system improvement and structural sustainability. Especially in the Netherlands, traffic management accommodation is becoming more and more important. On the one hand, road pricing is waiting to be implemented. Traffic demand is difficult to curb under current conditions. On the other hand, the possibilities for infrastructure expansion are very limited due to spatial, environmental and financial constraints. This is how the Dutch Ministry of Transport came to adopt a three-pronged approach of 'utilization, construction, and pricing', with traffic management 'utilization' occupying a prominent place (Ministry of Transport 2005). Somehow, existing infrastructure has to accommodate increasing volumes of traffic, an efficiency leap depending primarily on a range of traffic management measures to enhance road network performance. In 2007 a specific traffic management policy framework sketched how this strategy would be pursued over the longer term (Ministry of Transport 2007; Rijkswaterstaat 2007). It was observed how the shift from a bottleneck-orientated to a network optimization approach had helped to prevent the Dutch congestion problem from escalating. But with even greater traffic volumes expected, development of new innovation trajectories was indicated to be necessary. The revolutionary changes in in-car intelligence were identified as unpredictable but promising developments towards further gains in congestion abatement and network reliability. As the above governmental sources point out, traffic management optimization has helped prevent the Dutch congestion problem from escalating. But to the public, the failure to solve the congestion crisis is obvious; the success of Dutch traffic management is debatable. In terms of traffic safety, however, successes are more convincing: the Netherlands has a good record in traffic casualties per vehicle kilometre. Nevertheless, both assessments of performance are rather superficial, disregarding the many factors which co-determine traffic flow and safety outcomes. As indicated in the previous section, a more systematic view is needed to assess traffic management performance. For instance, a systematic assessment would at least relate outcomes to growing traffic volumes. This adds the important nuance that traffic management optimization may not have reduced congestion levels themselves, but did manage to absorb considerable growth in traffic volumes (Annema and Vonk Noordegraaf 2009). It would also include many variables intervening between traffic management policies, on the one hand, and traffic flow and safety outcomes on the other. What is more, it would highlight the many side effects of traffic management policies. In the following, four of them will be briefly discussed: 'induced travel', 'problem shifting', 'system overload' and 'car dependency'. Consideration of these issues will not only enable balanced assessment of traffic management performance, it will also illustrate the general difficulties of accommodative efficiency-orientated strategies in a self-propagating system.

Induced Travel

The basic idea is that any increase in highway capacity reduces the generalized cost of travel, by reducing the time cost of travel. This applies especially to congested highways. In brief, 'induced travel' indicates how improvements in traffic handling can spur traffic generation. It is a feedback loop to be reckoned with, even when its exact significance is difficult to specify: the induced travel claim presupposes, for instance, elasticity in travel demand. This presupposition is contested (Noland and Lem 2002; Metz 2008a, 2008b), as travel behaviour is far more complex than such a rational choice frame suggests. Apart from the elasticity debate, it should be noted that different forms of 'induced travel' can be distinguished. Increase in highway capacity may have differing behavioural effects, ranging from changes in modal choice to changes in departure times.

Problem Shifting

As mentioned, 'induced travel' has many facets. Traffic may actually be induced or generated, but it may also be shifted in time and space. Traffic management can arrange for local traffic flow improvements, but such improvements will always have impacts on the wider road network. Ramp metering arrangements may, for instance, be succesful in securing highway circulation, but achieve this only at the cost of queueing on the access roads. In this way, bottleneck solutions tend to have their consequences 'downstream', or at a later time. In that sense, the term 'solution' can be considered a euphemism for these arrangements (Topp 1995).

On the other hand, the term 'problem shifting' downplays the gains to be achieved by local interventions. The detrimental side-effects of traffic do, of course, depend on the vicinity of residential areas, and some roads are more important for network performance than others. 'Problem shifting' can alleviate problems locally.

System Overload

Traffic management improvements may induce travel, and 'shift problems', as side-effects. But the improvements can also be actually self-undermining. Especially in the Netherlands, traffic management optimization has been successful in accommodating extremely high traffic intensities on limited infrastructure capacity. The problem of providing capacity proportional to growth could be said to have been tackled by intensification of use of the existing network. Intensification can be considered a very 'sustainable' way of development, but this success is Janus-faced: infrastructure is made use of at close to maximal capacity. Redundant capacity is almost lacking, which makes for a volatile, vulnerable road system: traffic incidents can have disproportional effects (Immers and van der Knaap 2007). Such disproportionate effects are common experiences for the Dutch public, regarding both road congestion and railroad operations: disturbances spread throughout the network.

Car Dependency

As mentioned, increased capacity can have different side effects. But it must be said that the degree to which these effects actually backfire is very situation-dependent. This depends, for instance, on the behavioural responses of travellers. And, apart from the short-term effects that cast doubt on anti-congestion achievements, the possible long-term consequences need a mention in their own right. The short-term 'induced travel' effect, for instance, may affect settlement behaviour as well as travel behaviour. Seen in a longer time frame, spatial dispersal of activities is a behavioural response to be reckoned with.

Considering these drawbacks of anti-congestion policies, traffic management risks actually contributing to system lock-in, even though it improves the system. Its interaction with the mobility system's self-propagating dynamics seems unfortunate. To be sure, this claim of car-dependency reinforcement applies to anticongestion policies, not to traffic management per se. Traffic management need not be restricted to anti-congestion. Not only does it serve safety, it can also prioritize between transport modes, rationing waiting times at crossings. Its 'sustainability potential' is highly ambiguous, as it involves many sustainability aspects apart from congestion problems (Pel and Boons 2010). The side effects of anticongestion policies must be taken seriously, not so much to 'unmask' the failure behind apparent traffic management success, but especially to serve as illustrations of the more general difficulty of optimization-towards-sustainability.

This difficulty seems to be increasingly acknowledged, as the many pleas for mobility policy integration testify.

The Quest for Integration

If traffic management is to contribute to sustainability and avoid reinforcing the self-propagating dynamics of the mobility system, its side effects need to be dealt with. In a sense, the solution is easy: traffic management can facilitate traffic flow, but it can also erect barriers and limit road capacity under the heading of a 'differentiation in accessibility profiles'. But for obvious reasons, the scope for such restrictive measures is limited. The differing side-effects cannot all be addressed by the subsystem itself: even when 'shifting problems' and 'system overload' could in principle be solved internally, 'induced travel' and 'car dependency' can be considered inherent and inevitable side effects. They are strongly co-determined by structural conditions that transcend the accommodative traffic management subsystem.

In view of the limitations to the internal solution of traffic management flaws, outside help seems to be required: system integration (Hine 2000; Geerlings and Lohuis in this volume). Mobility system integration is the obvious response to the diagnosis of overall system dysfunction. Such an approach has become obvious once the 'predict and provide' paradigm was abandoned. Integration seems the true successor to the 'predict and provide' paradigm, especially as restrictive policies are prone to fail to the same limitations of optimization strategies (Bertolini et al. 2008). However, 'integrated transport policy' seems mainly obvious as a general idea. Integration of what with what? Potter and Skinner (2000) address this underspecification, and seek to contribute to better understanding. They present a distinction between levels of integration: functional or modal integration, transport and planning integration, social integration, environmental, economic and transport policy integration.

> Essentially the highest level holistic strategy may be described as one which brings together all of the above in a coherent way. While such a strategy contains little that is new, the high level of integration between different policy strands would be an important development. The aim is to ensure that environmental, fiscal and social measures are working in harmony to reduce the need for travel, and reduce the impact of journeys made. All of the many elements in social, economic, environmental, transport and land-use policies are integrated in such a way that the whole system has a greater value than the sum of its parts. This is a systems led or holistic approach. This level provides the best opportunity for a more sustainable transport system and is the benchmark against which all integrated transport strategies should be tested (Potter and Skinner 2000: 284).

This benchmark of integration essentially proposes a 'supersystem' as a yardstick for mobility system functioning. In such 'supersystem', even 'induced travel' and 'car dependency' might be solvable. The traffic-inducing shifts in 'generalized costs' generated by traffic management measures could be compensated for, for instance by pricing measures.

This 'supersystem' benchmark indicates how traffic management (and other forms of system optimization) could be cured from side-effects, and contribute to sustainability. But integrated mobility policy proves to be very difficult to achieve in practice, and not only at its highest 'holistic' level. In fact, May et al. (2006) find very little evidence of 'synergy', the theorized surplus value of integration. Such fruitful interactions between instruments seem to be rare occasions; complementarity between instruments they consider a more realistic goal (idem: 326). However, integration need not be pursued as a quest for synergy alone. Apart from the quest for synergy, integration can be pursued as 'removal of barriers'. Many differing barriers can be distinguished such as legal/institutional, financial, political/cultural, practical/technological (May et al. 2006: 321; Hine 2000). This strategy aims to identify barriers to implementation, and find a second instrument to overcome them (May et al. 2006: 320). In fact, the necessity to overcome barriers partly accounts for limited 'synergy', as it tends to entail compromises (idem: 322).

'Synergy' was claimed to be a rare occurrence, as 'overcoming barriers' tends to detract from these positive interactions between instruments. Apart from this difficulty, a further complication seems to be that its occurrence is difficult to establish. May et al. (2006) point out the difficulty of isolating the impacts of policy instruments. Synergy they consider harder to achieve with a single objective, as the instruments contributing to it will to some extent duplicate one another in their impacts (idem: 322, 326).

Apparently, the holistic benchmark for system integration suggested above is a standard remote from everyday practice. Jones and Lucas (2000: 185) describe how in the UK, transport has started to become acknowledged as a 'cross-cutting issue', and how this has led to the establishment of a broader approach to the appraisal of road schemes. This integrated approach shows a tragic mechanism (Teisman 2005), where integration ambitions turn into barriers (see also Verweij and Gerrits (2010), on organizational barriers to network-road management):

> While this approach is to be welcomed, in terms of its broadening of the criteria under which transport proposals are assessed, the particular structure of the framework often makes it difficult to link it directly with other sector responsibilities and initiatives. It may thus, inadvertently, in some respects be acting as a barrier to 'joined-up' policy appraisal (Jones and Lucas 2000: 186).

Still, they consider a common framework is 'ideally required' (idem: 191/192). The authors seek to find solutions for the apparent mismatch between the general integrated framework, on the one hand, and the particular sector responsibilities, on the other. It is suggested that indicators should be provided by the departments with prime responsibility for the relevant area. In some cases, the authors admit, such 'prime responsibility' is difficult to allocate, suggesting the establishment of a cross-departmental working group.

The tension between the aim for 'synergy' and the necessity to 'remove barriers' seems to be the basic difficulty in the pursuit of an integrated mobility policy. It is also evident in Hull (2008), when investigating cross-sectoral cooperation in UK local transport authorities. She explains the difficulty as follows:

> Sector-specific performance management creates competing agendas and the protection of empires in local authorities between the different teams. Visions of what a sustainable transport system might look like varies from sector to sector and, depending on levels of cooperation and communication, is 'translated' into transport planning practice in different ways in different localities (Hull 2008: 102).

What is striking is the apparent near impossibility to allocate prime responsibilities, and the difficulty to establish a clear set of indicators. Jones and Lucas's earlier suggestion of an interdepartmental working group seems optimistic, considering the above-mentioned barriers between sectors. It seems that mobility is more and more often acknowledged as a cross-cutting issue, but the implications of this might not be acknowledged to the full. As Hull notes, different sectors have their particular 'translations' of sustainability, the goal policy integration was meant to serve. The quest for integration may underestimate the fragmentation that these 'translations' indicate.

The Challenge of Societal Differentiation

The self-propagating dynamics of the mobility system are hard to tackle by optimization strategies alone. Accommodative policies typically suffer from side effects, as the traffic management example illustrated. The side effects create a need for mobility policy integration. However, this rather obvious solution strategy turned out to be difficult to bring about, as 'synergy' and integrated, joined-up appraisal run counter to institutional barriers. Hull (2008) drew attention to this by pointing out the different sectoral 'translations' of sustainability. In her analysis, integration failure seems not to be due to the difficulty of overcoming incidental barriers, or to overlapping measures that prevent 'synergy' from coming about. Deeper roots are indicated: institutional differentiation, with sustainable mobility 'falling through the cracks' of a fragmented society (Hull 2008: 101).

At first sight, differentiation and fragmentation do not seem to add much to integration research. These phenomena have been mentioned already under 'removal of barriers', albeit only implicitly. Fragmentation is the very lack of coordination that needs to be overcome; in that sense, the viewpoint of fragmentation is even presupposed. Are not integration and fragmentation just counterparts, bound to recur in any sustainable mobility consideration?! The brief review above, however, suggests not. 'Synergy' and 'removal of barriers' are notions stemming from the quest for integration, and so is the diagnosis of sustainable mobility 'falling through the cracks'. But the assertion of different sectoral frames with divergent 'translations' of sustainable mobility is essential. It pinpoints a condition that is essential from a governance point of view, namely the circumstance that in a differentiated society, actors entertain different world views. Sustainable mobility cannot be treated as a singular final destination of integration attempts, for lack of consensus on what it actually entails (see above for the different dimensions of mobility problems that actors may choose to emphasize or de-emphasize).

This is how the 'fragmentation view' adds to the integration debate: reasoning from the need for integration, fragmentation tends to be viewed as an incidental circumstance to be overcome (i.e. a barrier). But however understable in the light of integration ambitions, such a line of reasoning risks being mistaken in two respects. Firstly, 'fragmentation as a barrier' focuses on the negative side of societal differentiation. It focuses on means and hindrances, and can easily 'forget' the inherent difficulty of reaching consensus on the goals that integration is to serve. Secondly, reasoning from the quest for integration, fragmentation may seem to be an undesirable exception. However, fragmentation may actually be the rule. This turns the argumentation for the need for integration on its head. It brings us to consider that maybe it is the integration attempt that is disturbing everyday proceedings, rather than the other way around. 'Integration attempts as disturbance' articulates more clearly the added value of a 'fragmentation view' on integrated mobility policy. And apart from its surprise value, the viewpoint is not without foundation. Niklas Luhmann has provided it with a compelling line of argumentation, well beyond general philosophical considerations.

In modern societies, the argument goes, complexity tends to be overwhelming. Somehow, governing actors need to cope with this complexity; as Luhmann (Luhmann 1990, 1995) emphasizes, complexity needs to be reduced. Complexity reduction can be achieved by limiting the amount of societal interrelations observed, i.e. through selective observation. Selection can be expressed as a distinction between the relevant and the irrelevant relations. The irrelevant relations are ignored; they become the 'environment' to the 'system' of relevant relations. These system/environment distinctions are the means to cope with complexity. Stabilization of these system/environment boundaries prevents governing actors and organizations from being overburdened by outside pressures, and allows for continuity. An example of such complexity reduction seems to be the apparent neglect of 'induced travel' (see above): these indirect effects are notoriously difficult to predict. Including these aspects in traffic modelling would seriously compromise the accuracy and speed with which actual intensities and distributions can be modelled – actual traffic flow is complex enough!

Reasoning from the quest for integration, one might speak of unfortunate neglect, but there are reasons to exclude 'induced travel' from the equation.

These stabilized relevant/irrelevant distinctions entail a certain closure towards the environment, which is the price of the very complexity reduction that made it manageable. This is how social systems such as transport boards or spatial planning agencies become 'introverted'. They are self-referential, perceiving the world 'out there' through the lens of their relevant/irrelevant distinctions. The organizations governing the mobility system are self-referential, and *necessarily so*. In this way, fragmentation can be considered the rule rather than the exception.

An important consequence of self-reference is societal fragmentation into systems according relevance selectively, and into systems of *meaning*. As Hull remarked in the above, policy sectors make their particular 'translations' of what a sustainable transport system looks like. In this analysis, any societal order is the emergent result of the actions of a myriad of self-referential actors and organizations, all optimizing their own 'systems'. A 'sustainable mobility system', in other words, is unlikely to come about in the form of a unilaterally defined 'supersystem'. From a Luhmannian viewpoint, this benchmark seems hopelessly far removed from the reality of differentiated society.

A selfreferential system 'forgets' what aspects of reality it has excluded; it is suffering from 'blind spots'. This being the case, 'induced travel' is not only exogenized for pragmatic reasons, but the aspect is considered irrelevant altogether, filtered out by an organization's system of meaning. This is how self-reference entails relativism (Cilliers 2005), with the concomitant communication difficulties. The earlier mentioned 'barriers' to integration are deep-rooted in belief systems and communication channels. Indeed, the perspective of social differentiation can be taken as sceptical undermining of sustainability attempts (Luhmann 1989). Why for example aim for integration if the reasons to do this are hardly communicable to the parties involved? In the following section a more constructive approach is taken.

Transition Management: An Evolutionary View of Integration

From a Luhmannian viewpoint, it is hardly surprising that the 'quest for integration' finds many institutional barriers in its way: self-referential systems have their own particular ideas about what a 'sustainable transport system' looks like. According to this societal analysis, the integration sought for could only emerge over time, depending on the co-evolution of self-referential systems. The Luhmannian fragmentation view introduces an evolutionary view of system integration.

An evolutionary view on mobility system integration is promising (Bertolini et al. 2008). Such a framework is better equipped to capture the slowly emerging results of integration processes that may only surface after a considerable time. Seen as coupling between self-referential systems avoiding being overburdened by complexity, integration processes must generally be slow. One could think of the long-lasting divides between transport and spatial planning, for instance. These slow processes of changing systems of meaning are problematic for the evaluation process. As already discussed above, 'synergy' effects were difficult to establish, but it could very well be that evaluation simply took place too soon to capture the complexity of the phenomenon concerned (Sanderson 2000).

An evolutionary view of sustainable mobility thus seems promising as a way to appreciate the inertia of changing systems of meaning. And, instead of deploring the slowness or apparent failure of single integration attempts, it directs attention to potentially reinforcing interactions between a great many small or bigger changes.

Mobility system change occurs through a co-evolution of subsystems. This takes on board societal differentiation with a continued quest for integration. It is a basic premise of 'transition management', which will be discussed here as an evolutionary approach that seeks to reconcile integration ambitions with differentiation conditions. Transition management follows structural analysis, where the current situation is diagnosed as one of car-dependent lock-in (Rotmans 2003, 2006; Loorbach 2007; Avelino et al. in this volume). Lock-in has come about through co-evolutionary processes, such as the mutual conditioning of mass automobility and urban sprawl. In fact, TM is based on a societal model that encompasses far more than this well-known land-use-transport nexus (Wegener and Fürst 1999). The multi-level transition model (Geels 2002, 2005) distinguishes the 'landscape', 'regime' and 'niche' levels, the interplay of which determines social evolution.

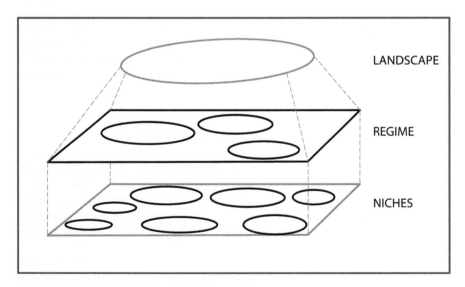

Figure 4.1   Multi-level model of transitions

The 'landscape' is the level of general societal changes, such as individualization and emancipation (as social processes) or changes in oil supply. The 'regime' refers to the dominant practices in a system. In the case of the mobility system, spatial planning doctrine and mobility policy are examples, but also taxation policy and social policy need to be mentioned. Finally, the 'niche' consists of new practices that challenge the regime constellation, including technological innovations as well as social movements. The multi-level transition model is a model of socio-technical change. This is how it is more encompassing than evolutionary land-use-transport models; it also includes cultural, technological and economic aspects of system evolution. For the mobility transition, it is important to note that this model integrates non-spatial dimensions in the analysis.

Transitions are structural long-term changes. The framework is comprehensive, but its evolutionary aspect clearly distinguishes it from blueprint planning approaches. TM seeks to steer the multi-level co-evolution towards sustainability; it theorizes both lock-in and lock-out. More precisely, TM seeks to promote lock-out as far as these evolutionary processes allow for such intervention. It thus acknowledges limited steering capacity, dispersed control and societal fragmentation. It does not strive for the complete integration of all determinants in the multi-level model. The 'supersystem' benchmark mentioned above thus differs from transition management ambitions, as it seems to entertain a more linear view of the mobility system. TM instead sees the mobility system as a complex adaptive system, and strives to use the possibilities for 'synergies' and 'leverage' (Senge 1999; Flood 1999) of such composed systems. Treating the mobility system as a composite, TM clearly operates from a 'fragmentation view'.

On the other hand, the quest for transitions reveals a strong integration ambition and an analytical emphasis on systemic wholeness. In this sense, TM is an approach that seeks to reinvigorate the 'quest for integration', rather than abandon the project. It specifically seeks to deal with so-called 'persistent', structural problems.

> There are no ready-made solutions for persistent problems and pseudo-solutions soon become part of the problem. Anticongestion policies, for instance, create space for more traffic, aggravating other problems. Persistent problems cannot be solved by current policies alone, nor can they be corrected by the market (Rotmans and Kemp 2008: 1009).

Not surprisingly, transition management mistrusts optimization strategies. Interestingly, it indicates that 'pseudo-solutions' can even be considered part of the persistent problem. This distinction between 'pseudo-solution' and 'sustainable' solutions is an important analytical category of the TM approach to persistent problems. The distinction is, of course controversial: congestion abatement measures may have side effects, but to many, they offer real solutions to a real problem. On the other hand, the 'pseudo-solution' verdict is understandable, once one endorses a structural problem diagnosis (see above). The 'pseudo-solution' category sharpens TM strategy with respect to the problems of side effects that are bound to occur in a differentiated society. At the same time, the category does presuppose some structural problem analysis, or even an implicit 'supersystem' benchmark.

To conclude, TM is a typical attempt to reconcile the 'quest for integration' and the 'view from fragmentation' perspectives on sustainable mobility. Its evolutionary approach is a promising way to manoeuvre between integration and differentiation. However, this manoeuvring yields tensions that have not gone unnoticed (Shove and Walker 2007, 2008). The very notion of a pseudo-solution entails the risk of letting in 'supersystem' benchmarks through the back door, despite earlier acknowledgement of differentiation. The tension need not, however, be treated in terms of inconsistency; it is also a practical challenge for governance and management (Pel and Teisman 2009). In the next section, this practical challenge will be addressed, referring to some transition processes described by other contributions in this volume.

'Boundary Judgements' in Mobility Transition Processes

TM seeks to reconcile the quest for integration with the circumstance of fragmentation. Of course, such ambition may seem naive: the acknowledgement of widespread and strong self-refence may dismiss it as a Tower of Babel project, bound to falter on communication breakdowns. But complete miscommunication need not be presupposed; system/environment boundaries can be permeable to varying degrees. The complexity reductions of the actors involved in mobility policy can even be expected to display overlaps and similarities, considering their shared orientation on overlapping and interrelated problems. The congruence of societal actors' system boundaries is an empirical question (see also the chapter by te Brömmelstroet and Bertolini in this volume), especially as these boundaries shift over time.

Luhmann's theory of societal differentiation gave the outlines of an empirical research programme. It suggests specific attention should be given to relevant/irrelevant distinctions, or system internal/external distinctions. But TM and similar integration attempts have a practical interest. They lead to questions such as how can these system boundaries be changed for the sake of integration and transition? What do they look like in actual mobility policy-making and how can they be detected? The 'view from differentiation' can be made operative in the form of 'critical systems heuristics':

> The idea is that both the meaning and the validity of practical propositions (e.g. solution proposals or evaluations) depend on assumptions about what 'facts' (observations) and 'norms' (valuations) are to be considered relevant and what others are to be ignored or considered less important. I call these assumptions 'boundary judgements', for they define the boundaries of the reference system

to which a proposition refers and for which it is valid. A critical employment of the systems idea requires that we understand and disclose the selectivity of reference systems (Ulrich 2003: 333).

What is important about the 'critical systems heuristics' approach is that it inquires about the ways in which actors make sense of and act in their daily practices. It is a way of questioning, usually targeted at individuals rather than organizations. The 'boundary judgements' of individuals may display differences with those institutionalized in the communication channels of organizations; Critical Systems Thinking can be used for analysis on both actor and institutional levels.

Disclosing the selectivity of reference systems helps to gain detailed insights into mobility policy integration processes, mapping the divergences in system definitions that may prevent mobility system integration. Asking the 'boundary questions' can help unravel the controversy concerning the role of the traffic management in the mobility transition. Some examples include the following. What problems are actors addressing? What problems could or should they be addressing? What are considered to be relevant side effects deserving attention? And what other policies can be considered relevant 'flanking measures'? *In what sense* is a certain policy considered a solution? *In what sense* is it a 'pseudo-solution'? CST can thus make relevant the 'view from differentiation', and examine the practices in mobility subsystems. Disclosure of the selectivity of reference systems opens up the scope for integration.

Many examples throughout this book describe the development of mobility policy integration processes, or even in explicit mobility transition attempts. The latter, in particular, illustrate the tensions involved with ambitious integration attempts in a differentiated society. For instance, the chapter by Gorris and van den Bosch describes the Rush Hour Avoidance (RHA) experiment (see also the chapter by Vonk Noordegraaf and van de Riet in this volume). In this experiment, it was attempted to persuade commuters to avoid the rush hour by rewarding them, an 'inverse' pricing measure. A key boundary question would be what problem is Rush Hour Avoidance trying to solve? At first sight, RHA can be considered an anti-congestion measure focusing on rush hour peak congestion. As explained above, RHA could therefore be considered a potential 'pseudo-solution'. But this is exactly where TM comes in, seeking to 'transitionize' the experiment. From the transition management perspective, the experiment could be part of a transition towards sustainable mobility. The experiments could be 'scaled up' (Gorris and van den Bosch in this volume) to integrate them in a transition strategy. Boundary questioning took place to raise the experimenters' awareness of the scope of the experiment. It was suggested that the project should be viewed in differing contexts such as:

1. the project context, and the context of possible extensions such as RHA 2, in which more participants would be recruited,
2. the ongoing (but somewhat stagnating) development of a Dutch road pricing policy, with which the project might interfere in different ways, and
3. sustainable mobility (idem: 11).

Viewing the project in differing contexts, and not only in terms of a 'sustainable mobility system', is exactly how TM can help navigate between integration and differentiation: seeking to integrate single measures in wider contexts, while acknowledging that participants have to implement such integration on the basis of their own particular system definitions.

TM continues the quest for integration from a long-term perspective, viewing integration as a result of co-evolution, rather than comprehensive planning. Such a long term perspective invites its specific boundary questions. The chapter by Avelino et al. in this volume has shown how difficult it is for actors to reconcile short- and long-term objectives. Especially striking is the way in which actors experience this tension, and how they make sense of their situations in terms of dichotomies. These typical examples of complexity-reduction confirm the theoretical expectation that the transition to sustainable mobility has to deal with fragmentation (see above). Moreover, they show how integration attempts can be informed by insights into actors' system definitions, in order to enrich 'supersystem' considerations stemming from the quest for integration.

Conclusion

The self-propagating dynamics of a car-dependent mobility system pose a serious challenge to mobility policy. Accommodative policies that seek to optimize the system bear the risk of becoming 'pseudo-solutions', as the example of traffic management congestion abatement illustrated. This is an important reason for the 'quest for integration'. Integration turns to be difficult to achieve in practice, however, and these difficulties may actually be underestimated by those who start reasoning from the need for integration. Luhmann's theory of societal differentiation turns the argumentation on its head, redirecting attention from the desirable to the possible. It explains that failed integration attempts are not incidental occasions as they always entail the risk of introducing overburdening complexity. It also explains why the benchmark of a mobility 'supersystem' is practically inconceivable, given the ongoing necessity to cope with societal complexity. And it also reminds us also to make use of what self-referential systems do best: optimization within boundaries. The differentiation-based analysis does not say that all integration efforts will be futile. Self-referential closure does not imply total incommensurability of sectoral frames. Integration is possible, but steering ambitions towards this aim will have to be modest.

Despite the challenges posed by differentiation, the need for mobility policy integration will remain. 'Persistent', 'structural' or systemic problems seem to call for nothing less than radical integration attempts aiming for structural system change. Transition management is an attempt to continue, or even radicalize, the quest for integration, while acknowledging the difficulty of such undertaking in a differentiated society. Its analytical category of the 'pseudo-solution' can become problematic, in that sense, as far as it imposes a 'supersystem' benchmark. Such a category is unlikely to be interpreted alike by all actors involved in a certain mobility policy.

Compatibility of system definitions is crucial in integration attempts. This is why Critical Systems Thinking could help manoeuvre between the quest for integration and the condition of differentiation. Disclosing system definitions that often remain implicit, it allows for realistic assessment of the scope for integration.

In the practice of 'boundary questioning', 'supersystem benchmarks' and 'pseudo-solutions' could be useful heuristic devices. In integration processes it would help to develop *situated* notions of 'pseudo-solutions' and 'sustainable' solutions. After all, this critical contribution is about opening up a discussion on these notions, rather than condemning actors for their lack of comprehensiveness. This lack of comprehensiveness is inevitable.

Chapter 5

Applying Transition Management in Ongoing Programmes and Projects in the Netherlands: The Case of Transumo and Rush Hour Avoidance

Teije Gorris and Suzanne van den Bosch

Introduction

The mobility sector faces problems related to oil dependency, security of supply, climate change, and traffic congestion. These persistent problems are a serious threat for our economic, ecological and social system and, overall, a threat for sustainable development. Although the environmental performance of the mobility sector has greatly improved over the past 30 years (e.g. higher efficiency, lower emissions), policy makers increasingly acknowledge the limitations to end-of-pipe solutions and the need for more structural change. The current way of troubleshooting and policy making that optimizes the current system is not providing the right framework for solutions. In the Netherlands different policy makers, scientists, and increasingly also industry, agree that we need a structural breakthrough (a new system) to overcome the persistent problems in sectors such as the mobility sector (Avelino and Bressers 2008).[1] Such a structural change in the mobility system is referred to as a 'transition' towards sustainable mobility. Transitions are defined as major shifts in 'regimes' of culture, structure, and practices, which are dominant in fulfilling societal needs such as mobility (Rotmans and Loorbach 2006). Transitions do not take place instantaneously. Instead, they evolve over long periods of 25–50 years (a generation). They are characterized by long-term changes that take place in different domains (e.g. technological, institutional, ecological, economic, socio-cultural), with many stakeholders involved, and there is no one stakeholder who has the control or power to force a breakthrough. Because of these characteristics, transitions can not be 'steered' by traditional linear incremental planning.

---

1 Policy makers in the energy sector (www.energietransitie.nl) and health care sector (www.tplz.nl) are also searching and learning about structural changes or transitions at a system level.

In co-production with the policy domain, Dutch social scientists have developed transition management (TM) as a new governance approach to influence transitions (Rotmans et al. 2000, 2001). A key concept in this approach is the TM cycle (Loorbach 2007), which can be characterized as a joint searching and learning process, focused on long-term sustainable solutions. This concept and other key concepts of TM are extensively described in the chapter by Avelino and Bressers in this volume. TM seems a promising approach for accelerating or managing the required transition towards a new mobility system. However, practitioners who are involved in programmes, processes, or projects that are aimed at transitions need supporting tools and practical guidelines (Raven et al. 2008; Caniëls and Romijn 2008).

The aim of this chapter is to demonstrate how theory about TM is translated into practice, in particular the practice of individuals and institutions that are involved in the Dutch transition to sustainable mobility. The chapter discusses the experiences of Transumo (TRANsition SUstainable MObility), its TM activities within the Transumo Transition Programme (TTP), the development of a specific instrument that is applied in this programme, and the experiences within the project Rush Hour Avoidance. Transumo is a Dutch platform including over 300 companies, local, regional and national governments and knowledge institutes that cooperate in the development of knowledge with regard to sustainable mobility.

We start by giving a brief introduction to TM and elaborate on the theory on experimenting within a TM context. We then give an outline of the overall Transumo research programme, reflecting on our quest for sustainable development and progress so far, and introducing the Transumo Transition Programme. Next, we go into a specific instrument (transitioning) with which we are experimenting. By describing a project case, we give further insight into our experiences regarding applying TM in ongoing practice. We conclude with a reflection on the tensions between theory and practice that follow from our experiences within the TTP, and specifically from applying the transitioning instrument. We close with recommendations for follow-up research and similar programmes that aim to contribute to transitions.

Transition Management and Experimenting

The mobility system is a complex system which can be seen as a complex interaction of different social subsystems. Relationships with spatial, economic and ecological systems are but a few examples of such interaction. Each system has a history of its own, through which the system has evolved to its current state, which sets the stage for a variety of stakeholders who are involved (with many inter- and intra-party differences). These characteristics make it difficult to practice steering by classical command and control. TM is a recently developed alternative steering approach that takes the characteristics of complex systems as a starting point. TM has been applied in several policy domains (e.g. energy and health care) and regions (e.g. Parkstad Limburg and Zeeland) in the Netherlands (Loorbach 2007).

TM is a young but promising field of science with its roots originating in complex systems theory, sociological theory, and governance (Loorbach 2007). This new field of science can provide means and instruments for the required transition in the Dutch mobility system (see also the chapter by Geerlings, Lohuis and Shiftan in this volume). An important TM instrument is creating space for frontrunners who can learn from each other and from experiments, including learning from failure. In this section we specifically go into the theory on experimenting within a TM context.[2]

Experimenting within the Context of TM

Experimenting is an important part of TM: creating partly protected spaces (niches) that enable experimentation with radically innovative practices, which fit within a certain transition pathway to a desirable future. Often these 'transition experiments' are conducted by niche players, but sometimes regime players are involved to anticipate barriers. *Regime players* are persons and organizations who represent the incumbent system ('closed-minded' to fundamental changes of the current system); *niche players* are persons or organizations (innovators) representing the new system (open-minded). The main objective is to learn from each other's perspective (social learning), and from the experiments with the aim to contribute to a transition. Because of the high risks of transition experiments, failure is always possible.[3] Learning experiences that are gained in a specific context (deepening) can be used in future experiments in other contexts (broadening). The aim of experiments in the context of transitions is to contribute to fundamentally changing the dominant practice into a sustainable practice (scaling up). These mechanisms of deepening, broadening, and scaling up are central theoretical concepts to understand how experiments can contribute to a transition (van den Bosch and Taanman 2006; van den Bosch and Rotmans 2008). We will now briefly introduce[4] these concepts.

---

2   For an elaborated description and reflection on TM, we refer to Part I of this volume.

3   Project failure can be a success in TM terms, whereas it is regarded as a failure in project management terms.

4   This introduction is a short version of a more extensive description (supported with a literature study) in van den Bosch and Rotmans (2008). Deepening, Broadening and Scaling up: A Framework for Steering Transition Experiments. Essay 02, Delft/Rotterdam: Knowledge Centre for Sustainable System Innovations and Transitions (KCT).

Deepening

The mechanism 'deepening'[5] is defined as a learning process through which actors can learn as much as possible about a transition experiment within a specific context. What actors learn about when 'deepening' includes shifts in ways of thinking, values and perspectives (culture), shifts in doing things, habits and routines (practices) and shifts in organizing the physical, institutional, or economic context (structure). These changes in culture, practices and structure are strongly related with respect to each other and their context. Through deepening in niches actors can also learn about this complex relation between culture, structure, and practices. Deepening can be understood as 'learning in a local context how to fulfill a social need in a new or deviating way'.

Broadening

The mechanism 'broadening' is defined as repeating a transition experiment in different contexts, and linking it to other functions or domains. What is repeated or linked are the new or deviating culture, practices and structures that are the outcome of innovation and learning processes (deepening). By extending what is learned to broader contexts or broader functions, the influence of the transition experiment is increased.[6] As a result of *broadening* the transition experiment gets diffused or adopted in a variety of contexts, or fulfils more social needs. Broadening can thus be understood as 'exploring new application domains or functions for a transition experiment'.

Scaling Up

The mechanism 'scaling up' is defined as embedding a transition experiment in – new – dominant ways of thinking (culture), doing (practices), and organizing (structure), at the level of a social system. What is scaled up is not the activity of experimentation, but the new or deviating cultures, practices, and structures that are being experimented with. Through scaling up a sustainable practice, and related culture and structure, the dominant way a social need is fulfilled is fundamentally changed, which extends the scale of the initial innovation project. Scaling up can thus be understood as making sustainable practices, and related culture and structures, that initially exist only at the level of experiments become part of the mainstream practice.

As the theory about transitions and transition experiments is still developing, a lack of sufficient practical tools and instruments is inevitable. Theory has not been

---

5   The mechanism 'deepening' should not be confused with 'deep' or narrow learning processes.

6   Influence is increased because the number of contexts in which the transition experiment influences how a certain societal function is fulfilled is increased.

put to test to its full extent. Similar to the object being studied, the study itself is one of experimenting and learning. In this volume, the chapters of Geerlings et al., Avelino et al. and Pel provide examples and a reflection on the experiences with TM in the transport sector so far. The next sections of this chapter will describe how TM has been applied in the ongoing Transumo research programme, and how theory about experimenting has been translated into a practical tool to support ongoing projects concerned with practising TM.

The Transumo Research Programme

As described in the previous section, TM is about, amongst other things, experimenting. In this section we describe the experiences of initiating and managing experiments within the Dutch research programme Transumo. We start by giving a brief description of the programme activities, including examples of projects, and then derive the main lessons with regard to translating theory on transition management into the practice of ongoing programmes and projects.

Transumo Activities

The main goal of Transumo is developing a knowledge network on sustainable mobility. It aims to contribute to a transition from the current inefficient mobility system towards a system that facilitates a stronger economic position, as well as giving ample attention for people and environment. 'This will be achieved by initiating, and establishing for the long term, a transition process that leads to the replacement of the current, supply driven, mono-disciplinary technology and knowledge infrastructure, with a demand driven, multidisciplinary and trans-disciplinary, participative knowledge infrastructure'.[7] The research and knowledge development activities of Transumo began in 2004 and have continued until 2009. Since the core business of Transumo is developing knowledge, Transumo cannot organize or force the transition itself. Instead, Transumo contributes by developing the knowledge that is needed to accelerate and steer the needed transition. A key condition is that the public sector, the private sector and knowledge institutes work and invest together in each project. This *triple helix* composition (university-industry-government) guarantees that knowledge development and application go hand in hand (doing-by-learning and learning-by-doing).

---

7   http://www.transumo.nl/En/AboutTransumo.aspx.

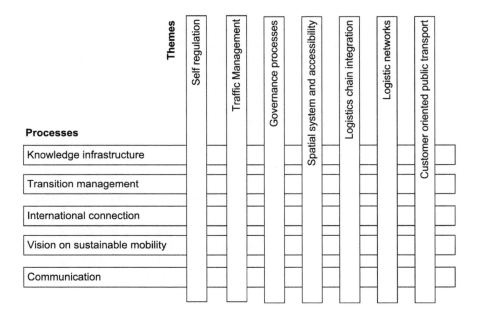

Figure 5.1   Transumo programme

The Transumo activities are organized as a matrix (Figure 5.1). Thirty-five projects are vertically clustered into seven themes covering a broad range of themes from traffic management, spatial developments, public transport, governance, supply chain management, both technological adjustments and organizational changes, and both macro- or meso-foci and micro-foci. Activities aimed at knowledge infrastructure development, communication and TM are organized horizontally.

The projects (described in Box 5.1), clustered into themes, are managed by a theme manager. The overall programme is managed by the Transumo Bureau. The Transumo Bureau is supervised by a supervising board. Transumo is partly (50 per cent) funded by the Dutch government ('BSIK' investment programme; an impulse programme to stimulate research and development in the Netherlands). The other half is financed by the participating organizations involved in the projects. The largest share of this group consists of business actors (on average approximately 50 per cent per project), followed by knowledge organizations (approximately 35 per cent) and governmental actors (approximately 15 per cent) (Bressers et al. 2008). When applying for the project portfolio of Transumo, the projects were required to satisfy multiple sustainability and transition criteria. They had to make visible that their project was a real contribution to the ongoing research in the field of sustainable mobility, and that their project fitted within the TM framework that Transumo had set itself.

Box 5.1   Transumo project examples

Transition towards sustainable traffic management (TRADUVEM)

The TRADUVEM project is inspired by transition theory and focuses on a breakthrough in the current traffic management system (multi-purpose steering). In doing so, the project organizes arenas with regime and niche players. Every stakeholder in the traffic management process, including the users of the traffic infrastructure, will be involved in this project. The result should be that, in sustainable traffic management a degree of involvement will be created, thus developing and co-creating a vision and roadmap towards sustainable traffic management.

Designing sustainable accessibility (DESSUS)

This project aims to contribute to the transition to sustainable mobility through the development of a 'Participatory Planning Support System' that enables more effective integration of spatial and transport planning. In particular, the aim of this project is to provide planners with tools by which they can – in interaction with stakeholders and consistently with individual user behaviour – identify aspects of the existing land-use and transport system that can be improved from a sustainable accessibility perspective (see also the chapter by Te Brommelstroët in this volume).

Effective Closed-loop supply chain Optimization (ECO)

The goal of this project is to define the field of global closed-loop supply chains, and position it in mainstream supply chain management and supply chain economics. Closed-loop supply chains are a relatively new research focus, while recovery initiatives are usually on a national or even smaller scale. Scaling up to global initiatives offers many opportunities, but is often hindered by legislation and lack of knowledge regarding concepts and best practices.

People-movers project (project stopped in 2007)

An initially technical project (implementing driver-less people-mover systems) was transformed into a transition project addressing the influence of people-mover systems on the spatial design and policy in urban regions. The goal of the project was to tackle the main barriers to realise the potential of people-movers: mapping the role of people-movers in the future urban environment, creating a toolbox for decision makers, broadening the application of people-movers by enabling them to mix with other forms of traffic, and validating the results in a demonstration project.

Each Transumo project is an experiment, like the Transumo programme itself. It is the use of TM in combination with the 'traditional' themes that makes the Transumo programme unique and innovative. Not included in the Transumo programme is specific research on alternative fuels and technologies.

In this section we elaborate on our experiences with starting and managing the programme, the projects themselves, and how TM has been put into practice and evolved.

Lessons Learned by Transumo

So far, Transumo has learned several lessons from its programme and project activities (Gorris and Pommer 2008). The lessons are described in chronological order, starting from programme initiation, and then shifting in focus from general programme management towards project management and execution (top-down). The lessons learned on the project level have also influenced the programme management (bottom-up).

- *Subsidy essential in programming multi-party research.* The programme is partly (50 per cent) funded by the Dutch government to strengthen the knowledge infrastructure. The other half is funded by the participating organizations, thereby creating partnerships and commitment. Without the subsidy concept, TM would not have been put on the agenda to this extent in the transport sector.
- *Bringing together regime and niche within programme management.* Initiating a programme based on the developing TM theory can be considered a transition itself. There was little experience in setting up a new programme based on TM. The supervising board (traditionally-orientated) was not convinced about the added value of TM. However, throughout recent years interest has grown, and is still growing within the different layers of the organization (niche players have managed to create space to practice TM). The main cause is the growing insight into the deficiencies of the traditional means (of project management) and their inability to solve the problems of today, let alone those of tomorrow. The first results seem to support the theory.
- *Multi-party formation is essential in many ways.* The mobility system consists of many actors, who are represented within the projects. Important stakeholders are involved from the start. It is a model of interaction and co-production. For most of the participating organizations, cooperating in a multi-actor formation (knowledge, policy, and market sectors together) was new. You might say that a multi-actor project start-up is a small success in itself. Combined with the financial model of operating in partnership, hidden agendas can be excluded.

- *Multi-party formation causes tensions between short-term and long-term ambitions.* Projects have to deal with multiple partners, who all have different interests, on different terms. Sometimes these might reinforce one another, but sometimes these also frustrate each other. Transition requires far-reaching innovations, but, because of the differences between short-term and long-term perspectives, project partners often only reach enough consensus to be able to work together, but this is not far-reaching enough to create knowledge and innovation for a transition process.
- *Spreading TM theory is essential.* All projects are content-orientated (research on a specific field), as well as contributing to a transition to sustainable mobility. Traditionally, most of the consortia and participating researchers are well experienced in managing a 'traditional' project focused on an innovative concept. None had experience of transition theory and management. Throughout the first years the call for transition support has become louder.
- *TM theory is not enough.* More and more project managers were having to face certain issues they could not solve themselves by means of traditional project management: issues raised by the regime (a Ministry which stands in the way of an innovation) or issues regarding cooperation within the private sector – in fact, those issues that are the cause of the present lock-in situation in the transport sector. Knowledge of the TM basics was not sufficient. Project managers were not able to make them applicable to their situation and the Transumo Bureau offered them more tailor-made support.
- *Joint vision is needed.* Parallel to the developments on the project level, it became clear that Transumo lacked a clear vision of sustainable mobility. That is, an integrated storyline, a storyline linking all 35 projects. The concept of sustainability in this context is defined as the balance between people, planet and profit. During the programme the focus on the planet aspect increased. However, it remains a goal to develop a vision of sustainability, and operationalize the concept.

Transition Programme: Increase of Transition Activities

The learning experiences discussed above and the progress and success of the Transumo programme were needed to create space for increasing the focus on TM theory and practice.

Halfway through its running time, Transumo intensified its TM activities and support for project managers in order to address the following type of questions. How can a 'normal' project be turned into a transition project? If transitions take place over a long period, how can tools be developed for monitoring them?

Together with leading experts in the field of TM and sustainability the Transumo Transition Programme was developed. DRIFT (the Dutch Research Institute for Transitions), CCT (Competence Centre Transitions), TNO (experts on transforming an innovation project into a transition experiment), AT Osborne (developing a vision and storyline), and CE (experts on sustainability) are participating in the programme. By joining forces on different aspects (monitoring transitions, transitioning methods, vision development, etc.), an integrated and potentially effective approach was developed, which aims to develop knowledge, tools and evidence on putting transition theory into practice. The approach is based on a framework that distinguishes three levels of transition activities:

- *Project level*: Aimed at project manager/participants and their competences. Project managers and participants learn to apply the TM basics in project and process management. During an intake session the project manager discusses his issues and need for transition support with transition experts. Together, they make a plan. The plan is implemented by means of several workshops where the project team and transition experts meet and discuss issues, and then suggest the next steps.
- *Programme level*: Aimed at the internal programme organization. Activities are geared to interconnecting the projects and developing a joined-up 'story', an overall philosophy and transition paths towards sustainable mobility. As stated before, Transumo lacks a joined-up story. Using vision sessions and organizing interaction between projects we want to develop our 'story'. At the programme level, activities on transition monitoring communication are incorporated.
- *Social level*: Aimed at the external programme organization. Activities are aimed at connecting Transumo to the 'outside world'. In order to connect our vision with institutions and regimes, we want to organize vision sessions in which important stakeholders meet and learn from Transumo experience.

Activities have started on all three levels. The next part of the chapter specifically describes the first experiences with one of the instruments used on the project level: the transitioning instrument.

Transitioning Instrument

In 2008 the Transumo Transition Programme (TTP) has had its first cases[8] involving the project level approach, specifically with the application of the *transitioning*[9] instrument (Emmert et al. 2006; van den Bosch and Rotmans 2008). The transitioning instrument is aimed at transforming existing innovation projects into 'transition experiments' with a high potential to contribute to a transition. The instrument was developed as part of a KSI[10] research project, and first tested within the TTP. The instrument translates theoretical concepts, which are developed within KSI research on transitions, into practical guidelines for practitioners who are aiming to influence ongoing transitions towards a more sustainable society. The key concepts within the transitioning instrument are the mechanisms deepening, broadening, and scaling up (van den Bosch and Taanman 2006), which were described in the previous.

Framework for Transitioning

Central in the transitioning instrument is a matrix that relates the mechanisms deepening, broadening, and scaling up to the process and substance characteristics of innovation projects, which results in six main challenges for managing transition experiments (Table 5.1). These management challenges are further specified in concrete management guidelines (Table 5A.1), which are aimed at supporting the successful management of transition experiments.[11]

---

8   Cases in which the transitioning instrument was applied are the Transumo projects European Networks (EN) and Rush Hour Avoidance (RHA). The first experiences with the RHA case are described in the next section.

9   The concept of 'transitioning' was introduced by Jan Rotmans as a general concept that refers to actively transforming existing activities into activities that can contribute to a transition. With regard to activities at the project level, transitioning refers to 'broadening the scope of innovation projects, in terms of process and content, by relating them to a societal challenge'.

10   KSI is the Dutch Knowledge network on System Innovations and transitions. It comprises over 80 researchers from a dozen universities and research institutes with specific knowledge and expertise of transitions and system innovations (www.ksinetwork.org).

11   The management guidelines that are presented in Table 5A.1 are an elaboration of the guidelines that were developed by Martin van de Lindt and Suzanne van den Bosch (2007) as part of the development of the transitioning instrument.

Table 5.1   Management challenges related to the guidelines for transition experiments

Steering dimensions / Project characteristics	Deepening Learning as much as possible from a project in its context	Broadening Replicating and linking to other contexts and functions	Scaling up Embedding in dominant ways of thinking and doing
Process	*From:* realizing results *To:* searching and learning	*From:* coincidental links *To:* directed linking	*From:* operational... *To:* strategic management
Substance	*From:* incremental innovation *To:* developing new ways of thinking and doing	*From:* context-specific results *To:* adapting to other contexts	*From:* handing over results *To:* changing dominant ways of thinking and doing

Source: Emmert et al. (2006); van den Bosch and Rotmans (2008).

Showcase: Rush Hour Avoidance

This section discusses recent experiences with, and the results of, a first case on the project level of the TTP. We go more deeply into one of the Transumo projects by describing the project, its development, and transition dilemmas, the approach followed and the preliminary results. We specifically describe the process of transitioning this project, which was started by the project consortium, and further supported by the TTP. We end this section by giving a brief insight into how the follow-up workshop has been planned and evaluate the first experiences with the transitioning instrument.

Rush Hour Avoidance (RHA) Experiment[12]

Rush Hour Avoidance ('Spitsmijden' in Dutch) was set up as an experiment to examine whether car drivers can be persuaded to avoid the rush hour by positive stimuli.[13] The mechanism to do this is to provide commuters with a reward for 'good' behaviour, which is contrary to the mainstream way of punishing people for traffic usage. The first phase of the Rush Hour Avoidance experiment consisted

---

12   All information on Rush Hour Avoidance can be found on www.spitsmijden.nl. In their contribution to this volume Vonk Noordegraaf, van de Riet and Annema go into attitude change and policy learning regarding Rush Hour Avoidance.

13   More information about the experimental design of Rush Hour Avoidance can be found in Knockaert et al. (2007).

of a pilot (RHA 1) aimed at creating new insights into the mobility behaviour of commuters in relation to positive stimuli.

This first pilot was conducted on 50 weekdays in October to December 2006, during which 340 frequent car drivers looked for alternatives to driving in morning traffic over the stretch of the Dutch A12 motorway from Zoetermeer to The Hague. They were rewarded (by either a financial reward or credits for a free smart phone) if they were successful in avoiding the rush hour, compared with their initial behaviour. This type of positive stimuli had a significant effect on changing driving behaviour. The number of participants driving in peak morning traffic was reduced by about 50 per cent. While the initial objective was to stimulate 6 per cent of the pilot participants to avoid the rush hour, the result revealed a 50 per cent avoidance. The first phase of the RHA experiment therefore was a success (it confirmed the hypothesis that a reward system persuades car drivers to avoid the rush hour) (Spitsmijden 2007a). Another aspect of the success was the successful deployment of the technical system and the organization of the back office. And finally, there was the successful cooperation between local, regional and national governments, several private parties and three universities. After the first phase of the RHA experiment, the perspective of this project consortium was broadened from 'avoiding the rush hour' to contributing to the transition to sustainable mobility in the Netherlands.

The second phase of the experiment consisted of a follow-up pilot (RHA 2) to explore in more depth the long-term effects of the experiment on behavioural change. This second pilot also involves employers, and actively promotes public transport as a behaviour alternative. The third phase aimed scaling up RHA 2 from 800 to 5,000 participants (RHA 3).

The development of the RHA experiment can be characterized as a TM process, in which an initially limited mobility experiment was succeeded by a second experiment that is explicitly connected to the transition challenge of realizing sustainable mobility. This process was the result of active process management of RHA, which broadened the scope from project to process, and from the pilot to an open search-and-learn process about the transition to sustainable mobility. It resulted in a statement from the Dutch Minister of Transport, Public Works and Water Management to the Dutch House of Representatives that more RHA projects should be stimulated.[14] More RHA projects took off from 2009 onward. At present there are still RHA projects running.

In the first phase of the RHA experiment, several sessions were also organized to discuss TM with the project steering group. This inspired the RHA consortium, but TM as a method or specific TM goals were not defined in the RHA 1 project objectives (Spitsmijden 2007b). The project consortium did, however, include

---

14   Source: Letter from the Dutch Minister of Transport, Public Works and Water Management to the Second Chamber, about 'A Different Way of Paying for Road Use' (ABvM), 30 November 2007.

several researchers who focused on the contribution that RHA could make to a transition to sustainable mobility. This research is part of RHA 2.

Transition Dilemmas Resulting from the First Pilot of RHA

The results of the first RHA pilot conducted at the end of 2006 were promising. Even though this first pilot was set up as a small 'laboratory' experiment, instead of a broader transition experiment, it had a significant impact.[15] The organizations within the RHA consortium applied the financial reward instrument at various locations. And the Ministry of Transport, Public Works and Water Management responded by stating that it aims to experiment with the RHA concept within the context of a differentiated kilometre pricing system. Other organizations outside the RHA consortium also started to develop financial reward instruments. And newcomers, such as NS Dutch Railways, participated in taking a closer look at the possibilities of the RHA concept in relation to the train.

However, after the initial success, RHA faced several 'transition' dilemmas with regard to deepening, broadening, and scaling up the experiment. One dilemma was choosing strategically between further research and market implementation. To learn as much as possible (deepening), the follow-up of the RHA experiment would require a more integrated approach with more space for experimentation concerning the conditions for success and possible side effects. Furthermore, in order to scale up, the experiment needs to learn about and overcome technical, legal and fiscal scaling-up issues. Another dilemma concerns the scaling-up process: should it be guided by the project consortium, the Transumo programme, or external actors? With regard to broadening, RHA needs to position itself with regard to similar initiatives. It is clear that RHA is much broader than a solitary financial reward instrument, and can only be used as a stand-alone measure temporarily. The aim of the consortium is to connect RHA to a transition to new mobility arrangements in which rewarding and pricing go hand-in-hand within the same system.

To address these dilemmas in the second phase of the RHA experiment, the Transumo Bureau has offered the RHA consortium additional support from the Transumo Transition Programme (TTP). Because the TTP was looking for cases to develop its tools, a joint search and learning process was started to connect transition theory and TM to the practical experiences of RHA. In a joint meeting, RHA participants together with additional TM experts (who participated in the TTP) explored how the transition dilemmas and questions could be approached. The meeting finally recommended that the next step should be to position the RHA

---

15   This success was the result of the active process management approach of RHA that is comparable with several TM principles (e.g. conducting an actor analysis, involving both regime and niche players, cooperating with the external environment, and stimulating public communication).

experiment with regard to its context, and with regard to a vision of sustainable mobility.[16]

First transition Workshop with RHA

In close interaction between the TTP and RHA, a first transition workshop, entitled 'Rush Hour Avoidance: success, context and vision', was prepared and organized at the beginning of 2008. As this workshop was a first experiment for the TTP as well, TTP participants were also participating (and not just facilitating or organizing) in the workshop. Using participative and interactive methods, the RHA and TTP participants:

1. discussed the RHA context and vision of sustainable mobility;
2. updated an actor analysis that the RHA consortium conducted at the project start-up (2006);
3. further explored the actual relationships between RHA and the context and vision; and
4. obtained more knowledge of the transitioning instrument.

During the first part of the workshop, the participants worked on landscaping their context (relevant developments in policy and technology) and discussed their visions of sustainable mobility. One of the outcomes was that a coherent vision of sustainable mobility in the Netherlands does not yet exist. During the workshop the building blocks for such a vision were created, such as 'living, working, mobility without compromising other generations or places'.

Secondly, an actor analysis was updated in which the most important actors and their activities were listed. A follow-up is needed to categorize these actors again in 'critical' or 'dedicated' and in 'regime' or 'niche'.

The third part of the workshop was about addressing how the RHA consortium is influenced by the images of context and vision and vice versa (how can RHA be of influence on the context and vision of sustainable mobility). The conclusion was that the RHA Steering Group should mainly focus on conducting the project as such (layers 1 and 2). This raised a question about who was going to connect the project to its broader context (layers 3 and 4). The RHA consortium already includes several (influential) persons who provide a connection with the external environment.

The last part of the first transition workshop with RHA included a discussion on the 'transitioning instrument',[17] aimed at enhancing the project success and the perspective to scale up (Box 5.2).

---

16   Source: the report 'Intake Transitie Ondersteuning Spitsmijden', 12 December 2007.

17   As described earlier in the chapter, the application of the transitioning instrument was tested in practice for the second time (the first test involved the Transumo project European Networks). The discussion on the instrument was bi-directional: 1) the

Box 5.2   Possible examples of deepening, broadening, and scaling up in the RHA project

---

Deepening

Learning about the effect of a financial reward system (a change in structure) on the mobility behaviour of car drivers (a practice) in a local context.

Broadening

Linking to other mobility domains (public transport, car sharing) and other societal needs (not only sustainable mobility but also housing, spatial planning and corporate social responsibility).

Scaling up

Scaling up RHA would imply that avoiding traffic rush hour changes the dominant practice of commuters, and positive stimulation of sustainable mobility becomes part of the dominant culture and structure of companies and government.

The six management challenges for transition experiments (Table 5.1) were presented as a framework for setting up a project and conducting activities for deepening, broadening, and scaling up. The project manager of RHA recognized the six management challenges, and perceived the framework as an important framework for sustainable project, process and programme management. He and the other workshop participants stated that the theoretical framework will become stronger if the six management challenges are elaborated in practical guidelines. In the last part of the workshop, a sub-group made a first attempt to develop some initial guidelines:

> ***Deepening process.*** Allocate time, budget and resources for the learning process; leave space in the project plan for a broader perspective; call for 'helping troops' in time (to guarantee the quality of learning).

> ***Broadening process.*** Set up the project with a separate shell for the context (in RHA the context is addressed in a separate work package). In other words, specific TM goals must be part of the project plan/results and budget, and 'connector' needs to be appointed.

---

applicability and development of the instrument in general; and 2) the application of the instrument for the RHA case.

Scaling-up process. Organize the project and process management in parallel, with a connection (different agenda, same objectives); appoint a 'figurehead'; and involve key actors, let them do the work!

Deepening substance. Recognize that the project is not a goal in itself but part of a broader development; and learn about new business models.

Broadening substance. Visualize other projects, specify new actors in RHA 2 (do not stay with old actors just for convenience); and learn about the difference with RHA 1.

Scaling up substance. Specify the present context and the relevant actors; and think about new business models and financial structures.

Second Transition Workshop with RHA

While only a small part of the first workshop had been dedicated to discussing the transitioning instrument and framework, it was perceived as potentially useful. On the basis of the experiences of the first workshop, and previous experiences with applying the instrument, a second transition workshop with RHA was prepared. The position and use of the instrument within the workshop is aimed at supporting the RHA consortium with their transitioning process, while at the same time the RHA consortium supports the development of the transitioning instrument. The proposed outline for the workshop from TNO/KSI would be as follows.

In advance of the workshop, all RHA participants are requested to score the project in an elaborated matrix of the transitioning framework (Table 5A.1 in Appendix 5A). This matrix consists of several statements with regard to 'ideal' project and process characteristics on the three dimensions: deepening, broadening, and scaling up. The sum of these scores can be illustrated in the transitioning framework with the six management challenges for transition experiments (Table 5.1). This method was previously tested in another Transumo project case (European Networks), and proved especially valuable for discussing priorities with regard to setting up transition activities for deepening, broadening, and scaling up the experiment.

The first part of the workshop will consist of an interactive (structured) group discussion to determine the main priorities in order to increase the impact of RHA on the transition to sustainable mobility. The individual scores are used as input for this discussion. The result of this first part will be a set of shared priorities.

The second part of the workshop uses the identified priorities to develop strategies for deepening, broadening, and/or scaling up the RHA experiment. An initial idea is to use a 'roulette game' as a method for high-speed subgroup discussions, in which each subgroup answers a set of transition questions that together add up to a strategy and related activities.

The last part of the workshop consists of a plenary session to discuss the results and translate this into short- and long-term actions.

Evaluation of the First Experiences with the Transitioning Instrument

Given the aims with regard to applying the transitioning instrument in the RHA experiment (as described before), important evaluation questions concern:

- whether the instrument helped the RHA consortium; and
- whether the development of the instrument was helped by testing it with the RHA consortium.

Because of the limited experience with applying the instrument, these questions can not yet be fully answered.

With regard to the first question, RHA was presented with one of the first releases of the transitioning instrument. From the point of view of the RHA consortium, at present the added value of applying the instrument in the RHA experiment is limited. This is because the RHA consortium has already incorporated TM principles in a separate workflow on TM (including several transition researchers). Also at the time of introducing the transitioning instrument, an additional workflow 'external relations and scenario development' was being developed. These workflows overlap with the transitioning instrument: the steering dimension 'deepening' is covered in the TM workflow and the dimensions 'broadening' and 'scaling up' are covered in the workflow 'external relations'. The RHA consortium is currently focusing on these workflows to contribute to the transition to sustainable mobility. However, they recognize the potential value of the transitioning framework, and are interested in the further development of the instrument.

With regard to the second question, the testing of the transitioning instrument with the RHA experiment added to the development of the instrument. Testing the instrument in practice with an actual case and dilemmas proved to be fruitful. The transitioning framework (Table 5.1), which was presented in the first workshop, provides valuable theoretical concepts to support ongoing practices. Parts of these concepts are already being applied in the sub-projects of RHA 2 and the workflow 'external relations and scenario development'. However, to support a further translation of theory into practice, the project manager of RHA suggested the transitioning framework should be enriched with practical guidance for the specific RHA context. Another lesson learned from RHA is that the transitioning instrument should distinguish between projects that are still at the beginning of a transitioning process and projects like RHA that are already actively working on contributing to a transition. In this way the transitioning instrument might support different type of projects in different phases of development.

Four more general lessons can be drawn with regard to the ability of the instrument to translate the theory on transition experiments to practice. First, initial experiences within the RHA project (and also European Networks) show that the project participants recognize the management challenges for transition experiments (Table 5.1). Second, the framework provides project managers and participants with a new perspective on addressing these challenges; and the transitioning instrument enables them to make strategic choices with regard to focusing more on activities aimed at learning (deepening), repeating and linking (broadening) and/or embedding (scaling up). Third, the distinction between process and substance relates to existing project management language, and supports practitioners in focusing on the concrete characteristics of the experiment. Fourth, to provide practical value to practitioners the transitioning instrument should include a set of supportive 'transition tools' (such as how to set up a transition arena), and should also pay attention to the competences that are needed for handling these tools.

Conclusion

Half way through its running time, the Transumo Bureau deployed its so called Transumo Transition Programme (TTP), including the specific transitioning instrument. This chapter has tried to provide insight into the first results of putting TM theory into practice at the level of both the programme and the specific Rush Hour Avoidance project. The potential added value of TM is that it provides steering principles to programmes and projects that aim to contribute to sustainability transitions. However, the case also illustrates the tensions resulting from the high ambition of translating recent theoretical transition concepts into existing practices in the search for sustainable mobility.

As TM theory illustrates, TM is about a continuous process of searching, experimenting, and learning. The experiences of Transumo with initiating and managing a programme on the transition towards sustainable mobility, includes experimenting with bringing regime and niche players together, combining traditional project management with TM, and cooperating with researchers and practitioners who are experimenting outside their fields of expertise and disciplines. Translating TM theory into practice is a long-term process of interaction between theory and practice, and between societal, programme and project level scales. We have outlined the lessons learned by Transumo, which have resulted in further applications and directions for the development of the transitioning instrument aimed at supporting projects with their contribution to transitions. The initial results of the case Rush Hour Avoidance (RHA) illustrate how developing practical transition tools is a search and learning process, and at the same time shows the potential of an instrument in which theorists and practitioners, TM, and process and project management can meet.

The case of the TTP and the RHA project reveal some important tensions in putting transition theory into practice. Within several layers of the Transumo programme there appeared to be a tension between classical project and programme management and transition management (e.g. short-term versus long-term perspective; realizing results versus experimenting and learning). It took a great effort to grow support for TM activities within the programme and project management (because of the scepticism about the added value or lack of time and budget in terms of traditional project management goals). This tension will always remain to a certain extent, resulting as it does from multi-actor projects, where some of the participating organizations will expect success in traditional project management terms (related to the fact that organizations need a return on investment to survive). Furthermore, successful experiments (such as RHA) are also necessary to create space and resources for future experiments, thus enabling a TM approach of continuous experimenting, searching and learning.

At the programme level, another tension between theory and practice is that the timing of TM activities in practice deviates from the TM cycle (Loorbach 2007). For example, the TM cycle starts with developing a vision of sustainability and the Transumo practice started with setting up projects without a precise vision of sustainable mobility. The RHA case shows that Transumo projects could use a broad vision of sustainable mobility that provides direction and guidance, and at the same time a vision development process can make use of building blocks that are developed in projects such as RHA.

Supporting practice with theoretical concepts that are developed within the context of a relatively young science (such as 'transition science') results in tension as well. Theorists are limited in supporting practice because they are required to contribute to theory development (expressed in scientific publications), and practitioners are expecting ready-to-use solutions (panacea). This tension shows that the interaction between theory and practice is limited by institutional borders. However, 'transition science' is aimed at crossing these borders with a 'mode 2' approach of developing knowledge (Rotmans 2005). This is resulting in a growing field of transition researchers[18] who are developing their concepts in strong interaction with practice, and at the same time, a growing field of 'transition professionals'[19] are conducting practical activities to stimulate transitions in strong interaction with science. This brings forward several challenges for follow-up 'mode 2' research aimed at putting transition theory into practice. However, we also acknowledge the limitations of researchers and practitioners within the dynamics of modern society (which will not allow the rapid realization of a sustainable society). On the basis of the experiences within the TTP (including the specific transitioning instrument), the following recommendations for follow-up TM research and practice can be derived:

---

18   www.ksinetwork.org.

19   The term 'transition professional' is used by the Competence Centre for Transitions (CCT) to refer to people who are engaged in transitions in a professional manner. At present in the Netherlands, hundreds of people are involved daily in realizing one or more transitions. Since 2006, transition professionals can follow a Masterclass Transition Management, facilitated by the Erasmus University Rotterdam (www.transitiepraktijk.nl).

- Integrate TM principles in the programme management right from the start or set up a separate programme to experiment with TM (creating a niche) within existing programmes and embed these learning experiences in the overall programme;
- Distinguish between transitioning experiments right from the start and transitioning ongoing experiments that have a specific need for transition support (instead of a top-down supply of transition concepts, make use of bottom-up demand);
- Cooperate with intermediate organizations with transition expertise (such as the Competence Centre for Transitions (CCT) or TNO) that can provide an interface between transition science and practice, and can facilitate the development of practical transition instruments and tools;
- Support projects not only with instruments and tools but also with competence development or a pool of experts with specific TM competences;
- Develop transition instruments and tools in cooperation with practitioners who are participating in projects, including projects that either feature or lack TM approaches or expertise.

Appendix 5A

Table 5A.1   Management guidelines for transition experiments

Steering dimensions / Success Criteria	Deepening — Actions aimed at learning as much as possible from the experiment in the specific context	Broadening — Actions aimed at repeating the experiment in other contexts or connecting to other functions and domains	Scaling up — Actions aimed at embedding the experiment in dominant ways of thinking, doing, and organizing
Process			
Space in budget and planning	allocating resources (time, money, knowledge, etc.) to an open search and learning process	allocating resources to interaction with other domains and partners	allocating resources to (early) involvement of key actors at a strategic level
Space in the process	building in space for reflection on and adjustment of the vision and learning goals	building in space for reflection on the connection to the broader context	building in strategic reflection on barriers and opportunities in dominant ways of thinking, doing and organizing
Quality of learning process	organizing a broad, reflexive and social learning process	focusing the learning process on how experiments can reinforce each other	focusing the learning process on how learning experiences can be embedded in dominant ways of thinking, doing and organizing
Supportive incentives/ assessment mechanisms	developing supportive incentives/ assessment mechanisms that increase the quality of learning	developing supportive incentives/ assessment mechanisms that stimulate interaction with other domains and partners	developing supportive incentives/ assessment mechanisms that stimulate feeding back results to key actors at a strategic level
Competences of project participants	selecting project participants with an open mind and willingness to learn	selecting project participants that are able to look outside the borders of their discipline and are strong 'connectors'	selecting project participants that are able to communicate and 'anchor' project results at a strategic level

Table 5A.1   Continued

Strategic management	the management guarantees that project results are related to the societal challenge	the management guarantees the interaction with other domains and partners	the management guarantees connection to key actors and developments at the strategic level
Substance			
Connection to societal challenge	connecting project goals explicitly to social (transition-) goals	cooperating with partners and developing new partnerships to realize shared social goals	adapting to the sense of urgency with regard to societal challenge
Sustainability vision/future perspective	project participants share a long term sustainability vision	developing an overarching sustainability vision to provide guidance for different experiments	drawing attention to the sustainability vision at a strategic level
System analysis (dominant culture, practices, structure in sector)	project participants share perspective on dominant ways of thinking, doing and organizing in the sector (from which the experiment deviates)	identifying similar experiments and potential new partners, application domains and functions	identifying key actors with power and willingness to influence dominant culture, practices and structure
Learning goals/ desired changes (innovation)	formulating explicit learning goals with regard to desired (interrelated) changes in culture, practices and structures	repeating the experiment in other contexts and experimenting with new functions is part of the learning goals	anticipating and learning about barriers and opportunities in dominant culture, practices and structures is part of the learning goals
Intended results	distinguishing results in generic and context specific	sharing results with other experiments and potential application domains	stimulating structural (regime) support and resources for results

Source: Based on Van de Lindt and van den Bosch (2007).

Chapter 6

Short-term versus Long-term Dichotomies: Applying Transition Management in the A15-project

Nanny Bressers, Flor Avelino and Harry Geerlings

Introduction

The previous chapters of this book have shown how the method of transition management (TM) is being applied in ongoing projects. As explained in Chapter 3, TM is a model for working towards systemic change, and aims to stimulate system innovations for societal change towards a more sustainable future. This can be carried out by bringing actors together (the transition arena), and by developing of future visions, problem awareness, and steps to take today to reach the desired future (transition paths). Different authors indicate that several tensions exist when applying the theory of TM in practice. Gorris and Van den Bosch observe, in Chapter 5 of this book, an important tension that exists between project management and TM, which relates to the tension between short-term and long-term results. These are, however, not the only tensions, or dichotomies, that occur in the application of TM. In this chapter we will demonstrate that there are many more dichotomies, with a different character, and which have an effect on the application of TM and the achievement of long-term objectives. For these purposes, it is important to highlight that TM is both a scientific approach and a governance model, aimed at bringing actors and perspectives together to achieve sustainable change.

As could already be gleaned from the previous chapters, TM is not an easy or straightforward process. The dichotomies that TM attempts to overcome may even be further reinforced in the application process. The objective of this chapter is to distinguish how actors in specific cases (the Transumo programme overall, and the A15-project more specifically) deal with 'short-term' and 'long-term' perspectives, and what challenges and lessons can be distilled from this for the ongoing development of transition management.[1] The research method that was used is a mix between participant observation and action research (Greenwood and

---

1   All three authors have been actively involved in the Transumo programme and the A15-project. Two of the authors were involved in the preparation and organization of two 'innovation-sessions' in the A15-project. Data-collection took place through participant

Levin 1998). This chapter starts with a description of the research area: the Port of Rotterdam and the study area. Within the A15-project, the focus is in particular on one specific trajectory: the 'innovation impulse'. The empirical findings on this innovation impulse, as an application of TM, are then discussed. From these results we derive a list of dichotomies that relate to the tension between the short term and long term. Following on from this, we discuss the relevance and implications of these findings for the ongoing development of TM.

Complexity in the Region: The Port and the A15-motorway

The Spatial Organization

The Rotterdam Port area (Figure 6.1) is an area of major economic importance for the Netherlands (about 5 per cent of the national employment, and about 10 per cent of the GDP is generated in this region). Rotterdam is Europe's largest logistic and industrial hub (Port of Rotterdam 2008). 'Maasvlakte' is the name of the port and industrial zone built on reclaimed land in the region of the Port of Rotterdam. It was created because more space was needed in the Europoort – the complex of ports and industrial areas that was created in 1957 between the city of Rotterdam and the North Sea. The Port is thus growing, and from an economic perspective it is seen as important that the ongoing growth of the port is facilitated. However, the handling capacity of the Port is bounded by the transport capacity of the available infrastructure. In the Port there are five major transport modalities: road, rail, coastal and inland shipping and pipeline. Most freight is transported by road, but increasing congestion lengthens travel time considerably. This not only increases the transport costs of transporters and shippers, but also has a negative impact on the international competition position of the Port.

As well as longer travel time and congestion, there are also impacts on the regional environment. Air pollution and noise put pressure on the quality of life in the region. In the neighbourhood of the A15 motorway that runs from the Maasvlakte eastwards, there are several urban areas that suffer from pollution and noise. In the short term, between 2010 and 2015 a large-scale road expansion from two to three lanes is planned for busiest parts of the highway (Geerlings et al. 2009). However, this extra capacity will only be a temporary solution. The ongoing expansion of the road capacity with additional lanes is not considered a sustainable solution in the long run: in the light of the expected growth in transport it enhances capacity only temporarily. Apart from that, traffic is expected to increase further, as the government has decided to invest in an expansion of the Port area.

---

observation in both internal and external project meetings, interviews and document reviews.

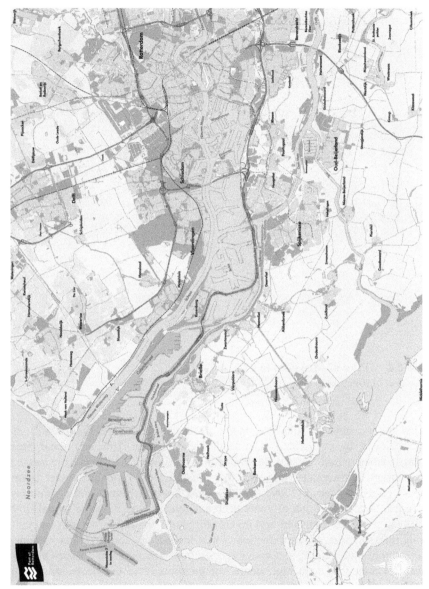

Figure 6.1   Map of the current Rotterdam Port area and its surrounding road network

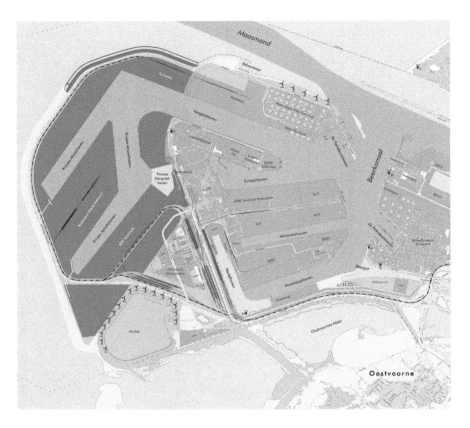

Figure 6.2   Plan of Maasvlakte 2
Source: Port of Rotterdam.

This enlargement of 400 km², called Maasvlakte 2 (see Figure 6.2), is being achieved by reclaiming new land from the sea. This additional area will provide increased growth possibilities for the Port, and hence, increased transportation. Furthermore, the extra infrastructure will probably attract latent transport (Geerlings et al. 2009), which means that more sustainable solutions are needed. One could think of many different solutions, such as the modal shift policy (e.g. more rail transport and inland shipping), increasing the efficiency of existing infrastructure, the introduction of new technology, logistical innovations, organizational innovations, and better cooperation. The combined issues at play in the Port area lead to a high degree of complexity in the decision-making processes and complicate the determination of future directions. Actors have to make decisions under great uncertainty, while many other actors are also making strategic decisions and choices (Ostrom 1990: 210). The Port is hence a good example of an area with complex problems (or: 'wicked' problems) (see, for instance, Rittel and Webber 1973; Rotmans 2003: 38). Decision-making in such a complex setting would be aided by the cooperation of actors, in order to avoid counterproductive action and conflicting stances.

The A15-project: Organizing Innovation

In Chapter 5 of this book, Gorris and Van den Bosch described the Transumo programme extensively. Transumo is a tripartite programme, where business actors, knowledge actors and several governmental actors are working together to achieve an impulse for the transition towards sustainable mobility. According to Bressers et al. (2009), Transumo has, in terms of individual actors, most business actors, followed by governmental actors, and science parties. Governmental actors lag somewhat behind in terms of involvement. Tripartite working is consistent with concepts such as the 'triple helix organization' (Etzkowitz 2003). In a triple helix organization, roles start shifting, and business, science, and government partially take over each other's tasks (whilst maintaining their primary functions) to achieve their shared objectives. The Transumo projects also represent this triple helix structure. A good example of this is the project entitled '*From Maasvlakte to Hinterland: Sustainable Freight Transport as Challenge*' or *the A15-project* in short. In this project more than 250 stakeholders, including both public and private organizations, the Port Authority, research parties, local government and pressure groups participated in order to meet the challenge of finding sustainable solutions for accessibility and environmental problems in the Rotterdam Port region from 2020 and onwards. Thirty of these stakeholders were more closely involved, and were part of the project's consortium. As the previous section indicated, at present the A15 is the main transport vein from and to the hinterland, but suffers increasingly from congestion as a result of the ongoing transport and traffic growth. Furthermore, the surrounding environment suffers from air pollution and noise. The participants in this joint project considered a wide range of technical and organizational measures and calculated their expected effects on the regional mobility system and the local environment in 2020 and 2033, in order to tackle the accessibility and sustainability challenges ahead.

The researchers in the consortium (who mainly came from the academic world and specialized consultants) were responsible for collecting the data and analysing it by means of document reviews, statistics, traffic modelling, interviewing, and collecting, analysing and applying quantitative data (with regard to traffic and environmental effects in the A15-region) in traffic models and scenarios. They were also responsible for identifying possible solutions in close cooperation with the 250 stakeholders in order to deal with the problems and make recommendations based on these possible solutions.

The results of this work were presented in 'reports and deliverables' in which the project results and visualizations thereof were formalized on paper. Three groups (steering group, management team, and knowledge workers) met independently of each other on a regular basis (once every few months) to discuss goal-setting, planning, task-division and the conclusions presented in the 'deliverables'. Besides those meetings, there were also 'open' meetings, to which 'semi-outsiders' were invited. These 'semi-outsiders' included all the stakeholders formally involved in the project, as well as actors with an evident stake or interest in the theme of the project (e.g. researchers, consultants, company representatives, government officials, environmental activists). These open meetings provided a forum in which the 'insiders' presented their vision for the future, project results and 'deliverables', and the 'outsiders' were asked to react, comment, discuss and give input with regard to a specific theme.

This consortium of participants in the A15-project together explored and discussed many possible solutions, some of which were analysed in more detail. After the environmental and traffic-related problems had been studied and presented in several 'deliverables', the focus turned to identifying possible solutions. One of the inside parties put together a 'long-list' of possible solutions on the basis of input from interviews with stakeholders, a meeting with all the companies that were involved in the project, brainstorms in the 'open meetings', and the expertise of the researchers. This 'long-list' was first reduced to a 'short-list' (Table 6.1), based on expert judgments regarding the specific measures', scoring on criteria such as accessibility and feasibility.

The effects of these measures on both the traffic and environment were calculated and compared with the autonomous development. The investigated solutions ranged from dynamic traffic management, night distribution, innovative public transport, inland terminals for short-sea shipping to new infrastructural works. The combined package of these measures applied to road, rail and water and was estimated to result in a 25 per cent decrease in traffic flows on the A15 in 2020 in comparison with the reference situation (Kuipers et al. 2008). Although this result was considered promising by the project participants, some critical remarks were made with respect to the nature of the measures and the working method that was followed.

Table 6.1   Overview of the 'Modern Classical' measures

	Short description of the measures
1	A west-side river bank connection (Oranje Tunnel)
2	Innovative passenger transport (including transfer centres, reward system, new bus concepts
3	Separate driving lanes – combined with mobility and chain management, reward systems, cleaner engines, green wave, guided vehicle concepts
4	Night distribution – combined with rewarding, quiet freight cars, chain management
5	Innovative modal shift – combined with container transfer centres

Whilst this first 'package of solutions' was in the process of being formulated in a 'deliverable', both 'insiders' and 'outsiders' expressed their criticism of the list of solutions in terms of not being new, innovative, or radical enough. This point was brought up as explicit criticism by many outsiders, both in the open meetings on the 'traditional trajectory' and in the two sessions on the 'innovation impulse'. Not only was the first 'package of solutions' not considered innovative enough, it was also found to lack strategies on *how* to implement these solutions. As such, the persons responsible for the deliverable decided to give this first 'package of solutions' the title of 'Modern Classical'. The second round aimed to give more attention to environmental aspects and innovation. There had been several discussions and disagreements in the management team about the extent to which the innovative participatory methods from TM would be appropriate to apply in this second round of the project. Finally, it was decided to have two parallel trajectories during the second round. One was referred to as the 'main trajectory' or the 'traditional trajectory', the other was called the 'transition trajectory' or 'innovation impulse'. This resulted in the following project set-up, as illustrated by Figure 6.3.

Figure 6.3 illustrates how the innovation impulse ran parallel to the 'normal' trajectory. The next section discusses the rationale behind this and the organization of the innovation impulse.

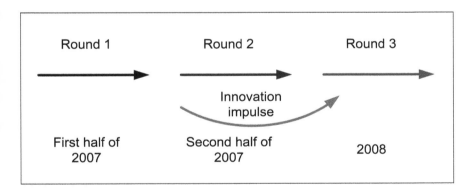

Figure 6.3   Project set-up of the Transumo A15-project

Applying Transition Management: The Innovation Impulse

The starting point for the 'innovation impulse' was that it was deemed necessary to achieve (higher) ambitions in the project, which were not yet achieved in the first phase. More innovative measures were found to be both possible and necessary. The project participants were thought of as too strongly connected to daily practices, and therefore strongly embedded in the current way of thinking and working. This supposedly would limit their potential to come up with new and creative ideas (Kuipers et al. 2008). The alternative trajectory, parallel to the main trajectory, was then initiated, to give an innovation impulse to the project, by using the expertise and creativity of 'outsiders'. This innovation impulse trajectory was *inspired* by concepts of TM, although the organization of a fully-fledged TM process was hampered for practical reasons. The innovation impulse had to be prepared, acted out, and translated into a deliverable within three to four months (September 2007 to December 2007), during which there were two sessions with the group of 'innovative outsiders', who were all selected and interviewed in September and October.

This meant TM was not fully implemented. The participants chose to take the two-track approach (visualized in Figure 6.3): to hold on to the 'modern classical project approach', while making space for an 'innovative transition trajectory'. In the literature on TM (Loorbach 2007) the term 'two-track approach' serves to underline that a TM process is not necessarily intended to replace mainstream (government) policy: they can 'coexist'. With time and patience, the transition movement may spread out and have a transformational influence on the (mainstream) policy. For a project, such a two-track approach is a rather 'safe' choice to make: if something good comes out of it, one could integrate the results in the 'normal' trajectory, but, if the transition management approach fails, not much would be lost.

The process of the two sessions was guided by a professional process manager from an advisory organization and five facilitators from Erasmus University Rotterdam, TNO and Delft University of Technology. The innovation-trajectory was not financed out of the budget of the A15-project, but entirely out of additional money received from the Transumo organization. From an original long list with up to 40 names and organizations, over 20 people were approached to participate in the innovation sessions. All those people agreed to participate in at least one of the two planned sessions, and most met this promise. Participants came from a wide variety of organizations, such as small businesses, large business firms, universities, governmental departments, journalism, environmental organizations, overarching multi-actor organizations, consultancies, and so on. Prior to the sessions, most participants were informed about the project and the innovation impulse in a semi-structured interview, in which information was also acquired regarding the views of the participants on the Rotterdam Port area, and the potential solution pathways they had in mind.

The two innovation sessions took place in October and November 2007. The first session was meant to help the participants to get to know one another, and then evaluate and contribute to the package of measures of the first phase of the main trajectory. The second session focused on going deeper into the content and developing new and innovative solutions and ideas. To stimulate this creative process, several measures were taken to assure the participants this was not just yet another boring business meeting. Both sessions took place in an artists' atelier in Rotterdam, and the rooms were decorated with several mobility symbols, such as traffic signs, and quotes from the interviews were pasted on the wall in order to stimulate discussion. Several exercises were carried out in order to break through fixed beliefs and positions.

The results from this session were as follows. One of the main points the innovators came up with while reflecting on the Modern Classical measures was that the focus should not be solely on technical innovation, but also on organizational innovation. For instance, what organizational innovations are required for the successful implementation of technical solutions?

During the first workshop six recurring fundamental issues with respect to the Rotterdam Port development in relation to transport could be identified:

1. Purpose of the A15 project. Is the project mainly about accessibility? Is sustainability a limiting condition or a main objective?
2. The function of the Port area – working versus living. Should the area be used for industry, logistics and other related port activities only and should nearby citizens be persuaded to live somewhere outside the port region?
3. The role of the Rotterdam Port. Should Rotterdam focus more on value-adding activities instead of container transshipment? Or, should Rotterdam focus more on cooperation with other Northwest-European ports?
4. Organization and government. What should be the role of government? And what can be expected from the private sector?
5. Logistics. Is the logistical sector too much focused on short-term solutions instead of on designing better systems for the mid- and the long-term?
6. Modal shift. Is a modal shift from road to rail and inland shipping achievable? And, if so, what part of the expected transport growth can it account for?

These results were further explored in the second session. In this second session, people were asked to write on post-it notes what their desired future perspective was, and what would be the turning point that would lead to that perspective. After writing this down, they were asked to place the post-it notes on the timeline on the wall, hence choosing whether their perspectives were to take place in 2027, or maybe 2057, or any other year between 2007 and 2057. All this resulted in the presentation of three future perspectives, at the end of the second session.

First, *the A15 was proposed as an experimental seedbed for small-scale innovations.* The innovators proposed not to invest in widening the A15, but rather in the following:

- the prevention of unnecessary mobility (by, for instance, teleworking);
- better use of existing infrastructure (congestion charge, pricing);
- facilitation of other modalities of transport (e.g. pipelines, inland waterways, rail, investments in public transport).

The point of departure in their plan was the assumption that automobiles will become more sustainable (i.e. low or zero emission and/or more fuel efficient) in the near future, so the problem is not so much about environmental issues, but about accessibility. Second, *new organizational forms were proposed for infrastructure and mobility.* The innovators started from the assumption that they should not enroll too easily in thinking about technical solutions, but rather focus on organizational innovations. They noted that power relations between the relevant actors in the Port area are traditional, and that it appears difficult to pinpoint a problem owner. These and other observations brought the innovators to the idea of a modal director or manager in combination with the distribution of slots for road transport. Various factors influence the price of slots including time, work/private, comfort, reliability, environmental quality, and modality. Third, the *Rotterdam Port area was proposed as motor of a bio-based economy.* The innovators were challenged to smartly adapt to future changes in freight streams worldwide. First, they dwelled on a number of worldwide trends with respect to the energy supply, the Chinese economy, and developments in Eastern Europe. Consideration of local trends and local opportunities like the Rotterdam Climate Initiative and the presence of large refineries in the Port are leading to shared support for Rotterdam as the motor of a bio-based economy. The assumptions behind this idea were the worldwide rise of biofuels and the opportunity to invest in other related port activities that generate more added value than container transshipment. Consequently, the innovators designed a sustainable transport system based on their future port perspective.[2]

The results of the innovation impulse were collected and presented in project deliverable D16 (Lohuis et al. 2008). By then, the project management had gained some confidence in the trajectory, and the results were welcomed. They served as a starting point and inspiration for the set-up of the third phase in the project trajectory, together with the results from the 'normal' second-phase trajectory, which had been presented in deliverable D15, and the management presented measures under the three keywords: Dynamic, Sustainable, and Daring.

---

2   Further information about the developed measures and ideas can be found in deliverable D16.

Empirical Findings on the Innovation Impulse

In this section the researchers analyse the short-term and the long-term perspective in the A15-project based on observations in and around project meetings *in both trajectories*, the two deliverables that came out of *both trajectories* in the second round, and interviews that were conducted for the innovation impulse.

Observations in and Around the A15-project Meetings

One of the general observations in the A15-project relates to the excessive use of transition terminology. The project documents (proposals, plans and reports) were filled with the terms 'sustainability', 'transition management', 'system innovation' and 'transition to sustainable mobility'. During the actual meetings, however, these words were used much less, and sometimes not at all. Transumo provided a format in which project documents had to be delivered. The participants had to specify how their project would contribute, or had contributed, to the transition to sustainable mobility, which system innovations were involved, and how TM was applied. 'Sustainability' was defined in terms of 'people, planet and profit'. In the meetings, the competitive position of the Dutch transport sector and the economic value of logistics were treated as a given by most project participants, because of the economic importance of the Rotterdam Port.

In order to comply with the 'people-planet-profit-balance', participants emphasized the 'side-effects' of economic optimization that are indirectly beneficial for the planet and people. 'Increasing efficiency' and 'combining freight loads' primarily leads to cost reduction and the speeding up of traffic flows (good for profit). It does, however, also lead to 'less transport' (in terms of less kilometres), and therefore also to 'less noise' (i.e. good for people), and 'less emissions' (i.e. good for the planet). In this way the goals of accessibility and economic optimization were framed in terms of sustainability. Both insiders and outsiders mentioned this point in project meetings, frequently emphasizing that accessibility was the primary focus of the project, and that the long-term sustainability aspect was missing.

In the discussions about long-term system innovation and sustainability in the meetings during the first round, or when participants called for more innovativeness or more attention for the ecological aspects, other participants responded in terms of pragmatic considerations such as the limited budget, scope and time frame of the project, or strategic considerations such as the demands of the steering group. Moreover, during the meetings there were significant disagreements about the extent to which the project should focus on a long-term or a short-term perspective. These disagreements were related to certain tensions between project participants with differing backgrounds, such as researchers and company representatives, environmental organizations and company representatives, consultants and researchers, members of different research institutes, and individuals representing different departments within one organization.

These disagreements can be illustrated with several anecdotes, one of which relates to a meeting of the 'business representatives'. Although the semi-governmental environmental organization participating in the project had been invited to the meeting, the representative of that organization was not present. At the reception following the meeting, a business representative loudly and publicly commented on the absence, concluding that it was good because 'at least this way we can keep it pleasant'. Another anecdote relates to an open meeting in which dozens of 'outsiders' were invited to discuss sustainable freight transport and the accessibility of the Rotterdam Port. One representative of an environmental organization commented that the A15-project was nothing but a 'toy' of the Rotterdam Port Authority. A governmental representative commented that yet again it showed that Transumo-projects were nothing but 'a hobby for professors'.[3]

While Transumo-projects explicitly aim to bring research and practice closer together in an effort to reach societal objectives, in the reality of this project it seemed that the gaps between researchers, consultants, businesses and environmental organizations were actually enlarged as conflict emerged and stereotypes were confirmed. One of the most striking stereotypes relates to the short term and the long term. Stakeholders had the tendency to separate each other into '*those that think short- term*' and '*those that think long-term*'. We will come back to this particular tendency later on, as it was explicitly confirmed during the interviews.

Another striking feature during the meetings on the 'traditional trajectory' was the relatively technological approach, especially in comparison with the broad project goals. The focus on technical measures, and the use of rather technological calculation methods, was sometimes at odds with the goal of creating solutions in the Port region for sustainable development. During most of the knowledge workers' meetings, the discussions predominantly revolved around who was going to use what data through the use of what computer model. Fundamental discussions about goals or strategies in the project were mostly confined to the management team and the steering group, and hardly discussed with the knowledge workers. There was a strong division between the production of knowledge and deliverables, on the one hand, and the political and strategic discussions, on the other.

The most striking observation in and around the project meetings concerns the way in which 'insiders' referred to the two parallel trajectories during the second round (regular trajectory versus the 'innovation impulse'). As described in the previous section, these interviews and sessions were prepared, organized, and reported by five 'facilitators' (and one senior process-manager who was hired to lead the discussion during the sessions). It so happens that these five facilitators were the youngest people involved in the A15-project.

---

3   The anecdotes come from Avelino's field notes.

What Participants Write ... (the 'Deliverables')

The original package of measures and solutions for the A15-region (the 'Modern Classical trajectory') presented relatively short-term measures, such as the distribution of goods at night and the dedication of separate driving lanes on the road, but the two more recent deliverables (D15 and D16) focused more on the long term. According to one deliverable *'an important point of departure is that the Modern Classical trajectory did not give any attention to the design of the area under study in the long term'*. This increased focus on the long term coincides with an increased focus on sustainability. Whereas the project started with a focus on accessibility, within the basic conditions of sustainability the deliverable from the general trajectory now also proposed *'that sustainability is a strategic chance for the future development of the port'*.

Hence, the focus within the project, whether it was the general trajectory or the innovation impulse, focused increasingly on sustainability and long-term measures. Both connected different kinds of solutions and measures to the shared ideals of accessibility and sustainability. D15, the deliverable of the general trajectory, connected long-term goals to a more accentuated version of the goals from the Modern Classical trajectory, plus five new themes, in which several measures were presented. D16, the deliverable of the innovation impulse, presented three ideal images as new ambitions for the project.

1. the A15 as an experimental seedbed for small-scale innovations;
2. slot management as an innovative form of organization; and
3. Rotterdam Port as an engine of the bio-based economy.

D16 classified these ideal images as presenting the contrasts between long-term and short-term effects, the future long-term perspective being represented by the image of the bio-based economy, while the A15 as an experimental seedbed consisted of measures that could be carried out 'tomorrow'. This contrast is also represented by a quote of one of the participants who noted that *'we have to think long-term, and act short-term'*.

The deliverables published therefore seemed to present the long term and the short term as a dichotomy between concrete actions (short-term) and ideal visions or strategic opportunities (long-term goals or ideals). However, as was also mentioned in the deliverable of the innovation impulse the contrast between the short and the long term is a false distinction. Long-term perspectives which are not connected to taking actions in the present are illusions. Hence, the deliverables appear to be hovering between describing the dichotomy between the short term and the long term, and yet also point to the interaction between the two.

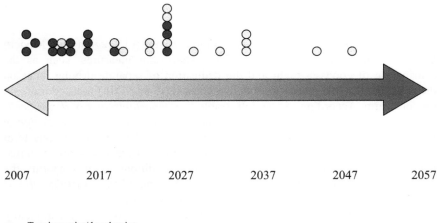

2007   2017   2027   2037   2047   2057

● Turning point/ breakpoint

○ Future perspective

Figure 6.4   Timeline exercise, second innovation impulse meeting

Other dichotomies are also demonstrated in the deliverables. As the report recognizes, there are significant tensions between transition management, on the one hand, and project management, on the other. On the basis of other sources, one can connect this to the often-made assumption that TM is solely a long-term focus perspective, while project management is about the short term. Although the report claimed otherwise, many of the project participants did not seem to share this view because in achieving transition or system innovation it is about beckoning long-term future images, on the one hand, and possibilities to take steps in the right direction 'today', on the other.

In general, the two deliverables demonstrated that the tension between short-term and long-term perspectives was problematic in the project. Apart from the abovementioned tendency to dichotomize, there also appeared to be problems surrounding the definition of the 'long term'. While one person viewed the long term to be 2020, someone else would regard this is as the short term. In the timeline, hardly anyone mentioned perspectives beyond 2037, indicating that even the innovators had trouble thinking truly long-term. In conclusion, the two deliverables showed us the tendency to dichotomize in the project, and the problems around long-term thinking.[4]

---

4   However, it appeared to be less the case in the deliverables than is revealed in the data acquired from interviews and participation. This might be because written sources usually have multiple authors, who restrict each other's individual perceptions, and hence moderate each other's views.

What Participants Say ... (in Interviews)

For the organization of the innovation impulse, different insiders were interviewed. These included participants in the steering group (responsible for the quality control of outcomes), the management team (project leaders responsible for the outcomes) and the researchers. Several 'outsiders' were also interviewed: some participated in the innovation sessions, others participated in the open meeting of the 'regular trajectory', while others participated in all meetings. In the interviews, these participants were asked to comment on the following topics in relation to the A15-project:

- goal-setting;
- relation between the short and the long term;
- embedding in Transumo;
- application of transition (management) concepts;
- relation between the different trajectories;
- transfer of knowledge; and
- power relations.

In the interviews it became apparent how differently the participants thought about all these issues. When asked to define what the 'long term' or the 'short term' was, participants gave strikingly different answers. Interpretations of the short term varied from 'today', 'tomorrow', 'the next four years', 'until the end of this project', '2010', '2015' or even '2020'. Interpretations of the 'long term' varied from 2010 to 2050. Some saw 2020 as clearly long-term while others saw it as mid-term or even short-term. In the interviews, participants also commented on the interpretations of others. For example, one participant commented that 'the long-term vision of the Ministry is about 2020, but that is actually too short-term because real change can only happen after that'. The one thing that all participants agreed on, however, is that the tension between the short and the long term was one of the major challenges in the project. It was emphasized that this tension was a topic of discussion in all the different groups and that questions on whether to focus on the short or the long term kept returning in the project discussions.

As one participant concluded in an interview, the problem in the project was not so much that the long term was lacking, but rather that the dimension of time in itself was lacking. Both in the innovation meetings and in the interviews, other participants also commented that the 'package of solutions' was too much an *enumeration* of possible measures (which is in a way inherent to the chosen process of going from a 'long-list' to a 'short-list' to a 'hot-list'). These solutions were presented as a static 'package' but not placed 'in time'. Ironically, the same participants who produced the package of solutions had a rigorously planned process on how to produce that output (planning in which they agree who should have what ready when). This output became the goal of the project, but the output *per se* – the package of solutions – was not placed in time at that time (in terms of which solutions could be implemented when and by whom, how this related to the timing of other solutions, and how all this related to the actual substantive goal). This was only done in Phase 3 of the project, when the seven themes were connected to stakeholders and participants for their implementation.

The most striking observation in the interviews was that participants separated other participants and stakeholders into 'those that think short-term' and 'those that think long-term'. Especially business companies were mentioned by all participants as the ones that think short-term or only care about today and tomorrow. While most participants emphasized that this short-term thinking was a problem – as they believed it impedes innovation and change – they did not blame the companies for it. Short-term thinking was believed to be inherent to business actors. Explanations such as the short-term demands of shareholders (in the case of large companies), the highly competitive market, and the small profit margins in the transport sector (in the case of smaller companies) were given as a reason for this. Business '*cannot afford to think long-term*', one respondent commented.

As many of the stakeholders in the A15-project were companies, there was a problem according to the participants that long-term thinking was undeveloped. Many of the stakeholders seemed rather uninterested in the long term and more interested in short-term solutions. All participants described and emphasized this dilemma. As mentioned before, it was one of the main reasons to set up the parallel trajectories. There was also a formal task division as there were various other projects around the A15 that dealt with short-term solutions, while this A15-Transumo-project had been explicitly assigned to deal with the long term. However, as a participant stressed, it was inherently difficult to think long-term in this specific project because the problems on the A15 were already very urgent. Short-term solutions were deemed necessary and urgent by the majority of the companies in the region.

When asked how the relation between the short term and the long term was dealt with or managed, participants gave various answers. Some emphasized that the project had two groups that came from different worlds – one that thought short-term and another that thought long-term – and that these two different worlds would simply '*never find each other*'. Others emphasized that there was a lack in the project of people who could build bridges between the two ways of thinking. One participant stated that by simply putting these two different groups together and making sure that each 'gets a bit of what he wants', they would meet in the middle and make concessions.

Retrieving Dichotomies

As the previous section demonstrated, even though all the participants seemed to agree that considerable tensions and dilemmas in the project arose from a short-term focus versus a long-term focus, they actually had very different ideas on what the words 'short term' or 'long term' entailed in terms of actual calendar dates. This suggests that the perceived tension between the short and the long term might have been about something other than the actual temporal aspect. Indeed, another observation is that the participants explained the tension between the short term and the long term by explicitly referring to tensions between other dichotomies. For instance, all mentioned the tension between the 'accessibility target' and the 'sustainability target'. Even though most emphasized that these targets were not mutually exclusive and could reinforce each other, they still emphasized that certain stakeholders wanted the project to focus on accessibility, while others wanted to focus on sustainability. Subsequently, 'those who mostly wanted sustainability' were characterized as 'those who thought long-term', and 'those who wanted mostly accessibility' were characterized as 'those who thought short-term'.

In many interviews it was emphasized that either the majority of the stakeholders or at least the most dominant stakeholders deemed accessibility a more important focus of the project. One participant, however, pointed out that, while accessibility was actually really the goal of the project, sustainability was accepted by everyone as a necessary condition, and that 'conditions are actually more important then goals' because 'goals are flexible, while conditions are hard'. Other participants, mostly those who were only involved in the 'innovation-impulse', described the A15-project as an accessibility project focused on short-term technological solutions but 'disguised' as a sustainability project.

So far, none of this is too surprising. First, it is a human tendency to think in terms of dichotomies and categories. Second, the concept of sustainability has an inherent long-term dimension, so the association between one and the other is evident. Third, the tension between sustainability and economic targets such as accessibility is also common, and so are suspicions that the sustainability discourse might be a disguise for other interests. Yet the list of categories that are associated with the long term versus the short term is even longer. Although many associations make sense, not all associations are self-evident or necessarily logical. For instance, many participants associated the short term with technological solutions and the long term with organizational and cultural strategies. This is not self-evident. As a matter of fact, one could argue that in some cases, solutions in the technological or infrastructural sphere require 'more time' to be achieved than, for instance, organizational measures.

Another interesting connotation of the long term was the idea among participants that a long-term focus is the same thing as a slow process in the project. Stakeholders and outsiders – mainly companies – mostly complained about the project 'being slow and taking too long'. Insiders tended to conclude that this meant those critics were 'too impatient to think long-term'. There is, however, an obvious difference between a long-term *content* focus (e.g. how could the Port develop during the next 30 years?) and a slow *process* within the project (e.g. what are we doing in the project in the coming weeks?). A long-term content focus can perfectly well be combined with a quicker process. One of the reasons that the long term was associated with a delay in the progress of the project had to do with the project's focus on quantitative research outcomes and traffic models, in which the effects of the measures were calculated. This was considered by many to be the core output of the project: the concrete, objective and scientific results. Other outcomes, such as future visions and strategies (formulated in the course of a participative process by the stakeholders), were considered creative and fun, but vague and normative, and therefore not 'counted' as 'project results'.

The parallel trajectories and the respective deliverables appeared to reinforce this interpretation, and also confirmed the idea that the long-term focus leads to 'vague outcomes' that cannot be translated into concrete project results (i.e. calculating them in scenario models) while a short-term focus safeguarded a successful project output. Ironically, the deliverable that was quantifiable (D15) took much longer to be prepared and written than the deliverable that was not quantifiable (D16). While certain insiders tended to associate the calculation in traffic models with action and actually doing something (in the sense of getting things done and producing output), outsiders – especially companies – associated this with 'yet another' theoretical exercise instead of a plan for action. Along these lines, there were many other associations with the short term and the long term. Based on the observations in documents, meetings and interviews, a list of associations was derived (Table 6.2).

There was a tendency in the A15-project to place participants in one column or the other. Those who were in favour of concrete project results were also in favour of a short-term focus, and therefore a focus on accessibility. The distinction between the two columns was mostly confirmed and reinforced rather than broken down. Especially as the participants emphasized the differences between those characteristics that 'fitted' in one column and those that fitted in the other, rather than pointing out the similarities between them in the common endeavour to search for ways to deal with these dilemmas.

Table 6.2   Long- versus short-term and other dichotomies

Associations with 'Short Term'	Associations with 'Long Term'
Present	Future
Accessibility	Sustainability
Economic interests	Societal interests
Technological focus	Organizational focus
Transport Planning	Spatial Planning
Optimization	Innovation
Business actors/consultants	'The rest' (government, NGOs, scientists)
Content	Process
Applied knowledge	Fundamental knowledge
Concrete	Abstract
Operational	Strategic
Vested interests/regimes	Suppressed interests/niches
Consistency	Flexibility
Conforming to fixed paradigms	Challenging and changing paradigms
Action, 'doing something'	Reflection, 'thinking about it'
Fast process/quick project outcomes	Slow process/no project outcomes
Local (low level of aggregation)	National and Global (high level of aggregation)
Pragmatic	Idealistic
Incremental	Radical
Tolerant	Judgemental
Bottom-up	Top-down
Quantitative/traffic models	Qualitative/images
Objective	Subjective
Serious 'Work'	Creative 'Fun'
Insiders' expertise and experience	Outsiders' naivety
Solutions/measures	Ideas/visions
Is/'how things are'	Ought/'how things should be' (normative)
Project management	Transition management

The Relevance for the Development of Transition Management

Many of the participants in the A15-project saw the long-term perspective and the short-term perspective as mutually exclusive. They associated the difference between the short and the long term with various other dichotomies. These dichotomies were confirmed and reinforced by the majority of the participants. This meant that many discussions about the 'short term' versus the 'long term' seemed to be about something other than the actual temporal aspect. This 'thinking in dichotomies', and their confirmation and reinforcement as observed in the A15-project, can be considered problematic if the challenge is to find a middle way between each of these dichotomies and to link them to one another. In this connection, the most striking observation is that a 'long-term perspective' – in terms of what happens between now and the future – could theoretically be a tool to bridge many of these dichotomies. This is, however, impossible as long as the long-term perspective is only associated with one side of the dichotomies (the 'future' and everything that is intangible or faraway). In terms of the development of TM the results also demonstrated the associations that people have with TM: long-term, abstract, process-orientated, and normative.

TM *literature*, however, positions itself explicitly as the opposite of solely long- term, only process-orientated, or just interested in a narrow image of sustainability. TM aims to do the following:

1. link sustainability to other targets such as accessibility through a participative process, in which economic, ecological and societal stocks and flows are explicitly compared and discussed (Rotmans et al. 2001);
2. integrate process and content (Loorbach 2007); and
3. bring in the long-term temporal perspective that relates the 'now' to the 'future', and links current actions to future ambitions through transition scenarios, backcasting techniques and 'transition paths' (Sondeijker et al. 2006; Loorbach 2007).

As this analysis has made obvious, however, the participants did not see TM in this way. Instead, most of them associated TM only with *one side* of the dichotomies (the right-hand column): thinking about the *future* solely, a *process* tool that denies the content, something that is *only* about the ideal of sustainability and not about other economic or societal targets. As such, the most important challenge for TM is to explicitly position itself as an approach that *breaks through* dichotomies, and offers concrete techniques to do so.

Continuing with the retrieved dichotomies, another sharp distinction between TM and a perceived opposite was found: project management versus TM. There is a certain tension between the paradigm of project management – which is based on setting fixed targets, task division (fragmentation) and sticking to the time planning – and the paradigm of TM – which is based on an explorative goal-setting, integration, adaptation, and learning. Despite this tension, it is not a matter of choosing one or the other. TM does not replace project management: it is rather a form of *process management* that *includes* project management. In the A15-project some participants were used to the 'project management' paradigm and, on that basis criticized other participants for not being quite as strict on time planning and budget.

TM offers insights and suggestions for process management at the meta-level of a project, i.e. how to safeguard coherence and a sense of unity in the bewildering variety of stakeholders, steering groups, management teams, expert meetings, working groups, deliverables and administrative reports. The idea of a distinction between project management, on the one hand, and TM, on the other, therefore, indicates that the project participants' understanding of TM remained limited, despite the innovation impulse and the Transumo transition activities. It is too easy to simply point to project participants and claim that 'they just do not get it'. Rather, an important lesson for TM is that the level of abstraction might be too high for many professionals.

Apart from the problem of the abstract character of TM and the perceived long-term focus, which deviates from 'common project management', another problem associated with TM is the degree of normativity. The idea of a 'sustainability vision' appeared to scare off various participants because of its normative tone. This brings us to another dichotomy associated with the short term versus the long term: the distinction between 'is' and 'ought'. The 'is' versus 'ought' dichotomy (or pragmatism versus idealism) relates to one of the most fundamental debates in social science, between those that 'describe' and 'explain' and those that 'prescribe' and 'predict', i.e. between those that call for an understanding of how things 'are' and those that emphasize the understanding of how things 'should be'.

This tendency can also been seen in governmental and consultancy discourse, in which it is emphasized that the important thing is to 'act' on the basis of pragmatic understanding of the way things go, rather than taking a paternalistic approach to decide how things should go. This is related to the preoccupation with 'what companies find important', and the tendency to accommodate them instead of 'telling them' what they should do differently. TM, however, aims to go beyond this dichotomy between 'is' and 'ought'. It is not about knowing with absolute certainty how things are exactly at a specific point in time, nor is it about deciding how things should be in the future. It is about a process of figuring out together what we *can do* with regard to our common future (Avelino and Rotmans 2009).

Conclusion and Reflection

This analysis demonstrates the multiple challenges that TM faces in practice. First, it needs to be explicitly rebranded as a tool to break through dichotomies, instead of being an approach that reinforces dichotomies. We chose the word 'rebrand' carefully, thereby demonstrating that TM never intended to become only part of the right-hand column of the dichotomy table. However, several practitioners at the operational level do associate themselves with this right-hand column – as illustrated in the A15-project – and therefore TM needs to become aware of these associations and position itself explicitly as neither of the two columns.

Second, TM was considered to mismatch with project management: the two were seen as conflicting types of management, with differing objectives and approaches. TM should respond to this by integrating project management actions better into the TM-model. After all, it is unlikely that professionals will leave all project management behind, as it is an important frame of reference for them. Project management is inevitable in real-life projects, which also means TM should become more open to the practical demands project managers face.

Third, TM was considered too abstract and too normative. The latter may be inherent in the approach, as allowing normativity and an action perspective is one of the things that distinguishes TM from other system theories. There will always remain a certain degree of differences in taste between actors (are they open to normative approaches or not). However, the degree of abstract terminology and thinking can be improved. For this, it would help to further emphasize that TM is not simply a generic process tool that can be applied equally to all sectors, but that it is mostly a flexible and reflexive tool that can be designed to fit the demands of the sector or region under research. By adding sector-specific considerations the abstract nature becomes less, and it becomes easier for professionals to relate to the discussion.

This reflexivity principle of TM, which is emphasized in numerous scientific publications (Rotmans et al. 2001; Loorbach 2007; Kemp and Rotmans 2009), should be more explicitly communicated in the context of practical applications by professionals. Achieving a more sector-specific fit can reduce the need for abstract and generic applicable terminology, and hence make it more accessible for professionals. This can aid them in breaking through dichotomies. Even then, the dichotomies may never entirely vanish, but if TM can achieve its ambition to connect the two worlds by better communicating and involving practitioners at the operational level, it may be able to construct bridges for the future.

PART II
Climate Change, Transport Energy Use and Emissions

Chapter 7

Characterizing the Impacts of Uncertainty in the Policy Process: Climate Science, Policy Construction, and Local Governance Decisions

Deb Niemeier, Thomas D. Beamish, Alissa Kendall, Ryken Grattet, Jonathan London, Carolyn de la Pena and Julie Sze

Introduction

Local governments in the U.S. have a unique place in the implementation of greenhouse gas (GHG) mitigation and adaptation strategies. Because of the historical importance of property rights in American law and governmental tradition, decisions at the local level can directly influence the ways in which development occurs through zoning and because they structure how urban landscape activities are regulated they represent a critical link in government response to climate change. For example, unlike some states (Florida, Rhode Island, Massachusetts), in California all land use decisions are made by county and municipal governments alone. Yet despite the importance of local land use authority, we know very little about how uncertainties and risks associated with climate change and the policy regimes being suggested play out in local governance and decision-making processes.

A recent example illustrates this point. In February of 2009, a local government, which passed the first solar ordinance in the nation and has long been considered among California's most environmentally progressive rejected a project to retrofit an existing 90-year-old house; the retrofit would have improved its energy efficiency by more than 70 per cent over a standard remodel. The decision, while seemingly 'irrational' when thinking globally about carbon reduction made sense given local political constraints and community values. The decision to turn down the retrofit reflected both a desire to retain a historically important 'California bungalow' roof style and at least one local politician's desire to limit the number of political battles in a quest to develop good will around a looming infrastructure project – the largest ever undertaken by the city: implementation of a city-scale solar collector field.

Because the effects of GHG emissions have generation-long lag times and are inequitably experienced across the globe, the need for reducing near-term emissions is very difficult to communicate. We rely on characterization of *potential or future* impacts to spur action, yet this characterization necessarily carries with it large degrees of uncertainty that may, on the surface, reduce the sense of urgency for near-term mitigation and adaptation. As a society, we have very little experience grappling with economic decisions for which consequences occur decades or centuries later, and virtually no organization is designed to consider these consequences (PSMCRDS 2009).

With new feedbacks in the climate system suggesting a much faster rate of change than anticipated (Lawrence, Slater et al. 2008; Rignot, Bamber et al. 2008), it is critical that we quickly unravel the interactions between science, the policy process, and public interests (actions and motivations), many of which hinge on characterizations of risk and uncertainty, in order to structure successful policy strategies. Further, we must be able to quantify the impacts of the convergence of these forces on the construction, implementation, and even enforcement of policies that target reductions in GHGs.

In this chapter, we explore the ways in which uncertainty arises as a recurrent feature of the policy life-cycle. We characterize the state of knowledge and identify key research questions across three key points of interaction and communication: between science and policy, between different layers of government, and between local implementers and their communities. We position this review in the context of changes in California. Given the size of its economy and population, California is arguably the single most critical player in the U.S. in terms of addressing climate change. Legislation passed in 2006 and known as AB 32, the first of its kind, sets an ambitious GHG emissions target of 1990 levels by 2020 with further reduction, 80 per cent of 1990 emissions by 2050, mandated by Executive Order (Schwarzenegger 2007). While AB 32 was far-reaching, California just recently passed an even further reaching bill Senate Bill 375 (SB 375) (Steinberg 2008), which mandates the Air Resources Board (ARB) to set GHG targets at the regional level. The legislation is incentive-based, lacking penalty or sanction for noncompliance. Communities are charged with developing their own strategies for achieving targeted reductions in GHG emissions. This landmark bill addresses the issue of local land use control to mitigate a global problem by tackling urban sprawl and promising to produce a more efficient region (Yamamura 2008). The importance of local decision-making in reducing energy demand through land use, building design and transportation is indisputable (Kaswan 2009). Local governments can serve as vehicles of policy innovation, initiating change both horizontally (local to local) as well as vertically (local to regional to state to federal) (Engel 2006). But innovation in local governance, and the ability to spread this innovation, depends on many factors, not the least of which is the magnitude of the risks that residents and policymakers alike attach to a potential new regulatory approach (Galle and Leahy 2009).

Decision-making and Uncertainty in Context

Confronted with a preponderance of evidence, governmental agencies, commercial and local interests, and communities are struggling with how to define mitigation and adaptation strategies that can reduce the impacts of climate change. A key challenge is to bridge scientific and social constructions of risk. Constructing adequate policy and regulatory approaches requires characterization of both 'acceptable risk' as well as 'acceptable response to the risks'. Yet, for a number of interrelated reasons the creation and implementation of climate change policy is no simple task. Given the potentially radical, life changing issues and outcomes climate change policy must tackle, the number of vested interests and stakeholders involved in the debate over policy form and content is virtually unlimited. Reflecting this diversity, the creation, implementation, and enforcement of climate change policy reflects an overlapping mix of agencies and jurisdictions (e.g. see Adelman and Engel 2008; Kaswan 2009), along with commercial and civic 'interests', which seek to have their view (and preferred remedy) of the 'climate change problem' recognized in any new or modified policy mandate.

Further complicating efforts, the policy process includes institutions that take form as related but distinct regulations and laws, norms and values that are less formally represented, or are simply tacitly held assumptions, suppositions, and beliefs that organize practitioners and the public into like-minded enclaves. Historians and sociologists have documented the ways in which individual and group aspirations and political divisions influence how scientific data and technical knowledge is valued. This is particularly true in moments of uncertainty when alliances shift rapidly: individuals seeking 'social currency' and 'technological assimilation' may regard particular data as true (or false) because of the status they themselves can acquire through those assessments (de la Peña 2007; Traweek 1988; Marvin 1990; Fouche 2003; Dumit 2005). As a matter of course, any climate change directive must make its way through this warren of complex and competing interests and institutions that make basic policy initiatives difficult even under favourable conditions, when the parties involved ostensibly agree on the problem and the policy-based remedy to solve it. In total, these dynamics can insulate the local policy process from public influence and confound efforts to develop policy that aligns with statutory mandates.

This process of enclave thinking or groupthink (Janis 1983) is exacerbated when the public is confronted with high levels of urgency and uncertainty; policy makers and public interests typically rely on already institutionalized regulations, norms, and assumptions – those with which they are familiar – to reduce doubt and ambiguity and render the new, uncertain problem manageable (Meyer and Rowan 1977; Edelman, Uggen et al. 1999; Beamish 2000; Beamish 2002a; Beamish 2002b). For example, consider the target exercises specified in AB 32 and SB 375. The state level targets mandated by AB 32 are highly specific: 1990 levels by 2020. Likewise, regional targets under SB 375 for metropolitan areas are equally detailed and unambiguous. Yet their implementation will be anything but unambiguous or specific. Each mandate will confront local contexts in which community members have ample cause to be uncertain about climate change: they are bombarded by media-generated competing definitions of the causes of climate change and appropriate strategies for personal and collective action. Yet, these same communities will often have a great deal of certainty about the value of a particular design or land use approaches that will ultimately impact their ability to mitigate the effects of climate change. Attitudes toward property rights and government intervention in planning (e.g. see Pendall 2001) as well as fiscal conditions (Thomas 2006) may play as significant a role as social and economic class as predictors of action.

Put simply, the range of potential policy strategies likely to be both considered and implemented by local governments is currently unknown. Coupled with inputs in the form of scientific and policy metrics and constructs that reduce complexity (thus, increasing user accessibility), and interactions with community groups that have their own internal value systems and frequent distrust of external actors, the implementation of mandate streams will necessarily produce varied outcomes. Acknowledging these real world conditions destabilizes the usual means by which we model, interpret, and portray the move from scientific understanding to policy construction (PSMCRDS 2009). As demonstrated with our opening example, when transitioning from traditional frameworks for evaluating local policies to evaluative frameworks which necessarily hinge on climate change, the net result can be the acceptance of local policy actions that in seeking to reduce uncertainties, may actually be at cross-purposes with the intended goal, or even when in-sync can result in unexpected or diminished outcomes (Abbott 2008).

Variability in Local Policy Decisions

If our goal is to better understand and characterize the ways in which uncertainty emerges from the policy construction and implementation processes and how this uncertainty impacts local and individual decision making, then we must rethink the ways in which we account for the variability inherent to local policy development and within implementation outcomes among communities. This leads us to characterize the policy process – as we know it today – as a system comprising three intersections (Figure 7.1): between science and policy; between different levels of governance and between science, local implementers, and community interest groups. Each of these intersections directs empirical attention and anticipates a range of guiding research questions. In addition, we must also rethink what we consider to be the effects of these intersections on local decision-making practices and actual (or estimated) changes in emissions.

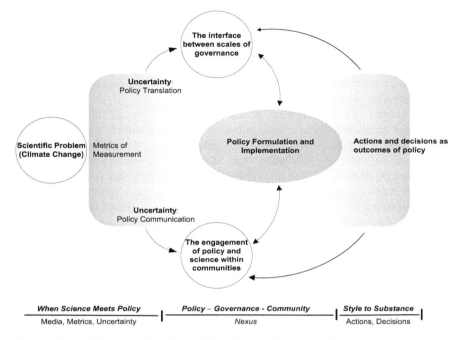

Figure 7.1   Characterization of the climate change policy process

Thus, we consider how scientific knowledge, its diffusion downward through layers of government, and its reception (and, potentially contestation) within local communities affects whether governance practices change and whether those practices actually result in desired reductions in GHGs. In the following sections, we discuss the state of the knowledge and identify research needs in each of these areas.

When Science Meets Policy: Metrics and Media Representations

While the fundamental mechanisms of climate change causes are well understood, the process of climate change and its effects are complex and uncertain. As is true more generally, communication of scientific knowledge regarding climate change to lay audiences poses significant challenges. As a result, there is a premium on development of simplifying language, symbols, models, and constructs to make what is known comprehensible. Often scientific knowledge is reduced to metrics and media representations that assist scientists and other knowledge brokers with narrating the problem and with the design of the solution.

In the policy discussions of climate change, the policy-makers have relied heavily on available metrics, constructs and models to help establish the urgency and usefulness of mitigation or adaptation strategies. But all indicators and metrics necessarily reduce the level of detail and occasionally the accuracy of the communication. For example, GDP, perhaps the most well known of economic indicators, exemplifies this trade-off between the benefits of a simple metric and a loss of fidelity. Consider that all sectors of the economy and all types of expenditures are bundled into a single performance indicator, obscuring variability in performance of one sector compared to another.

For climate change, scientific, policy and lay audiences all rely on the same metric for measuring climate change performance at national, regional, system or technology scales – carbon dioxide equivalent (CO_2e) emissions. Notably, CO_2e is an indicator of *cause* rather than an indicator of *effect*, since it is simply a measure of GHG emissions normalized to the most common GHG, CO_2. This characterization of emissions, rather than their impacts, as an indicator of climate change avoids assessment and prediction of the effects of climate change.

There are two potential benefits to using a simplified causal metric, (i) a great deal of uncertainty is stripped from the discourse on climate change policies by quantifying causes rather than effects, and (ii) as the focus remains on preventing climate change, causal metrics characterizing emissions may be more salient to new technology development and policy implementation. Unfortunately, this choice of indicator may also introduce some unintended consequences that distort the actual climate effects of different mitigation or policy strategies. Consider, for example, the overwhelming use of the IPCC's global warming potential.

Since the mid-nineties, global warming potentials (GWPs) proposed by the IPCC have served as the primary mechanism for normalizing GHGs into CO_2e values. A GWP converts non-CO_2 GHGs to CO_2-equivalents based on their relative impacts. GWPs have been widely employed in policy-relevant research and data collection such as the *Inventory of U.S. Greenhouse Gas Emissions and Sinks: 1990–2007* (US EPA 2009) and also in policy development and implementation such as the *Kyoto Protocol* (United Nations Framework Convention on Climate Change 2008) and California's AB 32, whose rulemaking looks to the IPCC's GWPs for numerous GHG inventory and accounting activities.

The IPCC selected cumulative radiative forcing (CRF) as the basis for calculating the relative impact of GHG emissions in its widely used GWPs. The first step in calculating CRF requires identifying the radiative efficiency (RE) of a gas, and the decay function that defines its lifetime in the atmosphere. When multiplied, these two parameters equal the instantaneous radiative forcing (RF) of a gas in the atmosphere. CRF is calculated by integrating RF over a time horizon. GWP for a gas is calculated by taking the ratio of the CRF of that gas and the reference gas, typically CO_2. The IPCC defines this as:

$$GWP = \int_0^{TH} RF_i(t)dt \, / \int_0^{TH} RF_c(t)dt$$

where c refers to CO_2, TH denotes the analytical time horizon, and i refers the GHG of concern

Source: IPCC 2001.

The use of CRF to normalize GHG emissions to a reference gas necessarily precludes consideration of the effects of increasing GHGs in the atmosphere. Figure 7.2 shows the impact chain for greenhouse gases and climate change. As indicated in the figure, the basis for GWP calculation is limited to the first few steps in the impact chain and does not predict warming, much less the impacts of global warming on human systems.

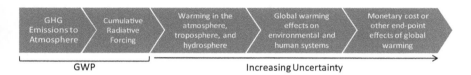

Figure 7.2   Chain of climate change impacts

The overwhelming use of GWPs to convert GHGs into CO_2e values leads to a number of potential distortions in capturing the effects of GHG emissions. First, the prevailing use of GWPs with 100-year time horizons in GHG inventories and mitigation strategies can distort preferences for emissions profiles, particularly if time horizons over the next 20–50 years are most important for preventing irreversible changes to the climate system and environment. For example, CH_4 has a very high 20-year GWP of 72, but a GWP of 25 if evaluated at a 100-year time horizon. Thus, the selection of a shorter or longer time horizon for evaluating GWPs could change the preference for mitigation strategies that reduce CH_4 over CO_2, or the converse.

The practice of summing GHG emissions over time in CO_2e values has other ramifications in climate mitigation strategies. For example, in studies estimating the contribution of land-use change emissions to the carbon-intensity of biofuels, ignoring the timing of land-use change emissions and other emissions that occur early or in advance of the biofuel life cycle significantly underestimates the global warming effect of the biofuel as measured by CRF (Kendall, Chang et al. 2009; M. O'Hare et al. 2009). Despite the shortcomings in current metrics and the need for alternative measures that are more closely linked to policy and economic dimensions (Fuglestvedt, Bersten et al. 2003), there is no clear successor in terms of an indicator that draws broad support (Shine, Fuglestvedt et al. 2005). The example of distorted preferences for one emissions profile over another is just one of many ways that the selection of a metric for quantifying climate change performance can influence the outcome of a policy, or a policy's effectiveness of a technology in meeting the ultimate goal of mitigating climate change.

Metrics are seen as attractive because they are thought by both scientists and policymakers alike, to reduce uncertainty in the translation of scientific knowledge into policy. However, as the discussion above suggests, metrics frequently introduce additional uncertainties, by obscuring nuances and distorting the science. The existence of multiple metrics can also incite battles about which measures are most appropriate; in turn, policymakers are then required to take sides, which can politicize debates about metrics, undermining the claim of autonomy.

However, not all of the scientific communication in policy discussions about climate change policies occurs around metrics. The growth in cultural productions (documentaries, novels, cartoons and art) related to global climate change mirrors the historical rise in atmospheric carbon dioxide seen in *An Inconvenient Truth* (Ziser and Sze 2009): consistently low numbers preceding a spectacular hockey stick-like increase (e.g. see Boykoff and Mansfield's (2009) graph of newspaper coverage of climate change between 2004 and 2009). The work in cultural productions provides narrative arguments (e.g. heat waves and hurricanes) and symbols (e.g. polar bears stranded on melting icebergs) that emerge in policy discussions as powerful rhetoric to develop climate change initiatives and are promoted by social movement organizations to mobilize citizens to support those initiatives. While the links between media representations and the scientific knowledge about climate change can be more or less explicit, they are frequently presented alongside discussions of metrics and scientific findings.

The addition of the influence of popular culture on environmental issues in public life (Boykoff and Boykoff 2007; Chilvers and Evans 2009) means that scientific knowledge and its assorted metrics are also embedded in media, books, and film and translated through various forums to the local decision-making process (Ziser and Sze 2009). Many of the media sources of information on climate change represent critical avenues for transmitting information to constituencies with less access to traditional scientific media (Boykoff 2008); in fact, the balanced approach taken by much media in the early 2000s may have actually lead to greater skepticism regarding the existence and seriousness of climate change (Boykoff and Boykoff 2004; Krosnick, Holbrook et al. 2006).

Celebrities continue to emerge as spokespersons for scientific knowledge about climate change. Boykoff and Goodman (2009) go so far as to suggest that the creating celebrities around climate change has enabled new and extended networks of celebrities that critically shape how we understand science and knowledge as a general public, and that these spaces are highly contested, underpinned by loose facts and an action strategy that can be highly politicized. Moreover, like the way metrics have generated further uncertainties centering on which metrics are best, media representations also have the potential to engender debates in which scientists and policy-makers must take sides, such as whether *An Inconvenient Truth* 'got the facts right'. Instead of media representations of science clarifying debate they become the focus of further conflict.

In this domain, some of the important research questions revolve around how scientific knowledge is filtered and translated through popular culture and policy discourse in ways that can mitigate or enhance uncertainty:

- How does the science of climate change influence discussions about the implementation of local and regional goals? More specifically, how have metrics and media representations been used within those discussions? How has a state-level policy been translated into targets for local and regional action? What are the limitations of relying on the particular metrics and representations that have been employed?
- How does uncertainty influence the selection of a metric or development of certain constructs, and how does that metric or construct in turn influence policy and climate mitigation strategies? For example, does use of IPCC GWPs inflate the promise of certain 'low carbon' technologies for local decision-makers and implementators?
- How do popular representations of 'metrics' of climate change in the US media impact the public's perception of scientific data or measurable impacts or even 'appropriate' responses to climate change? Two particularly salient examples are the proliferation of references relating Hurricane Katrina to climate change, and popular images of polar bear habitat destruction. And how does this political and media lens affect the application of science in the policy arena?
- How have metrics, constructs and model development and acceptance (by policy-makers and scientists) played out historically for systems with significant uncertainty? In particular, have elements with higher uncertainties been set aside or simplified to allow for greater certainty in the system as a whole? If so, what are these elements and what are the implications of such strategic decisions?

The Interface Between Levels of Governance

The critical question in this domain is 'What shapes the way in which uncertainty is approached and discretion is wielded in different local governmental and community contexts?' and by related, 'What accounts for variability in the alignment or lack of alignment between broader-level policy principles and more site-specific implementation practices?' Here, local systems of governance reflect how regulatory agencies communicate and translate policy from one domain to another; such as the interface and translation that occurs between the abstract, legislative processes (e.g. federal and state policymaking) and the actions taken by local governments and regulatory agencies (i.e. implementation and enforcement) (Pressman and Wildavsky 1979; Sabatier 1986; Bardach 1998). Whether and how translation happens to a great degree reflects the structure of inter-governmental relations as well as the relations between the communities and constituencies they represent. In the case of California, how a regional governance structure operates and how it aligns with or opposes local communities as they work to implement SB 375 will greatly impact their success in choosing the right kinds of policy instruments for their community.

There are also other regional, state, and federal entities as well as commercial firms and social movement groups that supply information, pressure, and support for local governments and communities that also influence implementation of policies such as SB 375. Finally, there are differential levels of expertise expressed by different local governments that also influence the shape and outcome of policy translations. Emissions levels, for instance, are often considered and debated by citizen planning boards – without anyone on the boards having scientific expertise and decisions may actually diverge from common wisdom. Alternatively, some local governments may be generally resistant to what they perceive of as interference by outside entities or have decision-making traditions that work to buffer their approach to implementation from outside influence.

In brief, then, the translation activities that characterize and constitute the process of policy-in-between the policy-on-the-books (e.g. SB 375) and policy-in-action (e.g. local climate mitigation plans) can result in a significant degree of variability in implementation and thus outcomes (Jenness and Grattet 2005). We contend that accounting for patterns in how different locales respond to new climate change policies requires disentangling how policy-in-between translations affect policies-in-action. Only from this can we then assess whether and to what degree policies-in-action cohere with and accomplish what the original policy-on-the-books was drafted, in abstract, to achieve.

Reflecting these influences, we identify five dimensions to the policy-community nexus that reflect important avenues for additional research:

- What is the structure of intergovernmental relations within the region and how does each local government fit within that set of relations? How do leaders within local government conceive of the distinctive customs and traditions of their organization and their community. (How do they answer the question 'What kind of local government are we?')
- How do local governments view their relationship to higher level governance structures that might be charged with achieving GHG reductions? How do they balance the need to attend to what they perceive to be community interest with the need to collaborate on regional issues?
- How does the regional government conceive of their member communities and what effect does this have on how they implement new land use policy? Policy implementers approach their charge and the communities they represent differently based on the social and political terrain they confront that reflects both contemporary community agency interactions and local memories of past dealings and outcomes.

- How have (or not) regional governance structures formally involved local community members and civic groups into the implementation process and what effect has this had on how they implement policy? How successful are policy implementers, in proactively pursuing risk communication and community inclusion campaigns as a way of reducing the chance of local resistance and increasing 'community buy in'?
- How (and why) have civic groups mobilized to influence policy implementation processes in the past and what effect has this had on present day implementation? And related, how do local community groups perceive the regional governance structures and related parties, how do they vary, and to what degree have these variant impressions influenced policy implementation?

The Engagement of Policy and Science within Communities

Often lost in the discussion of climate change is the way in which the lay-public (i.e. ordinary citizens) choose to act or not to act. How both the science and the policy associated with climate change are received by local citizen groups and officials is an important consideration for determining how policies will unfold. Research on communities and their interface with the policy implementation processes suggests that the introduction of new policies, especially those that are deemed essential or threatening (or both), provides the pretext for the evaluation and reflection on what a community 'stands for'; its collective beliefs and views of how best to secure the future, and its collective reconstructions of the past (Levine 1982; Walsh 1988; Kroll-Smith and Couch 1990; Freudenburg and Pastor 1992; Wynne 1996; Beamish 2001; London, Starrs et al. 2005; Grattet and Jenness 2008).

However, collective identity is not monolithic and, in fact, communities may vary in the degree of contestation about 'what kind of community' they are. Such contestation can provide the seeds for dissent about the priorities reflected in policy and the possibly even the validity of the science on the subject. For example, in local discussions, debates, and deliberations concerning climate change policy, which social groups and groupings are considered valid stakeholders as well as valid sources of knowledge? Introducing collective identity into the discussion of climate change policy raises questions concerning the place of race, class, gender, sexuality, age, nationality, mobility, and other markers of cross-cutting collectivities in policy decisions and implementation processes. What groupings will be recognized as legitimate and who will bear the greatest (or least) and why? Historians and social critics have documented the tendency for such knowledge to be produced by and for individuals who have most social and cultural capital (Chinn 2000; Green 2001), but this may be more or less contested within individual communities.

The reaction on the part of communities can veer far outside of the standard 'rational decision making model' or even ensuring exclusiveness (Danielson 1979), both of which have long been relied on to characterize policy implementation processes. Instead, communities have been found to reflect what may best be called 'contextually rational individuals' who do indeed conduct cost-benefit utility calculations but also bring to bear other considerations such as local traditions, civic identity, and shared expectations concerning the proper exercise of government authority and role of citizen participation in policy and decision-making (Thomas 2006). In short, varied constructions, understandings, and relations among policy administrators and the lay-publics they seek to serve will shape how climate change policies are locally received and thus implemented. As a consequence, compliance can be facilitated or undermined by the way science and policy is received locally.

Moreover, citizen groups not only engage with local policymakers about the implementation process they also engage with the science upon which the policies are putatively based. Community distrust of science and scientific institutions, based on perceptions of disrespect of their local knowledge and disregard of local interests and values can also hamper effective communication of scientific information and the development of collaborative partnerships (Corburn 2005; Liévanos, London et al. in press). Local communities (city councils, planning commissions, community action groups) have ways of processing scientific data *that are a priori to any given policy initiative and that thus influence local engagement with the science of climate change.* At the same time, climate change models that reliably capture global dynamics can leave great gaps in certainty as to specific local effects. Thus, local discussion, debate, and action on issues involving complex scientific data, multiple variables, and tentative predictions, all characteristics of the climate change issue, involve a high degree of uncertainty. This endemic uncertainty allows for a range of stakeholders to present locally plausible arguments that reflect both their understanding of the science of climate change *as well as their exercise of local cultural authority* based, for example, on their race, class, and gender (Marvin 1990) or their own attitudes and beliefs about the existence and causes of global warming (Krosnick, Holbrook et al. 2006).

Uncertainties surrounding both the science of climate change and who is and is not recognized as a voice in the construction of climate change initiatives and implementation processes portends social conflict. For example, the recent death from heat stroke of a pregnant Latina farm worker[1] (where neither the farmer nor labour contractor had provided sufficient shade or water) has been raised by environmental justice activists in the Central Valley of California as evidence that their communities have a clear and embodied stake in climate change. While the certainty claimed by these advocates may be questionable, what is unquestionable are the ways in which they construct systems of social meaning and forces of social mobilization using the media, scientific data, and their own embodied politics. These bases of meaning and mobilization also signify the ways in which climate change is embedded within broader discourses of equity, of efforts for human

---

1   http://www.npr.org/templates/story/story.php?storyId=91240378.

dignity, and of regional identity and how understanding these dimensions can help policy makers and scientists incorporate the concerns of this key constituency.

How climate change policies and scientific knowledge are reconstituted locally requires examining both the structural and cultural aspects of the civic environments in which policymaking and decisions take place. It also requires an understanding the broader history of how laypeople have constructed scientific knowledge and technological expertise in the United States and the ways that lay construction of scientific knowledge and technological expertise can vary within and across communities. Moreover, it highlights the importance of considering the intersection of race, class, and gender, the actions of environmental justice social movements globally and within communities. To understand how framing and collective identity unfold in local decision-making, research streams should ask:

- What is the structure and culture of community civic life? What are the implications of profiles and dynamics of race, ethnicity, class, and gender? How does this differ by community? What consequences do those differences have on the design of policy and its implementation?
- What knowledge, mobilized by which actors is considered legitimate in climate change policy? How does the science applied make certain bodies more visible, and others less/invisible?
- How are factors of scientific uncertainty identified, contested and applied in the framing and outcomes of these conflicts? How is certainty produced? How does this model of certainty and its production implicate other agendas (e.g. equity, empowerment)?
- How is the 'global' frame itself produced as a social and cultural artifact and applied through the conflict – how is it positioned relative to other frames (e.g. local economic development, local environmental impacts, aesthetics)?
- How do issues of social equity interact with the production of the global frame and also the production of certainty as a scientific and a social fact?

From Style to Substance: Actions and Decisions as Outcomes of Policy

Thus far, we have described the different intersections that we think should focus analyses of the local design and implementation of climate change policies. We now turn to a consideration of how to best characterize the outcomes of the factors and processes we have described. In other words, how should researchers think about the dependent variable in climate change policy studies? Here it is important to distinguish between policy actions taken at the local level (e.g. revision to land use decision-making criteria), which represent policies meant to aid the implementation of broader policies (e.g. SB 375), and the actual decisions that local bodies make in applying new policies to particular cases (e.g. zoning). Both are outcomes. However, the former does not necessarily lead to improvements in the latter.

Despite the best of intentions, the literature suggests that even when there are overarching frameworks in place, there are often vast disparities between the intent of established goals, plans, and policies and the actual implementation of such plans (Pressman and Wildavsky 1979; O'Toole 2004). That is, even when policy and plan are in sync, implementation – by this we mean the actual decisions made regarding conformance with such instruments as zoning ordinances or design guidelines – may in fact be inconsistent (Waldner 2009). Local government with declining or stagnant revenues, even those presumably cooperating (McCarthy 2003), may in practice slip and slide around policies in an effort to maintain competitiveness (Wolman 1996), lending credibility to the phrase '*how* we regulate something is almost as important as *what* we regulate' (Sovacool and Brown 2009: 317).

Thus it is critical to look at both local policy actions and patterns of decisions in concrete cases as outcomes of climate change policies. Both can vary in ways that are informative of the effects (actual or symbolic) of climate change initiatives. For example, although there can be little doubt that local governments have taken up the call to arms on climate change: more than 900 mayors have signed the US Mayors' Climate Protection Agreement, committing their local jurisdiction to GHG emissions reductions below 1990 levels. Some have argued that the grassroots mobilization is substantial, pointing to GHG efforts at the subnational level that alone represent between 43 per cent and 89 per cent of the affected populations (Lutsky and Sperling 2008). Yet arguing that decentralization translates to systematic action on reducing GHG emissions is naïve at best. Even on issues that have been around for a long time, e.g. sustainability, local progress continues to be largely unfocused and unorganized, lending uncertainty as to whether any measureable real progress has been or can be made. In fact, very few cities have actually initiated the long-term planning that would indicate a stronger commitment toward increased sustainability. In contrast, numerous local governments are implementing chunks of what should be part a larger overarching framework, such as green building programs and energy conservation measures, in a piecemeal fashion (Saha and Paterson 2008).

Policy actions alone are not sufficient. They must lead to coherence across local settings and they must reshape decision-making in meaningful ways. Thus, we argue that understanding how local governments will respond to climate change requires that we close the policy implementation loop by increasing our knowledge on how policy transitions in the other intersections (science and policy: levels of governance) connect to actual decision-making outcomes by local city officials and city staff. There are two obvious levels from which to examine decision-making related to zoning and code enforcement. The first level draws on decisions that are made by elected officials and revolve largely around variances to zoning. In many cases, this aspect of decision-making reflects the tensions that surround the potentially large land use changes (e.g. agriculture to residential) that are frequently needed to accommodate development.

There is a well-formed literature exploring the relationships between zoning decisions and land prices and development (e.g. see Thorson 2003). But our opening example of a house retrofit points to the need to examine decisions at the individual project level to ensure that local government structure transitions to a body capable of continued progress toward climate change goals. Rodiek (2009) has argued that the economic, technological and political systems currently employed to make land use decisions must be fundamentally reconfigured. He suggests that many of the environmental issues currently faced by society reflect superficially constructed political accommodations that do not allow science to be properly weighted.

On the second level of decision-making, local government staff routinely makes decisions that can have significant impacts on the ability of cities to reduce or mitigate their GHG emissions. Variations in how policies are actualized by local government staff can be characterized by the general philosophy toward enforcement and the types of strategies that are practiced and the way in which resources are allocated between them (e.g. technical assistance versus incentives versus deterrents) (May and Burby 1998). The operational features embedded in the city staff or organizational structure can limit innovation and different departmental aims can lead to inconsistent outcomes (Burch 2009). Precedence is also extremely important to most cities, which leads to path-dependent decision-making and the strict adherence to guidelines in seemingly routine cases.

With climate change, individual inconsistencies between stated goals, plans, and policies and the actual project approval and building code enforcement process, which represent the city staff translation of policy, can actually lead to approvals that diminish a community's ability to reduce or mitigate its GHG emissions. New understanding and research is needed in:

- How do local governments structure their actual project approval processes and how rapidly and in what ways these organizational structures and processes change when new policies are adopted;
- What kinds of policy actions produce discernible impacts on land-use decision-making and in what circumstances are those actions undermined by the intersections described above?
- Through the years, cities have enacted numerous ordinances and area specific design guidelines – how do these converge or diverge in terms of the project approval process? Do certain aspects of design take precedence over others? Who determines these priorities and how are they reflected in staff reports and staff assessments?

Concluding Comments

Reconstructing the urban landscape to reduce environmental impacts presents a significant challenge to society and cuts across social and cultural divisions (Sze 2006; Beamish and Luebbers 2009) as well as the structures of governance (Scruggs 2003). Perhaps the most critical issue, and one of the least understood, is how mitigation and adaptation decisions will be made at the local level, and with what consequence. With state and local level policy and regulatory developments, land use and local government action are at heart of how GHGs reductions are to be achieved. Without a better understanding of the decision-making process and how global, national, and state policy initiatives translate into locally implemented reforms, our ability to predict outcomes, such as reductions in future GHGs, is severely limited.

We have argued that the subnational initiatives, like California's AB 32 and SB 375, provide an unrivaled opportunity to significantly improve our understanding of how uncertainty is identified and managed in local governance and community responses to legislatively directed changes. Without question, decision-makers require new information and alternative ways of thinking about managing resources when faced with climate change (Committee on Human Dimensions of Global Change 2009), but to be effective, a much greater understanding of the needs of these institutions and the deliberative processes that inform community decisions must be developed.

We have argued that uncertainty is inherently embedded in the communication and interaction between science and the policy process, between levels of government, and between local implementers and their communities. Policy-makers, businesses, and scientists rely on metrics, conceptualizations, constructs and schemes to translate the performance or condition of complex and sometimes obscure systems into comprehensible values. As these translations begin to take hold in the policy development arena, uncertainty increases related to the communication itself, the forms of metrics, and the way these metrics translate into policy measures. In short, community-based certainties (e.g. historic design is better than modern design) interact with science and policy uncertainties to produce outcomes that can derail progress toward reducing GHG emissions.

As the policy process moves into the governance domain policy advocates begin to strategize on policies that will, in theory, both achieve a desired outcome and be compatible with local preferences. In the abstract, policies tend to be constructed with the assumptions that their costs and benefits will be uniformly distributed and experienced across locations and populations, and that local decision-makers are assumed to make rational decisions regarding the costs to benefits and proceed to implement based on the positive utility associated with compliance. However, as we've shown, research in sociology, sociolegal studies, public administration, and public policy tells us that the policy implementation process is seldom if ever this simple or reflective of comprehensively rational decision makers. Variability in implementation, and thus outcomes is the rule rather than the exception (e.g. see Diver 1980; Hawkins 1984; Hutter 1989). This is especially true for laws and policies that lack enforcement authority and instead rely on voluntary compliance (Burby and Paterson 1993; Deyle and Smith 1998). Most laws and policies contain some degree of ambiguity and many knowingly include slack to permit local decision-makers discretion in implementation (Edelman, Uggen et al. 1999; Grattet and Jenness 2005). Acknowledging that ambiguity, discretion, and variability in implementation and outcomes is insufficient for understanding the form and content of implemented and enforced policy, nor does it sufficiently explain how closely implementation of the policies conform to the spirit and intentions of the original policy mandate.

With the changing relationships characteristic of contemporary society, new forms of grassroots politics have also emerged. And, in fact, current trends in state funding as well as the way in which resources are being allocated will push communities to develop new approaches to collective decision-making that are more collaborative and less formal-institutional in nature. What is more, in response to top-down policy directives – even those that appear from above as 'public goods' – grassroots groups may organize around shared interests that frequently result in new grievances and identity formations. In the process of organizing, grassroots groups also acquire technical expertise, either through organizational building or networking with outside groups. The move away from government control and predictable paths of problem definition, negotiation, and implementation opens up divergent interpretations of social problems and the competition between different frames of understanding (Mauss 1975; Hilgartner and Bosk 1988).

Since citizen participation – whether in an official capacity or as protestors of a given policy – is the primary means by which communities influence implementation decisions, it is imperative that we understand how communities understand both specific initiatives, such as AB 32 and SB 375, as well as the policy implementation processes itself. This imperative gains further weight when the manner by which citizen forums are generally conceived by knowledgeable policymakers: as neutral frameworks for decision-making even though they privilege formal professional policy discourses over local values and preferences (Sandercock 2000). Because of its assumptions and preferences, the current community participatory model has largely overlooked or ignored the broader cultural, social, and political dynamics within which all policy implementation efforts are embedded. Obviously, this model greatly limits community involvement in policy initiatives and furthermore hazards undermining the legitimacy of the supposed public good policy mandates as well.

As evidenced by the increasing numbers of local GHG inventories being developed, climate change policies such as AB 32 and SB 375 reflect scientific consensus and are fast becoming a fact of social, economic, and government life. This makes it critical that we understand how the science of climate change is interpreted and translated into policy vis-à-vis locally embedded social and political systems that reflect years of accumulated knowledge, assumptions, and unique preferences, which in turn strongly influence the form and content of local climate change actions (Beamish 2002). In addition, the urgency of a coordinated and comprehensive reaction to climate change trends amplifies not only the unpredictability of this process but also our need to understand whether or not our current efforts at climate change mitigation will indeed result in significant reductions where they count – on the ground where they are generated. The kinds of policies that will be needed to adequately respond to climate change will likely require substantial changes in the way in which we live our lives, and thus represent a significant threat to what many might refer to as their quality of life. In light of all of this, there is a critical and urgent need to better understand the interaction between science, the policy process, and public interests and how these relationships influence the creation, implementation, and enforcement of policies that target climate changes.

Chapter 8

Public Acceptance of Hydrogen Technologies in Transport: A Review of and Reflection on Empirical Studies

Nicole Huijts, Eric Molin, Caspar Chorus and Bert van Wee

Introduction

It is increasingly acknowledged that the rapidly growing energy demand, urgent environmental problems and depletion of fossil fuels demand immediate and global action (International Energy Agency 2007). Examining the field of transport, one of the major sources of energy and environmental problems worldwide, both researchers and policy makers have often suggested replacing fossil fuels with other, more sustainable energy carriers, such as hydrogen, bio fuels or electricity stored in batteries. Of these alternative carriers, hydrogen is increasingly recognized as a potential future energy carrier leading to a sustainable future energy system (e.g. Banister 2000; European Commission 2006).

More specifically, hydrogen-powered fuel cell vehicles are expected to offer potential solutions to a number of problems related to transport and/or energy use, such as noise, air pollution, global warming and the security of energy supply (Banister 2000; European Commission 2006; Ball and Wietschel 2009). Traffic noise is likely to decrease if fuel cells instead of internal combustion engines are used for propulsion. Also the level of emissions, which is known to influence global climate change and local air quality, can be reduced by using hydrogen as a fuel in transport.[1] Finally, reducing fossil fuel use potentially increases the security of supply by reducing our dependency on finite stocks of fossil fuels and avoiding geopolitical struggles resulting from this dependency.

However, before hydrogen can be successfully implemented as an energy carrier in transport, a great number of barriers need to be tackled, such as the lack of refuelling infrastructure, the high costs of fuel cells and of low-carbon hydrogen production, technology immaturity, safety issues and public resistance (McDowell and Eames 2006). The first barrier, a lack of refuelling infrastructure,

---

1   Note that the actual emission reductions strongly depend on the source of energy that is used for the production of hydrogen (e.g. Ball and Wietschel 2009).

is likely to prove a difficult one to overcome. The installation of hydrogen refuelling stations requires a great deal of investment and will only be worthwhile if hydrogen is used by many vehicles. Car drivers, however, will not find hydrogen vehicles attractive if there is no ready access to fuel (e.g. Struben and Sterman 2008). This chicken-and-egg problem could be overcome if government policy support stimulates both the installation of fuel stations and the use of hydrogen cars up to a certain 'critical mass'. Struben and Sterman (2008) also argue that the same chicken-and-egg problem applies to the availability of spare parts and the repair services associated with hydrogen fuels. Costs and safety issues may be diminished by technological research (Edwards et al. 2008), which is increasingly taking place in scientific institutes as well as in industry. The European Commission (2006) also indicates that hydrogen-related safety issues are expected to be tackled by setting regulations, codes and standards. However, all these investments in terms of time, effort and money from the side of industry and the government are deemed to have only a very limited effect if the public disagrees with the use of hydrogen as an energy carrier in transport. Reasons for diverging public opinions might include a greater perceived safety risk (as suggested by e.g. Bain and Van Vorst 1999) or because of a general preference for vehicles other than those fuelled by hydrogen. Therefore, while enormous investments need to be made in research, development and implementation, it is of critical importance to gain knowledge about hydrogen acceptance among the general public, both in the role of citizens and consumers. Reacting to this need, a number of empirical studies into the public acceptance of hydrogen technology in transport have been published in recent years.

The goal of this chapter is to critically review this body of research into the public acceptance of hydrogen as an energy carrier in transport.[2] In line with the approach adopted in most of the available studies, we focus on quantitative studies. The contribution of this chapter to the literature is threefold. First, after having presented our selection of empirical studies, we review and reflect on terminologies that have been applied in these empirical studies. Specifically, we argue and illustrate that the current use of terminology is inconsistent across studies and provide definitions of and distinctions between terms based on wider research on technology acceptance. Second, we review the theoretical frameworks adopted in the studies and argue that what is often lacking is a clear theoretical foundation underlying performed measurements and explanations of obtained results. Several theories from the field of social psychology are presented, showing fruitful avenues for improving hydrogen acceptance research.

---

2   During this chapter's review process, another review of empirical findings, which includes identifying gaps in research, has been provided by Ricci et al. (2008). Compared to that study, we focus more heavily on quantitative studies and discuss more elaborately the terminology and theoretical approaches adopted in the reviewed studies.

Third, we highlight the main empirical findings presented in these studies, showing that hydrogen buses have received positive acceptance so far, and showing that several variables have been found to influence acceptance. We suggest that more research is needed to better understand the role of the several variables. The last section presents conclusions and recommendations for further research.

Selection of Empirical Studies

Empirical hydrogen acceptance papers were collected from scientific journals up to May 2008. An additional search using the snowball method provided extra papers. In total, 11 journal papers and one conference paper were found. Table 8.1 shows information on the retrieved publications, including the specification of the type of hydrogen application for which the studies measured acceptance.

As Table 8.1 shows, most of the studies concern transport applications; only two studies measure acceptance of other types of applications as well (Molin 2005; Zachariah-Wolff and Hemmes 2006). We will not discuss the empirical findings on these other applications.

Eight studies deal with acceptance of hydrogen buses. Six of these studies were connected to a hydrogen bus project that was actually implemented, five of which concerned fuel cell buses and one concerned a bus with an internal combustion engine (ICE). The study on the ICE hydrogen bus (Hickson et al. 2007) also stands out in terms of being the only study that was entirely outside Europe; the hydrogen bus study of O'Garra et al. (2007) also provided data from Perth in Australia, as well as three European cities. Two of these studies and the four other studies measured acceptance of other applications than buses, including hydrogen cars (Molin et al. 2007; Molin 2005), hydrogen taxis (Mourato et al. 2004; Zachariah-Wolff and Hemmes 2006), hydrogen vehicles in general (O'Garra et al. 2005) and hydrogen refuelling stations (O'Garra et al. 2008).

Table 8.1   Overview of the 12 selected studies regarding public acceptance of hydrogen technologies

Paper (authors + year)	Hydrogen application	Location and year of data	Nr. of respondents	Kind of respondents
Haraldsson et al. (2006)	Fuel cell public transport bus on hydrogen	Stockholm, 2004	518	Bus passengers before operation of fuel cell bus
Heinz and Erdmann (2008)	Fuel cell public transport bus on hydrogen	Amsterdam, Barcelona, Berlin, Hamburg, London, Luxembourg, Madrid and Reykjavik, 2006	2,833 (reasonably divided over the eight cities)	Hydrogen and other bus passengers and people in public places
Hickson et al. (2006)	Hydrogen bus with internal combustion engine (ICE)	Winnipeg, 2005	369	ICE hydrogen bus passengers
Molin (2005)	Hydrogen investments in general, hydrogen buses, hydrogen cars, hydrogen mobile phones and hydrogen for home cooking	Netherlands, 2003	612 (of which 205 were not given any information, while 407 got positive, neutral or negative information)	Citizens
Molin et al. (2007)	Vehicles driving on biodiesel or hydrogen or hybrid vehicles	Amsterdam, 2006	75	Car drivers at two fuel stations
Mourato et al. (2004)	Hydrogen taxis	London, 2001	12 (in two focus groups) and 99 (in 6 different taxi stands)	Taxi drivers
O'Garra et al. (2007)	Fuel cell public transport bus on hydrogen	Berlin, London, Luxemburg, Perth, 2003–2004	1,090 bus users and 360 non bus users	Bus users and city residents
O'Garra et al. (2005)	Hydrogen vehicles	London, 2003	414	London residents

Table 8.1 Continued

O'Garra and Mourato (2007)	Hydrogen buses	London, 2003	531	London residents
O'Garra et al. (2008)	Hydrogen storage and refuelling facilities at existing vehicle refuelling stations	London, 2003	346	Households near existing commercial refuelling stations
Saxe et al. (2007)	Fuel cell public transport bus on hydrogen	Luxemburg, Hamburg, London and Stockholm, 2004 and 2005	508 and 507 fuel cell bus passengers and 200 fuel cell bus drivers	Bus passengers before and after one year of operation of fuel cell bus
Zachariah-Wolff and Hemmes (2006)	Hydrogen buses, natural gas blend with hydrogen, micro-combined heat and power at home, hydrogen fuelled taxis	Netherlands, 2003	This paper uses the same data as Molin (2005)	Citizens

Review of and Reflection on the Use of Terminology

Looking at the papers, it shows that the terms *acceptance, perception, attitudes* and *preferences*, as well as *knowledge, awareness, familiarity* and *need for information* were often used. In this section, we will look at definitions or, when absent, at the implicit use of the words to gain a better understanding of how the terms are used in the papers. Then we will look at the wider available literature to find suggestions for improvement. We grouped together the first four terms, all representative of the wider understanding of acceptance, and the last four items, all related to knowledge which could influence acceptance.

Acceptance, Attitudes and Perception

Terminology in the selected papers   The use of acceptance and seemingly related words in the selected papers are presented in Table 8.2. These words were gathered from the title, abstract and body of each paper.

Two findings stand out from reviewing the papers. First, explicit definitions are very rarely given, and none of the papers provides a definition for acceptance. Two papers (Molin 2005; Zachariah-Wolff and Hemmes 2006) provided definitions for the words attitude, perception and willingness to use. The other papers only implicitly provided interpretations of the terms, by the measurements taken. Second, Table 8.2 shows that a myriad of terms and measurements were chosen and often even seemed to be used interchangeably. Acceptance or acceptability, for example, was measured by asking for opinions, attitudes, beliefs and willingness to use, and sometimes even by asking for preferences, WTP and willingness to use. In addition, the terms support and opposition were used. The objects of acceptance measurements concerned actual hydrogen projects or suggested future applications of hydrogen; some papers combined both measurements. *Attitudes* were measured in many different ways, asking for people's opinions on a wide array of topics and with many different answering scales, such as opinions towards the transition to a hydrogen economy (the scale went from bad to good), trust in safety regulation (from disagree to agree), need for information (from no to yes) and support (choice options were support, opposition, indifferent or need more information). The term *perception* was often used interchanged with associations, beliefs and attitudes. Furthermore, it was used for opinions with respect to the use of hydrogen in general and the respondent's own use of hydrogen or for opinions with respect to aspects directly related to the use of the technology, such as the safety of hydrogen vehicles and aspects indirectly related to the use of the technology, such as emission reduction.

The inconsistency of the usage of terms between papers, as well as the fact that the meaning of terms is often not made explicit in the papers, hampers the understanding of the wider value of the studies for interested readers.

Avenues for improvement – terminology in wider literature   Several studies, in the field of psychology in general or research into acceptance of other technologies, have yielded insights that can provide useful starting points for improving the understanding of the reviewed terms. Based on these studies, we will suggest clarifications for the terms acceptance, acceptability, attitudes and perception.

While the term acceptance was used most often, the term acceptability was also used in one paper. From comparing the several papers it is not clear what the difference is between these two terms. Schade and Schlag (2003) discussed the distinction between the words acceptance and acceptability in the context of urban transport pricing strategies, noticing that these two words were often used with several meanings and without clear definitions. The authors made a distinction between the two terms by saying that acceptance refers to attitudes after the introduction of the technology or measure, while acceptability is the prospective judgment to introduction in the future. These definitions do not include behaviour, or do not distinguish attitudes from behaviour. We propose, therefore, using the term acceptance for actual behaviour in reaction to the technology, and acceptability for attitudes towards the technology and towards possible related behaviours. This is more in line with Wolfse et al. (2002), who describe a framework for the acceptability of controversial technologies. They suggest that acceptability considers people's willingness to consider the technology seriously and acceptance refers to the formal decision to implement the proposal.

Furthermore, papers usually use one term for acceptance, ignoring the heterogeneity that the term acceptance can encompass. Wüstenhagen et al. (2007), for example, described three different kinds of acceptance in the context of sustainable energy technologies: socio-political acceptance, community acceptance and market acceptance. Socio-political acceptance concerned acceptance at the broadest, most general level, including acceptance of both policies and technologies; it concerned acceptance by citizens, stakeholders and policy makers. Community acceptance was defined as local stakeholders' acceptance of locating renewable energy projects. Market acceptance concerned the adoption of the innovations. For *public* acceptance, which is our concern here, we suggest that three similar types should be distinguished:

1. socio-political acceptance, which can be defined as political and social behaviour by the public in reaction to national or even international (e.g. in the European Union) policy making;
2. citizen acceptance, which can be defined as responses to situations where the public is faced with the use of technology in one's living areas as a result of others; and
3. consumer acceptance, which can be defined as the public's reactions to the availability of innovations on the market (in other words, the purchase and use of products).

Table 8.2   Terms and measurements in papers on acceptance, perception, attitudes and preferences or indications of those

Paper (authors + year)	Terms used in the papers	Definitions or, if absent, measurements taken
Haraldsson et al. (2006)	Attitudes, acceptance	WTP (willingness to pay) extra for a bus ticket when fuel cell buses are used instead of conventional buses (yes/no)
Heinz and Erdmann (2008)	Public acceptance, public attitudes	Preference for hydrogen or conventional buses: support, opposition or indifference with respect to substitution of conventional buses by hydrogen buses
Hickson et al. (2006)	Public perceptions, consumer perceptions, acceptability	Perceptions related to hydrogen as a fuel (good or bad idea)
Molin (2005); Zachariah-Wolff and Hemmes (2006)	Acceptance, willingness to use, perception, attitude	Attitude, defined as an evaluative component denoting whether a transition towards a hydrogen economy is good or bad; perception, defined as what is thought about or associated with hydrogen; willingness to use, defined as the extent to which one is willing to use several hydrogen applications; perceptions of and associations with hydrogen
Molin et al. (2007)	Preferences	Preference for a car based on the following attributes: fuel type, CO_2 reduction, change in fuel price, change in purchase costs, detour for a refuelling station, range and motor performance
Mourato et al. (2004)	Preferences, support	Taxi drivers' WTP for participation in a pilot project with hydrogen fuelled taxis; support for the introduction of greener fuels and technologies in the taxi fleet
O'Garra and Mourato (2007)	Preferences, WTP	WTP for hydrogen fuelled buses

Table 8.2   Continued

O'Garra et al. (2007)	Preferences, WTP, acceptability, attitudes with respect to support and oppositions	WTP extra per bus fare for hydrogen buses; WTP extra tax for large-scale introduction of hydrogen buses; attitudes about whether bus demonstration projects were a good idea
O'Garra et al. (2005)	Awareness and acceptability, perceptions, associations, support, opposition and beliefs	Support for or opposition to the introduction of hydrogen powered vehicles in London; beliefs about technical solutions to environmental problems; the first word that people think of when they hear the word hydrogen (perception)
O'Garra et al. (2008)	Support, opposition, attitudes, acceptance, acceptability	Attitudes towards hydrogen vehicles and the installation of local storage facilities at existing refuelling stations near to people's homes; social costs associated with a new facility, calculated from adding up the time that each chosen 'protest' activity would take
Saxe et al. (2007)	Acceptance, WTP, attitude/ opinion	WTP extra for a bus ticket when fuel cell buses are used instead of conventional buses (yes/no); change in attitude/opinion of passengers and bus drivers during the project (feeling more positive or more negative during the project); change in attitude/opinion of bus operators concerning whether the technicians can keep the bus running without assistance

To illustrate the proposed terminology for city buses, the public can have attitudes (acceptability) and behaviour (acceptance) in reaction to (1) the implementation of extra national taxes to realize hydrogen city buses (2) the realization of these buses and refuelling stations near their dwellings, and (3) the availability of hydrogen buses, giving the public the option of being a passenger in these new buses. It is expected that people have different attitudes and behaviours for these different hydrogen-technology related events. For example, it was found that people have a different opinion about underground carbon storage when they were asked about it in general versus when it concerns usage of this technology within their own living environment (Midden and Huijts 2009).

The word attitude is regularly used in the papers, referring to many different measurements. We would like to suggest definitions from the field of psychology. Eagly and Chaiken (1996) defined attitude as 'a psychological tendency that is expressed by evaluating a particular entity with some degree of favour or disfavour'. Also Ajzen (2001) stressed the evaluative component of attitudes, stating that this evaluation is measured on scales like 'good-bad, harmful-beneficial, pleasant-unpleasant'. Additionally, Crano en Prisline (2006) suggest that attitudes represent evaluative integrations of cognitions and affects experienced in relation to an object. So we suggest to use the word attitude for evaluative judgments. For attitudes in the context of hydrogen acceptability and acceptance, Molin (2005) and Zachariah-Wolff and Hemmes (2006) defined attitude as an 'evaluative component denoting whether a transition towards a hydrogen economy is good or bad'. Attitudes may, however, also concern evaluations towards other aspects, such as characteristics of the technology and specific reasons to implement the technology (e.g. climate change). In economics the term preferences is often used. Attitude is different from preferences in the sense that attitudes measure peoples' evaluation of something, without explicitly referring to a certain set of alternatives. Preferences are always dependent on the alternatives from which people have to choose.

Another term that has come up several times is perception. The interpretation of this word in the reviewed papers concerns a broader use than is common in the field of psychology. Psychologists usually use a definition that is directly related to sensation: perception involves the interpretation of sensations, giving them meaning and organization; sensation refers to the immediate and basic experiences generated as stimuli fall on our sensory systems (Matlin and Foley 1997). This definition from the field of psychology is more 'a quick immediate and intuitive cognition' (Merriam-Webster Incorporated 1997), while hydrogen acceptance studies seem to use a wider definition such as 'a mental image' (Merriam-Webster Incorporated 1997). Terms used in psychology for this are attitudes (see above) and beliefs. A belief can be defined as a 'conviction of the truth of some statement or the reality of some being or phenomenon especially when based on examination of evidence' (Merriam-Webster Incorporated 1997). Ajzen (2001) connects beliefs and attitudes by saying that 'beliefs that are readily accessible in memory influence attitude at any given moment'.

Table 8.3   Measurements of knowledge, awareness and familiarity per paper

Paper (authors + year)	Terms used in the papers	Knowledge-related items in papers
Haraldsson et al. (2006) Saxe et al. (2007)	Knowledge/ familiarity, need for information, awareness	Familiarity with the fact that there is a fuel cell project; wanting to have more information concerning hydrogen and fuel cells
Heinz and Erdmann (2008)	Need for information	Attitudes towards substitution of conventional buses by hydrogen buses: support, opposition, indifferent, need for more information
Hickson et al. (2006)	–	–
Molin (2005); Zachariah-Wolff and Hemmes (2006)	Hydrogen knowledge	Being able to answer nine questions correctly, about the properties of hydrogen, the applications of hydrogen in vehicles, and about the emissions of hydrogen fuelled vehicles (true of false)
Molin et al. (2007)	–	–
Mourato et al. (2004)	Having heard of, familiarity	Having heard about fuel cells; familiarity with information provided about fuel cells
O'Garra and Mourato (2007)	Awareness (self-reported)	Self-reported awareness about hydrogen vehicles: having heard about hydrogen vehicles
O'Garra et al. (2007)	Knowledge/self-reported awareness	Having heard that car companies were developing hydrogen vehicles
O'Garra et al. (2005)	Knowledge, awareness	Environmental knowledge: three test questions on the relation between the hole in the ozone layer and climate change, car use as a source of pollution and greenhouse gas emissions from transport as a source of global warming; self-reported prior awareness: having heard of hydrogen vehicles and fuel cell vehicles
O'Garra et al. (2008)	Knowledge (self-reported); need for information	Self-reported knowledge on hydrogen vehicles: having no knowledge, weak knowledge or fair to strong knowledge; attitudes towards the introduction of hydrogen vehicles in London: oppose, support, indifferent or need for information

We suggest making the meaning of terms more explicit in studies and taking the proposed definitions in mind when studying the public acceptance of hydrogen technologies.

Knowledge, Awareness, Familiarity and Need for Information

Terminology in the selected papers   Table 8.3 gives an overview of knowledge-related terms in the selected papers.

Several papers mentioned and measured knowledge or related items. The terms that were used included awareness, familiarity, having heard of something and need for information. Clear definitions, distinguishing the knowledge-related measurements from each other, were not given in any of the papers.

Knowledge was tested in many different ways. First, knowledge was tested by checking the ability to answer test questions correctly. These tests comprised several items that combined knowledge about environmental problems, the physical properties of hydrogen and the consequences of different fuels. Second, some studies asked for self-reported knowledge, asking people to indicate how much they knew about hydrogen, fuel cells or other related issues. Third, the terms awareness and familiarity were used and seemed to measure being knowledgeable about events or information. Fourth, several studies investigated the need for more information. We can conclude that also for knowledge-related items, a myriad of words and conceptualizations were used. The meaning of the terms and the wider implications of the findings were often not elaborated on.

A reflection on the terminology   We will now reflect on this diverse use of the terminology and suggest some definitions for terms and distinctions between meanings of terms by using dictionary information and findings from knowledge-related studies in other research fields. First, the difference between the knowledge indicated by the participants themselves and the knowledge measured by tests needs to be understood. It is unlikely that these two items have perfect correlations, and it is even uncertain whether they have reasonable correlations, since people may not be very good at judging their own knowledge as compared to other people's knowledge and may have a different perception of what knowledge is than the researcher. This may be illustrated by a meta-study in the field of genetically modified food acceptance, which compared the two ways of measuring knowledge in American and European studies (House et al. 2004). Self-rated knowledge was called subjective knowledge and knowledge calculated from the percentage of correctly answered test questions was called objective knowledge. The study showed that the two knowledge measurements did not measure the same construct in the gathered studies; the average correlation between the two items amounted to only 0.36 ($p < 0.01$, $n = 309$). The study also showed that the two knowledge measurements correlated to different variables; while both objective and subjective knowledge correlated with education, subjective knowledge was also correlated with religion, location of the respondents and willingness to eat

GM food products. Based on these findings, we suggest making a distinction between objective knowledge and subjective knowledge when trying to explain the role of knowledge in the formation of hydrogen acceptance.

Second, awareness was examined by posing the question whether people had heard of hydrogen and fuel cells or whether they were aware of certain developments or projects. Familiarity, on the other hand, was elicited by asking for familiarity with certain information. It seems that these measurements are quite related. The dictionary definition of awareness (Merriam-Webster Incorporated 1997) that is closest to the way the awareness is used here is 'having or showing realization, perception or knowledge'. This definition includes the term knowledge and therefor gives an overlap with the factor knowledge. It is suggested to use the term awareness only in the context of having realization of the existence of an object (like 'having heard of it') and to use the term knowledge when people know specific facts. For familiarity the definition is 'close acquaintance with something' (Merriam-Webster Incorporated 1997). While awareness seems closer to mental processes or mental constructs, familiarity seems closer to experiences. The term familiarity can be used as a realization of the technology based on personal experience with hydrogen technology, such as having already used a hydrogen vehicle, or other more extensive involvement with it, like having read a lot about the subject.

Third, several of the selected hydrogen papers reported the need for more information. Need for information was measured on two different scales. One scale was an agree–disagree scale, thereby determining the amount of information need in general. The other scale asked people either to give an outspoken opinion by choosing support or opposition, or not to give an outspoken opinion, by choosing need for information or indifference. This way of measuring need for information will indicate whether people feel knowledgeable enough to support or oppose the use of hydrogen technologies. The two ways of eliciting need for information are different by nature and can elicit different responses from people. They cannot therefore be directly compared. We suggest that a general interest in information, and the specific need for information in order to give an answer to evaluative answers to questions should be distinguished in order to be able to answer certain acceptance questions.

Based on these deliberations, we suggest that the following six knowledge-related factors need to be distinguished:

1. objective knowledge;
2. subjective knowledge;
3. awareness of the technology, or related aspects, in the sense of having realization ('having heard of it');

4. familiarity with the technology, in the sense of having had personal experience of it;
5. interest in more information; and
6. need for more information in order to be able to answer acceptance questions.

Review of and Reflection on the Use of Theories

Looking at the selected papers, we noticed that often a strong theoretical framework was lacking; important theories and theoretical notions were often not explained. Most authors did refer to findings in previous hydrogen and/or acceptance studies. Molin's (2005: 115) study was the only paper that described a causal model which was 'loosely based on attitudinal theories that can be found in psychology literature'. Acknowledging the theoretical knowledge base per se does not increase the value of a paper; however, applying these theories to improve the distinctions between the concepts, as well as putting the results in a larger context and explaining the value of the outcomes, will increase the value of the research.

Although the studies did not describe relevant theories, they did seem to make several implicit assumptions. This was most clear for three different topics that are related to well-known theories in the field of psychology:

1. the relationship between attitudes, intention and behaviours;
2. the influence of psychological constructs such as associations and trust on acceptance; and
3. the role of knowledge, awareness and familiarity.

In this section, we will describe the implicit assumptions more elaborately and we will reflect on theories that can improve the understanding of the available results and the quality of future studies. Due to the limited use of theories in the selected papers, we will mainly elaborate on the reflective part.

The Relationship between Attitudes, Intentions and Behaviours

In general, when talking about acceptance, it is often hoped that not only the attitude but especially the behaviour of people is positive towards the technology. For example, it is hoped that people will use the hydrogen bus once it is implemented and that people do not protest against a hydrogen refuelling station that has been planned by policy makers. In order to indicate current behaviour or predict future behaviour, attitudes are often measured, even though the connection between attitudes and behaviour is usually not explicitly discussed. The same counts for the relation between intentions and behaviour. Several of the selected papers on hydrogen acceptance measured attitudes and intentions to behave, as can be seen in Table 8.2, but of these studies, only Molin's (2005) paper explicitly postulated that attitudes influence intentions to use, and intentions to use influence behaviour. However, a specific theory on this topic is not explicitly used to choose and support the measurements. We will describe the dominant model for predicting planned behaviour in the field of psychology and other theories that complement or criticize this theory, in order to present current insights into the value and role of attitudes with respect to behaviour.

First, the widely applied theory of planned behaviour (Ajzen 1991) says that attitudes towards behaviour influences the intention to behave, which in turn influences the actual behaviour. This shows that attitudes influence behaviour indirectly rather than directly, via the intention to behave. Second, the theory postulates that also subjective norm and perceived behavioural control influence intention to behave. This means that attitudes are not the only predictors for intention to behave. Third, moods and habits can also influence behaviour (see e.g. Ajzen 2001), showing that also other variables can have additional explanatory power for behaviour. While the theory of planned behaviour is a model that predicts planned behaviour, i.e. following from thoughtful decision making (Crano and Prislin 2006), it is increasingly being recognized that people often show automatic behaviour, habitual behaviour, or behaviour influenced directly by feelings. Adding these variables to the model could increase the predictive value of an acceptance model.[3] Fourth, the predictive value of the applied model is also strongly influenced by the way variables are measured (Armitage and Connor 2001). For example, attitudes have to be consistently measured with the specific behaviour. Fifth, the attitude needs to be strong (stable and resistant to change) in order to have a relatively high predictive value of later behaviour (Ajzen 2001); it needs to be recognized that often hypothetical cases are studied and people's attitudes and intentions will not be the same in reality (Crano and Prislin 2006).

We will illustrate a few of these insights in the case of hydrogen vehicles. People's car behaviour can be predicted by asking a number of people about their intentions to buy a car and by asking about their attitudes towards the car. This can be done in a very specific way by asking people about their intention to buy a specific car within a specific timeframe in a specific location, which can be predicted by their attitude towards buying the specific car in the specific time frame and the specific location. The actual buying behaviour could, however, also be influenced by the idea that the vehicle is not available at short notice because of rumours that the time between ordering and receiving the vehicle is too long (perceived behavioural control is low). In addition, the intention to buy the car will also depend on the image of the vehicle that prevails among colleagues, neighbours and friends (this is related to social norm) and on the past behaviour of buying cars since, for example, people who are used to visiting a Ford garage are not likely to switch to Toyota (habit). And if people expressed their attitude when

3   A meta-study (Armitage and Connor 2001) has shown that the theory of planned behaviour on average predicted 39 per cent of the variance in intention and 27 per cent of the variance in behaviour in 185 studies up to the year 1997.

it was not a very strong attitude, the attitude is likely to have changed by the time they actually buy a new car.

Recognizing the value of measuring attitudes is important for studying hydrogen acceptance. We suggest that future studies are improved by, first, using extra predictive variables, especially for the case that behaviour is not planned, second, to attend the specificity and strength of measured attitudes and intentions, and, third, to measure actual behaviour or try to simulate real life events so that the predictive value increases.

The Role of Associations, Trust and Affect

Several papers measured variables such as associations and one paper measured trust. The presence of many positive associations and the limited presence of negative associations were sometimes seen as a sign of acceptance. Trust was found to be related to acceptance. Related theory on these factors was not discussed in the reviewed papers. Both trust and associations seemed to concern intuitive notions, especially in the case of affective trust or distrust reactions and instant, free associations. In the field of psychology, a growing body of research discusses the role of intuitive processes for attitude formation and for behaviour, including trust, associations and affect. We will discuss these here.

Dual-processing theories (e.g. Smith and DeCoster 2000) postulate that there are two pathways in thinking that lead to behaviour. One pathway is the rational or analytic one, where reasoning leads to attitudes towards an object and to behaviour, while the other pathway is more intuitive and based on heuristics, leading to automatic or spontaneous behaviour. Heuristics can be considered short-cuts in thinking, where instead of spending the time and energy that rational thinking takes, people use faster and more efficient routes in their mind, basing their decisions and behaviours on previous experiences, feelings or other easily retrievable mental objects related to the situation or object. In general, it is assumed that both pathways are used together to come to attitudes and behaviours. Using associations to form your opinion or basing your reaction on trust and affect rather than a deliberate processing of size and likeliness of the effects, can be considered examples of heuristics or short-cuts in thinking that influence attitude formation.

Several studies investigated the role of associations, trust and affect for acceptance of technologies. Visschers et al. (2007), for example, showed that semantic associations with other risks are found to influence the perception of a new risk. Trust is shown to influence the perception of both the risks and benefits of technologies (e.g Siegrist 1999; Siegrist and Cvetkovich 2000, studying acceptance of biotechnology), leading to an inverse relationship between the perceived risks and benefits. The same effect was also found for the variable affect, influencing the acceptance of nuclear power (Peters and Slovic 1996). It has been found for trust that this factor plays a particularly important role in attitude formation for relatively new and unknown technologies (Siegrist and Cvetkovich 2000; Midden and Huijts 2009), when little information is available to deliberate upon. More intuitive factors, such as affect and associations are more likely to influence attitude formation and behaviour where relatively unknown technologies are concerned and we therefore suggest including these factors as determinants for acceptance in hydrogen acceptance studies.

The Role of Knowledge-related Items

Knowledge-related variables were treated in the papers, sometimes as a finding by itself, sometimes as a predictor for an acceptance measurement. Several authors found that higher scores on the knowledge measurements led to higher acceptance measurements. That can easily lead to the idea that more knowledge automatically leads to higher acceptance and that knowledge can be increased by providing information. For example, O'Garra et al. (2005) suggested that 'there is a strong need to raise awareness [knowledge] among the London public specifically about hydrogen and fuel cells, as this seems to be key to public acceptance of H2-based technologies'. We acknowledge that knowledge can play an important role in acceptance, although the influence of knowledge on acceptance is not as straightforward as is sometimes thought. The positive relationship between knowledge and acceptance could also be caused by the fact that the people who already had an interest in hydrogen informed themselves more thoroughly, or had a technical education and therefore have more knowledge and also a more positive attitude towards technology in general. We can therefore not assume that increasing knowledge automatically increases acceptance. In other fields of technology acceptance, for example windmill acceptance, the findings did not indicate that people with a low acceptance have less knowledge: on the contrary, 'objectors actually appeared to be extremely well informed' (Ellis et al. 2007: 520). More research into the effect of knowledge in an experimental setting is suggested to gain a clearer view of the relationship between knowledge and acceptance. To increase understanding, we will first discuss some theory on the effect of knowledge.

Two mechanisms could block the positive effect of information on acceptance. The first mechanism is that people do not use information to change their opinion in a positive direction. Instead they may judge information based on whether it corroborates their opinion and consequently either strengthen the opinion they already have, or, if the information does not agree with their opinion, disregard it (Marsh and Wallace 2005). People may also discard or even oppose information provided because they distrust the providers of the information (e.g. Cvetkovich et al. 2002). The second reason for the possible limited positive effect of information on acceptance is that people often do not choose to study the available information at all. Ter Huurne (2008) showed that some people actually avoid information. She mentions several reasons for information avoidance. One reason could be that the gap in information is either too small or too large. If the gap is small, people might feel they can bridge the gap themselves, so they do not need to get information from others. If the gap is large, people could fear an emotional risk. This could include fear of bad news, fear of failure, or fear of increased uncertainty, fear of being incapable of making adequate decisions. Another explanation may be the principle of least effort: people can reduce effort by avoiding information acquisition and processing (Payne et al. 1993).

Whether more knowledge leads to more positive acceptance or not, it will probably lead to more stable opinions (Daamen et al. 2006), which would give more definitive answers to how accepting people are of hydrogen technologies. They may still be positive or negative attitudes and behaviours, but it can also lead to neutral attitudes and behaviours, because people realize the complexity of the topic (Hibino and Nagata 2008) and can therefore not make up their mind one way or the other.

Based on these findings we can conclude that knowledge is important, but that providing information is not a straightforward solution leading to increased acceptance from the lay public. Besides the ethical aspects of using information to influence people, information might not always (Hibino and Nagata 2008) reach the public, and when it does, it does not automatically increase acceptance. More research is needed to find out the circumstances in which people take up information and how information and the context of the information influences acceptability and acceptance.

Review of Empirical Findings on
Acceptance, Acceptability and Determinants of These

In the light of the discussed terminology and theories used in the papers, we will give a summary of the findings divided into acceptance-related findings (including all the different terms that have been used) and the determinants of acceptance.

Findings for Acceptance

In this section we will summarize the findings of three categories, namely acceptability and acceptance, willingness to pay (WTP) and knowledge. As a result of the larger number of hydrogen bus studies, these results are mainly related to this hydrogen application. It should be kept in mind that different hydrogen applications will elicit different attitudes, different benefit perceptions and different safety perceptions.

All studies found high acceptability rates for hydrogen fuelled buses; the acceptability number ranged from 68 to 95 per cent of participants (O'Garra et al. 2007; Hickson et al. 2007; Heinz and Erdmann 2008; Molin 2005). Small percentages (about 1 to 3 per cent) of participants particularly objected (O'Garra et al. 2007; Hickson et al. 2007), mainly because of safety concerns, even though other studies found that a sizeable group mentioned negative associations with hydrogen in general, such as 'bomb' and 'explosive' (Zachariah-Wolff and Hemmes 2006). Overall, this indicates high support for hydrogen buses and little influence of the perceived safety issues. People often seemed to associate hydrogen fuelled buses with environmental friendliness (Hickson et al. 2007; Zachariah-Wolff and Hemmes 2006; O'Garra et al. 2005) and assigned a positive rating of the comfort of the bus, compared to that of conventional buses (Haraldsson et al. 2006). Quite a large proportion of people, however, indicated that they needed more information before they could actually decide whether they supported or opposed the technology. Acceptability or acceptance of other applications in transport, such as taxis or boats, has not been measured and requires further research.

Stated willingness to pay extra for hydrogen fuelled buses has also been measured by several studies. Stated willingness to pay is used to predict consumer acceptance or adoption, but does not equal actual consumer acceptance. Two studies measured willingness to pay in two very different ways. O'Garra et al. (2007) measured the specific amount that one was willing to pay extra. This was measured in four cities at the same time. After explaining that hydrogen buses would emit zero air pollution, be less noisy and more efficient than conventional buses, the average WTP for bus tickets per city varied between €0.27 and €0.40 (€0.32 on average). The average extra annual tax that London and Perth residents would alternatively be willing to pay for these buses was €24 and €16 respectively. These numbers are reasonably close to each other, showing only moderate differences between the cities. The study also showed, however, that 24 per cent of all participants were not willing to pay anything extra, which is a considerable proportion. Haraldsson et al. (2006) measured in Stockholm only whether people were willing to pay more, rather than how much more they were willing to pay. Two measurements were taken during a hydrogen bus project. It was found that no less than 63 per cent of the bus passengers were not willing to pay extra at the beginning of the project and 61 per cent after one year. There was therefore not much change in the number of people that were willing or not to pay extra for hydrogen buses between these two points in time. The number of people not willing to pay more was much higher in this study than in the study by O'Garra et al. However, due to the different ways of measuring the WTP as well as the diverging circumstances, it is not possible to really compare these findings. A very different but cost-related measurement in a third study (Zachariah-Wolff and Hemmes 2006), measured the public's reaction to higher costs, which were not specified. The reaction to the suggested higher price of using hydrogen buses instead of diesel buses was that 37 per cent of the Dutch participants in the study changed their preference from hydrogen buses to diesel buses (the preference for the hydrogen bus over the conventional bus went down from 95 per cent to 58 per cent).

Only a few studies have looked into the willingness to pay for private vehicles and taxis. One study, using discrete choice modelling, specifically provided insight into how people balance the different drawbacks and benefits of private vehicles in theoretical situations (Molin et al. 2007). The results indicated that both a higher fuel price and a higher vehicle price each decreased the preference for a hydrogen vehicle over the current vehicle; however, a strong CO_2-emission reduction of 30 per cent did offset the extra purchase costs of €1,000 but was not enough to offset 50 per cent extra fuel costs. Another study in London investigated taxi drivers' willingness to pay for a hydrogen fuelled taxi. In this case, 69 per cent were willing to pay extra for a vehicle with extended range and a lower fuel price, even with only 10 available refuelling stations in the city (Mourato et al. 2004).

WTP values could be more extensively researched for different conditions of hydrogen use and for different circumstances. Difference in WTP values can result from several factors. In the first place diverging WTP values result from the differences in the questions asked to the participants, as we saw in the bus-related studies. Other reasons for differences are often related to the context of the WTP question (see Sevdalis and Harvey 2006, who have been measuring context effects). First, WTP will be influenced by the way that the hydrogen bus is introduced to the respondents in the study, for example as reducing air pollution (as in the study by O'Garra et al.) or without introduction. Second, WTP for one specific option will be influenced by whether people are aware of alternative technologies. Third, WTP will be influenced by the way that extra costs are charged. For example, charging the whole population for using hydrogen to fuel the entire stock of public buses might be more acceptable than charging specific groups of people for single buses. Finally, measured WTP values might also be different from actual WTP values because people are less aware of the consequences of their choice in hypothetical situations than in real life situations (e.g. Hensher et al. 2005). See also Mitchell and Carson (1989) and Carson et al. (2001) for an extensive review of the pitfalls associated with retrieving WTP responses to hypothetical choice situations. These factors will likely also influence acceptability and acceptance findings.

Knowledge-related items were measured in diverse ways in several studies. The studies showed quite consistently that the respondents had little knowledge of hydrogen technologies and the properties of hydrogen itself (Zachariah-Wolff and Hemmes 2006; Molin 2005; O'Garra et al. 2007; O'Garra et al. 2005; Mourato et al. 2004) and/or many respondents would like to have more information at the time of the research (24 to 73 per cent of the respondents, Haraldsson et al. 2006; O'Garra et al. 2005; O'Garra et al. 2008; Heinz and Erdmann 2008). These findings indicate that little is known about people's acceptability and acceptance when people are more informed and feel they have sufficient knowledge.

Based on these findings, hydrogen bus acceptability by bus users if the bus does not cost extra for the user is quite positive. However, the findings are inconclusive for diverse price schemes, for citizens living near bus routes and refuelling station locations, for socio-political acceptance and for different kinds of acceptance for other hydrogen applications than buses.

Possible Determinants of Acceptance

Several potential determinants of influence to public acceptance were measured in the reviewed papers. Two categories that were also distinguished in previous sections are:

1. psychological variables (such as attitudes and preferences towards aspects of the technology, general attitudes such as environmental attitudes, associations and trust);
2. knowledge-related items (such as prior knowledge about the topic, awareness of the projects).

A third category is discussed in several papers, but has not been part of the terminology and theory sections. This concerns demographic and situational variables (such as education and distance from a refuelling station). We will look at the measurements for these determinants in more depth per category.

Psychological variables   Reactions to characteristics of a hydrogen vehicle were measured in two studies that differed in hydrogen application, level of experience, and in type of measurement (attitudes vs. preferences). Hickson et al. (2007) measured hydrogen bus passengers' attitudes with respect to riding comfort, noise level and temperature comfort, based on personal experience. They found that a majority of their respondents rated the comfort of the hydrogen bus more highly than a conventional bus, while a minority judged it as being equal. Molin et al. (2007) measured car drivers' stated preferences for future cars, based on various characteristics that future cars might have, and found that the perceived utility of cars was influenced by fuel type, the amount of CO_2 reduction, fuel price, the purchase costs of a new vehicle, the detour necessary to reach a refuelling station and the range of the car, but not by decreasing the motor performance by 20 per cent. The respondents valued hydrogen as a fuel higher than biodiesel and even more highly than hybrid vehicles. Due to the large differences in the setup of the two studies, we cannot compare the results, However, while the first study did not show a correlation between the rated items and the acceptance of hydrogen buses, the second study explicitly studied the influence of aspects of the hydrogen-fuelled car on preferences, showing which characteristic had most influence on the choices that people indicated.

One example of general attitudes and beliefs that are possibly, but not necessarily related to hydrogen in transport is environmental concern. This psychological variable has been measured in several ways and has mainly been tested in WTP studies. O'Garra et al. (2007) found that giving high priority to public spending on solving environmental problems positively influenced WTP extra for hydrogen buses in two out of four cities and that the frequency of donations to environmental groups or organizations also positively influenced WTP in three of the four cities. So, this factor did not influence WTP values in all cities. The measurement of the attitude towards the priority of solving environmental problems with public spending was not significantly influential when considering whether to support or reject the introduction of hydrogen vehicles in London (O'Garra et al. 2005). For taxi drivers, WTP for acquiring a fuel cell taxi in the future was found to be influenced by concerns about the perceived personal risk of suffering health problems from air pollution, while WTP for participation in a fuel cell taxi pilot project was not influenced by these environment-related concerns (Mourato et al. 2004). These diverse findings show that environmental attitudes do influence stated WTP answers, but this does not seem to occur in all contexts. The diversity in environmental attitude-related questions makes it difficult to make a comparison between the studies and draw stronger conclusions. We suggest a more thorough approach to measuring the effect of environmental concern.

Three of the 12 papers asked the respondents for their associations with hydrogen. O'Garra et al. (2005) elicited free associations using open-ended questions. Both Zachariah-Wolff and Hemmes (2006) and Molin (2005) measured free-associations with open-ended questions, as well as close-ended questions, asking the respondents to indicate to what extent they associate terms such as 'dangerous' and 'environmentally friendly' with hydrogen, on a Likert-scale. The latter measurement seems to be very close to the attitude measurements described in the previous section. Related to these measurements, Hickson et al. (2007) asked two open-ended questions about perceptions related to hydrogen as a fuel: one on the positive aspects of hydrogen as a fuel ('good points') and one on the negative aspects of hydrogen as a fuel ('bad points'). Of the three studies measuring associations, only Molin calculated the correlation between the close-ended associations with hydrogen and, on the one hand, attitudes towards the general use of hydrogen and, on the other hand, indirectly with willingness to use hydrogen applications. He found a positive correlation between the association 'environmentally friendly' and both (1) attitude measurements towards the use of hydrogen, and (2) willingness to use measurements with respect to hydrogen applications. He found a negative correlation between the association 'unsafe' and both (1) the attitude measurements on hydrogen use in general, and (2) willingness to buy and use hydrogen applications. Based on the measurements summarized here, the meaning and role of associations is not quite clear.

Trust was measured in one paper. O'Garra et al. (2008) found that trust in safety regulations positively influenced support of local development and decreased opposition towards a hydrogen storage facility near the respondent's home. Although this variable has been measured in only a single study, it seems to be relevant for more situations and transport applications and therefore should be further researched.

Knowledge-related items Several studies measured knowledge-related items, but not all of them explicitly studied and explained the relevance of this variable. Saxe et al. (2007), for example, measured the need for information and noticed that the number of respondents needing more information went down from 44 to 36 per cent after running a hydrogen bus project for one year. The influence of the need of information on WTP was not measured. Heinz and Erdmann (2008) and O'Garra et al. (2008) asked people to choose between support, opposition, indifference and the need for information, indirectly assuming and enforcing that the need for information is opposite to indicating acceptability in terms of support, opposition or indifference.

Five studies measured the influence of knowledge on acceptance. Molin (2005) and Zachariah-Wolff and Hemmes (2006) measured the influence of positive, negative and mixed information on attitude, using the same dataset. Molin found that positive information had a positive influence on intention to use and negative information had a negative influence on intention to use. The latter was larger in effect size, so it was not surprising to see that mixed information, containing elements of both positive and negative information, also had a negative influence on intention to use. This was an indirect effect; the perception of safety was an intermediate variable. This means that information influenced the perception of safety which in turn influenced intention to use. Molin also measured the knowledge level of people before giving the information and found that this prior knowledge level also positively influenced attitudes. The findings in this study indicate that balanced information does not always increase acceptance; it can also decrease acceptance. Zachariah-Wolff and Hemmes found that the three different types of information influenced different perception items, which is probably a direct result of the content of the different compositions of the information blocks. O'Garra et al. (2005) measured, first, the influence of whether people had heard of hydrogen and fuel cell vehicles. The results indicated that having heard of hydrogen vehicles and to a smaller extent having heard of fuel cell vehicles had a positive influence on support of the introduction of hydrogen vehicles in London. Second, they measured the influence of environmental knowledge by asking whether the respondent knew that the ozone layer is not the main cause of climate change. The researchers did not find an additional explanatory effect for this knowledge-related item. O'Garra and Mourato (2007) found significant positive correlations between, on the one hand, knowledge about hydrogen vehicles and, on the other hand, WTP for the air and noise pollution reduction associated with the introduction of hydrogen buses in London. O'Garra et al. (2008) measured self-reported knowledge on hydrogen vehicles and found that people with self-reported prior knowledge on hydrogen were four times more likely to support than oppose local developments with respect to hydrogen refuelling facilities. These studies show that several knowledge-related measurements, such as self-rated knowledge, information, or having heard of something, can influence acceptance items. Several studies showed a positive relation between knowledge and acceptability and acceptance-related measurements, although sometimes no relation was found. Molin's study showed that providing information, which can be assumed to increase knowledge, does not necessarily increase acceptability and acceptance. Considering the limited knowledge that people have now, it is important to understand the effect of information, increased knowledge, and a feeling that one knows enough to form an opinion.

Demographic and situational variables Many of the studies measured demographic variables and several studies reported correlations with acceptance. O'Garra et al. (2005) found that gender, age and income did not influence support for hydrogen vehicles, while gender and age did have an influence on prior hydrogen and fuel cell knowledge. Men had a higher score on both knowledge items than women. Higher age had a positive influence on prior knowledge of fuel cell vehicles. O'Garra et al. (2008) found that a higher age increased opposition and decreased support of local hydrogen storage at existing refuelling stations. They also found that a higher income marginally decreased opposition but did not increase support and, finally, that gender did not significantly influence opposition or support. Molin (2005) used structural equation modelling[4] to provide information on the direct and indirect effects of demographic variables on willingness to use. The study showed that respondents' age, gender and education level had a direct and/or indirect influence on the intended use of hydrogen applications. Age had a reasonably strong negative direct and indirect influence on intended use of hydrogen applications. The indirect effect of age concerned a negative influence on the perception of environmental friendliness, which had a positive influence on attitude and intended use. Both gender and level of education had an indirect influence on intended use. Men and higher educated people, on the one hand, had more knowledge of hydrogen than women and lower educated people, which led to a more positive attitude towards the use of hydrogen and to a higher intention to use hydrogen applications. On the other hand, men and higher educated people perceived hydrogen applications as more unsafe than women and lower educated people, which had a negative influence on attitudes towards hydrogen use and intention to use hydrogen applications. Combining both effects, men and higher educated people had a slightly higher willingness to use than women and lower educated people. We can conclude that the findings of the studies on the influence of demographic variables are quite diverse and sometimes even contradictory. This may be caused by using different measurements for the same concept, or because it concerns different hydrogen applications. A more thorough study of the relation between demographic variables and acceptability and acceptance is needed.

Zachariah-Wolff and Hemmes (2006) looked at the influence of demographic variables on more specific, single perception and attitude measurements. They found that educational level, age and gender influenced a number of perception and attitude measurements. Educational level, for example, positively influenced the perception

---

4   Structural Equation Modelling (SEM) enables a simultaneous estimation of direct and indirect effects, controlling for correlation between covariates.

that hydrogen was environmentally friendly and the attitude that 'investments in hydrogen buses are good', while it negatively influenced the attitude 'we should convert to hydrogen when fossil fuels run out'. The age of the respondents had a negative influence on the perception of environmental friendliness and a positive influence on the attitude measurement 'we should convert to hydrogen when fossil fuels run out'. The *middle* age levels had higher values than the lowest and highest age levels for perception of inexhaustibility of hydrogen and for attitudes that 'hydrogen buses are good' and that 'introducing hydrogen is good for the environment'. Gender was found to influence only hydrogen perceptions: men had higher scores on both positive and negative perceptions (including 'environmentally friendly', 'inexhaustible fuel', 'explosive' and 'dangerous'). None of these demographic variables were shown to influence perception of expensiveness or the attitudes 'eliminate negative effects before hydrogen' and 'convert to hydrogen as quickly as possible'. This detailed information can provide insight into the specific beliefs of groups of people and can possibly explain differences in findings on the effects of several demographic variables.

Demographic variables also influenced WTP measurements. Mourato et al. (2004) found that education and age positively influenced WTP for a fuel cell taxi, but did not influence WTP for participation in a pilot project. O'Garra et al. (2007) found that income and age, but not gender and university education, had in some cases a significant influence on WTP extra for hydrogen bus fares or extra tax, but not for all four cities. London respondents with a higher income indicated a slightly higher WTP. Older people indicated a significantly lower WTP in Berlin, London and Luxembourg. Finally, O'Garra and Mourato (2007), using the method of quantile regression, found that income and the frequency of bus use had a positive influence on WTP, while age and university education had a negative influence on WTP. Gender had no significant influence. Interestingly, only some lower WTP values were influenced by the frequency of bus use, age and university education. Apparently, people that indicated willingness to pay a reasonable amount of money were influenced by other factors than people that were willing to pay nothing or only a small amount of money. Here we also find diverse findings.

One situational variable is the distance to a potential hydrogen refuelling station. This distance was found to be relevant for acceptability of hydrogen refuelling stations: residents living 200 to 500 metres away from a hydrogen refuelling station are more opposed to the proposed installation of hydrogen storage facilities at existing refuelling stations than people living less than 200 metres away from the location (O'Garra et al. 2008). Another situational variable is the current frequency of bus use. O'Garra et al. (2007) asked for the bus use frequency but found no correlation with WTP to support the introduction of hydrogen buses in the city. Hickson et al. (2007) did notice that frequent bus users (more than four trips per week) had a more positive attitude towards using hydrogen as a fuel than less frequent bus users.

Apparently, demographic and situational variables influence acceptance in certain situations or in certain acceptance measurements. More thorough research could combine and compare the measurements of different situations and hydrogen applications.

Conclusion and Discussion

Hydrogen is a potential solution to problems related to transport, energy use, the environment and the security of the energy supply. However, several barriers need to be overcome before successful implementation can be realized, including possible negative public acceptance. The aim of this chapter was to critically review the available quantitative hydrogen acceptance studies in the field of transport and to provide suggestions for improvement. We have briefly reviewed the use of terminology and theory in the selected papers and provided suggestions for improvement, by referring to general psychological theories and wider literature on acceptance. Finally, we reviewed the actual findings on acceptance and determinants of acceptance and indicated knowledge gaps.

First, with respect to terminology use, we noticed that terms were not used in a coherent and consistent way across the studies. We discussed the use of the terms acceptance, acceptability, attitude, perception, knowledge, awareness, familiarity and need for information, and suggested usage of terms based on literature. A more explicit use of terminology and related measurements, in studies, indicating what concepts mean and do not mean, would improve the readers' understanding.

Second, we noticed that the majority of the studies lack a firm foundation in relevant theoretical frameworks. We suggested that future studies provide more scientific underpinning by making use of several theories developed in the field of psychology, for example dual-processing theories and the theory of planned behaviour. This will be helpful because it will provide a more complete overview of the underlying mechanisms and determinants and because it will increase understanding of the wider implications of the findings.

Third, we have briefly summarized the findings on public acceptability, acceptance and determinants. Since most of the studies focused on acceptability with hydrogen buses, we can draw some careful, tentative conclusions with respect to this. The findings on this topic suggest that test projects with hydrogen buses, as well as the idea of future hydrogen bus projects, receive positive attitudes among the public. However, it should be kept in mind that most of these bus projects and related studies took place within large cities and towns in Europe and might not equal the acceptability in other places. Within the studies the findings were also quite diverse. The knowledge level of the respondents in all the studies was quite low and people often indicated they needed more information. Based on the discussion of theory on knowledge-related factors, we realize that this might imply that acceptability and acceptance may easily change. More research is needed for acceptability and acceptance for consumer acceptance of private hydrogen vehicles, for citizen acceptance (for people living near bus routes and refuelling station locations) and for socio-political acceptance.

Fourth, several determinants of hydrogen technology acceptability and acceptance have been measured in the selected studies. Demographic variables were found to have varying (positive, negative or no) influence on acceptance. Environmental attitudes and knowledge measurements mostly showed a positive correlation with acceptance, but also here diverse findings were presented. Other variables which were measured but whose influence still needs to be confirmed were, first, situational variables such as distance from house to a refuelling station and frequency of bus use, second, psychological variables such as attitudes and perception towards technical aspects of hydrogen applications, associations with hydrogen and trust in actors involved with implementing hydrogen applications and, third, knowledge-related items such as the need for information and received information. Although the studies provided a useful palette of relevant influences on acceptance, none of the studies have measured these influencing factors in a comprehensive way.

While this chapter has focused on the person-related factors that influence acceptance (socio-demographics and other person-related situational variables, psychological variables and knowledge-related variables), obviously also other more general situational circumstances will influence acceptance. This includes the way that the technology is introduced (e.g. by whom, which brand, which object, forcefully or with the consent of all parties, etc.), the way that the hydrogen is produced (from oil, gas or more sustainable sources), the exact design of the technology (materials used, shape, safety standards, etc.), the available alternatives and their characteristics (including other energy carriers like bio fuels and electricity), and other societal circumstances (e.g. the perceived severity of the expected and believed climate change, price and availability of fossil fuels and alternatives, etc.). Finally an important role will also be played by the way that society as a whole frames and talks about the problems that we face, the desirable pathways for future energy and transport systems, and the availability of and views about possible alternatives. These are important factors influencing acceptance that need to be studied and elaborated on in future research.

Besides terminology and theory use, which we focused on in this review study, several other study-related factors can influence the acceptability and acceptance findings. One factor which can influence findings relates to the study design, such as the introduction of the interview, and the choice of answering scales. Furthermore, and even more unavoidable, language differences will influence the comparability of the results and the transferability of the findings to other language areas. Finally, we need to note that the findings also strongly depend on the appropriate choice and use of methodologies. We will not elaborate on that here; methodologies used in hydrogen research are discussed by Yetano Roche et al. (2010).

Note also that we have focused on quantitative studies. While quantitative studies have benefits, especially as they provide quantitative results representing the opinion of a larger population and the relative strength of influencing factors, these studies are also criticized for the fact that they cannot grasp the entire complexity of the problem and do not give people the opportunity to formulate the issue in their own words (e.g. Ricci et al. 2008). Qualitative research provides a valuable addition to quantitative research in understanding people's underlying reasoning and beliefs. We refer to the work of Ricci et al. for a review and more insights from qualitative research on hydrogen technology acceptance.

All in all, we conclude that acceptance of hydrogen is probably not a major barrier for the successful implementation of hydrogen as a fuel in public transport buses, but that more insights are needed to fully understand the determinants of acceptance and the interrelation between these factors, and more insights are needed into the acceptance of other transport-related hydrogen technology applications. Furthermore, insights are needed into acceptance under diverse conditions (for example, differing in the way that hydrogen buses are introduced or the way that the extra costs are retrieved from the public) and about the factors influencing information processing and attitude changes resulting from information uptake. Finally, we advise researchers to make more thorough use of theories, to use terminology in a clearer and more consistent way, to study all possible determinants in a more comprehensive way, and to discuss the transferability of results.

Chapter 9

Transport-related CO_2 Emissions –
Deconstructing the Trends

Yusak O. Susilo and Dominic Stead

Introduction

Using National Travel survey data from the Netherlands and the UK, two countries with similar economies and comparable levels of car ownership (see for example European Commission 2008), we examine how passenger transport emissions are divided across society and how similar this distribution is across these two different countries. We also examine trends in individual travel patterns and CO_2 emissions over time in these countries. We construct a simple classification of individuals based on their travel patterns and CO_2 emission profiles with the aim of identifying the key socio-economic characteristics of individuals with high and low emission profiles in these two countries. By looking across a series of data since 1990, the chapter also examines the extent to which the socio-economic characteristics of the main contributors of CO_2 emissions are similar in these two countries. Trends in opinions about the effectiveness and acceptability of various measures to address transport-related CO_2 emissions are then examined according to several socio-economic characteristics in order to help to understand how opinions might differ between individuals with different emission profiles, and to contribute to the development of more targeted policies for transport CO_2 reduction. The chapter is intended to lay the groundwork for further investigation and consideration of the stratification of transport-related CO_2 emissions and a more targeted approach to policy-making in this area.

This chapter draws on data from the UK and the Dutch National Travel Surveys (NTS) which provide detailed information about individuals, households and their trips for the last three decades. The Dutch NTS data have been collected continuously by Statistics Netherlands since 1978 using travel diaries. However, because of some differences in the way of recording certain variables before 1990, this chapter only uses NTS data from 1990 onwards. The UK NTS has been carried out as a continuous survey since 1988 and annually contains data for over 5,000 addresses (ESDS 2007). Because of accuracy and comparability issues, this chapter only uses the UK data from 2000 and 2004 datasets.

Emissions of CO_2 per person are calculated for four different years between 1990 and 2005 at five-year intervals for the Netherlands (1990, 1995, 2000 and 2005) and for two different years for the UK (2000 and 2004) using information from NTS data about each trip (mode, distance, fuel type, vehicle age, occupancy and speed) together with vehicle emission factors from COPERT, a computer programme to calculate emissions from road transport developed for the European Environment Agency (Ntziachristos and Samaras 2000). For journeys by public transport modes, information about mode and distance only are used to calculate CO_2 emissions using typical emission factors according to analyses by van den Brink and van Wee (1997) for the Netherlands and figures from Transport Direct (2008) for the UK.

National Trends in Transport Energy Consumption and CO_2 Emissions

Between 1990 and 2005, total greenhouse gas emissions in Europe declined very slightly (EEA 2007). Emissions from transport however increased by almost 30 per cent during this period, of which 90 per cent were produced by road transport (ibid). In the Netherlands, CO_2 emissions from land-based transport increased by 25 per cent (Statistics Netherlands 2006): an increase of more than 2 per cent per year. This is in contrast to the greenhouse gas reduction targets agreed under the Kyoto Protocol, where the target of a 6 per cent decrease in greenhouse gases between 1990 and 2008–12 was agreed for the Netherlands.[1] Fortunately, other sectors in the Netherlands have not experienced such high increases in CO_2 emissions as in the transport sector, and emissions of other greenhouse gases have been reduced. Emissions of CO_2 from commerce have increased since 1990 but to a lesser extent than the transport sector, whilst emissions from households and industry have fluctuated but remained fairly stable during this period (Figure 9.1a). The net effect is that emissions of all greenhouse gases from the Netherlands (excluding those from air transport) have been stabilized between 1990 and 2005 (Netherlands Environmental Assessment Agency 2006). However, further increases in CO_2 emissions from the transport sector, now the largest and fastest growing source of CO_2 emissions in the Netherlands, may thwart the achievement of the Kyoto greenhouse gas emission target for the Netherlands as well as the European Union's more recent greenhouse gas reduction target for 2020 (European Commission 2007a). The UK also experienced similar trends. Transport is the only sector whose carbon emissions were higher in 2005 than they were in 1990, a period in which reductions achieved by other sectors of the economy helped deliver a cut in total UK carbon emissions of just over 5 per cent (Figure 9.1b).

---

1   Emissions targets under the Kyoto Protocol were set using a five-year end-point (or budget period) between 2008 and 2012, rather than a single year. The argument for this budget period was to help smooth out short-term fluctuations in economic performance or weather, either of which could spike emissions in a particular year.

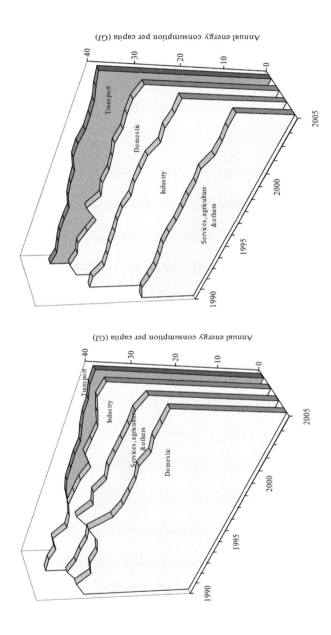

(a) Annual energy consumption per capita in the Netherlands[1]

(b) Annual energy consumption per capita in the UK[2]

Figure 9.1   Energy consumption by sector in the Netherlands and in the UK, 1990–2005

Source: [1]Statistics Netherlands (2006). [2]Commission for Integrated Transport (2007).

Passenger transport currently accounts for more than half of the greenhouse gas emissions from the transport sector in both countries (Netherlands Environmental Assessment Agency 2006; Commission for Integrated Transport 2007) and the great majority of passenger transport emissions originate from road-based transport. In 2005, more than 90 per cent of all CO_2 emissions from land-based passenger transport originated from cars. Note that emissions from air travel are not included here – there is a lack of data concerning the contribution of air transport to national CO_2 emissions (and emissions from air transport are excluded from the Kyoto Protocol targets and reporting). It is important to recognize however that air transport is an increasingly significant producer of greenhouse gas emissions, mainly CO_2, since it is a rapidly growing sector and also has a greater effect on climate change as a consequence of being released at altitude, which adds to radiative forcing (Penner et al. 1999).

Whilst car-based journeys dominate CO_2 emissions from land-based transport, only around half of all trips in the Netherlands are actually made by car (Figure 9.2). A further 45 per cent of all trips are made by bicycle or foot and around 5 per cent of trips are made by public transport. In other words, just under half of all trips contribute to 90 per cent of all CO_2 emissions (i.e. those by car) and a similar proportion of trips (i.e. those by bicycle or foot) produce no CO_2 emissions. In the UK, the proportion of car journeys is higher – but still not proportional with its share of emissions. One of the most noticeable differences between the modal split in the two countries is the proportion of journeys by bicycle. In the Netherlands, more than a quarter of all journeys are by bicycle whereas only 1 per cent of journeys are by bicycle in the UK.

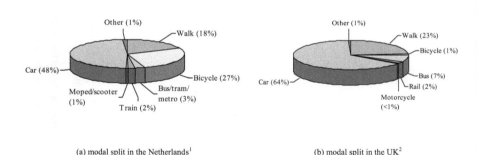

(a) modal split in the Netherlands[1]   (b) modal split in the UK[2]

Figure 9.2   Modal split of personal travel in the Netherlands and the UK, 2005

Source: [1] Statistics Netherlands (2006). [2] Department of Transport (2007).

Individual Trends in Travel and CO_2 Emissions

Recent Travel Trends in the Netherlands

In many ways, individual travel patterns in the Netherlands did not change substantially between 1990 and 2005. According to Dutch NTS data, average travel distance per person per day, travel speed and time spent travelling all remained fairly constant during the 15-year period between 1990 and 2005. What did change however is the average number of trips, which decreased by 14 per cent during this period,[2] and travel-related CO_2 emissions, which increased on average by 16 per cent between 1990 and 2005. The increase in CO_2 emissions per capita can be mainly attributed to decreases in travel distance by less energy intensive modes (e.g. bicycle and public transport) and increases in travel distance by certain energy-intensive modes, and more frequent trips for certain purposes, such as commuting. Estimates of annual CO_2 emissions using the average daily emissions calculated for 1990, 1995 and 2000 correspond well with official data for annual emissions (Figure 9.2), despite the fact that NTS data only record travel information for one day. Interestingly, there is a constant share, about 30 per cent of the population, from 1990 to 2005, who did not use motorized transport in any observed days. This share increased from 30 per cent in 1990 to 33 per cent in 2005 (more information on Dutch personal travel trends can be found in Susilo and Maat 2007 and Susilo and Stead 2008).

Recent Travel Trends in the United Kingdom

In the UK, the number of trips per person fell slightly between 1995 and 2005, whilst the average distance travelled increased slightly. This reflects an increase of 7 per cent in average trip length over the same period. Interestingly, the average trip time increased between 1995 and 2005 by 9 per cent to 22 minutes. As a result, the average time spent travelling increased from 369 hours per person per year (about an hour a day) to 385. The number of trips by bicycle and on foot declined by over 15 per cent between 1995 and 2005 (Department for Transport

---

2   The decrease in the average number of trips may be mainly due to various changes between 1990 and 2005 in data collection methods and definitions of journeys (van Evert et al. 2006). Very short trips, such as short distance walks, which were recorded in the earlier version of the survey, were removed in later surveys. Some frequent trips that are part of work activities (e.g. delivery workers's or taxi drivers's trips) were recorded as one trip. However, since the total travel distance and time were still recorded, this adjustment would not significantly influence the emissions and energy calculation in this study (Susilo and Stead 2007).

2006). Unlike the Netherlands, the proportion of zero emission travellers (100 per cent non-motorized travellers during the observed days) in the UK is relatively low: 8.6 per cent in 2000 and 9.8 per cent in 2004. This is due to higher car usage rate in UK than in the Netherlands and the longer survey duration in the UK than in the Netherlands. As a result, the British are responsible for 17 per cent more transport emissions than Dutch, with lower number of trips, higher travel time and similar travel distance.

Gender

Between 1990 and 2005, there has been a consistent and substantial difference in transport-related CO_2 emissions between men and women in both countries (Figure 9.3a). Men account for around two-thirds of these CO_2 emissions whilst women account for approximately one-third. The growth in CO_2 emissions has however been higher for women than men during this 15-year period, suggesting a slight trend towards convergence. Travel distances covered by men are also consistently and substantially higher than those of women (Figure 9.3b). As in the case of CO_2 emissions, men account for around two-thirds of all travel distance whilst women account for approximately one-third. On average, men also spend 10–20 per cent more time travelling than women (Figure 9.3c). In terms of the number of trips however it is women who consistently make slightly more trips than men (Figure 9.3d).

Employment

People in full-time employment account for more than 50 per cent more transport-related CO_2 emissions than those in part-time employment and more than double the CO_2 emissions of people who are not in employment (Figure 9.4a). In the Netherlands, between 1990 and 2005, the highest rate of growth in CO_2 emissions has taken place amongst people in full-time employment. CO_2 emissions from people who are not in work, on the other hand, did not increase during this period. Similarly, people in full-time work consistently travel furthest and spend most time travelling whilst people who are not in work cover the shortest distance (Figure 9.4b) and spend the least amount of time travelling (Figure 9.4c). Interestingly, people who work part-time consistently make more trips (Figure 9.4d).

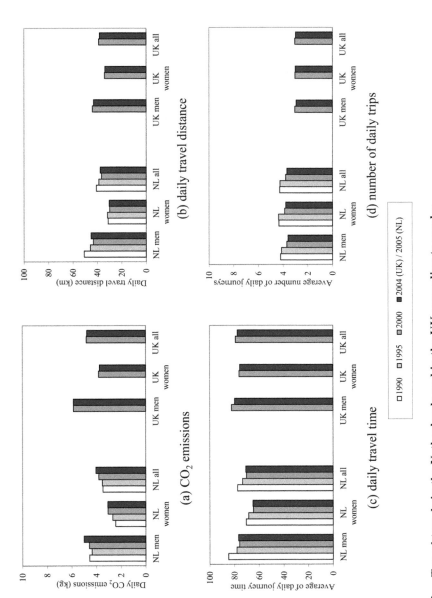

Figure 9.3 Travel trends in the Netherlands and in the UK according to gender

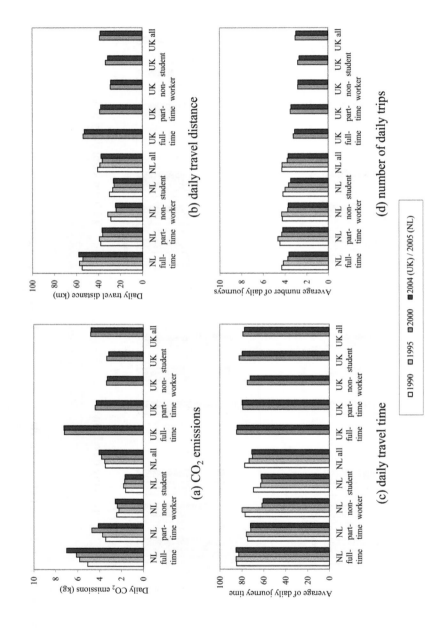

Figure 9.4 Travel trends in the Netherlands and in the UK according to employment status

Income

Transport-related CO$_2$ emissions are consistently and substantially higher for people with higher personal incomes (Figure 9.5a). In the Netherlands, the rate of growth of CO$_2$ emissions between 1990 and 2005 for people with higher incomes[3] has been much faster than for people in other income categories. People in the low-income category[4] account for less than one third of the CO$_2$ emissions compared to people in the high-income category. Similar observations can be made for travel distance and travel time: people with high incomes travel longer distances and spend more time travelling whilst people with low incomes travel shorter distances (Figure 9.5b) and spend less time travelling (Figure 9.5c). Although people with higher incomes also make slightly more trips than others, the difference in the number of trips between different income groups is fairly low (Figure 9.5d).

Household Structure

In the Netherlands, residents of households containing children (under the age of 18) account for lower levels of transport-related CO$_2$ emissions compared to residents of households without children (Figure 9.6a). In the case of UK households, this difference is less clear. In the Netherlands, CO$_2$ emissions of households with children increased substantially between 1995 and 2005,[5] which indicates a possible trend towards convergence in CO$_2$ emissions between different household types. In terms of travel distance, residents of households with more than one adult and no children consistently travel further (Figure 9.6b). The relationship between household composition and time spent travelling is unclear (Figure 9.6c). What is clear however is that, in the Netherlands, between 1995 and 2005, residents of households with children consistently spent the least amount of time travelling than the residents of other household types. In terms of the number of trips, residents of households containing children make the most number of trips whilst residents of households containing no children make fewer trips than average (Figure 9.6d).

---

3   For the purposes of the analysis presented here, the higher personal income category in the Netherlands was defined as €30,000 (net) or more per year for 1990 and 1995, and €35,000 (net) or more per year for 2000 and 2005. Whilst the higher personal income category in the UK was defined as more than £20,000 (gross) per year.

4   For the purposes of the analysis presented here, the lower personal income category in the Netherlands was defined as less than €15,000 (net) per year whilst the lower personal income category in the UK was defined as less than £10,000 (gross) per year.

5   No data are available for 1990 due to differences in the way household variables were collected.

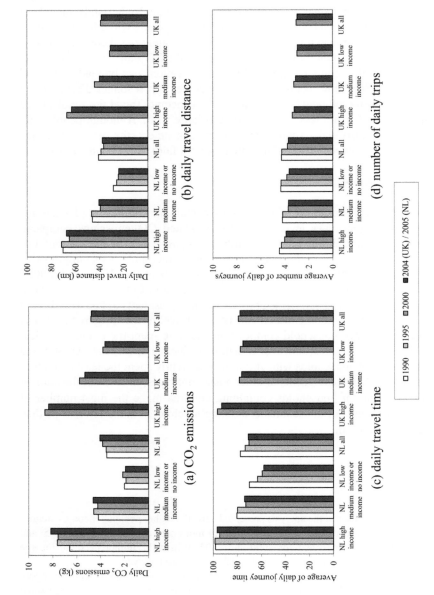

Figure 9.5 Travel trends in the Netherlands and in the UK according to personal income

Legend: □ 1990 □ 1995 □ 2000 ■ 2004 (UK) / 2005 (NL)

(a) CO₂ emissions — Daily CO₂ emissions (kg)

(b) daily travel distance — Daily travel distance (km)

(c) daily travel time — Average of daily journey time

(d) number of daily trips — Average number of daily journeys

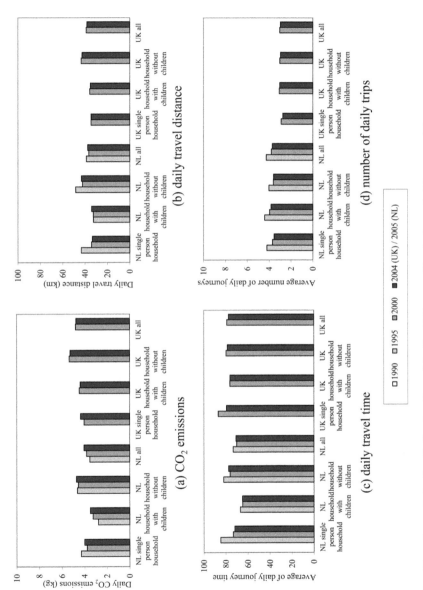

Figure 9.6   Travel trends in the Netherlands and in the UK according to household composition

Classification and Analysis of Individual CO_2 Emission Profiles

Having looked at some of the recent national trends in transport energy use and CO_2 emissions in the Netherlands and the UK, we now make a simple classification of individuals based on their CO_2 emissions and examine how emissions have changed over time within each group in both countries. Here we differentiate between five groups (quintiles) of individuals based on their daily transport CO_2 emissions. A sixth group containing 'zero emission' travellers is also identified: individuals in this group made all their journeys recorded in one day by non-motorized modes (i.e. by foot or bicycle).[6]

Looking across six categories of respondents classified according to their CO_2 emissions (Figure 9.7), three key trends over time are apparent. Firstly, the proportion of individuals in the zero-emissions category stayed fairly stable over time and, rather surprisingly, increased slightly between 1990 and 2005: in the Netherlands, 30 per cent of survey respondents were found in this category in 1990; in 2005 the proportion of respondents in this category was close to 33 per cent. In other words, around one third of the survey respondents generated no travel-related CO_2 emissions on the day that they were surveyed. In the UK, this zero emissions travellers are only about 3 per cent of survey respondents. This is also due to the fact that the UK NTS observed a longer period than the Dutch NTS, which increases the chances of travellers to change their mode from non-motorized to motorized modes. Nevertheless, if we explore further day-by-day emissions from the UK dataset, less than 10 per cent of day-trip in the UK has zero CO_2 emissions.

Secondly, the proportion of car trips for all categories of respondents stayed quite stable between the observed periods (not shown). In the Netherlands, about 13 per cent of respondents are responsible for almost 60 per cent of transport emissions, whilst in the UK this proportion of emissions were produced by 20 per cent of the respondents. On average, British respondents produced 800–1,000 grams CO_2 emissions more per day than Dutch respondents during the observed period.

Thirdly, looking across all examined periods, the top quintile of respondents (classified according to their CO_2 emissions) make between 10 and 20 per cent more journeys than average, undertake significantly more journeys by car than average (and fewer by foot, bicycle or public transport), spend about twice the average amount of time travelling (at twice the speed), cover more than three times the average distance and produce about three to four times the average amount of CO_2 emissions. The lowest quintile of respondents, on the other hand, make fewer journeys than average (by around 10–15 per cent), make significantly more journeys by public transport than average, spend substantially less time travelling

---

6   Individuals in the 'zero emission' group all made one or more journey. Individuals making no journeys on the day of the survey were excluded from this analysis.

(at a lower than average speed), cover less than a quarter of the average distance and produce around a fifth of the average amount of CO$_2$ emissions.

Comparing the socio-demographic characteristics among different groups of respondents, the main polluters were the same types of people as might be expected: men rather than women; higher rather than lower income groups; members of smaller households; and people with access to private vehicle (85 per cent of their trips were using a private vehicle). Interestingly, while zero CO$_2$ emissions travellers in the Netherlands were dominated by women, this is not the case with British respondents (Table 9.1). This is undoubtedly a consequence of much higher levels of accessibility by foot/bicycle in the Netherlands compared to the UK.

Table 9.1   The characteristics of zero-emissions travellers and the highest quintile of CO$_2$ emissions

Zero CO$_2$ emissions travellers		Highest quintile of travellers	
UK NTS	*Dutch NTS*	*UK NTS*	*Dutch NTS*
Slightly more men than women, relative high proportion of younger people, unemployed, larger household size and people below average income Very low proportion of people aged between 25 and 64, people with above average incomes, and people access to a car	Relatively high proportion of women, younger people (aged 24 or under), older people (aged 65 or older), people with below average incomes Relatively low proportion of people aged between 25 and 64, people with higher education, people with above average incomes, people with access to a car	More men than women Fewer younger respondents More respondents aged between 25 and 64 Fewer older respondents More full-time workers Fewer students Smaller household size More respondents with access to a car More than 85% of all trips by car	More men than women Fewer younger respondents More respondents aged between 25 and 64 Fewer older respondents More full-time workers Fewer students More respondents with higher education Fewer respondents with children More respondents with access to a car More than 85% of all trips by car

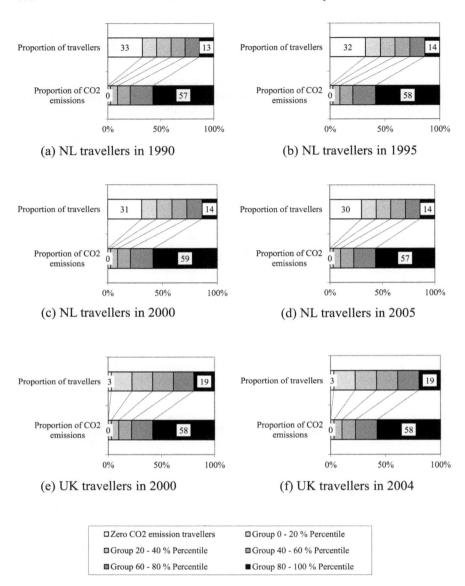

(a) NL travellers in 1990   (b) NL travellers in 1995

(c) NL travellers in 2000   (d) NL travellers in 2005

(e) UK travellers in 2000   (f) UK travellers in 2004

☐ Zero CO2 emission travellers	☐ Group 0 - 20 % Percentile
☐ Group 20 - 40 % Percentile	☐ Group 40 - 60 % Percentile
☐ Group 60 - 80 % Percentile	■ Group 80 - 100 % Percentile

Figure 9.7   Proportion of travellers against their transport CO_2 emissions

Quantitative Analysis of Individual CO$_2$ Emissions and Socio-economic Factors

To test the above explanatory analyses and to examine the influence of socio-demographic variables on transport CO$_2$ emissions, regression analyses were performed. These analyses were carried out for four points in time for the Netherlands (1990, 1995, 2000 and 2005) and two points in time for the UK (2000 and 2004) in order to determine whether the influence of the variables were consistent. While the R^2 values for the analyses are all relatively low, the results show reasonable consistency across the four years examined.

In the Netherlands, variables such as full-time employment and car availability became more important over time (between 1990 and 2005) for CO$_2$ emissions (Table 9.2). In the UK, car availability became more important over time (between 2000 and 2004) for CO$_2$ emissions (Table 9.3). In both the Netherlands and the UK, men consistently account for more CO$_2$ emissions than women (Tables 9.2 and 9.3). Income and household size variables appear to be less significant in the UK than the Netherlands.

Policy Implications, Acceptability and Effectiveness

As we have shown in the previous section, certain types of individuals tend to produce much more CO$_2$ emissions than others. In this section, attitudes of various types of individuals toward various transport policy are explored based on the results of the 2007 Special Eurobarometer Survey on transport policy (European Commission 2007b).[7] This survey contains a number of insights into public attitudes regarding policies for reducing transport-related energy and CO$_2$ emissions across different socio-economic groups (and also between different countries in Europe). The survey highlights for example some clear differences in attitudes across different socio-economic groups concerning the types of measures that could be used to address transport-related CO$_2$ emissions. While only a limited number of measures are considered here, it is recognized that a much greater variety of policy instruments are available to tackle transport-related CO$_2$ emissions (see for example the contribution by Hickman et al. in this volume).

---

7   Special Eurobarometer surveys are carried out regularly on behalf of the European Commission to gauge public opinion on a wide range of subjects (recent topics have included attitudes to climate change, radioactive waste, the European common agricultural policy, and European development aid).

Table 9.2 Regression analysis of individual CO_2 emissions with socio-economic variables, in the Netherlands, 1990–2005

	1990		1995		2000		2005	
	Coeff.	t-stats	Coeff.	t-stats	Coeff.	t-stats	Coeff.	t-stats
Constant	481.63	1.95	1,113.96	8.34	792.32	2.32	104.32	0.68
Male	974.57	8.76	683.62	14.29	554.57	3.50	730.14	10.85
Age < 25	57.87	0.21	453.33	3.78	848.21	2.28	1,333.41	8.17
Age 25–44	119.24	0.54	127.64	1.12	394.14	1.22	886.80	6.50
Age 45–64	287.99	1.39	200.50	1.92	400.43	1.41	449.63	3.87
Full-time worker	1,278.97	8.39	1,333.34	17.33	2,244.62	9.20	2,378.51	22.31
Part-time worker	423.95	2.40	422.96	4.97	1,753.76	6.28	645.23	5.33
Student	667.36	2.82	98.17	1.16	328.47	1.17	37.28	0.31
2-person household	-166.94	-0.88	-113.23	-1.18	-120.43	-0.47	-123.64	-1.18
3-person household	-285.14	-1.36	-281.95	-2.61	-689.71	-2.23	-1.28	-0.01
4-person household	-426.68	-2.14	-541.73	-5.07	-621.69	-2.03	-342.52	-2.67
5-person household	-646.77	-2.86	-508.10	-4.31	-825.00	-2.32	-388.42	-2.59
6+ person household	-1,059.57	-3.36	-542.48	-3.81	-784.13	-1.68	-176.81	-0.86
Households with children	N/A	N/A	-323.01	-4.92	-49.62	-0.23	-281.85	-3.12
Higher education	629.14	3.64	735.04	8.17	691.55	2.47	728.35	6.05
Tertiary education	265.54	2.20	47.08	0.67	198.79	0.93	45.01	0.48
High income	1,899.14	8.22	2,376.74	21.95	1,583.04	4.63	2,112.50	13.93
Medium income	378.41	2.74	247.47	3.41	-297.24	-1.39	208.98	1.95
Car availability	2,206.00	17.97	2,341.11	35.16	2,449.89	11.67	2,721.79	29.43
N	13,040		97,877		112,741		50,155	
Mean	3,479.29		3,526.10		3,816.84		4,044.04	
SD	5,566.92		6,873.69		23,595.19		7,106.74	
R^2	0.113		0.101		0.009		0.129	
Adjusted R^2	0.112		0.101		0.009		0.129	

Table 9.3   Regression analysis of individual CO$_2$ emissions with socio-economic variables, in the UK, 2000 and 2004

	2000		2004	
	Coeff.	*t-stats*	*Coeff.*	*t-stats*
Constant	2,072.92	6.18	1,668.46	7.95
Male	1,113.68	5.52	1,269.61	10.36
Age < 25	-656.84	-1.65	387.43	1.59
Age 25–44	-117.79	-0.29	587.75	2.39
Age 45–64	634.43	1.84	768.43	3.60
Full-time worker	1,919.84	5.41	1,480.87	7.02
Part-time worker	656.49	1.92	226.53	1.06
Student	387.96	0.60	-318.35	-0.86
2-person household	850.10	2.60	138.98	0.69
3-person household	123.20	0.30	172.03	0.68
4-person household	464.28	1.05	221.15	0.82
5-person household	571.39	1.09	111.37	0.36
6+ person household	665.33	1.05	119.46	0.33
Households with children	534.73	1.61	50.10	0.26
High income	375.22	1.15	157.15	0.85
Medium income	2,648.65	7.02	2,403.56	11.20
Car availability	518.80	2.00	1,470.25	9.37
N	7,420		18,447	
Mean	4,802.54		4,763.58	
SD	8,331.75		8,119.97	
R^2	0.067		0.077	
Adjusted R^2	0.065		0.076	

In terms of the types of *measures to improve traffic problems* in urban areas, there are some noticeable differences in attitudes by gender, age and level of education. A higher proportion of men than women favour measures such as public transport improvements, vehicle access and parking restrictions and charges for road use (Table 9.4). On the other hand, a higher proportion of women than men favour measures such as speed limits. Older respondents are more likely to favour measures such as public transport improvements and speed limits more than younger respondents. Conversely, measures such as vehicle access and parking restrictions and charges for road use are less favoured by older respondents. More educated respondents are more likely to favour measures such as public transport improvements and speed limits, and are less likely to favour measures such as vehicle access and parking restrictions and charges for road use. Overall, measures such as public transport improvements are favoured most, whilst measures such as road charging are least popular.

Table 9.4   Support for measures to improve traffic problems in urban areas according to the socio-economic characteristics of respondents

	Better public transport (%)	Restrictions in city centres (parking, access for private cars or trucks) (%)	Speed limits (%)	Charges for road use (e.g. city tolls) (%)	No need for improve-ment (%)	Other (%)	DK/NA (%)
Sex:							
Male	49.1	17.9	12.5	5.8	6.3	5.4	3.1
Female	48.0	15.9	20.3	3.9	5.5	2.3	4.2
Age:							
15–24	47.6	20.2	17.1	6.8	4.3	2.1	1.9
25–39	50.7	18.6	15.5	5.0	4.3	3.0	2.8
40–54	53.1	15.1	13.3	5.0	6.4	4.4	2.8
55+	43.1	15.4	19.9	3.6	7.4	4.7	5.9
Age of completing education:							
15	44.3	12.1	21.2	2.5	7.6	4.9	7.4
16–20	47.7	17.4	17.2	4.7	6.2	3.4	3.5
20+	52.6	18.2	12.5	5.7	5	4.1	1.9
EU27	48.5	16.8	16.5	4.8	5.9	3.8	3.7

Source: European Commission (2007b).

There are a number of similar differences in attitudes concerning *measures to reduce CO$_2$ emissions from road transport* according to gender, age and level of education. A higher proportion of women than men favour measures to restrict the use of cars and increase information to promote the purchase of more fuel efficient vehicles (Table 9.5). On the other hand, a higher proportion of men than women favour tax incentives to promote the purchase of fuel efficient vehicles. Older respondents are more likely to favour measures to restrict the use of cars than younger respondents. Conversely, measures such as increasing information to promote the purchase of more fuel efficient vehicles are less favoured by older respondents. More educated respondents are more likely to favour measures such as tax incentives to promote the purchase of fuel efficient vehicles, and are less likely to favour measures such as restricting the use of cars. Overall, measures such as restrictions on vehicle sales and tax incentives to promote the sale of more efficient vehicles are favoured most, whilst measures restricting the use of cars are least popular.

Table 9.5   Support for measures to reverse the rise of CO$_2$ emissions according to the socio-economic characteristics of respondents

	Introduce restrictions to the use of cars (%)	Only allow the sale of less polluting vehicles (%)	Promote the purchase of fuel efficient vehicles by giving better information (%)	Promote the purchase of fuel efficient vehicles through tax incentives (%)	DK/NA
Sex:					
Male	9.8	33.2	15.5	33.2	8.2
Female	11.6	36.7	17.1	26.8	7.8
Age:					
15–24	11.5	34.7	21.0	28.6	4.2
25–39	8.7	33.9	17.0	35.3	5.1
40–54	10.1	34.3	15.2	32.9	7.5
55+	12.6	36.7	14.6	23.7	12.4
Age of completing education:					
15	14.1	38.1	14.2	20.9	12.6
16–20	9.8	34.4	17.0	31.0	7.9
20+	9.9	33.9	15.8	34.7	5.7
EU27	10.8	35.0	16.3	29.9	8.0

Source: European Commission (2007b).

The 2007 Eurobarometer Survey on transport policy reveals some differences in the *preparedness to pay for using less polluting transport* according to according to socio-economic variables such as gender, age and level of education. Overall, more than half of all respondents are prepared to pay more for travel in order to use less polluting transport. Men are less prepared than women to pay more to use less polluting transport (Table 9.6) and more women than men are prepared to pay above 10 per cent more for travel in order to use less polluting transport. However, somewhat at odds with this is the statistic that more men than women are prepared to pay up to 10 per cent more for travel in order to use less polluting transport. Older respondents are the least prepared to pay more to use less polluting transport. Younger and more educated respondents are the most prepared to pay more for travel in order to use less polluting transport.

Preparedness to pay for congestion through road tolls is also examined in the 2007 Eurobarometer Survey. Just over a third of all respondents agree that road users should pay for congestion through road tolls (Table 9.7). There is little difference between men and women in support for road tolls to pay for congestion and environmental damage. Younger and more educated respondents are more likely to favour road tolls; older respondents and those who have received less education are least likely to favour such tolls.

Table 9.6   Preparedness to pay more to use less polluting transport according to the socio-economic characteristics of respondents

	Not prepared to pay more (%)	Prepared to pay up to 10% more (%)	Prepared to pay above 10% more (%)	DK/NA
Sex:				
Male	43.2	42.3	10.8	3.7
Female	38.9	47.9	7.7	5.5
Age:				
15–24	34.4	49.7	12.1	3.8
25–39	40.5	45.7	10.3	3.4
40–54	41.2	46.9	8.3	3.7
55+	43.8	41.6	7.8	6.8
Age of completing education:				
15	46.5	40.7	4.9	7.9
16–20	44.3	44.5	7.1	4.0
20+	35.5	47.2	14.0	3.2
EU27	41.0	45.2	9.2	4.6

Source: European Commission (2007b).

Table 9.7   Opinions about whether road users should pay for congestion and environmental damage through road tolls according to the socio-economic characteristics of respondents

	Agree (%)	Disagree (%)	DK/NA
Sex:			
Male	34.9	60.8	4.3
Female	34.5	58.9	6.6
Age:			
15–24	41.2	55.9	2.9
25–39	34.7	61.7	3.6
40–54	32.3	63.0	4.7
55+	33.9	57.3	8.7
Age of completing education:			
15	32.7	58.0	9.3
16–20	32.0	62.7	5.3
20+	36.1	60.3	3.6
EU27	34.7	59.8	5.5

Source: European Commission (2007b).

Conclusions

In the United Kingdom and in the Netherlands, as in most countries, transport energy use and CO_2 emissions continue to grow and may thwart the achievement of the national greenhouse gas emission target agreed at Kyoto as well as the European Union's more recent greenhouse gas reduction target for 2020. The transport sector in both countries is currently responsible for about a fifth to a quarter of all national CO_2 emissions, and passenger transport currently accounts for more than half of the greenhouse gas emissions from this sector. While car-based trips dominate CO_2 emissions from passenger transport, only around half of all trips in the Netherlands and 60 per cent of all trips in the UK are made by car. Thus, certain trips produce a disproportionately high amount of CO_2 emissions whilst other trips produce zero emissions.

Using the UK and the Dutch National Travel Survey, this chapter has identified trends in transport-related CO_2 emissions over time and examined the relationships between individual CO_2 emissions and socio-economic variables. The analysis results reveal that the proportion of individuals with zero-emissions from transport in the Netherlands has consistently stayed around the 30 per cent mark and actually increased slightly between 1990 and 2005. Respondents in the highest quintile produce more than four times the average amount of CO_2 emissions whilst those in the lowest quintile produce less than a quarter of the average amount of CO_2 emissions. The difference in average CO_2 emissions between the highest and lowest quintile is typically around 20-fold. There is thus a relatively large proportion of people producing very low quantities of CO_2 emissions, and a small proportion of people producing the majority of the emissions: half the population is responsible for about 10 per cent of travel-related CO_2 emissions whilst another 10 per cent of the population is responsible for almost half of all travel-related CO_2 emissions. While in the UK, 60 per cent of the population is responsible of 20 per cent of the emissions whilst another 20 per cent of the population is responsible of the 60 per cent of the CO_2 emissions.

The socio-economic characteristics of the six different categories of respondents grouped according to their travel-related CO_2 emissions are in line with results of other studies into the socio-demographics of transport emissions (Anable et al. 1997; Brand and Boardman 2008; Greening et al. 1997; Greening 2004). Recent European public opinion surveys on transport policy reveal that attitudes regarding policies for reducing transport-related energy and CO_2 emissions vary quite considerably across different socio-economic groups. In some cases, the groups responsible for high CO_2 emissions are the most supportive of measures to reduce these emissions. Similar findings were noted some decades ago by Crossley (1983) with respect to household energy consumption, when he reported a tendency for people 'with attitudes in favour of energy conservation to actually use more energy in the home' (Crossley 1983: 538). In the case of other types of policies however the opposite is true: the groups responsible for high CO_2 emissions are the least supportive of measures to reduce these emissions, especially measures that primarily impact upon the group's own travel choices (rather than measures that mainly affect other groups).

One of the implications of the results is that the reduction of CO_2 emissions in the upper quintile by a given proportion (say 10 per cent) will lead to a larger reduction of CO_2 emissions than a reduction of CO_2 emissions by the same proportion for all other four quintiles. Achieving reductions in the upper quintile is not likely to be easy however. Various instruments (e.g. fuel pricing, vehicle inspection and maintenance programmes) are considered to be regressive which may therefore affect the greatest emitters the least. Achieving reductions in the upper quintile requires a targeted approach using policies that are specific to the characteristics of the individuals in this category (e.g. multiple car owners, regular car-drivers, frequent flyers), such as taxation on multiple car ownership, incentives for shared vehicle ownership, reductions in speed limits and fiscal incentives for using alternative modes of transport. If nothing else, we hope that this chapter has helped to understand the current distribution of transport-related CO_2 emissions in parts of Europe, and has stimulated the need for more debate about targeted policies to address individual emissions.

Chapter 10

Modelling the Potential Transport CO_2 Mitigation Impacts of Available Policy Interventions

Robin Hickman, David Banister and Olu Ashiru

Introduction

Transport policy analysis is facing new challenges. In the past, it has been possible to take a short term perspective and assess options over a relatively short period on time (5–10 years), perhaps discounting over a longer period (30 years). With the new focus on climate change and the need to reduce levels of carbon consumption in transport, different analytical approaches are required. The future appears uncertain in many respects and analyses need to incorporate the potential for different future projections. This covers issues related to climate change, health, wider environmental factors, low carbon energy supply, security of energy supply and most recently financial meltdown. Recent difficulties in finding a consensus for change at the international level (cf. Copenhagen) means that the onus has also moved to national and city governments to develop more local strategies for carbon efficient lifestyles.

The use of scenario analysis can be important in this respect, as it is accepted that the long term (and possibly now even the short term) is subject to rapidly changing events, and the risks of following particular paths become much higher, or pathways may become redundant after important events. Scenarios allow different 'visions of the future' to be identified and discussed, and pathways to be developed that meet strategic objectives through the combination of a range of policy options. There is an explicit recognition of future uncertainty and risks associated with following particular pathways.

This chapter considers some of the issues involved in scenario building and presents a selection of likely impacts resulting from a range of different policy interventions promoted individually and in combination. It draws on work carried out in *the VIBAT-London project (Visioning and Backcasting for Transport in London[1]), hence is based on the London context. The study examines what* actions will need to be taken in London, both in behavioural and technological terms, to reach carbon dioxide (CO_2) emission reductions in the transport sector of 60 per cent by 2025 and 80 per cent by 2050 (as compared with 1990 levels). *A transport and carbon simulation model (TC-SIM)* is developed within the project, and this allows users to simulate changes to different aspects of the transport sector, and to create alternative pathways to reduced CO_2 emissions. The backcasting approach is used in the analysis, where future images of the future are developed and analysed by 'casting back' policy pathways to current years. A strategy and programme to achieve a forward-looking aspiration can hence be developed. The commentary in this chapter is developed in five key sections as follows:

- Developing the baseline;
- Modelling approach;
- Modelling assumptions and potential impacts by policy package;
- Towards 'optimum' packaging;
- Conclusions and unresolved issues.

Developing the Baseline

The type of thinking and approaches used in scenario analysis have become increasingly relevant in the light of recent events in the financial markets and the need for huge amounts of capital to be pumped into the banking sector, and the consequent impacts on the world economy, growth and employment levels, and uncertainty and confidence. The conventional assumption in forecasting approaches, and the starting point for the backcasting approach, is to develop a 'business as usual' (BAU) projection, based on different assumptions in the growth of gross domestic product (GDP) and other factors. The current economic climate suggests that GDP will contract and that the previously assumed levels of growth will be much lower in the future, at least in the next 10–15 years (Rothengatter 2009). This may mean that it becomes 'easier' to achieve challenging targets for CO_2 reduction, as the BAU is lowered. This new dimension needs to be built into all scenario analyses and models. In addition, it is becoming clear that travel is not only related to changes in GDP, but more importantly to the changes in global trade,

---

1   The VIBAT London project (Hickman et al. 2009a) was carried out by the Halcrow Group; University of Oxford, Transport Studies Unit; and Space Syntax. It was funded by the UrbanBuzz programme (www.urbanbuzz.org). More details can be found at the project website: www.vibat.org.

in real income levels and aspirations. The growth in long distance international freight (and aviation) is driven largely by trade growth, and the shorter distance travel (and aviation for leisure travel) by increases in income levels. New thinking is required to understand the potential for change, and this type of flexibility is embedded in the London study. There is a real opportunity under the changed economic circumstances, with constrained financial opportunities, to conceive transport planning in a different manner. The 'optimality criterion' used within the following analysis relates only to transport CO_2 reduction, but there are of course wider aspirations within the general sustainability objective.

The first stage of the assessment is to understand historical CO_2 emissions in the transport sector in London and to project a BAU future. Considering ground-based transport in London only (ignoring external travel and international air and shipping travel), this means that emissions in 2006 are at around 9.6 $MtCO_2$ (million tonnes of carbon dioxide), rising to around 11.7 $MtCO_2$ by 2025. The increase in transport emissions under the BAU scenario is largely due to the forecast population increase, as per capita emissions remain similar. London is quite different to many places in the UK and further afield; per capita traffic growth has been flat in recent years, even in outer London. Even modest traffic growth levels might be further reduced over the next 15 years by lower levels of income growth and higher levels of unemployment in London.

London's Climate Change Action Plan (CCAP) (GLA 2007) adopts a cross-sectoral 60 per cent CO_2 emission reduction target by 2025 on 1990 levels. This was adopted as a forerunner to the current UK national target for an 80 per cent reduction in CO_2 emissions by 2050 on 1990 levels (Climate Change Act 2008). The VIBAT London project assumes the transport sector delivers its 'fair share' of the 60 per cent reduction target by 2025 and 80 per cent by 2050 – an ambitious assumption. The gap between BAU projections and strategic target is dramatic, both in terms of its scale and in terms of the increased uncertainty of the trends. In addition, there is the need for policy makers to have a clear understanding of the likely mitigation impacts that can be achieved from the available policy interventions.[2]

---

2   A parallel measurement of CO_2 emissions would also include the development of carbon budgets – the 'area under the line' – and this may lead us towards a quicker response to reducing emissions. The temptation with end state targets is to delay the response. This chapter however concentrates on achievement against end state targets.

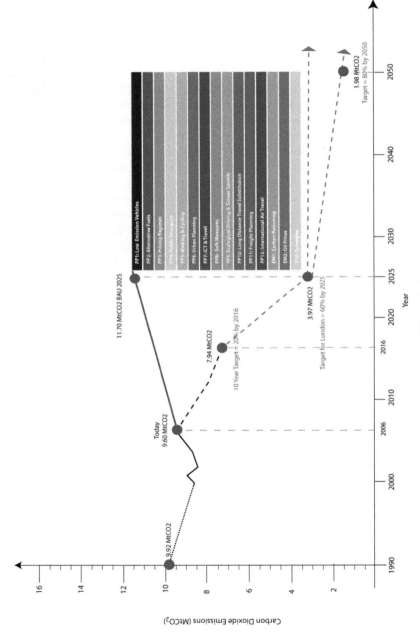

Figure 10.1 Available interventions to reduce transport CO$_2$ emissions

The range of interventions on offer in the transport sector is very wide. An inventory of measures has been developed, covering over 150 individual policy measures. These are then grouped, where mutually consistent and complementary, into policy packages (PP). These include:

- PP1: Low emission vehicles
- PP2: Alternative fuels
- PP3: Pricing regimes
- PP4: Public transport
- PP5: Walking and cycling
- PP6: Strategic and local urban planning
- PP7: Information and communication technologies (ICT)
- PP8: Smarter choice soft measures
- PP9: Slower speeds and ecological driving
- PP10: Long distance travel substitution
- PP11: Freight transport

Each policy package can be applied at a variety of levels of intensity – typically simplified as a 'low', 'medium' or 'high' level of application. Each will deliver a different level of CO_2 mitigation relative to the baseline and projected BAU transport emissions (Figure 10.1), over different periods of time. Hence the analysis incorporates some of the 'carbon wedge' mitigation thinking, as developed by Pacala and Socolow (2004), into the backcasting methodology. A grouping of policy packages, at particular levels of application, is conceived here as a 'scenario'.

Modelling Approach

In general it can be assumed that any intervention aimed at reducing transport CO_2 emissions will be targeted at one or more of the following travel metrics, which are seen to be central to the sustainable mobility paradigm (Banister 2008).

- Reduction in the number of trips
- Reduced trip length
- Mode shift
- Increased vehicle efficiency and occupancy

Each of the policy packages also impacts upon one or more of the above. Composite CO_2 emission impacts can be calculated by scenario. The modelling behind TC-SIM has been developed to allow quantification of the potential impacts of a range of policy interventions in multiple combinations. Table 10.1 outlines the approach taken to modelling the impacts of policy packages.

Table 10.1   Assumed impacts by policy package

Policy Package	Reduced Trip Length	Mode Shift	Fewer Trips	Increased Vehicle Efficiency	Composite CO_2 Emissions
PP1: Low emission vehicles	–	–	–	□	□
PP2: Alternative Fuels	–	–	–	□	□
PP3: Pricing Regimes	□	□	□	?	□
PP4: Public Transport	–	□	–	–	□
PP5: Walking and Cycling	–	□	–	–	□
PP6: Urban Planning	?	□	□	–	□
PP7: Information and Communication Technologies	?	?	□	?	□
PP8: Smarter Choice 'Soft' Measures	?	□	□	–	□
PP9: Ecological Driving and Slower Speeds	–	–	–	□	□
PP10: Long Distance Travel Substitution	–	□	–	–	□
PP11: Freight Planning	□	□	□	–	□

Notes: □ Modelled within TC-SIM London v.3; ? Not modelled, but potential impact; – Assumed no impact.

For example, PP1 low emission vehicles and PP2 alternative fuels only impact on vehicle efficiency; PP3 impact on reduced trip length, mode shift, fewer trips and potentially vehicle efficiency (the latter is not modelled in TC-SIM London).

A range of data sources are used within the modelling, including commissioned runs from a highway model (the London Travel Survey strategic model, LTS) and a public transport model (Railplan),[3] based largely on scenarios from T2025 – particularly the reference case Scenario 1 and full programme Scenario 4. Other datasets used within the modelling include the latest Department for Transport (DfT 2008) vehicle/speed CO_2 emission factors, Department for the Environment, Food and Rural Affairs (DEFRA) modal CO_2 emission factors and London Plan (GLA 2009) spatial planning assumptions. More details of the schemes assumed under the business as usual (BAU) reference case and Scenarios 1 and 4 are included in the Annex. The following system architecture is used within the modelling:

---

3   Both models are developed and run by Transport for London and associated consultants.

- A Flash based active-x graphical user interface;
- Data input and underlying modelling assumptions provided by means of a comma separated text file and an xml file;
- Comma separated text file contents are provided by a detailed spreadsheet based Transport Carbon Calculator (TC-SIM CALC).

For all policy packages and enabling mechanisms the CO_2 reductions are computed relative to the BAU reference case. This is conventionally driven by assumed GDP growth rather than the more uncertain future that is now faced with negative or low growth rates. If no policy package is selected this is the equivalent of selecting the BAU option. Tailpipe emissions only are considered, and travel only within the Greater London boundary. More details on the modelling methodology are available in a working paper (Ashiru et al. 2009).

Modelling Assumptions and Potential Impacts by Policy Package

The policy packages are considered below in terms of assumptions by level of application, with comparative benchmarks, most likely trajectory[4] and aspiration.[5]

PP1: Low Emission Vehicles

The take up of low emission vehicles, based largely on hybrid technology, is likely to be very important to reducing emissions. Because most CO_2 emissions derive from the car fleet, the achievement of targets is greatly reliant on the penetration rates of low emission vehicles into the fleet. Full introduction of an average car fleet of <100 gCO_2/km by 2025 and/or 2050 requires massive investment by car manufacturers and changes to consumer purchasing patterns.

The current best generations of new vehicles have emissions levels of below or around 100 gCO_2/km (the Toyota Prius hybrid emits 89 gCO_2/km; the Volkswagen Polo Blue Motion diesel emits 91 gCO_2/km). Relying on the low emission vehicle option may be high risk as there is no guarantee that the vehicles will penetrate the market to any great degree. The current consumer trend in the UK is for higher specification and heavier vehicles, which emit more CO_2, though there has been a recent preference for buying smaller vehicles, perhaps as a response to the recession. Recent reductions in average fleet CO_2 emissions have largely been due to dieselization rather than the introduction of hybrids, and diesels tend to be driven for longer distances. There are major issues concerning the costs and

---

4   Based on authors' view of current trend and/or investment pattern.

5   Defined as minimum requirement to achieve 'optimised balance' strategic package delivering a 60 per cent reduction in transport CO_2 emissions on 1990 levels. Wherever possible implementation should aim to deliver a higher level of application to cover the eventuality that implementation is not as successful as we envisage.

feasibility of converting the whole of the London car fleet to hybrids, and a poor understanding of incentives required to allow mass market take up. There are, however, major roles here for the UK and EU governments in terms of legislating for mandatory emission targets, the motor industry in delivering them, and for changes in consumer purchasing patterns. For London, the major legislative changes required concerning this policy package fall beyond the Mayoral remit, i.e. rely on the EU or UK governments to act. London has to concentrate on applying complementary measures – low emission zones, preferential parking areas for low emission vehicles, or perhaps altering the specification of the congestion charge to focus on emissions, and applying this over a wider area (see discussion under Policy Package 3).

Table 10.2   PP1: low emission cars assumptions

Variant 1: Passenger Fleet Cars	
Benchmarks	Example vehicle emissions factors: Toyota Prius, hybrid 1.8l, 89 gCO_2/km; Volkswagen Polo Blue Motion, diesel 1.2l, 91 gCO_2/km; Vauxhall Corsa, petrol 1.2l, 137 gCO_2/km; Volkswagen Golf, petrol 1.4l, 149 gCO_2/km; Renault Espace, diesel 2l, 196 gCO_2/km; BMW 5-series, petrol A8, 178 gCO_2/km; Maserati Granturismo, petrol M6, 385 gCO_2/km; Ferrari 612 Scaglietti, petrol, 470 gC)2/km. Average total passenger car emissions in the UK are around 175 gCO_2/km (2010).
Most likely trajectory[1] to 2025	120–130 gCO_2/km
Aspiration to 2025	120–130 gCO_2/km

Variant 2: Heavy Goods Vehicles	
Benchmarks	The more fuel efficient HGVs emit <1,000 gCO_2/km (fully loaded) Average HGV CO_2 emissions are around 1,100 gCO_2/km. Often tonne-km metrics are used within freight analysis.
Most likely trajectory to 2025:	900 gCO_2/km
Aspiration to 2025:	750–800 gCO_2/km

Note: [1] that these 'trajectory' and 'aspirational' figures apply to the total vehicle stock and not just new vehicles as highlighted in the 'benchmarks' and new EU regulations.

PP2: Alternative Fuels

Additional benefits can be obtained if alternative fuels are used in conjunction with petrol and diesel hybrids. There are many possible alternative fuels on the market – including compressed natural gas, liquid petroleum gas, methanol, ethanol, biodiesel, hydrogen and electricity (Khare and Sharma 2003). Many alternative fuels can be used on their own; others can be blended with existing fuels and used in vehicles without any major modifications to the engines. The International Energy Agency (2004, 2009) suggests that, by 2030, some 20–50 per cent of all fuels in transport could come from alternative sources, though this is now assumed to be very optimistic. Major issues here are the land take and water consumption, and the infrastructure required to support mass market use of alternative fuels. More recent estimates assume 5–10 per cent of fuel sold as alternatively fuelled would be more realistic. The electric car has much potential, for city driving in particular. In London the G-Wiz is available, and theoretically could emit (virtually) zero emissions if the source electricity was clean. There are major issues however to be overcome in developing electric vehicles that are attractive and deliverable to the mass market.

Table 10.3   PP2: alternative fuels

Benchmarks	Alternative fuel penetration is impressive in some countries, e.g. Brazil (50% ethanol using 'flex' vehicles which run on a proportion of gasoline and ethanol). Current UK levels are at 2–3%. The RFA (2009) recommends a limit of 5% renewable transport fuel by volume by 2013.

Most likely trajectory to 2025:

Variant 1: Car
0–35% total fleet alternative fuelled – 5% as most likely, 'low-medium' application.
TC-SIM modelling assumes:

Fuel Type	BAU	Low	Medium	High
Petrol	85%	80%	60%	35%
Diesel	15%	20%	25%	30%
LPG	0%	0%	5%	10%
Electric	0%	0%	5%	10%
Biofuel	0%	0%	5%	10%
Hydrogen	0%	0%	0%	5%
Total	100%	100%	100%	100%

Variant 2: HGV Freight
0–50% total fleet alternative fuelled – 10% as most likely, 'low-medium' application.
TC-SIM modelling assumes:

Fuel Type	BAU	Low	Medium	High
Petrol	0%	0%	0%	0%
Diesel	100%	95%	75%	50%
LPG	0%	5%	5%	10%
Electric	0%	0%	10%	15%
Biofuel	0%	0%	10%	15%
Hydrogen	0%	0%	0%	10%
Total	100%	100%	100%	100%

Variant 3: Bus
0–40% total fleet alternative fuelled – 15% as most likely, 'low-medium' application.
TC-SIM modelling assumes:

Fuel Type	BAU	Low	Medium	High
Petrol	0%	0%	0%	0%
Diesel	100%	95%	60%	0%
LPG	0%	0%	5%	0%
Electric	0%	0%	5%	0%
Biofuel	0%	5%	30%	90%
Hydrogen	0%	0%	0%	10%
Total	100%	100%	100%	100%

Aspiration to 2025:	Over 15% of the car fleet, 40% HGV fleet and 40% bus fleet are alternative fuelled, assuming land take issues can be resolved.

PP3: Pricing Regimes

Congestion charging or area-wide road pricing can also make a substantial difference to travel behaviour, whether operated within central London or beyond. In combination with other policies, road pricing on an environmental basis (i.e. the charging relates to the carbon emissions profile of the vehicle and the number of passengers), can give clear signals to consumers to switch to more efficient cars or to other modes of transport.

Table 10.4   PP3: pricing regimes

Benchmarks	The existing congestion charge scheme covers part of central London (western extension has been removed).
Most likely trajectory to 2025:	Continuation of present scheme – political difficulties in widening application. TC-SIM modelling assumes: • Variant 1: Existing congestion charging scheme (Reference) • Variant 2: Greater London-wide congestion charging scheme (congestion based) – (a) Inner London and (b) Outer London • Variant 3: Greater London-wide congestion charging scheme (emissions based) – (a) Inner London and (b) Outer London • Variant 4: Private parking charging schemes (independent to variants 1–3)
Aspiration to 2025:	London wide emissions-based scheme as part of a wider UK emission-based pricing scheme.

PP4: Public Transport

Public transport investment is critical in allowing consumers to choose carbon efficient means of travel. There is already an extensive public transport network in London, with extensive investment plans in the current T2025 Reference Case (2007 Spending Review), and larger still in the later scenarios within Transport 2025 (T2025) (TfL 2006).

Table 10.5   PP4: public transport

Benchmarks	Current high level of investment. Crossrail, the east-west rail link across London, will add 10% to the overall capacity of the public transport network and an additional 5.8 million passenger kilometres to peak capacity. The full Rail 2025 proposals will increase capacity on the rail network by 35–40%. The Public Private Partnership (PPP) package on the Underground network (LU) will deliver an average capacity enhancement of 25% across the LU (TfL, 2006).
Most likely trajectory to 2025:	Potentially Scenario 4 within T2025. TC-SIM modelling assumes: • Variant 1: business as usual application (T2025 Reference Case investment strategy), • Variant 2: medium intensity application (T2025 Scenario 4 investment strategy), e.g. including Crossrail, • Variant 3: high intensity application (T2025 Scenario 4+ investment strategy), e.g. including potential LRT schemes in outer London, • Variant 4: fare level reductions (independent to variant 1–3).
Aspiration to 2025:	Higher level of investment than T2025 Scenario 4.

Note: See Annex 10.1 for list of schemes by scenario.

PP5: Walking and Cycling

Similarly, investment in walking and cycling facilities and the streetscape and public realm makes carbon efficient means of travel more attractive, particularly for short journeys. London-wide, people make seven million journeys on foot every day. Walking is hence an important means of travel, and accounts for about 25 per cent of all London's journeys (GLA 2009). Despite this, investment in the pedestrian environment is traditionally low relative to other modes. London's streets need to be made more amenable and attractive in design terms to encourage pedestrian use and there are many initiatives underway. The growth of cycling in London is critical for attracting trips from the private car and, perhaps to a lesser extent, the public transport network. Less than 2 per cent of trips in London are made by bicycle, compared with 28 per cent in Amsterdam (GLA 2009).

Increased cycling (and walking) provides benefits through reduced congestion, pollution and improved health. There is already a fairly extensive walking and cycling network in London, with some investment plans in the T2025 Reference Case, and larger still in the later scenarios in T2025.

Table 10.6   PP5: walking and cycling

Benchmarks	Relatively good walking and cycling facilities and networks in London, however limited compared to some continental European practice.
Most likely trajectory to 2025:	Potentially Scenario 4 within T2025. TC-SIM modelling assumes: • Variant 1: business as usual application (T2025 Reference Case investment strategy), • Variant 2: medium intensity application (T2025 Scenario 4 investment strategy), e.g. including cycle hire scheme and London Cycle Network investment, • Variant 3: high intensity application (T2025 Scenario 4+ investment strategy), e.g. including additional London Cycle Network investment.
Aspiration to 2025:	Much higher level of investment than T2025 Scenario 4.

PP6: Urban Planning

Urban spatial structure, at the strategic and local scales, can be extremely influential in determining the main characteristics of travel – the numbers of trips made, journey lengths and mode share. Urban structure thus provides the underlying 'physical rationale' for travel (and consequently a major part of transport CO_2 emissions), alongside wider influences such as socio-economic and attitudinal/cultural characteristics. Despite this, urban planning is often underplayed as a tool in traffic demand management strategies (Banister and Hickman 2006; Hickman and Banister 2007). Dispersed and low densities, which are evident in suburban areas in London, certain preclude the use of public transport, walking and cycling, and tend to facilitate private car dependency.

This package focuses on using urban structure to support sustainable transport, with higher density development clustered around an upgraded public transport system, and urban areas master planned to vastly improve their urban design quality and attractiveness for living and working, and use of walking and cycling (Hickman et al. 2009c). There is complementary heavy investment in public transport and walking and cycling facilities. Extensive application of this package has a major impact, but largely over the medium term, as decisions on the location of new housing and other developments, take place gradually over time. These decisions have a substantial effect on both distances travelled and modes used.

Table 10.7   PP6: urban planning

Benchmarks	The London Plan develops higher density and growth aspirations, with some focus on outer town centres, but majority of growth planned in the Central Activities Zone and east London.
Most likely trajectory to 2025:	London Plan strategy TC-SIM modelling assumes: • Variant 1: business as usual application (London Plan), • Variant 2: medium intensity application (London Plan +), e.g. including higher densities around key public transport interchanges and improved public realm, • Variant 3: high intensity application (London Plan ++), e.g. including higher densities around public transport interchanges in outer London and improved public realm.
Aspiration to 2025:	Much greater use of urban structure, beyond even the aspirations of the London Plan, with greater intensity of development in certain locations, including outer areas, to encourage use of public transport, walking and cycling. An 'urban structure index' and strategy can be developed to optimize the application of density, settlement size, development location, mix of use, jobs-housing balance, accessibility and street layout in order to enable sustainable travel (Hickman et al. 2009c).

PP7: Information and Communications Technology (ICT)

This option explores the potential for CO_2 reduction through the application of ICT, either in or on travel. The former includes measures to increase operating efficiency and vehicle occupancies, and the latter measures that reduce travel by providing an electronic alternative to physical travel. The current application of these types of measures is at very low/formative levels of 'intensity' and the levels of transport CO_2 reduction are limited. Travel tends to adapt, with different types of activity taking place, including more travel in many places, rather than a simple substitution of physical travel for electronic interaction. Hence the rebound effects tend to be large here. There is more potential in future years as the 'network society' is developed and becomes established.

Table 10.8   PP7: information and communications technology (ICT)

Benchmarks	This type of activity is largely unexplored in the transport sector, or at least not well understood, in terms of potential to reduce transport CO$_2$ emissions. There is experience in telematics and much take up of electronic social interaction means, yet little knowledge as to long term transport CO$_2$ impacts. Certainly the package is not being utilized at the mass market scale to directly influence travel patterns and energy consumption or emissions.
Most likely trajectory to 2025:	Higher level of ICT application than at present, but not particularly targeted at achieving reduced transport CO$_2$ emissions. TC-SIM modelling assumes: • Variant 1: low intensity application – similar low levels of application as at present, • Variant 2: medium intensity application – improved levels of application, with ICT applications used to target the reduction of emissions in and on transport. E.g. telematics applied to directly reduce CO$_2$ emissions, • Variant 3: high intensity application – major change to level of application, with a real focus on using applications used to target the reduction of emissions in and on transport. E.g. local telecentres used to reduce long distance commuting.
Aspiration to 2025:	A high intensity effort to use ICT to reduce transport CO$_2$ emissions.

PP8: Smarter Choice Behavioural Measures

This option includes workplace and school travel plans, future changes in car ownership (including leasing and car clubs), car sharing, travel awareness and personalized travel planning programmes (Cairns et al. 2004). There is some overlap in definition with previous packages, such as ICT. These types of measures provide an important support to other packages, and they also have an important impact on reducing CO$_2$ emissions in their own right.

In implementation terms there is a developing programme – the DfT Sustainable Travel Demonstration Towns programme has implemented smarter choice measures in Darlington, Peterborough and Worcester. The evidence suggests that bus trips have increased by 10–22 per cent, walking trips increased by 10–13 per cent and cycling trips increased by 26–30 per cent. Car trips have reduced by around 9 per cent (Sloman et al. 2010). TfL is similarly implementing smarter choice measures, funding a programme since 2002. £5m is being spent in Sutton as part of the Smarter Travel Sutton programme. The objective here is to reduce car mode share by 5 per cent (TfL 2007).

Table 10.9   PP8: smarter choice 'soft' behavioural measures

Benchmarks	The Sustainable Travel Demonstration Towns programme has led to successful results and offers a model for practice in other areas. More widespread application, spatially and across the population cohorts, has however been slow and is likely to be difficult at the mass market scale.
Most likely trajectory to 2025:	Higher level of application than at present, but still exists as a 'tangential' part to other transport planning. TC-SIM modelling assumes: • Variant 1: low intensity application – similar levels of application as at present, with ad-hoc investments spatially, • Variant 2: medium intensity application – improved levels of application, with behavioural measures seen as central to transport planning. All urban centres receive Smarter Travel Sutton scale of investment, • Variant 3: high intensity application – major effort with behavioural measures applied across whole population; levels of investment and awareness increase.
Aspiration to 2025:	A high intensity effort to use smarter choice measures to reduce transport CO_2 emissions. Behavioural understandings of transport, and subsequent interventions, become central to the transport planning discipline.

PP9: Slower Speeds and Ecological Driving

Much of conventional thinking in transport is designed to speed traffic up, as congestion and delay are seen as 'wasted' time, resulting in loss of time that could be productively used on other activities. It has, however, been demonstrated that lower speed limits, and less lane switching, may allow traffic to flow more smoothly, thereby increasing capacity. There has been a clear move towards lowering speed limits in residential areas (home zones) and in other locations (e.g. around schools or on routes with important design quality), where priority has been reallocated to people. Lower speed limits can also have major safety benefits. Potter et al. (2001) advise that drivers of both cars and goods vehicles could typically save between 5–10 per cent on their fuel bills by adopting more fuel-efficient driving behaviour, and in some cases, a 20 per cent improvement in fuel economy could be achieved. There are therefore strong incentives to reduce the speed of vehicles from certain perspectives in some locations.

Lower speeds need to be combined with awareness programmes and better driving techniques to reduce fuel use. Ecological driving skills have been developed in the Netherlands and Germany and include simple measures such as driving at moderate speeds, avoiding excessive acceleration and harsh braking, changing gears at low engine revolutions, driving in the highest comfortable gear at any given speed, avoiding unnecessary use of in-car equipment (especially air conditioning), keeping tyres inflated and reducing unnecessary loads.

This package has the potential for substantial immediate and long term benefits if take up is high in terms of reduced speeds and changed driving styles. Slower speeds provide extensive savings, for example, with potential for some 15–20 per cent reduction in carbon emissions if a maximum speed limit of 80 km/hr is introduced on motorways and trunk roads, with lower speeds on other roads (with effective compliance). Although the fuel use and speed value curves for new cars are flatter than those for older cars, there are considerable fuel savings from lower speeds. The difficulty with this package, similar to many other packages, is in effective implementation and enforcement in the mainstream market.

Table 10.10   PP9: slower speeds and ecological driving

Benchmarks	Some slower speeds in residential areas in London, but not on strategic route network. Some ecological driving practice in the Netherlands and Germany, and developing niche activities in the UK.
Most likely trajectory to 2025:	Higher level of slower speeds and ecological driving application than at present, but remains a 'low intensity' effort. TC-SIM modelling assumes: • Variant 1: low intensity application – similar levels of application as at present. Limited use of home zones and slower speed limits in selected residential areas, • Variant 2: medium intensity application – improved levels of application. 20 mph zones across all residential areas and ecological driving training, • Variant 3: high intensity application – widespread take up of ecological driving and lower traffic speeds throughout London. Measures applied across whole population; levels of awareness increase.
Aspiration to 2025:	A high intensity effort to use ecological driving and slower speeds, targeted at reducing transport CO_2 emissions

PP10: Long Distance Travel Substitution

This package deals with long distance travel within London, and considers the Greater London part of the journey only (the extent of the trip within the urban area boundary). The increase in long distance travel within the UK, particularly by short haul air travel and air freight transport, causes particular concern for CO_2 emissions. The modal share of air transport is still very low but growth rates are much above those of all other modes. Also air transport is operating with a type of 'extraterritorial' status, being exempted from taxes that in national contexts are charged to all other modes. Long range leisure travel and airborne freight transport are growing at a high speed on the basis of the present cost situation. As increasingly important economic structures are relying on cheap air transport, attempts to internalize at least a part of the considerable externalities will become increasingly difficult in future years. Individuals are also becoming used to the availability of inexpensive, short-haul flights. This growth is being driven by growth in real income levels and in the globalization of economies, at least until recently. Rail has the potential to offer a serious alternative to air travel over distances of around 300–500km, particularly if High Speed Train (HST). The considerable improvements brought by HST on a limited number of national and international routes, together with faster services on existing infrastructure (e.g. with tilting technology and new signalling), technical harmonization, organizational cooperation and strongly improved conditions for competition, means that there is considerable potential for long-distance rail-air substitution (beyond the current Eurostar service) and even co-operation with HST serving air travel for longer distance travel.

Table 10.11   PP10: long distance travel substitution

Benchmarks	Some use of HST (Eurostar), but limited HST networks in the UK. More extensive networks in continental Europe.
Most likely trajectory to 2025:	Higher level of travel substitution application than at present, but remains a 'low intensity' effort. TC-SIM modelling assumes: • Variant 1: low intensity application – similar levels of investment as at present, • Variant 2: medium intensity application – selective one or two new routes targeted with HST investment, • Variant 3: high intensity application – dense network of HST targeted at reducing transport CO$_2$ emissions.
Aspiration to 2025:	A high intensity effort to use travel substitution to reduce transport CO$_2$ emissions.

PP11: Freight Transport

The freight sector has a major role to play in helping to reduce transport sector CO$_2$ emissions. McKinnon (2007) gives a good overview of the issues. Load factors are particularly important in the freight sector – the use of average emission factors in analysis can over simplify the analysis. In terms of the prevailing trends, HGV CO$_2$ emissions account for the highest proportion of freight emissions (79 per cent). They appear to have risen by over 5 per cent between 1990 and 2005. There are, however, some difficulties in finding good quality data in this sector, hence uncertainties remain as to the trends. A declining CO$_2$ intensity per tonne-km for HGVs can be attributed to a reduction in empty running, net consolidation of loads and improved fuel efficiency. Aggregate emissions continue to rise over time.

There is a range of measures to help reduce emissions in the freight sector. McKinnon discusses a number of areas, including improving handling factors (number of links in the supply chain), reducing length of haul, improving mode share, proportion of empty running, fuel efficiency and choice of fuel/power source. These can be considered in terms of subsidiarity (local production and knowledge transfer) and dematerialization (miniaturization, advanced logistics and distribution networks, load matching and material consumption). All can lead to savings, some substantial.

Table 10.12   PP11: freight transport

Benchmarks	Limited understanding of sector and application of measures to reduce CO_2 emissions.
Most likely trajectory to 2025:	Higher level of package application than at present, but remains a 'low intensity' effort. TC-SIM modelling assumes: • Variant 1: low intensity application – similar levels of application as at present, • Variant 2: medium intensity application – greater focus on improved handling factors, reduced empty running, fuel efficiency and improved mode share, • Variant 3: high intensity application – much improved handling factors, reduced empty running, fuel efficiency and improved mode share targeted at reducing transport CO_2 emissions.
Aspiration to 2025:	A high intensity effort to use freight transport planning to reduce transport CO_2 emissions.

Towards 'Optimum' Packaging

The TC-SIM model for London allows us to select different pathways towards carbon efficiency in the transport sector. Different policy approaches can be selected and optimized as to their efficacy in reducing CO_2 emissions. There can also be consideration of political realism, i.e. what can be implemented. The level of emissions reduction we want to achieve is selected and the variety of policy measures (both technological and behavioural) are examined so that the most effective combinations can be selected. There are multiple future policy pathways available.

Table 10.13 'Optimized balance'

Policy package	Comment	% of VIBAT London target by 2025
PP1: Low Emission Vehicles	High: 100g CO_2/km car fleet; 800g CO_2/km heavy goods vehicles	18.3
PP2: Alternative Fuels	Car low, Freight medium, Bus medium	2.0
PP3: Pricing Regimes	Emissions charging scheme – high; medium parking charging	9.9
PP4: Public Transport	High investment strategy; medium fare reduction	11.3
PP5: Walking and Cycling	High	2.1
PP6: Urban Planning	High	3.9
PP7: ICT	Medium	1.0
PP8: Smarter Choice Soft Measures	Medium	1.6
PP9: Slower Speeds and Ecological Driving	Medium	3.1
PP10: Long Distance Travel Substitution	Medium	0.6
PP11: Freight Transport	High	1.3
EM2 Oil Price	High – $140 barrel	5.1
Progress against VIBAT London target (60 per cent reduction in CO_2 emissions)		60.3

Note: Within the BAU for London, the T2025 Reference Case (Scenario 1) is normally used'; * An additive principle is mainly used in the modelling – assuming additive impacts.

The difficulty soon apparent is that very considerable efforts are required across the whole range of policy packages if strategic targets are to be met. As noted previously, the targets may be more easily achieved if the expected growth rates in the economy are lower than anticipated.

There is uncertainty over the scale of change required, given the longer term expectations of economic growth and the shorter term realities of reduced growth. Whichever future happens, there is a need to develop incentives and mechanisms for changing behaviour. These incentives include the successful delivery of low emission vehicles; and much greater investment in public transport, walking and cycling; more efficient designs for urban form and neighbourhoods; smarter choice behavioural measures, for a range of different stakeholders (involving businesses, schools, hospitals, the public sector, as well as individuals); slower speeds and ecological driving; and carbon efficiency in freight.

The strategy discussed here is to take a very ambitious approach and use all policy levers available to (almost) the full potential. The assumption within the simulation is that a very high degree of successful implementation is possible. This enhances the CO_2 reduction potential of the optimized strategy and hence this attains the target of a 60 per cent reduction in CO_2 emissions (Table 10.13, Figures 10.2 and 10.3).

The optimized strategy envisages that a deep reduction in CO_2 emissions will only result if large gains are achieved from both technological and behavioural change. Individuals have high concern for the negative effects of car use, and believe that urban liveability and lifestyles will improve if public transport, walking and cycling are used to a much greater degree. They are concerned that we will not achieve the forecast gains in technology and behavioural change. They see holding vehicle km (at present levels), with large gains from technology, as the best way to achieve CO_2 reduction targets. The findings are thus positive: the strategy achieves the required 60 per cent reduction target. However, the inclusion of the vast majority of packages applied to a high level of application may be very unrealistic and ambitious (certainly based on previous experience of application).

The scenario also shows the high interrelationships between supposedly distinct technological and behavioural measures. Many options – for example the penetration of low emission vehicles into the vehicle fleet – involve technological dimensions (the development of new car technologies) and behavioural (changed consumer purchase patterns). The technological-behavioural dichotomy is thus a little misleading and distracting. Perhaps a more important point, and the key conclusion, is that a 60 per cent emission reduction is possible in the transport sector in London. But this requires major effort, including investment beyond that considered even in T2025 Scenario 4 (which was itself a very ambitious strategy). Exhortation at the margins will not lead to the required level of change in travel behaviour and transport CO_2 reduction – i.e. we need to move beyond simply 'encouraging' people to change their behaviour. London is one of the leading cities in investing in public transport and in charging for car use. But even here, there is a long way to go. Achieving deeper cuts – up to 80 per cent and 90 per cent – would be exceedingly difficult in the transport sector. Much of travel would need to be electric and clean, and much more local, and/or involve higher levels of electronic interaction than at present.

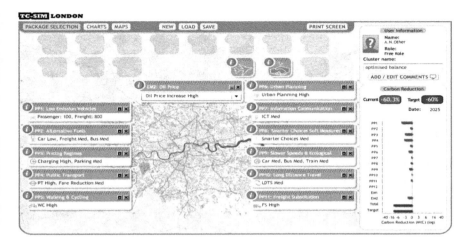

Figure 10.2   TC-SIM 'optimized balance' mode

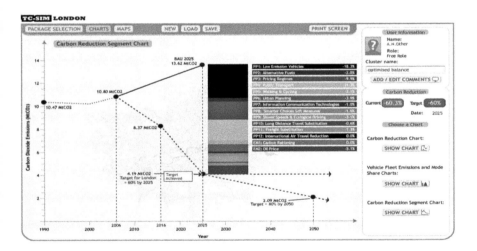

Figure 10.3   TC-SIM optimized balance segment

Conclusions and Unresolved Issues

This chapter addresses some issues that are problematic in terms of finding appropriate solutions. There is a need for cities to lead the way in developing carbon efficient lifestyles, particularly with the recent difficulties in finding a consensus for change at the international level. Cities can certainly push a more radical agenda than seems possible at the international level. But even in the leading cities, such as London, there is an enormous gap between the current strategic 60 per cent emissions reduction targets and BAU trends. There are huge difficulties in implementation and the scale of required change is being hugely underestimated. This becomes even more evident if transport is expected to deliver its 'fair share' of the targets, or if we move beyond the 60 per cent aspiration cross-sectorally.

Even with the current economic difficulties and the expectations that in the short term (the previously assumed) BAU will not take place, past experience has shown that after a short period the old patterns of growth in travel are broadly reinstated. Perhaps the current recession is sufficiently large for the dynamics to change and for a new BAU pathway to appear. In this case it may be easier to achieve the targets set in London and elsewhere as the scale of change is reduced. There are still the baseline figures for 1990 from which the targets are set, but the BAU is reduced, thus making targets smaller. There may also be negative feedback effects as there is less money available for adopting the new technologies and for public (and private) investment in new transport systems, and the urban infrastructure and buildings more generally.

Reducing transport emissions is thus a very complex problem; it involves us understanding the sociological factors behind people's rationales for mobilities (Urry 2007), and will require huge investment and social change. There are multiple policy pathways towards substantial improvements in carbon efficiency in the transport sector. All represent significant breaks against current trends.

1. The clear message is to work more effectively across the broader range of policy packages available and at a higher intensity of application relative to current trends. There are financial and behavioural implications here. Any analysis also needs to explicitly accept the greater uncertainties that are now apparent as a result of economic recession, but this new situation needs to be taken as an opportunity for change. Investment in longer term 'green' projects will mean that London emerges from the recession in a stronger position as a leading low carbon city. The most appropriate 'Keynesian stimulus' is in the emerging green technology sector, and this includes carbon efficient transport.
2. Low emission vehicles and alternative fuel penetration are likely to remain the most important policy levers as they tackle carbon efficiency in the dominant mode of travel (the private car). The main difficulty here is in achieving any level of success in penetration to the mass market. The motor industry and government need to develop mechanisms to achieve this,

including mandatory targets for manufacturers. However there is much reticence to move radically away from the current business model. The $<100gCO_2$/km car should be developed as a mandatory target for an agreed future year, say 2025, so that the whole fleet matches or betters this figure. The difficulty, it appears, is in agreeing targets by manufacturer, as some produce fleets with high levels of emissions.

3. There is also much potential in the behavioural measures, including pricing regimes, increased use of public transport, walking and cycling, ecological driving and slower speeds, and more efficient freight transport. Urban planning, smarter choices and soft measures have clear roles to play in their own right, but also perform very important roles as supporting measures to other policy packages, enabling higher levels of effectiveness in implementation. Again the difficulty is in implementation, certainly when applying measures which are difficult in political terms, or in moving ad-hoc practice to the mass market.

4. In empirical terms, there is also little current understanding concerning synergies between policy levers, packages and scenarios. Much further analysis is required on this issue, but the TC-SIM model does help in putting together the different policy packages in a form that enables decision makers to discuss and decide which combinations might best suit their needs.

Some interventions may continue to prove difficult to implement – pricing regimes and mass market alternative fuels, for example. Perhaps the most demanding future area will be in engaging the public in substantial behavioural change. Lifestyle change is notoriously difficult to engender at the mass market scale. High intensity application of all policy measures is required if we are to achieve the ambitious headline targets.

There are a number of areas which are important to carbon efficiency in transport, but remain very poorly understood and developed. These might be termed 'enabling mechanisms'. The first is rationing – transport could, in theory, be included in a rationing mechanism (beyond the Emissions Trading Scheme) which sought to reduce emissions. Though also very difficult to implement in the present political climate, a more carbon constrained world might necessitate more effective action here, including a rationing scheme at the business or individual level. Second is oil price (and linked with the 'peak oil' debate). Over the past 30 years there has been some stability in oil prices – at relatively low levels – but recently this has changed with high volatility and some concern we are reaching a period of peak oil. There is much debate in the literature about the future supply of oil. Estimates for the peaking of oil supply range from '2007–08' to 'after 2010' (World Energy Council) and '2025' (Shell) (Strahan 2008). Oil peaking is likely to result in dramatically higher oil prices as suppliers and consumers react to perceived supply shortages. The consumer is shielded to a certain extent by the high tax component in the price of petrol and diesel. Nevertheless, a large increase in the cost of oil impacts markedly on the price of petrol and diesel. Large price increases are likely to dampen the demand for travel using oil and provide clear signals to industry and consumers to increase efficiencies. Large price increases would, therefore, perversely 'help' achieve high intensity application in the preceding packages. There are, however, very large difficulties in terms of acceptability of large price increases (with the public and business).

Although the focus of this chapter has been on travel within London, there is a considerable amount of air travel in and out of London as the city is a global hub on the international aviation network. This represents an additional (huge) problem, namely the carbon costs of international air travel. It can be demonstrated, using the TC-SIM model, that the ambitious targets for carbon reduction in the transport sector for London can be achieved if aviation is excluded from the calculations. If aviation is included then the future targets become impossible to achieve.

Air travel is growing at an ever increasing rate, particularly short-haul travel, but also long-haul, and beginning to emit relatively high aggregate levels of CO_2. There is strong consumer demand for growth in air travel and a strong business lobby to increase supply. Politically we seem to be a long way from even addressing the problem. This would include reducing the demand for particular types of journey (largely through awareness initiatives) and reducing supply (largely through restricting airport growth and encouraging short haul air travel to be taken by rail). The topic is however 'complicated' in implementation terms. The air industry lobby is powerful and manages to keep consideration of 'reducing supply' (literally) under the radar. Within 5–10 years, depending on the growth of air travel, the size of the air sector will demand a revised policy approach if CO_2 reduction targets are to be achieved within transport and cross-sectorally.

The responsible governmental action would be, at least, to consider the likely options now. If the growth of short haul and long haul air travel is still deemed as 'untouchable' then this demands a more urgent response in ground-based transport. The UK Committee on Climate Change (2009) has recently started to consider these issues, and similar issues are found in international shipping. The difficulty is that the pathways for deep reductions in the ground-based transport sector, though theoretically possible, are looking very unlikely. This puts greater pressure on the domestic, industrial and power supply sectors to make greater contributions to carbon reduction targets, with transport having a lower target. This depth of inter and cross-disciplinary policy pathway analysis to achieve strategic aspiration – and differentiated by context – is not being carried out to any degree. Unfortunately we continue to fiddle while the climate warms up.

Annex 10.1   T2025 public transport modelling scenarios

Scenario 1: T2025 Reference Case	
National Rail	Channel Tunnel Rail Link to St. Pancras Chiltern Railways upgrade Heathrow Express extension to Heathrow Terminal 5 London Overground phases 1 and 2: East London line extension from Dalston to West Croydon and Crystal Palace and Gospel Oak to Barking line upgrade Rail reliability – increase journey times by 4.5%
LU	Piccadilly line extension to Heathrow Terminal 5 PPP line upgrades on Waterloo & City and Jubilee lines Reliability – an average 30% drop in capacity and 10% increase in on-train times on all lines not fully upgraded by March 2010, i.e. Victoria, Northern, Piccadilly, sub surface (Circle, District, Metropolitan, Hammersmith & City) and Bakerloo lines
DLR	DLR Bank to Lewisham three-car upgrade DLR extension to Woolwich DLR Stratford International – Canning Town
Bus and Transit	Bus service increase of 2.4% to be achieved by 2010 Greenwich Waterfront and East London Transit schemes phase 1
Other	Thames Gateway Bridge Smart transport measures – modest investment assumed Rail, Tube and bus fares increase by RPI to 2025
Scenario 2: Full PPP + Scenario 1	
LU	Full public private partnership (PPP) improvements (Upgrades of Victoria, Northern, Piccadilly, sub surface (Circle, District, Metropolitan, Hammersmith & City) and Bakerloo lines)
Scenario 3: Crossrail + Scenario 2 (which includes Scenario 1)	
National Rail	Crossrail

Annex 10.1 Continued

Bus	Increase in bus supply of 20% from 2006 to 2025
Scenario 4: Crossrail2 + Scenario 3 (which includes Scenario 2)	
National Rail	Rail 2025: Capacity enhancements to existing lines and East London line extension from Surrey Quays to Clapham Junction Thameslink programme Crossrail 2
DLR	DLR capacity enhancement – Poplar to Stratford DLR extension to Dagenham Dock
Light Transit	Thames Gateway bus transit schemes (further phases of Greenwich Waterfront and East London Transit) West London Tram and Cross River Tram Tramlink extensions
LU	Northern line segregation of services Enhanced line upgrades beyond PPP
Bus	A further increase in bus supply of 20% (total 40% 2006 to 2025)
Congestion and Emissions Reduction Plan	A package of measures to reduce congestion and emissions, including smart transport measures, vehicle technology change, a Climate Change Action Plan and a national road user charging scheme in London
Other	Silvertown Link

Source: Transport 2025, TfL 2006.

PART III
The Role of Information in Policy-making

Chapter 11

The Role of Information Contestability in Evidence-based Policy in Planning and Transport

Marcus Wigan

Introduction

Many of the processes of strategic planning and transport have long been based on slow changing environments where much of the operational investment could reasonably be undertaken on the basis that, if the present was well understood, the projections were largely adequate to undertake quite significant investments. Remarkably, this has also been broadly true for the complex area of freight modelling and planning, where predicting the present and straightforward projections on the economic base or employment numbers have proved to be adequate for most purposes in the views of the majority of current customers for such information and analysis (Wigan 2005).

A recent TRB Taskforce aimed at improving the state of practice in this tricky area by addressing the needs of US Metropolitan Planning Organizations came to much the same conclusions (TRB, In Press 2011). While these rates of change and development have proved at a broad level to be reasonably workable in the past, better understanding of the long persistent roots for the political processes with which they have been entangled is beginning to emerge from studies of the development and influences of major projects across the world (e.g. Sturup and Low 2008).

The reasons that such systems have proved to be not *too* unsatisfactory in the past is because rates of change in society and infrastructure have not in general been very rapid. This is now changing, and the prospects of more rapid change, and certainly greater levels of turbulence, are now quite substantial.

The horizons for policy development, infrastructure decisions, and major construction now place a significant amount of this long period within the zone where rapid changes are now highly probable. The decade long processes common for major infrastructure policy formation, planning and implementation are now subject to considerable review during their lifecycle.

This is not only because the polices themselves are starting to feel the effects of climate change, oil price increases and the need to moderate and diminish carbon emissions, they are now also about to be subject to very different evaluation processes and greater levels of interdependency between the previously far more distinct areas of physical planning and transport provision.

For example, a major project put out for a Public Private Partnership (PPP) will typically involve a horizon of 25–30 years: as this means that PPP bids raised in 2010 will need to cater for the uncertainties involved right up to 2035–45, the costs will inevitably have to rise. That is if the projects do proceed. The frequency of major climatic events is rising and can be expected to increase further, leading to a greater need to have procedures and processes that can adapt to such major events. The need to invest in major transport projects to adapt to climate change and energy constraint requirements is also increasing in the face of these greater uncertainties just as physical planning is coming under pressure to respond to the same environmental changes. Direct energy costs are not the sole factor, the 'design in' that strategic planning strategies imply has even longer lead times and arguably an even greater final impact.

A considerably higher level of government flexibility management and responsiveness would seem to be warranted, to manage the shortfalls in the transfer of broad strategy planning to operational on the ground events. The balance between private and public investments and controls will need not only to respond to changes and shocks at the planning stage – but to remain considerably more responsive throughout the lifetime of the project than they have been in the past due to the increasing interactions of very different areas of planning and transport, and increasingly, additional areas such a energy. These too will tend to increase the contingency provisions and costs likely to be incurred and so raise the levels of PPP bids still further. Current levels of information sharing and flexibility are managed largely by contract between government and PPP partners, and these agreements are frequently far from transparent – and even less flexible.

So, if these compressed and interacting strategies and implementation programmes are to be managed under new public policy pressures, how do we reassess the governance frameworks that we need to apply? Clearly some rethinking of the balance and transparency in contracts will have to be reassessed, but most important the information on which such changes – as we must now begin to plan for not easily foreseen shocks and substantial changes – and make greater and more continuous efforts to involve the public as well. Turbulence in the social, political and physical environment needs to be factored in more realistically to governance arrangements to achieve this. Ways of making the whole system work more responsively are therefore needed, and this is likely to require changes in information governance in particular.

Physical planning theory has been moving steadily towards 'continuous engagement' approaches (Albrechts 2003), reflecting the response of that component of the public planning, policy and operational nexus, with aspirations towards greater substantive involvement of the publics. (Innes and Booher 2004). Shifts in the modes of governance are a source of continuing tension shifts as pressures for more participatory processes grow (Newman 2001).

Here we raise some of the issues involved, and focuses on improving the governance processes so that the private, public, commercial and systems have the capacity, information, ability and power to respond.

We contend that systems that meet these goals also meet good standards for governance under the present situation; even when major changes are not well catered for. They are pivotal in combination with evidence based policy frameworks, and underpin them. A pivotal concept is *contestable* evidence based policy: where the analysis systems and the information are shared more widely between the parties involved. The adjustments to governance that will be required to make such a principle workable can provide greater flexibility to the overall decision processes, and thus ability to adapt to environments that are now changing faster than the life of many projects.

Evidence-based Policy

There are three basic elements that underpin rational decision-making. It is not suggested that decisions are always, or even in most cases, based on rational decision making: there are many factors to consider, and even the best analyses may have to omit important political and other factors, and power is always a basic issue (Albrechts 2003).

Framing the information and engagement flows in a different way has now become possible with the rise in public education and data access, and relevant alternative models of Foucauldian power are rehearsed by Richardson (1996).

We argue from the rational discourse stance that the better the evidence base the more likely that policies adopted will link together and enable cumulatively workable and effective action – bearing in mind that both rational debate and sources of power will always be involved in various measure.

The First is Evidence-based Policy

Conviction politics may be very effective in an electoral sense, but implementation requires substantiation and planning – preferably based on a measure of reality. At the very least, the requirement for some form of supportive evidence and analysis is becoming one of the barriers to entry from interest groups. In complex areas such as urban transport this is arguably becoming a necessity.

As the pressures of climate change, real commitment to overall sustainability, and turbulence in the physical, social and political environments are now increasingly likely to increase, evidence based policy analysis and communications become more important. Many policies required for moves towards sustainability will have to change assumptions that previously could safely be assumed to be reasonably stable. This will inevitably demand major revision to be made to long-term plans on a regular – or possibly even continuing – basis.

A good example is the overall strategic plan for Melbourne Australia. This was aimed at 2030. It has already been seen to require a radical rethink, as many of the hoped for outcomes and mechanisms have proved to be less than reliable, and the responses of many parties over the first eight years have not entirely followed the expected pathways. The front end loading into the early stages alone of the participation process was not supported by the necessary sustainable and continued participation.

There were hints of that evident even at the beginning of the process, as the match between the budget support for any policies involving public transport simply did not meet the timescales, let alone the sums, involved over the first five years – which was necessary to secure the infrastructure developments to meet the longer term goals.

The arguments for evidence-based policy have long been won in principle. However, in practice in many places, progress has not been nearly so good. Perhaps evidence-based policy needs a continuing updating process to support it into the subsequent implementation epochs?

The Second is Contestable Evidence-based Policy

This, unlike the previous form, is not always welcomed or easy to secure the basis for. However the best means of neutralizing evidence based arguments is to simply produce your own. Inevitably it will be based on different premises, use different data and include and prioritize different factors. The net effect is often to set both aside and quickly return to pure politics and making a choice between the two 'expert' and 'independent' sources is virtually impossible to establish.

A very common strategy – by both – or even all – sides – in planning debates involving transport. However the key term *contestable* works its magic on this deadlock … if the different parties are using the same data, and even the same models (if such are needed), then the debate can be joined on an equal basis. It is no accident that access to models and data is not always available to all parties. Just as Freedom of Information has become a dispirited and often fruitless route to participation in meaningful debate, so too have various forms of intellectual property right assertions become part of the armory of Government – and has undermined the ability of many community sectors to join in on equal terms.

One of the missing links is the still-limited availability of public data in various forms to sustain the rational debates. The arguments are varied, from an assertion that data is a Government profit item, and so unavailable to the people who paid for it (Peritt 1995), to arguments of confidentiality, real or supposed, to debar critical items from any data supply. Others have taken a contrary view (Wigan, Rockliffe and Edgar 1996; Edgar, Rockliffe and Wigan 1996; Wigan 1999).

The term *contestable* means imply that all parties can have equal access to the data and information foundations for whatever is proposed. This is one of the goals of Open Government initiatives, which now are beginning to attract significant resources.[1]

The Third is Making Information Accessible

This is no easy task. Transport, planning – and especially urban transport of goods and people – is a very complex system and even full access to the raw data would not help more than a few groups to undertake their own analyses. However the implications of many transport and planning proposals are strongly spatial, and so can be very effectively summarized in maps showing locations and impacts and associated information in a digestible form.

The latter example is considerably more powerful than it looks. To secure complex data from a government or other holder is not a straightforward process, converting it into a form that one can analyse is often error prone and demands expertise, and undertaking analyses that are summarized in thematic maps is another step upward on the learning (and software acquisition) curve, demanding the ability to load into a Geographical information System or some kind, access suitable spatial descriptions of the area concerned, and the skills to be able to create appropriate thematic maps.

This accumulated list of requirements for software, funds and skills comprises a significant barrier to access – even if the data could be secured from government, and of the end user on the community could afford the fees often charged for public data.

While the major barriers have been access to the data in sufficient detail and in sufficient time, the substantial effort required to transform it into usable and communicable information has resented another form of barrier.

However it is now possible to build data observatories or specialized knowledge bases where the data is already loaded in, where analyses can be undertaken by end users over the web, and where dynamic thematic maps can be made be available to interact with and explore on line by anyone with internet access and a web browser. Initiatives of this kind are essentially a 21st-century development, and the resources required to create and populate them are steadily diminishing.

All these functions and more are encapsulated a number of Knowledge Base Frameworks, one example of which is the REORIENT Knowledge Base.[2] Dynamic thematic maps are accessible directly online plus many documents about the information contained in the maps. There are many facilities below the publicly available level[3] including full data analysis and map generation. Data Observatories offer another more introverted approach, now gaining ground,

---

1   An excellent example is the 2010 bundle of UK Government initiatives reported at www.data.gov.uk.

2   www.reorient.org.uk.

3   See https://www.reorient.org.uk/pdfs/RKB_NKBS%20Confhandout.pdf.

especially in the UK: two practical examples operating in the first decade of the 21st century are given later.

The key relevance to transport governance is that this approach to making public data available closes the loop between evidence based policy and the consultation processes required to make governance structures workable for a wide swathe of the community. It must be added immediately that the addition of an eGovernment interaction process (such as a WIKI[4]) is needed to realize many of the potential gains, and the more sensitive issue of including email group organizational tools – likely to be used most by lobby groups – may be a difficult issue for government organizations to feel able to handle appropriately, and their implied official endorsement. Nevertheless slow but steady advances are being made on this Web 2.0 style of government engagement.[5]

To date this has been handled largely by distancing and hand off to funded groups, such as the International Teledemocracy Centre at Napier University[6] (funded equally by British Telecom and the Scottish Parliament itself).

The brave use of a WIKI[7] for city Plan review started by the City of Melbourne is closely controlled as far as a WIKI can be, including stringent single visible identity verification (reflecting bureaucratic dislike for multiple legal and contextually dependent identities in favour of unitary ones with all their risks to the person and visibility requirements undermining some of the anonymity advantages). But it is indeed a brave initiative. There will be more. The contextual multiple identity issue (Wigan 2008, 2010) will become crucial in such mediations of power and change, and requires further attention.

There is a real potential to make sensitive data available in this form, as it aggregates over sensitive dimensions and this allows the implications of data to be shown that could not be built for the basic raw data as it would not be made available at all in some cases, and in many cases for good privacy and confidentiality reasons.

The existence and availability of such systems now means that the pressure is now on Governments to provide similar systems of this type so that the community can actively participate in the governance of transport. The information is usually complex and spatially specific – and this form of access means that the balance between government, professional and the broader community can be made more equitable, as the information withholding power of government can be contested.

Recent work has explored these issues and demonstrated the links between contestable evidence based policy, information and governance. Further development and communication of these concepts in the present form were

---

4   For example the use of a WIKI for City Plan review started by the City of Melbourne on 17 May 2008 to 14 June 2008 see www.futuremelbourne.com.au/wiki/view/FMPlan.

5   www.agimo.gov.au.

6   The original unit has recently moved to Leeds University, although an ITC continues at Edinburgh Napier University.

7   A WIKI is an interactive open website that any one with access to it can edit. The ReOrient project mentioned later used the Efurt Wiki (http://erfurtwiki.sourceforge.net/).

stimulated by the Nectar Conference in Rotterdam in 2008, focusing on Transitions to Sustainability,[8] as this mechanism (contestable evidence based policy) is an underused and under exploited strategic tool, likely to be an essential component of successful transitions towards sustainability, and an essential element in underpinning sustained participatory engagement sought by the physical planning profession.

Another stimulation for the need to make evidence contestable became clear through an examination of the links between security polices by governments and the governance implications (Wigan 2006), where the corruption of 'evidence based policy' was highlighted, and the need to ensure better transparency (contestability) further endorsed. A seminal quotation use there is from Harding (2008), who, discussing the failures of evidence based policy where contestability is lacking, states:

> Experience with evidence-based policymaking in Britain raises doubts about such claims. The British experience led to the term 'policy-based evidence', to describe the end result where government agencies filtered out information that was inconsistent with government policy.

It is clearly time that greater contestability was enabled with less asymmetric information access.

How is it Done? The Role of Data Observatories

Recent work has further explored these issues and demonstrated the links between contestable evidence based policy, information and governance. This mechanism is an underused and under exploited strategic tool, and further consideration of both the technical and political implications is necessary to be able to properly appreciate these issues and the power relations involved if they prove to be effective. While the present chapter cannot address all the aspects of supporting the governance processes involved, examples can be given of productive directions already available to be examined for their potential to support the enhanced contestable processes.

The first technical question, to ensure that this is at least a possible direction, is what are the tools needed to make data capture and asset, and not a problem for people? Some of the actors that need to be covered include:

---

8   Programme   at: http://traverse.sharepointsite.net/Transumowiki/Document bibliotheek/03%20Projecten/Transumo%20A15%20van%20Maasvlakte%20naar%20 achterland/03%20Output/05%20Rapporten,%20notities,%20verslagen/Programma%20 Nectar%20workshop%202008%20Transumo-A15.pdf.

- Governments at local and national level (endorsing the ready and readily interpreted access to such information);
- Transport and planning specialists (to create and populate such systems);
- Community activists with the educational background to make use of the materials;
- Human computer interaction specialists to design, learn and redesign such systems.

Clearly access to data needs to be made available in forms not tied to specialist analytical skills, which usually means a visual format, preferably interactive. Much of transport and planning is strongly spatial, and so a map is often an ideal base for such communication. Such communication is increasingly necessary between departments or divisions of large government bodies. Examples include local government bodies in the UK such as Milton Keynes Council[9] and the County of Norfolk[10] in the UK, and a larger scale and more specialized effort by Transport for London.[11]

Data observatories offer an integrated access to many of the large and unwieldy data sources that underpin strategic decision-making, and do so in a manner that makes the information usable. Simple transformations, such as percentage changes in population by district, and more complex ones such as measures of accessibility summarize information in a meaningful way. Further added value is the provision to both internal and external bodies (and interested parties) of an ability to drill down to areas of interest and to explore other aspects using such tools.

The pressures to create such systems are coming from the inside of organizations, and as yet not from pressure from outside. However Freedom of Information requests for such malleable information are rarely easy or inexpensive for an organization to handle, so there are benefits in making the borders of government organizations more porous in this manner.

Sharing data – let alone models – is an expensive mode of collaboration as it usually involves a fair measure of support and time, so a data observatory self-serve approach cuts the costs that would otherwise be incurred and makes the process viable. Political acceptability is quite a different matter – and intellectual property rights yet another.

Political acceptability of contestable evidence based policy will be slow, until there are clear gains seen to be secured from it, and so the incremental step of improving governance by data sharing in a structured manner is both a valuable step towards it the way and a desirable end in itself.

Governance structures will have to change to enable greater use of the skills in the community. The model of consultation that asks for comment on a limited set of alternatives and claims that this task has been completed when these submissions

---

9   www.mkiobservatory.org.uk.
10   www.norfolkdata.net.
11   www.tfl.gov.uk.

have been placed on a website without acknowledgement or review or response by the government – however common – is no longer a workable model of tapping community skills and expertise – or support.

The skills of the community are steadily increasing as educational levels rise, and the capacity to handle data and analysis have risen with the rapid penetration of computers and computer skills. Government has in general taken up some of the opportunities presented by computer-mediated communications, but has yet to move on to the next stage of information exchange.

eGovernment has made considerable progress in terms of dissemination and access to government services, but the problems and issues involved in handling large volumes of email have made it difficult to consider moving on to a potentially higher level of interaction through data and even model sharing.

The advantages of making such a move are evident, in terms of rational decision-making, engagement with highly skilled members of the community and a greater understanding within the community when changes in direction are required. Equally the disadvantages to government is that significant engagement in the much more highly informed responses will be needed, and this at a time when many governments have outsourced much of their data and analytical work to consultants.

The governance implications are that greater in house technical skills may once again be needed, also easing the negotiation of matters that are more and more interwoven across many areas of government.

The governance of information when treated in this manner takes on a catalytic role in the marshalling of broader resources addressing transport and planning strategies, and offers a positive direction in which to move policy governance frameworks.

One of the barriers to this generally desirable move is the use of copyright over government data, which can severely impact both current and future efforts to share information and understanding. A critical community resource is geospatial data, and in the UK at least this major community asset is tightly held by the UK Ordnance Survey, and is already the subject of major moves by the geospatial community in the UK (the Free our Data Campaign) as the evidence is that such a move is a net gain[12] to the community and has begun to bear fruit after a decade of professional lobbying efforts. Certainly the commercial net gains in the US from making public data public have been extremely large (Wiess 2002).

Technical tools that enable visualization, interactions, exploration and analysis of complex planning and transport data have been developed. Practical examples are very helpful as there are few such systems to explore to get a feel for what can be done – and thus appreciate how it can change the way the communities can work if they become more widespread.

---

12   A succinct and reasonably balanced discussion is at www.freeourdata.org.uk/blog/?p=154.

The first known such tool to support contestable evidence based policy work,[13] with its inclusion of multiple levels of security and interaction, and rich communications (email, WIKI, video conferencing, data handling, map editing, interactive mapping …) was the ReOrient Knowledge Base[14] system created at Edinburgh Napier University specifically to allow these mechanisms to be deployed to support a distributed project team with partners from Australia to America to work effectively. It was developed rapidly enough to be used within the first quarter of the Framework 6 Project, and the data access, analysis and visualization elements have continued to service a series of other EU Framework projects after the end of the ReOrient project.

Readers are encouraged to explore the public elements of the Reorient Knowledge Base (RKB) for themselves, as it illustrates how such a public facility can be implemented, albeit the way in which the author would do it now, six years later, would be much improved. A full data cube analyser runs as part of the secured segment of the ReOrient KB website illustrates the extent to which end user analysis and presentation could be freed as early as 2004, when this way set up.

Mapping data is pivotal as it not only encapsulates the most understandable and communicable form of information transfer, but is also the very essence of physical planning and transport. Its monopoly value is well understood by government large and small in many countries and its potential for raising further fiscal impost well appreciated.

For some time in the late 20th century, European governments sought to secure monopoly profits from geospatial data, and sound arguments were made for this (Perritt 1995) as well as making provision for it to be made freely available. The policy of the US Government is to make the basic Tiger files by the US Census Bureau data available, but in a form in dire need of detailed quality improvement for many purposes. It is then possible for third parties to charge for any added-value quality enhanced version. This policy of the US Census Bureau enabled the US to secure a dominant position in applied GIS applications and software. The mid-1990s position was lucidly stated in a keynote speech by Dodson (1995), although the position stated was a common complaint:

> The United States passed through this stage some years ago, and summarised the European position as a wide concern that the problems with data pricing were causing widespread practical problems, and a general feeling that the United States had made the right decision on data pricing. Why do other countries, on their own admission, lag behind in GIS? The principal culprit is cost reimbursement on GIS data. The message came through clearly at both conferences (Bordomer '95 and CoastGIS '95). Speakers repeatedly complained that data pricing policies are a significant barrier to entry.

---

13   In 2004.
14   www.reorient.org.uk.

The State of Victoria spent a considerable sum in sorting out the Cadastre, topography and road network GIS databases to a consistent quality, and the Victoria Treasury then commissioned a report on what principles should be used to price the product once it was completed, and subject only to maintenance (FDF Management 1996a, 1996b). This and other approaches to pricing transport data are summarized in the relevant URISA reference textbook by Wigan (1999).

While the pricing conclusions cited the unsatisfactory experience of monopoly pricing, the two contributions were the use of Ramsey pricing (to set prices appropriate to a product where its entire residual value was embodied in it being fully maintained, as distinct from a more conventional sunk cost recovery costing and monopoly pricing strategy) and a stochastic approach to robust price setting when the elasticities of demand were unknown (Edgar, Rockliffe and Wigan 1996).

Wigan et al. (1996) foresaw that such data would, at least in part, soon become contestable. This has indeed occurred in the subsequent 15 years, and a number of alternate road networks and other GIS data resources have been created, culminating on open source approaches to community data resource building.[15]

As a result the OGCD (now Land Victoria) GIS databases were subsequently licensed at economic rates by data providers and the community on a wide user base, having started with this strategy when monopoly pricing was the norm. The advent of Google Maps and other added-value GIS data resources was predictable, but not taken seriously at that time, nor the recommendation that a right of access to private data be secured, although contestability was a key recommendation by Wigan et al. (1996).

In the light of the current chapter, another aspect of the OGDC work was the proposal and a Freedom of Information uncharged right to the GIS data pertaining to an individual or his or her property. This was a radical proposal at the time, but now that the digital cadastre is the basis of verification of property ownership the issue becomes ever more pertinent. The need for such cadastral data to be able to contest planning proposals becomes ever more important, at a time when the community now has wide access to computing power and the ability and tools to make full use of both the data and the tools.

Thus there is now contestability of geospatial-related information at last, although constrained by the quality of the datasets if no access is available to the incremental updates as they occur.

The latest development is that the resources available to enhance and update geospatial data can now be 'crowd sourced', where the community itself updates the information and corrects and validates it. This undermines arguments that a monopoly like the Ordnance Surveys' is necessarily required. An example of a crowd sourced mass geospatial transport data collection and redistribution service is available in the Netherlands, where details covering a very large number bicycle-specific routes[16] have been contributed to on-line by members of the

---

15   e.g. www.openstreetmap.org.

16   www.demis.nl/home/pages/Gallery/projects.htm: now used by 12 provinces.

bicycle community. While this is a small example (albeit with over three million such edits, and adoption by a number of Dutch Provinces as a standard public service) it is in the spirit of the theme of this chapter: that better information-enabled governance has much to offer planning and transport policy and practice. The governance implications of this now widely used system threefold:

- It was originated by bicycle community (programmers at Demis);
- It was and is updated and refined continually by bicycle users themselves;
- The essential quality control is now done by bicycle users, but funded by a large number of Dutch Provincial Governments.

This now provides an simple operational example of full contestability of government planning and transport organizations, where both the base data and the analysis tools and their use are held by both Government *and* the community ... and where the technical skills, initiative and critical mass was achieved led by the community: later supported, but not controlled by, Government. Bicycle provisions and information are now fully contestable, and policy initiatives based on data and visually provided interactive support allows the bicycle users to lead rather than follow Government polices in this area.

As the rates of change in physical planning and for transport are now under great pressure due to the rapid onset of climate change impacts. There is a rising need to both plan *and* invest in a faster cycle that before as the changes speed up and compress the horizon over which the planning and implementation processes have available to meet the carbon emission reduction demands set by physics rather than by politics.

However the community must still be brought along within this process, and these will not be easy, as the Dutch programs piloting Transitions to Sustainability[17] are demonstrating.

A positive aspect of the emergence of contestable policy, supported by shared data, visualization and analysis tools, is that the expertise of the community can be engaged more fully and new models of consultation can be developed where the policy processes will need to have higher level engagements at an earlier stage in the process than in the past. This will not only bring the community along a little quicker, and accelerate planning and transport proposals processes to fruition, but will, if adopted, change the nature of the governance and policy formation processes.

Instead of the community being presented with limited pre-analysed and pre-filtered choices at the end of a proposal as 'consultation', the formation of choices can be enriched (not necessarily a smooth and uncontroversial process of course), and the understand of the necessity to make changes to policies will be better negotiated – and more quickly – as the common ground will be at a much higher level.

---

17   Covered in detail in other chapters in this book.

The underpinning of contestable evidence based policy is the sharing and data, visualizations and models. Visualized outputs from models an immediate grasp accessibility variations across a city) are often enough to enable the processes advocated. Recent developments in Augmented reality have already reached the iPhone,[18] and add another economic and widespread means of making policy and planning implications clearer to an ever-wider range of stakeholders. Such enhanced and helpful technical capacities will soon bring higher community expectations in their wake.

The question arises: how much data and from whom? If the host system has provision for multiple levels of security links may be drawn to data available to only certain parties accessing the resource. However it is perfectly possible to use the Clean Room protocols now adopted by major government agencies, where unit record data can be accessed by models to do some form of estimation of mapping – but only the (filters for privacy) results are presented back to the users requesting such explorations.

This clean room approach also permits private and commercial data to be utilized and integrated under a range of different formal agreements, constraining the manner and levels of aggregation of its deployment, and so expands the common space for all parties if desired.

The basic issue of this chapter is that evidence based policy is no longer enough. *Contestable* evidence based policy is becoming essential. As this depends not only on polices for access to data (and analyses), the details of the processes required to manage various levels, of privacy, commercial and other sensitivities have been summarized to show that they are no longer insuperable.

The planning theory aims for sustained engagement with participation coincide with our proposed emphasis on data and model sharing as an essential infrastructure for contestable evidence based planning.

Summary

Information governance in planning and transport needs to change for the community as a whole to be able to handle and respond to the complex issues now arising in transport and planning. The barriers include government control of basic public geospatial data, and the necessary changes in the mode of operation of government to secure these gains. If they are addressed, then wider resources of the community can be harnessed, engagement improved, and responsiveness enabled. These goals may not necessarily be seen to be in the interest of politicians, but are broadly a necessary and desirable change for the community, who increasingly owns and wishes to be engaged in transport and planning issues.

---

18   www.ismashphone.com/2009/07/innovative-examples-of-augmented-reality-on-the-iphone.html.

Contestability and transparency and now both needed even more in governance if we are to manage and maintain costs, large scale changes and the more and more probable and frequent major weather, social and resource disturbances. The means to meet the need for information sharing at higher and continuing levels are no longer serious technical obstacles. Adaptations to Governance have not yet followed but again, the technical barriers are now much lower and the need greater. Inevitably, such continuing contestable evidence based policy – and continuing adaptation – will meet its greatest resistance in Governance arrangements ... not because they are likely to ineffective – but because they probably will be. These governance issues need to be addressed to enable us handle the transitions to sustainability in a timely and effective manner.

The changes in governance and policy processes enabled by a contestable evidence-based policy framework to become possible are important, and a major potential contributor to transitions to sustainability in planning and transport. Emergent experience in this area also offers the opportunity to exchange the experiences as such models begin to emerge. Provision could profitably be made to develop an international network mechanism to enable, publicize, communicate, endorse and exchange such experiences. The complexity of the interacting long lead time polices in many areas of transport and planning now requires such rapid information, data management, operational experience and knowledge exchange through such a new networked community of practice.

Chapter 12

Encouraging Changes in Travel Behaviour Towards more Sustainable Mobility Patterns: The Role of Information

Anaïs Rocci

Introduction

A consensus about the threat of climate change and the damages caused by human beings and their lifestyles on the planet seems to be established (IPCC 2007; Stern 2006; Houghton 2004). Environmental issues are nowadays a priority in public policies. However, although public awareness increases, people still refrain from changing their behaviour towards more sustainable mobility (Rocci 2007; Flamm 2007; Anable et al. 2006; Tertoolen 1998; Kempton 1993). The research by Howarth (2009) demonstrates that even if a high degree of concern about environmental issues is expressed, this is not reflected in corresponding lifestyle choices.

In this paradoxical context, this chapter examines individuals' mobility practices[1] related to environmental values in order to grasp the potentials of change. It specifically focuses on the role of information in relation to both transport supply and environmental awareness and knowledge it relies on.

Based on two sociological research works carried out in Paris, France (Rocci 2007, 2008), this chapter demonstrates that information plays a significant role in change. First, it provides knowledge and tools to increase individuals' mobility abilities and to expand multimodal[2] practices. Second, it makes people aware of environmental issues and thus promotes the acceptability of behavioural change.

---

1   'Mobility practices' cover travel trips, travel patterns, modal choice and activities. They are the way in which an actor appropriates the field of possible actions in the area of mobility and uses it to develop personal projects. They refer mainly to daily travel in order to carry out activities (e.g. work, shopping, leisure, social activities) and to long distance travel made for leisure or professional purposes. For more reflections about the concept, see Urry (2000) or Kaufmann (2002).

2   Multimodal practices mean that people choose and use different modes of transport to travel depending on the type of trip.

But, information is not always sufficient as it is mainly delivered by the mass media on the occasion of sensationalist events. Thus, its efficiency may be dubious as people feel powerless to change a global phenomenon at an individual level. Information is better transmitted and assimilated when provided through social interaction. Therefore, actions to promote change from mobility management must provide tailored information and encourage people to act voluntarily.

Three points are examined here: (i) the role of information in making modal choice and increasing ecological concerns; (ii) the shortcomings of information; and (iii) efficient ways to convey information. Finally, a broader view of the results is presented in conjunction with experimental Voluntary Travel behaviour Change programmes.

Background

The gap between attitudes and behaviour is mainly caused by confusion on the causes of climate change and by the lack of personal connection to the global issue (Howarth et al. 2009; Rocci 2007; Poortinga et al. 2004). The scientific discourse is too complex and the global phenomenon too distant from the individual daily life (Golovtchenko and Zelem 2003). The willingness of individuals to change their practices appears directly related to the sense of responsibility which, in turn, is directly related to the perceived impact of their own practices (Howarth et al. 2009; Marsden 2009; Schultz 2001; Young 2000). Thus, there is a lack of information on the consequences of the climate change issue and on the practices to adopt to remedy it. People will undertake the necessary actions once they know what they should do, how they should do it and why they should do it (Ampt 2003; Young 1993).

For instance, a survey conducted by ADEME[3] in 2001 shows that only 10 per cent of French people could define correctly the Green House gas emission. The lack of knowledge and understanding of the issue could explain the lack of responsibility towards the environment (Fransson et al. 1999). For some years information on climate change and environmental issues has been increasing and many continuous surveys conducted in France and the UK for instance show that knowledge and understanding are in expansion (DFT 2008; Eurobarometer 2008; Boy 2007). But, information on climate change and environmental issues is mainly conveyed through the mass media, which is not sufficient (Howarth 2009).

Information on the environment could provoke a behavioural change if the individual sees the advantages in the change and if it is supported by the social norms (Tertoolen 1998; Rogers and Storey 1987; Wallack 1981). In this respect, the social networks are real channels used to convey information, knowledge and practices (Reagans and McEvily 2003; Rogers 1962). What people feel, think and do is based on forms of social relations between actors within a given social

---

3   The French Environment and Energy Management Agency.

situation (Burt 1987). Degenne and Forsé (1994) showed that the diffusion of an innovation depends on the mechanisms of interpersonal and societal influences. Social changes result from a social diffusion of innovations, values and practices (Alter 2002; Valente 1996; Rogers 1962). The theory of innovation diffusion attempts to explain how new ideas and practices spread through interpersonal contacts largely consisting of interpersonal communication (Burt 2000; Valente 1995; Strang and Meyer 1993).

Furthermore, some researches demonstrate that many people lack information about alternatives to the car (Jones 2003; Rose and Ampt 2003; Steg et al. 2001; Brög 1998; James 1998). The provision of transport services and infrastructure, including pricing and land use policies, are of limited value if people are unaware of the system improvements. In order to change their personal travel behaviour, people need to be aware of convenient alternatives to car travel (Brög et al. 2002). Brög and Erl (1996) have conducted a research in Germany on the potential for modal shift from car to public transport, walking and cycling. They show that 75 per cent of current car trips could be switched to alternatives (34 per cent to public transport, 26 per cent to bicycle and 15 per cent to walking). In about half of these cases there was a lack of information about the available alternatives or a general negative attitude towards these modes. When provided with targeted and personalized information, people come to recognize that alternative travel practices can be better for them than previous choices (Bonsall 2007). Sammer et al. (2006) studied the role of information and knowledge on the choice of modes of transport. Their results showed that the variables related to the information towards the public and to the state of knowledge on a transport system significantly influence the choice of a mode. The modal choice depends on the degree of uncertainty of the traveller's information and knowledge about the available transport modes. The authors also note that issues of mobility concern more the sources, techniques, and the increase of information than the infrastructures which are limited by the costs and the environmental impact.

Methodology

This chapter relies on two sociological studies based on qualitative in-depth interviews and carried out in the Paris Region in France. The first one is a PhD thesis (Rocci 2007) which deals with limiting factors to behavioural modifications, analysing mobility practices, impact and perception of political measures, and environmental awareness. The second study was carried out following the thesis and deals with the importance of information for changing, in relation to both the transport supply and the environmental awareness and knowledge (Rocci 2008).

The aim of qualitative surveys is not to get a representative picture of the population but to compose with a wide diversity of situations and practices in which 'gathering information' is important. The qualitative approach provides insight to quantitative data by means of a fine analysis of individual's behaviour and individual patterns of logic.

A variety of family, professional and geographic situations were examined, with almost the same number of women and men.[4] Ninety people were interviewed for the PhD research (40 in the Paris region, 20 in Nagoya and 30 in London) during 2005–07. For the Paris region, which is the focus of this chapter, people are from 20 to 57 years old with a majority of 25–35 years. This is important because it is a period of many changes in the life cycle (changes in terms of family, professional, personal and/or geographic situations). The Paris region covers six zones, and the respondents live and/or work in all the zones (some of them live and/or work in the centre, others in the inner suburbs or the outer suburbs). A diversity of modes used for daily mobility were examined (car, carpooling, car sharing, public transport, bike, electric bike, motorized two-wheelers). In the second research, 20 persons aged from 26 to 61 years old were interviewed in 2008. These persons live or work in the City of Paris or in the inner suburbs. A variety of family and professional situations were studied. The objective of this survey was to get persons in a situation of modal choice (not dependent on the car). The aim was to understand how people knew of the existence of the transport supply, and how they adopted new modes. Another criterion for the interviewed people was to have experienced a new mode of transport or intending to do so (public bicycle system, car sharing, electric vehicle, or whatever mode of transport to which he/she was not accustomed).

An important feature of this research is that some people have been interviewed several times in order to better identify the contextual and temporal factors of change (or no change) and to follow the process from the intentions to the action. Re-interviewing respondents enable observing changes in attitude and behaviour. The various interviews show the way in which interviewees plan to put their thoughts into action and the effects of situation, context, opportunity and social influence on the process. It then becomes easier to determine the effects of the various multi-factors, the systems of constraints, and the systems of actors in the process of change. In the first survey (Rocci 2007), certain people were in the midst of changing modes of transportation, either getting rid of a car or acquiring one. The persons who were in a process of change and those who accepted to be re-interviewed were questioned several times throughout the thesis research (2005–07) in order to track any changes. The interviews were generally spaced by about six months; sometimes the second one was a year later. In the second research, the impact of the interview method was explored as it delivers information and stimulates introspection.

---

4   The interviewees were recruited through different social networks, forums on the Internet, associations. Each interviewed person was asked to suggest one or more persons to be interviewed in order to diversify the social and geographical characteristics.

The Role of Information in Constructing Modal Choice and Increasing Ecological Concerns

Information may be a factor encouraging behavioural change as it can remove some limits. Information contributes to the construction of modal choice and mobility knowledge as well as to the rise of environmental awareness.

The Role of Information in Constructing Modal Choice

Multimodal transportation supply may encourage users to diversify their modal choices provided that the supply characteristics are known, integrated and monitored by users. Mobility practices have to be learnt. Mobility needs abilities and knowledge (e.g. notion of 'mobility capital'[5]). And a lack of abilities could be a limit to behavioural change. Thus, information is required to increase this knowledge.

A process of learning, appropriation and adaptation is necessary, but first of all people must be informed of the existence of a mode and of its functioning. For instance, most of respondents do not know how to use the bus. Thus, they are scared to try a mode they do not manage well even if it would be better for them to use it. It refers to a fear of something unknown, uncertain and uncontrolled.

> The bus is really something that I don't know, I don't know how to take it, I don't know the lines, and it makes me scared ... I don't know where the stops are, I badly understand the route, but it would be good if I tried because the stop is just down to my house! (Vanessa, age 28).

Also, some respondents do not know about car sharing, for instance, even though they would dream about such a system. This lack of knowledge limits the potential of change.

> Car sharing system? What is it? I don't know it ... (Jérôme, age 28).

> Renting per hour would be my dream! (Céline, age 27).

Another limit to behavioural modification is the force of habits. Most of the time interviewees do not compare the various options and do not look for other options. They support the mode they usually use and discredit the others. It appears that the persons who have not experienced another way to travel, and thus do not know another kind of mobility, do not look far and wide. For instance, using the car could be straightforward.

---

5   See for example the works of Allemand (2004), Kaufmann (2001, 2006) and the article of Rocci (2008b).

Actually, when you have a car, you don't get informed about the other modes of transport, it's the easy choice, the easy way out. I think people have their habits and they do not think about other possibilities (Daphné, age 26).

Indeed, some respondents who used to drive do not imagine that it would be easier with another mode of transport. They choose the mode they are used to, the one they master and that appears easier to them.

I didn't look for information about public transport because it was straightforward with my car (Cyril, age 31).

Furthermore, sometimes they tend to underestimate the constraints and the costs of the transport they use, and over-estimate those of other modes; hence the need for information. For instance, one of the interviewees really thinks that using the car is cheaper than using public transport. She considers only fuel prices and not the price of the car, the insurance and repairing costs.

Finally, my car is not more expensive than the subway and it is even cheaper because I drive every day for short distances only; and I pay 23€ for fuel every month, so it really costs me less than a public transport pass! (Alicia, age 29).

Those examples point out the fact that information is crucial to explore other alternatives. For instance, some respondents can imagine a lot of constraints in cycling, but only one try may be sufficient to change their mind and, then, they cannot do without it anymore.

The bike, you must try, and once you start you can't do without it! (Arthur, age 24).

The Role of Information in Increasing Environmental Concerns

To modify their behaviour people also need information on the environmental issues and on the practices to adopt. Indeed, the environment does generally not appear as a main criterion in respondents' choice of mode of transportation. It appears neither in other daily practices of consumption nor in their global choices of lifestyle. They act mainly according to a personal interest. But, though the environment is rarely the main criterion in modal choice, it could be added on top.

I do not choose public transit for ecological reasons, but if it acts on the environment, that is better! (Jérôme, age 28).

Thus, in that case, this factor does not produce a change, but it may at least favour it and reinforce the decision. These people would be willing to make efforts provided that they understand clearly the stakes and the reasons to make that change, and that they also have some personal benefits.

Most respondents incriminate the lack of information on the climate change issue and tend to produce justifications for not changing their practices. They ask for understanding better the climate change phenomenon and the individual contribution. They also ask for knowing the practices to adopt in order to curb it. Indeed, climate change appears too far from their daily life and, thus, they do not link their own behaviour to the global phenomenon. Most of them tend to be concerned by what is tangible. They need to see the short-term effects. The more global the stakes appear to them, the less powerful they feel.

> We hear about that but we don't see the short-term effects. So I do not feel concerned so much (Cyril, age 31).

> If I saw the consequences, maybe I'd pay more attention (Marion, age 24).

The sensitivity of individuals and their commitment to change their practices appear directly related to their sense of responsibility and the perceived impact of their own practices as it is also demonstrated by other research (Young 2000; Howarth 2009; Marsden 2009). Furthermore, respondents ask for a better understanding of the contribution of their lifestyle choices and their personal travel to climate change as well as of the positive impacts of the actions carried out to remedy it. Respondents do not know what to do and how to do it.

> I hear about it, but not enough to realize neither its importance nor what I can do (Aline, age 35).

> I don't know what I could do, what I should do! (Céline, age 27).

> If I can do some things that are good for the environment I will do so, but you must tell me what (Jérôme, age 28).

Information appears to be important here because the better a person is informed, the more (s)he will become aware of the environmental issues. As they keep hearing information on the subject, some respondents feel more concerned and try to modify their practices.

> Continuing to hear some facts we try to pay attention to certain things, and the TV broadcast we have seen dissuaded us a lot! (Céline).

Similarly, another interviewee became aware of the issues because of the many references to the climate change in the media.

It's because of the evolution it takes and the extent it takes in the media (Aline, age 35).

Indeed, some concerned people do pay attention to their own practices and, thus, try to modify their behaviour for ecological reasons. And this is partly because they have got the good information that makes them aware.

But, if information on ecological issues has positive effects on attitudes, the increasing awareness does not necessarily modify behaviour. Being informed and concerned is not sufficient. The process of change requires time for integrating and assimilating the information. Some respondents think that the information exists but then it is a personal process to mature the thinking. It is an evolution by steps, a long learning process in which information needs to be assimilated.

Now I think people are globally well informed and aware of the consequences. Then, they need time to integrate it (Anne, age 45).

I think now everyone has heard about it. I think the information is there but then, it's a personal process (Anne).

About the environment we know obviously, but ... it is a development of ideas (Camille, age 34).

Consequently, it appears that such environmentally-friendly practices have to be learnt and integrated very early in life. Indeed, some respondents adopt pro-environmental behaviour because they have integrated gestures through their education.

I think it is in my behaviour anyway. I have a behaviour that promotes public transit. I was educated that way (Martin, age 27).

The Shortcomings of Information on Environmental Issues

Information is not always sufficient, especially when it is mainly delivered by mass media. Most of the time, this kind of information is quite alarmist and sensationalist. Measures to increase public knowledge are of dubious efficacy as information on climate change and environmental issues is delivered through mass media and is often clouded by sensationalist portrayals. Thus, it may paralyse people rather than encourage them. And they would feel powerless because of the gap between the global phenomenon and the individual daily constraints. Information appears also less efficient when it is not individualized. In that case, it would probably not affect sufficiently the persons who are mainly concerned by what is tangible and by what affects them directly. Furthermore, information may have adverse effects. For example:

- It can be *redundant* and thus make people weary. Sometimes, information proves to be too dense and too redundant, and therefore to have no longer any effect. Respondents do not pay any attention to it anymore and feel weary. Environmental discourse is used so universally now that it loses its value and distorts the information. An interviewee gives the example of automobile advertising.

  The environment, I do not care! It is politically incorrect, but we are fed up with the environmental message in France! (Michel, age 53).

  It's a marketing selling point, but it's also an illusion because when we see ads for cars they give the feeling that they do not consume fuel anymore (Anne, age 45).

- Information may be *distorted*. You see the information you want to see, and therefore, you seek information that is in agreement with what you think without necessarily looking at the other opinions on the issue. A respondent clearly highlights such dangers: misinformation, incoherent speeches and so on.

  I think that with all the sources of information we have, when you want information you can find it, but you find the information you are looking for. Some information is not necessarily right and doesn't go in a good sense, it's dangerous (Camille, age 34).

Indeed, it appears for example that the information an interviewee relies on limits his sensitivity more than it increases it. According to his sources, one might not worry about CO_2 emissions from vehicles since in the western market French cars would pollute the least. Moreover, according to his sources the local pollution might not a problem anymore; it would have been much reduced.

  The French are very innovative in diesel engines. They are the western cars that consume less and emit less Green House Gas.

  We must demystify the pollution in Paris because the pollution has halved over the last fifteen years. Simply because cars pollute three times less than they did, with catalytic converters and so on (Michel, age 53).

- Information may be *contradictory*. On one side you hear people predict a catastrophic future, and on the other side some proclaim that it can be managed. A respondent got confused hearing some kind of messages, as illustrated below:

Sometimes there is a kind of contradiction in the information, it is deceptive. Recently it was said that the global warming has always existed and it will continue … Once I was chatting with a colleague, professor of history and geography, who told me that throughout history there have always been events like this. So, on the one hand they say it's normal: we go through a natural phenomenon, but the problem is that before there were no cars, not as much CO_2! (Samira, age 53).

• Information may also *discourage* when the efforts that people imagined environmentally-friendly appear useless. For instance, an interviewee is discouraged to sort the wastes since she watched a report which devalues all her efforts.

We watched this TV report which was terrifying! They said that over 90% of the sorted wastes cannot be recycled. They said that sorting the card-board boxes was useless because there was always someone who was not doing it in the right way (Céline, age 27).

Indeed, knowing that not everyone acts in the same way and, thus, that some people wreck your personal efforts may discourage. It is what this interviewee explains worth for macro as well as micro levels.

If we heard that countries do not all agree to sign these agreements [The Kyoto Protocol] … You will not hide the information but that doesn't really encourage (Martin, age 27).

Thus, information as transmitted through mass media has not significant effects on behaviour. The effects are more perceptible on attitudes and awareness. However, it appears that information conveyed by social interaction is more efficient because it is individualized and may affect directly the person.

Social Networks and Interactions, an Efficient Source of Information to Modify Travel Behaviour and Environnmental Concerns

People can get information both on environmental issues and practices and on transport supply from different sources and through different ways such as the media, the internet and interpersonal communication. But all this information appears to be efficiently conveyed by the social networks (influence of peers, influence of charismatic and trustworthy persons, education, transmission of practices and knowledge, word of mouth, social Web such as forums on the Internet and so on). Respondents learn from the others, ask for advices and experiment new practices under the influence of their peers.

If the media have a role to play in disseminating information, it is efficiently conveyed by the network and through social interactions as it is shown by respondents.

> I receive information by e-mail and I give it to my friends, colleagues ... Then it is spread. (...) I'm not useful at a big scale, but would everyone inform his/her networks, it would widen (Ondine, age 61).

> Talking with people, you learn a lot of things (Rémy, age 40).

Indeed, it can be observed that respondents can be influenced by and get information from their peers and their different networks.

Getting Informed by the Media and the Internet

Though the mass media information does not significant effects on changes, it is accessible to everyone. Everyone can acquire general information about the main daily environmental issues and/or the existence of new transport supply or services.

Among the respondents, in general, the traditional media (press, TV, radio) and the Internet are often used to hear or to search for information about climate change issues.

> I'm learning mostly with TV and then the Internet, newspapers (David, age 55).

Some interviewees notice the role of the press to popularize scientific articles. Some of them also get informed in films or specific TV reports.

> Cinema is a good source too, we saw 'The walk of the emperor' which deals this subject, the film by Al Gore, a film called 'One day on earth'... (Philippe, age 44).

Otherwise, the media and the Internet are means to communicate on new transportation supply. Several respondents knew about the new bicycle system, organized bicycle training, car-sharing and so on through the free newspapers. And some have got informed about the transportation system through leaflets.

> I have seen it in a newspaper, there was an article talking about the bikes, and they talked about Voiture & Co for car sharing. They also talked about bicycle training, so when I saw that, I thought great! (Denise, age 48).

> We found that [a flyer of a car sharing company] recently. I found this flyer on the Windscreen (Jean, age 51).

I looked for that system before selling my car, I had a flyer on my car (Aline, age 35).

Some interviewees look for information directly on specific websites. For instance, a person got information about Vélib – the public bicycle system in Paris – and the steps to subscribe to it by this way.

I looked on the Internet, on the Vélib website before it started. I watched what they offered, fares, how to subscribe … (Corinne, age 26).

Other interviewed persons have a look on transportation websites to define their routes. For instance, Pascal organizes his routes with websites in order to take the maximum of bicycle tracks. Interviewees explain that there are very few landmarks in the city to follow bicycle routes. Thus, tools on cycling facilities are essential.

I prefer cycle lanes, so I look at the website of the Paris City Hall to see what exists (Pascal, age 35).

Contrary to the car, there are very few signboards for cycling in Paris, so it's better to have identified the route by the Internet the day before, crossroad by crossroad (Eric, age 35).

Céline knows the exact duration of all her trips by Vélib, which are shown on her user account on the website. In that way, she can better manage her travel time and make sure not to exceed the first free half-hour of using this system.

You always wonder if you will not exceed the half-hour. So that's why I go to see on the website, so I know how long my usual trips are (Céline, age 27).

Some respondents use mobile tools on the way such as WAP and GPS. Jérôme never waits for the bus because he obtains information on schedules in real time on his mobile phone via the Wireless Application Protocol (WAP). However, using such information tools requires a prior knowledge of the mobility system.

I search for the departure time of the bus on the WAP by my phone. You look at Orange World and there is an application for RATP schedule, it's great and reliable. They say the next bus is passing in … from anywhere. I don't need to wait for the bus, I know when it arrives.

You have to know the number of the bus line, the direction and the bus stop. Three letters are sufficient, but it is necessary to know the name of the stop … (Jérôme, age 28).

Others use a GPS to move during their journeys. For instance, Céline always looks at the GPS when driving a car, and sometimes Camille takes it with her for cycling. Thus, users have to juggle with a range of information tools depending on the mode of transport they use.

The media, movies and so on are sources of information accessible to all, and the Internet offers a variety of information when people are ready to look for it. Professional networks or associations can be other sources of information. But, it appears that the best and easiest transmission of knowledge goes through the social networks.

Transmission of Practices, Values and Knowledge through Peers

The peers transmit learning, knowledge, information and may influence one's practices. This influence refers to *education* of values and practices. Some interviewees provide information around them to facilitate dissemination. For instance, an interviewee tries to transmit environmental values to her children, husband or colleagues. Another one recommends to his friends the Al Gore's film *An Inconvenient Truth* to raise their awareness.

> I got my friend to watch it and I've recommended it to many people. The demonstration is really strong and well done (Martin, age 27).

Sometimes, the family hands down some values, habits and knowledge. For instance, the parents of an interviewee had shared with him their knowledge and their environmental sensitivity. The transmission of mobility patterns and modal practices is generally done through education. Martin was educated in an 'anti-car' atmosphere.

> They made me read many things on that subject, they talked to me all the time about that, all this was common topics of conversation! (Martin).

> If my parents had no car it's because they were focused on ecology. My parents always told me that the car pollutes and is costly. They were against the car. So that's why I take public transportation at the maximum. I was brought up like that (Martin).

Similarly, Jérôme's parents always moved in public transit. They have handed their knowledge to monitor the public transit and buses network down to him. And Anne explains that she cycles probably because of her family's culture.

> My mother took only the bus! So I took the bus with her a lot and she taught me everything (Jérôme, age 28).

> Maybe it's because I have a family that has always been cycling, I have a grandmother who is still cycling at 90 years. I have always seen the model of people who said that cycling was not complicated (Anne, age 45).

But of course, this family transmission of values and attitudes is not always observable.

Another kind of influence can be an exchange of *advices* or *liking*. Some respondents obtained information on the working process of a mode of transportation via friends or colleagues. For instance, Corinne does not hesitate to ask her peers for advice on the best routes by bicycle. And Martin has been helped by friends for his first use of Vélib, the Paris bike-sharing system.

> It's a friend who told me that I could cycle through the hospital. I didn't know that, in fact it is safer because there are no cars (Corinne, age 26).

> I asked my friends if there was a bus terminal next, they brought me to a terminal, quickly explained me how it works and I went back by Vélib (Martin, age 27).

Some respondents enjoy so much using a mode of transport that they try to influence their peers to join them. It is the case of some interviewees who try to 'recruit' new members for the car-sharing system or to encourage their peers using the bike-sharing system.

> I like to encourage people to make a try and convince them that it is easy to take. Because they often do not realize how simple it is! (Camille, age 34).

Obtaining Advices Through Other Users

Learning how to practice a new mode of transportation seems to be done to a large extent among users themselves. For instance, users of the public bicycle system share advices, exchange of experience and help each other at the terminal or on the street.

> The more I share it's still on the street, when we are at the Vélib terminals. People do not understand; don't know how to use it. Here there is much talk, we help each other (Camille, age 34).

> I think training is necessary to know how to take a bike and it was made between users. We help each other at the terminals. Once I understood the system I helped many people to use it. Many people were lost, then I helped them by explaining: you do that, then this, this … (Martin, age 27).

Sharing Experiences Through 'Social Web'

The Internet and forums are also great means for diffusing information and sharing knowledge, experiences or advice.

> I looked at the forums to see discussions and to know how they did with the empty stations and full terminals ... I learnt tricks ... what the strategy is when we can't find a bicycle and, worse, when we can't park it (Corinne, age 26).

Anne wanted not to be isolated in cycling. Through these forums, she creates social links by exchanging experiences, addresses of places, advices about routes and so on.

> I ask: I have to go to this place, do you know how to get there fast? (Anne, age 45).

Besides, the discussions and debates Eric had on this kind of forums have led him to question his own behaviour and to change some practices.

> Keeping discussing on the bicycle on the forum of Cyclurba and Vélotaf, questioning has come up (Eric, age 35).

The last two points appear particularly relevant for persons who are already using alternative modes of transportation. Persons who belong to the same social group – using the same mode of transport or sharing the same values – can help each other or share information and advices. In that way, the interview technique, as it is also a social interaction, gives an example of how respondents can change their mind when providing them with information or making them think about their own practices.

Examples of Changes in the Respondents' Attitudes and Behaviour Over Time

The various interviews show the way in which interviewees plan to put their thoughts into action and the effects of situation, context, opportunity, social influence on the process. In the first survey, certain people were in the midst of changing modes of transportation. For example, Daphné, who was in the process of getting rid of her car, was questioned four times. Several factors led her to want to use her car less, mainly her social network, but at various moments elements of situation came to bear upon her decision to change.

She had quickly moved through the normal course of events for acquiring a car: a license at the age of 18, borrowing her parents' car, and purchasing a car after getting into employment. After a few years, due to an awareness of environmental problems enhanced by her social status through her responsibilities as a teacher

['As a teacher I have a role to play for raising environmental awareness ...'] and to the influence of 'pro-environment' peers ['I didn't feel integrated while I got my car, I felt excluded in a way'], she began to conceive of doing without a car.

> He tried to make me understand that the car was not useful. At the beginning that annoyed me, and finally I thought that he may be right. (...) And the fact that I saw people around me who acted for and who were very invested in this cause made me think: they can do it, so why shouldn't I be careful in what I do?!

Then, favourable conditions made her decision possible: a move to a city with good public transportation, less travel between various schools for her job and so on. Thanks to her social network, Daphné also experimented with other means of transportation: a colleague informed her of a direct bus line between home and workplace, and her boyfriend encouraged her to try using a bicycle to get around. She, thus, overcame her apprehensions and perceived all the advantages of these alternative means of locomotion. She reduced her use of the car considerably and planned selling it on expiry of her insurance policy.

However, in the second interview Daphné explained that her insurance agent had told her that she could stop her insurance whenever she wanted, which meant that there was no more prescribed time. Moreover, she could have a residential parking place just downstairs from where she lived. And a bit later, as circumstances had it, she again needed her car to move music equipment once a week. Thus, a new need and factors facilitating the use and possession of the car worked to make Daphné keep her car. In the third interview, she still had her car but she was again planning selling it, particularly because she was not entitled to a parking place any more, and parking became a major constraint. She finally took the first step to sell it by going to see a mechanic, but her intention was again thwarted: he dissuaded her, saying that the car was too old to be sold. Thus, Daphné still owns a car but she does not really use it individually and much less on a daily basis.

The process of change in her practices, which lasted approximately two years, was thus motivated by ecological values, the influence of her circle, and experimentation with other ways of getting around, encouraged by her peer group. However, the context and circumstances came into play, sometimes favouring her decision [bus line, parking place, insurance term ...] and sometimes inhibiting it [insurance cancellation cost, parking fees, no trade-in value ...].

Considering the interview as a social interaction, it can demonstrate how the transmission of information and the social relationship can influence attitudes and sometimes behaviour.

The interview provides information when mentioning elements that the interviewee did not know, such as the existence of certain modes or services of transportation. It appeared in particular that few people were familiar with car-sharing systems. Asking them a question raised interest among some interviewees and even a request for explanation. ['Car sharing? No, I don't know. What is it?']. The same appeared for the bike-sharing system: how to enroll ['I don't know how long it takes to make the request'; 'Do you make your request at the town hall or is there a special place to do it?'] or how to use it, for example when there is no slot to return the bicycle. It appears here that people can obtain information through social interaction and social networks.

Some interviewees such as Céline even modified their practices following the longitudinal interviews. In the first interview, she did not know about the car-sharing system whereas she had an occasional need of the car. Furthermore, she expressed how constraining it was to borrow her mother's car. During the course of the interview, she was informed about the existence of car sharing. And thus she started to think about this system, explaining that she will have a look at it. In a second interview, it became clear that she had subscribed to a car sharing system the day following the first interview.

> The day after our interview, I called them. In fact, the next day I had customers who asked me to go to see them at the Beauvais airport. So instead of going by public transport and having a bad time or instead of borrowing my parents' car, I called the company and said, 'I just saw your car rental system – is it possible to register in one day and get a car immediately? How does it work?' (Céline, age 27).

During the interview, respondents could also consider their own behaviour and attitudes. For example, Yan realized that travelling now by scooter instead of bicycle did not correspond to the environmental concerns in society.

> 'I bought a motor scooter. Maybe I shouldn't have …' 'Why? It's not going in the right direction! They install bicycles (Vélib') so that we use them and then what do I do, I buy a scooter and I give up my bicycle!' (Yan, age 31).

And calculating his travel budget during the interview, another person wound up questioning his car ownership.

> My budget? No idea! Do you want me to calculate it? … Maybe 5,000€ a year on the car, and we must do about 7–8,000 km a year. So it's completely unreasonable to have a car! It's a very large chunk of my budget, but I use it very little. There are too many expenses with a car that you can't reduce. So, financially speaking, if we were realistic, we should get rid of it (Philippe, age 44).

Thus, the social interaction which stems from the interview may modify attitudes and behaviour as it delivers information and stimulates reflection by making interviewees consider their practices and their concerns.[6] Some actions to manage change are presented below.

---

6   The effects of the interview technique raise methodological questions which are analysed in another paper (Rocci 2009b).

Proposed Actions to Manage a Change:
The Voluntary Travel Behavioural Change Programmes

Information appears an important factor of change, even if it has shortcomings. People do not always know the alternatives to the car, and do not always understand or consider the consequences of their own practices on the climate change issue.

But, to have influence on behaviour, information must be tailored and individualized. People need to be personally affected and to be aware of the personal benefits (e.g. time, financial, social, health, quality of life). It is worthwhile to encourage people to act voluntarily because if people decide to change their behaviour by themselves and, thus, want to achieve a personal goal, there is better chance to act and to modify behaviour.

Voluntary behavioural change programmes, considered as soft measures of mobility management, are often effective because many people lack information about alternatives to the car, even for journeys where good alternatives already exist (Jones 2003).[7] They are experiments or interventions which aim at encouraging users to modify their behaviour voluntarily, excluding the provision of major infrastructures, financial constraints, restrictive policies, penalties or sanctions (Ampt et al. 2006). Those programs consist of raising awareness, providing information, resources and support for people to try alternatives to driving their cars, working through empowerment and motivation (Brög and Ker 2008). The objective here is to give people, in an individualized way, the tools to determine their own decision and to provide the information required to make a well-considered decision. The ways to do it could be:

- Providing individualized information – giving a feedback to persons on the impact of their travels, for instance a feedback on their CO_2 emissions.
- Providing multimodal information – giving a toolkit about the different modes available such as bus and tram schedules, cycle routes, maps, and so on.
- Providing incentives to encourage experiments such as a free public transit ticket, a free bicycle day renting.
- Encouraging commitment to change in the view of the other participants or the family members.
- Arousing introspection through debates, discussions, interviews, personal feedback during the intervention process.

First experiments of those programmes were carried out in Australia under the banner of 'Travel Smart' (Brög et al. 1999; Ker and James 1999; Goulias et al. 2002). The different experiments conducted until now have been successful and have demonstrated that customized encouragement, motivation and information

---

7   See a literature review of Voluntary Travel Behavioural Change experiences (Rocci 2009).

draw a considerable increase of the use of alternatives. Besides, they offer many advantages: a lasting shift from private cars to other modes of transportation, changes in travel patterns, a better image of the alternatives to the car and an improvement of the level of information of the users, free and volunteer modal choice translated into loyalty and durability of new practices.

Nowadays, there is increasing attention being focused on these types of experiments throughout the world.

Conclusion

This research has highlighted the role of information in the process of change, regarding the supply of transport as well as environmental issues. Information is one essential factor of change and an efficient instrument for policies, but it is not sufficient. It has to be integrated in a global action plan based on three elements: information, coercion, incentives.

The results showed the importance of providing users with tools, such as much materials [device] as cognitive tools [stimulate introspection], to help them in changing. People ask at the same time for more tools and knowledge on the transportation options, and on climate change issues as well as practices to adopt. As individuals learn about the existence of other modes of transportation and how they operate, they may wind up changing or diversifying their practices and their modes of transportation. In this respect, information may contribute to the adoption of multimodal practices. The more informed on the existence and running of the various modes of transportation people are, the more willing to adopt multimodal practices they will be.

However, this is less obvious regarding the climate change issue. In that case, information is not always sufficient to make a real change in individuals' behaviour. It may be confusing or contradictory and thus reduce the expected effects. Similarly, too redundant information can cause a rejection. Nevertheless, a weak knowledge of the issue limits the awareness of individuals and hence their intention to change their behaviour. Thus, information contributes to raise awareness and to favour the acceptability of change.

Furthermore, a change would be better accepted, effectively achieved and longer-lasting if it is done voluntarily, provided individualized information is delivered. In comparison, coercion can only have short-term effects: remove the policeman and the bad habits come back straightaway because the attitudes and mentalities do not change. For change to take place, decisions must be taken individually and must achieve a personal goal.

In addition, information appears more efficient when delivered by social networks and transmitted by social interactions, partly because it is prone to social pressure. Indeed, social influence has a considerable impact on individuals' attitudes, practices and behavioural change. People would act in accordance to the group they belong to and listen to the people they trust. The most effective way of diffusing a message is by word of mouth (Stern et al. 1987). This would be efficient for changing behaviour towards more sustainable practices if the group's social norms and values support sustainable mobility practices.

Chapter 13

Land Use and
Transport Information that Matters[1]

Marco te Brömmelstroet and Luca Bertolini

Introduction

One of the key barriers to integration of land use and transport planning is the lack of a 'common language' (i.e. tools, instruments, indicators) that can support planners from both domains in developing shared visions and integrated strategies. Many of such tools and indicators have been developed in recent years, but not so many are implemented in practice. In this chapter a new, participatory development approach for PSS (Planning Support Systems) is proposed, termed MPS (Mediated Planning Support) that addresses bottlenecks blocking this implementation. It is founded on insights from knowledge management, system dynamics and software innovation and is applied in the Greater Region of Amsterdam. This chapter discusses the evolution of the PSS, highlighting the most useful elements which can be applied in other land use and transport planning projects. It offers insights for practitioners and researchers interested in land use and transport planning integration and for professionals that are dealing with supporting planning with information and technologies.

Supporting the Integration of Land Use and Transport Planning

A better integration of transport and land use planning is believed to be crucial in achieving more sustainable mobility patterns in urban areas and is advocated by academics (e.g. Banister 2005; Cervero 1998; Meyer and Miller 2001), professionals (e.g. Transportation Research Board 2004), governments (e.g.European Conference of Ministers of Transport 2002) and business (e.g. WBCSD 2001; WBCSD 2004) alike. Underlying this is the belief that if the land use and transport systems are reciprocally supportive, important benefits of mobility are increased (for example, improved access to activities and jobs, a higher standard of living, WBCSD 2004: 13), while negative impacts

---

1   This chapter is adapted from Te Brömmelstroet, M.C.G., and Bertolini, L. (2008). 'Developing Land use and Transport PSS: Meaningful Information through a Dialogue between Modelers and Planners'. *Transport Policy*, 15(4), 251–9.

(e.g. pollution, risk, congestion are reduced (see for example, Banister 2005; WBCSD 2001; WBCSD 2004)).

From planning theoretical considerations, such integration can be most fruitful if it occurs in early phases of the planning process (Friedmann 1987; Healey 2007). The minds of the planners in both domains are still open in these phases, which is needed to come up with innovative ideas and shared concepts and visions. The issues that are being dealt with here are also less contested due to their abstract nature. It is assumed that with shared LUT (Land Use Transport) visions and concepts in place, the chances of conflicting land use and transport plans and projects are significantly reduced.

Yet, in general, real integrated LUT planning processes are often absent in planning practice, especially in these early phases of planning (Banister 2005; Stead et al. 2004; Transportation Research Board 2004). Now both domains develop their own separate visions, scenarios, plans and projects focusing on either specific land use or transport issues. As a result, plans and interventions that are derived from these visions are often (unintended) suboptimal or, in the worst case, conflicting (e.g. car dependent development or unprofitable public transport systems).

A number of factors seem to explain this difficult integration. The cited studies name both institutional/procedural discrepancies (i.e. different planning institutions, financial arrangements) and substantive differences (i.e. different planning objects, information, knowledge). This is also recognized in recent, dedicated research projects such as DISTILLATE in Great Britain (Hull and Tricker 2006; Jones and Lucas 2005) and IMPACT in Sweden (TransportMistra 2007). Although we recognize that the institutional and substantive domains are strongly interrelated, the focus of this chapter is mainly on the substantive barriers.

There have been significant academic and professional efforts to develop common LUT concepts in recent years with the goal to bridge the substantive differences between the two planning domains. The outcome of this is a host of indicators or potential accessibility measures (see for example Bertolini et al. 2005; Geurs and Van Wee 2004), tools and instruments (e.g. Emberger and Ibesich 2006 and Waddell 2002). However, recent studies show that this information and these 'state of the art' instruments are hardly used to support LUT integration in planning practice (NICHES 2007; Te Brömmelstroet 2010). Especially in the early phases of planning there is still a deficiency of relevant integral information and tools (see Hull 2005; Jones and Lucas 2005; Te Brömmelstroet 2010). The tools that do find their way into planning practice are in most cases developed to support the analysis of trends, the evaluation of alternatives or the assessment of projects. Not many of them are able to support scenario-building, story-telling or visioning, all specific tasks in early planning phases (Zapatha and Hopkins 2008). This is not unique for land use and transport planning. The so-called 'implementation gap' is shown in many different studies on the (lack of) use of dedicated information and instruments to support (spatial) planning (see Brewer 1973; Couclelis 2005; Danziger 1977; Klosterman 1997, 2007; Langendorf 1985; Lee 1973, 1994; Stillwell et al. 1999; Uran and Janssen 2003; Vonk et al. 2005). Note that the gap is not only apparent in a wide range of planning domains, but it is also consistent as a trend over a long period of time.

Generally, two extreme types of reactions on this implementation gap exist (Meadows and Robinsons 2002). On the hand, notably planners argue that they do not need tools and instruments in strategic phases. Intuition and experience are enough. On the other hand, notably modellers suggest that current models fail to represent much of the complexity of real life and more sophisticated models have to be developed to convince planners to use them. We assert that in strategic phases an understanding of the crucial mechanisms of reality is crucial to develop efficient strategies, as these mechanisms can be counterintuitive. So supportive models are needed to enable the planner to learn and play with interventions, but they can only be used if they offer a better understanding to the planners; without understanding of the (key mechanisms in) the model, the planner can not learn and translate these lessons in more efficient strategies. The central challenge is to find this balance between complexity and understanding (Bertolini et al. 2005).

To address this challenge, we have taken an approach based on insights from several related academic fields and focus on linking the *existing* routines of planners in specific planning contexts and *existing* models in more meaningful ways. Following findings in the academic fields of knowledge management, software development and system dynamics (Checkland 2001; Checkland and Scholes 1990; Nonaka 1994; Nonaka and Konno 1998; Rouwette et al. 2002; Stapleton and Constable 1997; Van den Belt 2004) we hypothesize that such an approach can give us more valuable insights in how we can truly support the land use and transport planners in the very specific tasks of early planning phases. Firstly, these are insights in how planners work now, where they see chances of land use transport integration and what characteristics dedicated information has too have to support this. And secondly, these are insights in the different sorts of information and instruments, how they are perceived in specific situations and how they can be linked to the specific knowledge field of both land use and transport planners. A context-specific combination of these two kinds of insights seems crucial in bridging the 'implementation gap'. The approach that we have used for this is coined 'Mediated Planning Support' (MPS). The reference is to the notion of Planning Support System (PSS), defined here as an infrastructure that systematically introduces relevant (spatial) information to a specific process of related planning actions (based on Klosterman 1997). Our specific approach to its development is through a mediation process with modellers and planners.

The goal of this chapter is (1) to present MPS as an innovative development method to overcome the implementation gap of land use and transport integration tools and (2) to show the results of a first test case in the Netherlands in terms of the specific requirements for information to support integration of land use and transport planning in early phases. These insights are formulated as field-tested hypotheses that will have to be further tested in other cases based on a design-orientated research approach (see Pawson and Tilley 1997; Van Aken 2004, 2005).

In the following, we will start by defining differences that exist between the sort of knowledge used by land use and transport planners and how these hinder integration. Then, we will shortly discuss how instruments that attempt to bridge these differences are currently used and perceived by planners. Following that, the current debate on the implementation gap of Planning Support Systems is summarized, focusing on proposed directions for improvement. We then make the case that key concepts developed in the practice and literature of knowledge management, system dynamics and software development can serve as useful guidelines for this. We shortly introduce this body of work and modify it to be useful for developing PSS, and thus introduce the MPS approach. The body of the chapter addresses how the MPS method was used in integrated planning processes for the greater Region of Amsterdam. We will synthesize the general insights on the requirements for supporting information and close with conclusions on the developed LUT PSS, a methodological reflection on MPS and recommendations for further research.

A Definition of Knowledge

The substantive barrier between land use and transport planning is related to the differences in types of knowledge used in both domains, fostered by the differences in educational backgrounds and the dominant epistemological frameworks that are used. Before we proceed with the analysis of these differences, it is essential to define how we use the term 'knowledge'.

The existing literature provides no clear consensus about what precisely constitutes knowledge and how it is distinguished from information (Checkland and Holwell 1998). This chapter adopts the definition that knowledge is a meaningful collection of information, such that it can be used in a specific context (Ackoff 1989). For our argument, we will make use of a distinction between 'tacit knowledge' and 'explicit knowledge', a concept developed in the field of knowledge management (see Nonaka and Takeuchi 1995; Polanyi 1967). Here, explicit knowledge is characterized as easily codified, formalized and expressed in words and numbers. It can be shared in systematic language, maps and indicators (Nonaka 1994: 16). Tacit knowledge on the other hand is deeply rooted in action, meaning and personal experience in a specific context. It is harder to codify and share. Converting existing knowledge into new knowledge (such as separated land use and transport knowledge into integrated LUT knowledge) requires interaction between tacit and explicit knowledge in an iterative fashion (as is elaborated in Nonaka and Takeuchi 1995).

Differences in Land Use and Transport Knowledge

Substantive differences between land use and transport planning are not only related to explicit knowledge (for example, differences in indicators, theories and planning objects); there are also strong differences in tacit knowledge domain. We posit that these differences are 1) one of the primary reasons for the lack of implementation of existing LUT tools and 2) largely ignored in the development of these tools. Below we will shortly introduce these differences. The differences sketched below are somewhat extreme, in the sense that they show archetypes of two planning domains. We realize that practice is less black and white, but see this as a useful characterization.

However increasing attention for communicative approaches (see for example Banister 2008), scientific instrumental rationality still seems the predominant paradigm in the field of transport planning (Willson 2001). Therefore, transport planners tend to use more quantitative information concerning e.g. transport flows, levels of service and costs. They focus more on general theories and computer models and tend to have an engineering background (Willson 2001: 2). In general, transport planners focus on solving problems (i.e. congestion) and optimizing the transport system, without much attention for wider (social, economic) goals that can be achieved. In other words, the focus is on finding the means (e.g. congestion charge or highway extension) for a given goal (e.g. efficient functioning of the network). Transport planners often use predictive forecasting methods to deal with uncertainty in the future (Jones and Lucas 2005; van der Bijl and Witsen 2000; Wachs 1985; Zapatha and Hopkins 2007).

On the other hand, land use planners tend to use more qualitative spatial information about places and functions, work in more communicative settings and often have a background in design or the 'soft' social sciences. Today's predominant land use planning mode is (at least theoretically) based on communicative, deliberative rationality in which multiple stakeholders are included (for example, Forester 1999; Healey 1997; Innes 1995). The focus lies on confronting and bringing together multiple goals from multiple disciplines in inclusive strategies. They deal with uncertainty in the future in many different ways (planning, scenarios and visioning) (van der Bijl and Witsen 2000; Zapatha and Hopkins 2007).

The State of Practice of Current LUT Planning Support Tools

In 2007, an internet based survey was conducted among planning practitioners in the Netherlands that had experience in attempts to integrate land use and transport planning processes (Te Brömmelstroet 2010b). The goal was to explore patterns in the lack of implementation of existing tools and broad directions for possible improvement. Findings showed that the respondents (62 transport orientated, 60 land use and two unknown) think that current tools don't provide enough insight in LUT relations, that tools are often used to justify choices that have already been made, that the tools do not fit the planning process and that they are not well linked to the political decision making process. There is not enough support for the generation of alternative solutions and the tools are often implemented too late in the planning process (Te Brömmelstroet 2010b).

Four possible bottlenecks behind these problems were seen as (big) problems by more than half of the respondents;

1. the tools are not transparent enough,
2. they are not user friendly,
3. they are not useful in interactive settings and,
4. the communication value of the outcomes is too low to be useful in the planning context.

These findings echo those of the broader international debate on decision and planning support tools, where it was found that planners see most of these tools as far too generic, complex, technology-orientated (rather than problem-orientated), narrowly focused on strict technical rationality and incompatible with the unpredictable/flexible nature of most planning tasks and information needs (Bishop 1998; Couclelis 2005; Geertman 2006; Klosterman 2001; Lee 1973, 1994; Ottens 1990; Scholten and Stillwell 1990; Vonk 2006). Geertman asserts that the history of planning support tools shows a continuous mismatch between the characteristics of developed tools and characteristics of dominant planning traditions (Geertman 2006: 876). To break through this, Geertman proposes to focus on a better link with the tacit knowledge of the actors in the planning process, with relevant planning issues and with the context-specificities of the planning process, explicitness and transparency in underlying premises, methods and outcomes, and an adaptation of planners (for example, a more constructive-critical attitude towards models) (Geertman 2006: 877–8). Planning support tools should be an integral part of the planning process, they must meet context and user requirements (also proposed by other scholars, notably Lee 1973, 1994; Vonk 2006).

Towards a Better Link between Tool Demand and Supply

For the support of integrated LUT strategy development this means that the focus should be on developing a common LUT language that can bridge both tacit and explicit differences in real-life planning contexts Such a language should be understandable for all (land use and transport) participants on the level of general assumptions, input and output. To face this challenge we have to shift the focus from developing innovative explicit information to incorporating the tacit elements of knowledge, the context specifics of the LUT planning process and the user requirements.

Many other disciplines have dealt with similar challenges in the past. Based on lessons from these fields and integrating these with the context-specificities of planning support, a process framework was proposed that facilitates a constructive and structured dialogue between model developers and planners. This method is shortly introduced below. Then, a case study in which the framework was used to support LUT strategy development is discussed leading to some first findings on how to develop meaningful LUT knowledge.

Mediated Planning Support

The academic foundations of our framework (which we coin 'mediated planning support' (MPS)) are comprehensively discussed in a separate paper (Te Brömmelstroet and Schrijnen 2010). Here, we will limit ourselves to introducing the main elements of the approach (Figure 13.1). The core principles are:

- A iterative stepwise approach – to give structure, but take double-loop learning effects into account (Argyris 2005; Stapleton and Constable 1997);
- Experiencing, reflecting, conceptualizing and experimenting for every (sub)product, according to the learning cycle of Kolb (1984);
- Socialization, externalization, combination and internalization of knowledge incorporated in the entire process to link tacit and explicit aspects (Nonaka 1994; Nonaka and Konno 1998);
- Support of a trajectory from problem definition to defining strategies for an existing planning problem to stay close the questions of the client and make the PSS an integral part of the planning process (Checkland and Scholes 1990; Lee 1973; Vonk 2006);
- Constructive and continuous dialogue between planners and PSS developers (Meadows and Robinsons 2002; van den Belt 2004; Vennix et al. 1997);
- Focus on group learning to come to planning LUT strategies (Argyris 1999; Vennix et al. 1997);
- Use of as much standing technologies as possible to overcome acceptance bottlenecks (Vonk et al. 2005);
- Keeping it as simple as possible, but not simpler then necessary (Meadows and Robinsons 2002; van den Belt 2004).

With reference to Figure 13.1, a MPS process starts with a focus on the definition of the specific planning problem at hand (in this case the early integration of LUT planning on an urban regional level). At this point, also the group of participants has to be identified (land use planners, transport planners and preferably also stakeholders from both domains), followed by introductory interviews.

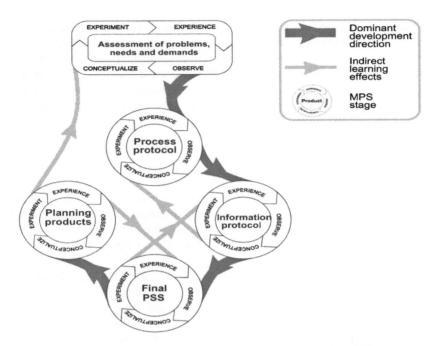

Figure 13.1   Framework for mediated planning support for LUT planning

In this way the participants' views of the planning problem and their expectations of the MPS process and its results are clarified. Subsequently, both a problem definition and a first design brief for a PSS have to be formulated. This is Step 1 of the MPS process.

A series of workshops follows where a planning product and a PSS (process and information) are simultaneously developed. This combination is important, as it creates a continuous testing ground for the intermediate results and fosters mutual learning effects. Working with the PSS also generates new insights in the user's needs. The second MPS step focuses on a *process protocol*, i.e. the necessary steps for arriving at a desired planning product. In the third step, the participants have to identify which information is useful and understandable in each step. In this workshop a first prototype of the common language (*information protocol*) is created. Through dialogue, the PSS developers and planners have to find out what kind of information is seen as useful in supporting the process protocol. By identifying where the information should be used, an information protocol is developed. These first two stages can be seen as a prototype development. Using the protocols and redefining them takes place in the next two stages.

In the fourth stage, this prototype is put to the test; the group of participants has to work with the PSS to arrive at the defined integrated planning product (the desired output is defined by the participants in the first and second stages).

Depending on how the group has defined the process protocol, this stage can stretch over multiple workshops. The fifth and last stage focuses on improving the PSS (based on the lessons learned) and on finalizing the planning product. The result is a *final PSS*.

As Figure 13.1 shows, the process has a dominant direction, but there are many recursive learning effects (the thin lines). For example, gaining new insights about an ideal sequence of planning steps can lead to a reformulated process protocol (learning by doing), which in turn can lead to new information needs.

Besides addressing the 'implementation gap' of PSS, such an iterative and inclusive approach is believed to foster interaction between tacit and explicit knowledge and to create improved relationships between planners and model developers (see also Ehrmann and Stinson 1999; Meadows and Robinsons 2002).

The next section will present a case study in which the MPS approach was used to develop a LUT PSS to support integral strategy development. According to the design orientated research approach, this case is used to find out how the MPS approach works in planning practice and what outcomes such a process would generate. These will have to be tested further in subsequent cases to ground them as 'technological rules' (following Pawson and Tilley 1997; Van Aken 2004). To come to these field-tested hypotheses different qualitative research methods and techniques were used before, during and after the workshops. These included participant observation, questionnaires and action research methods (Argyris et al. 1985). Two researchers of the University of Amsterdam and one from Delft University of Technology prepared and attended the workshops. One researcher was chairing and preparing the sessions while the other two were observing the participants. After each session, the participants were individually asked to reflect on the products and the process. In-depth interviews and meetings were held to clarify how the approach was received and what was gained through participating in it.

Mediated Planning Support Applied: The Case of Amsterdam

MPS was applied to support an integrated LUT strategy development process in the Greater Region of Amsterdam (Figure 13.2). This region is a semi-formal cooperation of 16 municipalities surrounding Amsterdam, encompassing about 1.4 million inhabitants. Amsterdam is the biggest and central city in this area. Leading job locations are located in the city centre, at the southern part of Amsterdam and near Schiphol airport.

The municipality of Amsterdam is the only Dutch municipality with their own fully functional transportation model – GenMod. It is a static and multimodal four step transportation model based on household surveys and mobility counts. GenMod does not represent the state-of-art looking at models available in research environments, but it can be seen as a common type of transport model applied for planning in the Netherlands (state of practice).

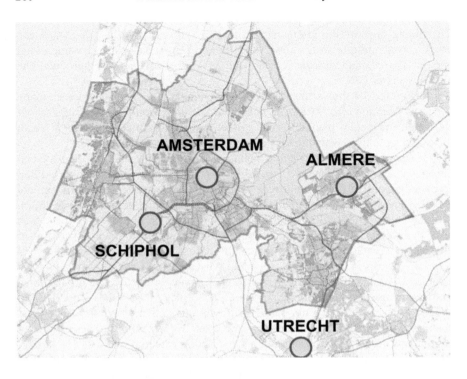

Figure 13.2   Greater Region of Amsterdam

Following the MPS principle of using as much as possible standing technologies and the belief of participants that while relatively simple, GenMod could still generate useful (i.e. complex and understandable enough) insights in LUT interaction mechanisms in early, strategic phases of the planning process, it was decided to use it as main source of information. GenMod covers 933 zones and includes extensive car and public transport networks. The model is capable of calculating transportation impacts for land use and transport developments in the Greater Region of Amsterdam. Recent test results have shown that the outcomes of the model are the best available in the Netherlands. Despite this, the model is not used to its full potential (especially in strategic phases of the planning process). It seems that the model is too narrowly focused on producing rigorous-calculation results, to be used as input for a technical rational planning process. Hence, it is not useful for the (also in Amsterdam much needed) support of LUT integration in early phases. In 2005 the Transportation Planning Department of Amsterdam (DIVV) and the University of Amsterdam thus started cooperation in a project aimed at increasing the usefulness of GenMod for the support of LUT integration in early phases of regional planning (for example, integral visioning). For this, MPS was implemented.

Involving approximately ten to fifteen participants, the MPS process included six formal meetings, from April 2006 to May 2007. Depending on the particular phase, the group of participants consisted of transport modellers, transport planners, land use planners (all from the Amsterdam municipality), land use planners from the regional authority (Stadsregio Amsterdam), representatives from the Dutch Railway company and researchers from the University of Amsterdam.

Developed MPS Products for LUT Planning Support

Below, we will discuss the developed products in the initial order of the MPS stages (Figure 13.1). This does not always reflect their order of development; due to recursive learning effects, often the products were redefined later in the process, as already discussed above.

Problem Assessment

The MPS for early LUT integration started with a session discussing current planning processes, focusing on bottlenecks blocking integration throughout the (cyclical) planning process. One of the conclusions was that transport planners see themselves reacting on already defined land-use plans, instead of jointly participating in earlier planning phases.

It continued with a discussion on the current planning process. According to the participants, planning is a cyclical process. It often starts with either a land use or a transport idea, followed by an internal discussion among (land use *or* transport) experts and stakeholders, where a shared vision is developed. Subsequently, risks, needs and opportunities are analysed and decision makers have to decide on a 'go – no go' basis, often followed by a 'benefit and necessity' discussion, which is a long process also involving citizens. This can either lead to the implementation of the land use/transport idea or to a new planning cycle. For concepts developed from a land use perspective there is often no support from the transport side and vice-versa, resulting in mutual competition and potential for conflict in later stages. Improving integration in the early phases (of concept development) would prevent such conflicts. As discussed below, in its current form GenMod is not suited to provide support for this.

A second session focused on discussing the planning problem that should be addressed in an integral LUT process. The participants agreed on working on alternatives to accommodate the economic growth that the region is expecting until 2030. This growth calls for an addition of 150,000 houses and 150,000 jobs. Also, the infrastructure faces a challenge to accommodate the corresponding traffic. Working on combined transport and land use alternatives was expected to create insights and lessons in to how these challenges can be coped with in an integrated fashion.

Process Protocol

In the following workshop the participants discussed which functional process could overcome the identified bottlenecks. The results of this discussion were interpreted by the researchers of the University of Amsterdam, who presented a process protocol in the next workshop. Again, this protocol was discussed (and used), eventually producing the one depicted in Figure 13.3a. Key characteristics of the process protocol are:

- The first planning step should focus on generating land use alternatives based on issues of accessibility and sustainability (derived from an analysis of existing urban development programmes/trends). In this step, existing land use constraints (for example, ecological protected areas) have to be considered in order to avoid the development of an overly idealistic LUT strategy.
- In the second step, the alternatives have to be tested on their network implications (e.g. level of service) and on the same indicators as in Step 1 to show the dynamics of these indicators. This will lead to an optimizing design exercise (but possibly also to more radical reframing) in which choices made in the various alternatives can be altered. Also infrastructure measures can be introduced here.
- The third step of the process protocol is to analyse and discuss the differences and similarities between the developed alternatives and consequences, in order to discern robust choices for future LUT systems (land use and/or transport planning decisions which are always beneficial) and interdependencies ('if we want this then we should do that' or 'if we do this then we can expect that'). This was considered more useful then drafting a 'best LUT plan'; supported by the belief that, while central and comprehensive planning of regional LUT developments is not feasible, being aware of broader implications is essential in order to decide and act consistently on specific issues as they appear (for example, infrastructural projects, local housing development plans).
- Learning effects can lead the participants (ideally also including information providers) to reconsider the LUT choices made earlier in the process (such as in the first developed alternatives).

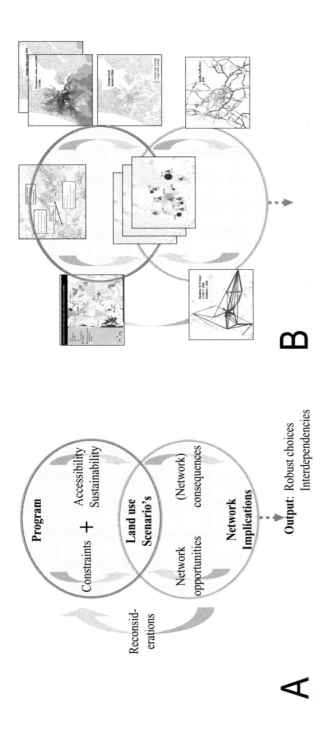

Figure 13.3 The process protocol (a) and the information protocol (b)

Information Protocol

The next step towards the LUT PSS was selecting the preferred information characteristics with the participants in relation to the envisaged process protocol. Discussions and individual exercises revealed that user needs in such a process were very different from the current characteristics of GenMod. The planners acknowledged that the explicit knowledge currently does not link to their tacit knowledge, as was also discussed above. They need a common language to discuss strategies, to sharpen concepts and ideas and to build visions. Characteristics as 'detail' and 'precision' are considered to be of minimal relevance. GenMod should be used to test existing insights and create new ones, instead of delivering 'facts' and evaluating existing plans and projects. Furthermore, GenMod is neither transparent nor user-friendly, generating a black box feeling. The model should not only predict future macro situations, but also create insight in LUT choices and opportunities. Finally, it was recognized that there are different layers of 'users' (i.e. citizens, stakeholders, experts) with different information needs, a feature that has to be included in a PSS.

The second step towards the information protocol was to judge and discuss the existing LUT information. In a workshop, the participants rated and discussed archetypical LUT maps and data that could be useful. A selection was made and related to the steps in the process protocol. The resulting information protocol (again after iterations of testing) is shown in Figure 13.3b. The important characteristics are:

- In the first planning step (constructing the land use alternatives), spatial maps are key. For the design of land use alternatives the participants wanted to know the spatial situation of indicators, such as potential accessibility (e.g. the number of people or jobs accessible from each zone within acceptable travel time) and sustainability (e.g. the number of people or jobs reachable within a direct distance of 5 kilometres[2]). Also spatial constraints have to be considered (e.g. valuable landscape features).
- The LUT information for the first step should in the first place function as a platform for discussions (linking tacit and explicit knowledge). For this purpose the information has to be (1) understandable for all participants, thus transparency of it is crucial (2) qualitative rather then quantitative and (3) simple rather than sophisticated.
- In the following step (showing the LUT consequences of the choices made) GenMod should calculate network consequences (e.g. level of service), network opportunities (e.g. for more efficient use) and the dynamics of the indicators used in the first step. This creates an understanding of

---

2   This indicator is seen as a proxy for sustainability, because it shows the number of activities within reach by slow modes (walking and bicycles), or by shorter trips on motorized modes (proximity).

which choices have a positive impact on the chosen indicators and which a negative one.

- In the third and final planning step (selecting robust choices and identifying interdependencies) the model should present clear overviews of all indicators and maps. These are then used to facilitate a closing discussion between the participants on the LUT lessons learned and to create a list of appropriate LUT choices and strategies.
- For these two latter steps, the information should sharpen existing ideas and can therefore be more complex. However, to be useful it should be (1) understandable, by explanation and discussion among the participants (2) more quantitative than qualitative and (3) transparent in its assumptions and calculations.

Final LUT PSS

The resulting product of the development approach was the final LUT PSS, a result of testing the proposed process and information protocol in the development of integrated LUT strategies. The participants were overall satisfied with the first version of the process protocol. It seemed that the alternative development and optimization supported an early integration of LUT planning.

The information protocol as depicted in Figure 13.3b was the subject of more group discussion. While everybody agreed on the usefulness of most indicators, the land use planners requested more transparency of the potential accessibility maps; what is included, what is excluded and what are the assumptions. According to one land use planner, flexible availability of other relevant information is required alongside these basic indicators. This is something that has to be improved in the final PSS, which is currently being developed in cooperation with the model developers and the University of Amsterdam. The focus lies on the creation of a 'GenMod light', with an increased interactive character and on better documentation to increase the transparency of the information.

Integrated LUT Strategies

The desired end product of the MPS process is not only the final PSS, but an integrated LUT strategy. In the case of Amsterdam, the participants agreed upfront that they did not want to create the best possible alternative from a LUT perspective, but foremost they wanted to improve their insight into LUT relations and the consequences of possible land use and/or transport choices and opportunities. The desired outcome of the process is a list of robust choices for future LUT systems (land use and/or transport planning decisions which seem to work in different scenarios) and interdependencies ('if we want A then we should do B' or 'if we do A then we can expect B'). Both lists should be accompanied by the corresponding information that was used (explicit knowledge) and discussions that took place (tacit knowledge). Such a product can then be presented to other municipalities in the region, to stakeholders and to decision makers.

An example of a robust choice in the case discussed was to concentrate land use programs along existing public transport infrastructure corridors. This was not an entirely new notion, but according to the participants the collection of information that was selected in the MPS approach provided clearer argument for this idea (currently not applied in land use planning!). Also, an expressed robust choice was to 'stop the expansion of the road network after the current A6-A9 link and optimize the regional public transport network of the Amsterdam region in combination with increasing the densities of the existing built-up areas'.

An example of a LUT interdependency that became evident in the process (as noted by a transport planner) is 'if we want to further develop the new town of Almere, *faster* public transport connections have to be developed (not mere capacity expansion) and development should occur only on the Westside of the existing town'. Interestingly and contrary to the official views, the developed land use alternatives also showed that from a LUT perspective the existing program could be developed almost without putting more pressure on Almere. The choice to build more houses there (the government plans to add 60,000 houses there before 2030), does not seem to be logical one from a LUT perspective. Such an intervention will probably result in unsustainable traffic on the road- and rail-links between Almere and Amsterdam. Creating more job opportunities in Almere seems to be a more robust choice. In the same vein, better housing location from a LUT perspective, and still acceptable form other perspectives, were also identified.

Conclusion and Discussion

This chapter started with signalling the importance of LUT integration and the lack of it in planning practice, especially in early phases of the planning process. It was argued that this was partly due to a substantive barrier. A survey among practitioners in the Netherlands showed that current instruments and PSS that attempt to overcome this barrier are not used, largely because of so-called soft reasons: tacit and explicit knowledge do not seem to match. These findings echoed general research on the implementation gap of PSS and it was proposed to follow guidelines suggested by other academic fields and to construct a structured dialogue between modellers and planners to develop and use existing LUT information for the support of early planning integration: Mediated Planning Support (MPS). This method was applied in the Greater Region of Amsterdam.

The outcome of the MPS process in Amsterdam is twofold; the LUT PSS (consisting of a process and an information protocol) and the shared LUT strategies. Below, we will summarize their main characteristics focusing on possible generic features applicable to other strategic LUT processes. These are presented as first 'field-tested' principles, which will be further tested in consecutive cases.

In closing the chapter, we reflect on the approach taken and suggestions for further research.

PSS for Strategic Land Use and Transport Planning

The process protocol (Figure 13.3a) provided a stepwise approach to get land use and transport planners in a cooperative process of developing shared strategies:

- Starting with a shared concept of the problem statement seems crucial; it can show the planners that the two domains have similar goals and can thus result in shared ideas or strategies.
- Developing alternatives in mixed groups of land use and transport planners is important to get diverging possibilities to solve the LUT problem, to support and guide the discussion between the planners, to learn about system dynamics and to test different strategies.
- The preferred outcome is a shared 'feeling' for the dynamics of LUT relations, as materialized in the identification of robust choices and important interdependencies. This enhances the learning effect (for participants) with a view on informing the negotiations where strategic decisions are made (i.e. by showing cross implications and trade-offs of such decisions).

The information protocol (Figure 13.3b) shows which kind of explicit information might be useful in which step of the strategy developing process:

- The generation of alternatives seems best supported by geographical mappings of the current situation. This means that some transport issues have to be translated in a geographical indicator (to improve understanding of their spatial implications).
- Simplicity is key: although the planners and modellers recognized that more complex measures are needed later in the planning process, simple indicators were deemed most useful in this early process. Much 'tacit' awareness about the complexity was already present at the table. Putting it in the indicator could even hamper a fruitful discussion.
- Network maps showing the functioning of important transport links are important for understanding the impacts of the generated alternatives (rather than helping generating them), so they can be compared and optimized (or more radically questioned).
- Most additional information should be provided in the form of a background database (such as on a laptop) that can be consulted during discussions; especially the indicators that show the dynamics between alternatives.

- In the final stage (selecting robust choices and identifying interdependencies) graphs are helpful in indicating the impact of certain interventions. It also helps to visualize the variation in impacts between the various alternatives. In particular maps showing the differences in geographical indicators seem to help planners grasp the internal dynamics of the alternatives. Where do certain effects occur when a certain intervention is planned?

LUT Strategies

The participants mentioned that the primary gain of this process is not (only) new LUT insights, but rather an increased (and perhaps most importantly a shared) awareness of the rationale behind LUT relations and choices. Or even, as one transport planner asserted: 'it created insight that existing ideas are not the only ones that make sense'. The participants also noted that the process perfected existing ideas and concepts, enriched their evidence-base and created a common language to address these issues. The transport planners emphasized that they now have useful process framework and guidelines, which might allow them to be involved in earlier phases of the planning process.

The MPS Approach as Mechanism

The process in Amsterdam has shown that working through the steps of the MPS framework results in a better fit between the existing transport model and the specific demands of LUT strategy development. Overcoming several of the identified bottlenecks (most notably increased transparency of the tool, increased interactiveness, improved communication value) resulted in more or better argued LUT insights, an improved fit with the planning process and improved support for the *generation* of alternatives, compared with the previous situation.

One of the key mechanisms seems to be the structured discussion and deliberation between the modellers and the planners. The planners feel that they now have more useful information that is understandable and that shows the crucial and relevant LUT relations. Due to the discussions in the workshops, all participants were fully aware of the limitations of the information and the assumptions behind them. This awareness seemed to be a condition for the creative use of the information.

During the process, much attention was given to how the information should be presented to be useful for the planners. The GenMod developers learned that spatial representation of transport impacts is crucial in supporting land use planners; increase and decrease categories ('better', 'similar', 'worse') communicate better than detailed figures and graphs are useful to compare different designs and interventions.

Importance of Context and Further Research

Unlike other regions, the Greater Region of Amsterdam can use a transport model that is managed by the municipality of Amsterdam. This unique situation makes it easier to adapt calculations and output to specific demands by planners. Also, the urban dynamics of the region are higher than that of other regions in the Netherlands, especially with respect to the expected economic growth in the coming decades, resulting in a greater sense of urgency. Moreover, the land use and transport planners in the region and the municipality of Amsterdam are relatively highly educated (Healey 2007) which might make them more capable and willing to work in innovative settings than those of an average municipality. Finally, the workshops only included planners (and one stakeholder), future cases need to include also decision makers and more stakeholders to see if such an approach can be applied in wider planning settings.

These characteristics may have important implications for the outcomes of the process and the potential to generalize them. Both the MPS approach as mechanism and the outcomes have therefore to be subjected to further testing in other contexts. The integration of more up-to-date models in the planning process should be also experimented with. Such research has to focus on how changes in context affect the usability of the MPS approach and if the LUT PSS features presented here are general principles or have to be adapted.

PART IV
Policy Evaluation

Chapter 14

Modelling Responses to Congestion Pricing in Tel-Aviv: An Activity-Based Approach

Yoram Shiftan and Issa Zananiri

Introduction

Congestion pricing is recognized as an integral part of managing any transition toward sustainable transportation, and it is becoming more and more popular as a policy measure to encourage people to shift from private-car use to public transportation (PT) or to change their travel time to off-peak periods. Such policies, however, can have other effects on travel patterns. They may encourage people to travel to other destinations or to change or cancel their activities altogether. In the long run, these policies may even cause businesses to move outside the existing business district, thereby dispersing activities and increasing dependency on private cars. Such a response may increase congestion and air pollution in the long term and, thus, reverse the effects intended in implementing the measure.

Congestion pricing should increase the attractiveness of the central business district (CBD) by encouraging people to change their choice of both travel mode and travel time without discouraging them from coming to the city centre. A successful policy should restrain commuting by car without hindering shoppers and people doing personal business. Commuters can shift only their travel mode and occasionally the time of day of their trip, but shoppers and other visitors can also shift their destination or even cancel their trip altogether, thus affecting the economy of the city centre.

The benefits and costs of car-restraint policies should be carefully studied before such policies are implemented. Benefits include reduced travel time and costs for some users; improved downtown amenities and potentially improved economic activity; reduced air pollution, noise pollution, and energy consumption; more productive land use and a reduced need to expand highways. Costs include a potential decline in economic activity, an increase in administrative costs, larger transit deficits, higher travel time and operating costs for users who change their travel patterns to avoid the restraint penalty, and potentially increased congestion outside the area where the measure is applied.

Finally, revenue from such policies should be considered neither a benefit nor a cost, but rather a transfer of resources.

To evaluate the potential benefits of car restraint policies and to learn how they function as a powerful transportation-planning tool, we need an improved understanding of individuals' responses to them and how those responses in turn affect traffic congestion, land use, and the vitality and value of the CBD. Understanding of travel behaviour and, in particular, of travellers' responses to various policies has recently been improved by the introduction of activity-based models. This chapter evaluates, by means of an activity-based approach, the potential response of visitors to the city of Tel Aviv in Israel to a congestion-pricing scheme that is being considered by the Israel Ministry of Transport.

Tel Aviv, the largest metropolitan area in Israel, serves as the country's main financial and cultural centre. The Tel Aviv Metropolitan Area (TAMA) stretches over 1,475 square kilometres and is inhabited by 3.2 million people. Given its geographical and economic position, the TAMA is a transportation focal point. Much of the traffic between the north and the south of Israel, as well as interconnecting traffic between the main cities (Jerusalem, Tel-Aviv, Haifa, and Beersheba), passes through the area. Thus, the metropolitan transportation infrastructure serves not just local and regional but also national traffic. The public transport system in Tel Aviv is based mostly on buses, which serve 93 per cent of the transit trips. Most buses share lanes with private vehicles; there are only 74 km of designated bus lanes, most of which are not physically separated from the regular traffic; there is, furthermore, insufficient enforcement to prevent trespassing. Train services in Tel Aviv are operated by the Israel National Railways company, and they include intercity as well as a few suburban lines. Modal split between private and public transportation trips is about 70:30 in favour of the private car.

Similar to many large urban areas around the globe, the city of Tel Aviv suffers from severe traffic congestion. Various congestion-pricing schemes are being considered for the purpose of easing congestion. These schemes vary according to three different geographical areas of coverage, three different times of day periods, three toll rates (of NIS 10, 20, and 30, where 1 EURO is about 5 New Israeli Shekels [NIS]), as well as the use of cordon (travellers being charged for crossing the area border) and area (travellers being charged for any movement within the area) charges.

Methodology

To better understand travel behaviour, research and practice are moving today toward activity-based models that treat travel as derived demand stemming from the demand to participate in activities. Travel choices, therefore, become part of a broader activity-scheduling process, which is based on modelling the demand for activities rather than merely the demand for trips. This new approach focuses on individual decisions regarding when and where to participate in what activities and for how long, taking into account time and space constraints. The explicit modelling of activities and consequent tours and trips along a time and space spectrum enables a more credible analysis of responses to policies and of their effect on traffic and air quality. Various metropolitan areas have developed or are in the process of developing new activity-based models for their metropolitan travel-demand model; among these areas are San Francisco (Bradley et al. 2002; Jonnalagadda et al. 2001), New York, Columbus (Ohio), Atlanta (Bradley and Vovsha 2005), Dallas/Forth-Worth, Sydney, the Dutch Albatros model (Arentze and Timmermans 2001), and the Travel Activity Scheduler for Household Agents (TASHA) model in Toronto (Roorda et al. 2008); moreover, various researchers have used this approach to study the responses of travellers to various policies (Shiftan and Suhrbier 2002; Davidson et al. 2007; Kitamura 1997; and Recker and Parimi 1999). Using an activity-based approach can reveal response behaviour that would not be shown under the traditional trip-based approach. For example, consider a person who travels from home to work during the peak hour in the morning, and then in the afternoon from work back home but needs to pick up his son on the way. A trip-based approach may show that with the introduction of congestion pricing this person would shift to transit; in reality, this is not a valid option in a case that the day-care facility does not have good transit accessibility because of the need to collect the child on the way back. Only activity-based modelling can take into account such considerations, and therefore it is likely to better estimate the response to congestion pricing.

This study develops and estimates an activity-based congestion pricing response model in order to better understand the complex response to toll pricing. Decisions to change behaviour are better explained in a whole daily-activity pattern and tour context than as trips in isolation.

For this purpose we developed a survey including revealed activity based data for one day, and a stated preference questions to obtain responses to potential congestion-pricing schemes based on the respondent's actual tour to the area where such a schemes was considered. The survey also asked respondents regarding their views of the suggested congestion tolls scheme. In each of the stated preference (SP) questions one of the congestion pricing schemes was presented to the respondent who had to choose among various alternatives, including mode and time shift, destination change, and trip cancelation. The data from this survey were used to estimate the activity-based congestion-pricing response model.

Data Collection

The targeted population of this study were drivers who enter or pass through the Tel Aviv area during the morning or afternoon peak hours; given the area's central location and role in Israel, this population can include residents from the whole country. The survey was designed and programmed as a web-based questionnaire. The sample was drawn from a given database of random individuals who are willing to respond to questionnaires and are paid for each questionnaire to which they respond. The socio-economic and demographic data of these respondents were already available in the database, and there was no need to ask such questions again. A total of 4,132 people responded to the survey, of which only 799 had actually entered the area being considered for congestion pricing in the past couple of weeks; this group filled out the stated-preference questionnaire. After cleaning the data for various problems, there were 793 records that were used for the model estimation.

Questionnaire Design

The questionnaire consisted of three main parts: (1) various general questions; (2) a travel diary, including details about a tour that involved travelling through the proposed toll congestion area; and (3) a stated-preference experiment regarding potential responses to various toll schemes. As mentioned, socio-economic and demographic variables were already available for the sample: age, gender, marital status, number of children, education, religious status, employment, and income. However, some general questions important for this analysis that were not available in the database were asked: Who pays for fuel and parking? Who will most probably pay for the congestion toll? Public acceptance questions were also asked, for which each respondent was asked to indicate on a scale from one to five his or her level of agreement with the implementation of the toll. Each respondent was asked, in addition, if the implementation of the toll should be conditioned on improving public transportation and on applying the revenue from the toll to improve public transportation as well as whether the toll would help ease traffic congestion.

The second part of the questionnaire asked respondents for details about their daily activity and travel patterns and specific details about each trip segment for the tour that include entering the area considered for congestion pricing; details included starting place and time, places visited, mode used, and costs and times of these trips. Respondents were also asked to estimate the time and cost of their tours if they were to use public transportation instead of their car.

Based on the actual tour that the respondent reported, the details of its time and cost under various congestion-pricing schemes for various response alternatives were developed and presented to the respondent. This was done automatically by the survey software, which randomly assigned some percentage change from the value of the actual tour taken for each variable and presented the respondent with the new value for each variable under each alternative. The respondent had to choose among five main alternative responses to the implementation of congestions pricing: first, pay the toll and continue driving without any change to one's travel patterns; second, shift to public transit; third, continue to drive but change the trip time; fourth, change the destination of the trip; fifth, cancel the trip altogether. Each scenario contained the following parameters: toll price in New Israel Shekels (NIS), travel time in car for the whole tour, and public transit travel time and cost for the whole tour. Each respondent was asked to respond to six different scenarios of potential congestion pricing.

Data Analysis

This section presents some descriptive statistical results for the three main types of data: socio-economic variables, scenario parameters, and the tour undertaken by each person.

Demographic and Socio-economic Data

The socio-economic data for the actual sample, presented in Table 14.1, shows a balanced distribution by gender. The distribution of the other demographic and socio-economic variables is consistent with the Census data and show that the sample is representative of the Israeli population.

Table 14.1   Socio-economic distribution of the sample

		Survey		NTHS	
		Number	*Percentage*	*Number*	*Percentage*
Gender	Male	401	50.2%	3,065	60.2%
	Female	393	49.8%	2,026	39.8%
Status	Married	467	58.4%	3,574	70.6%
	Single	259	32.4%	1,171	23.1%
	Divorced	64	8.0%	189	3.7%
	Widowed	9	1.10%	131	2.6%
Children	0	224	28.0%	3,351	68.5%
	1	98	12.0%	915	18.7%
	2+	477	60.0%	625	12.8%
Religion	Jew	753	94.2%	–	–
	Christian	3	0.4%	–	–
	Muslim	3	0.4%	–	–
	Druze	1	0.1%	–	–
	Atheist	40	5.1%	–	–

Table 14.1   Continued

Religious Status	Non-religious	484	60.6%	–	–
	Religious	309	38.7%	–	–
	(blank)	6	0.8	–	–
Education	Finished at least a Bachelor's Degree	324	40.6%	1,400	29.7%
	Junior College Degree	237	29.7%	658	14.0%
	High School Diploma only	204	25.5%	1,944	41.2%
	Did not finish school	29	3.6%	693	14.7%
	(blank)	5	0.6%	20	0.4%
Employment	Freelancer	121	15.1%	3,583	71.4%
	Employee	425	53.2%		
	Student	109	13.6%		
	Army service	29	3.6%	224	4.5%
	Unemployed	101	12.6%	1,210	24.1%
	(blank)	14	1.8%	0	0.0%
Age group	16–19	34	4.3%	99	2.0%
	20–24	111	13.9%	595	12.0%
	25–29	125	15.6%	646	13.0%
	30–34	117	14.6%	565	11.4%
	35–44	149	18.6%	1,250	25.2%
	45–54	149	18.6%	892	18.0%
	55–64	64	8.0%	490	9.9%
	65+	16	2.0%	429	8.6%
	(blank)	5	0.6%	0	0.0%
Income	High above Average Income	139	17.4%	–	–
	Higher than Average Income	69	8.60%	–	–
	Average Income	206	25.8%	–	–
	Lower than Average Income	187	23.4%	–	–
	Much Lower than Average Income	174	21.8%	–	–
	(blank)	24	3.0%	–	–
Geographical Distribution of Place of Residence	Jerusalem Area	62	7.8%	–	–
	South	59	7.4%	–	–
	North	80	10.1%	–	–
	Centre	592	74.7%	–	–

General Questions

Several questions were asked about who pays for the respondents' tour costs. The responses to these questions are shown in Table 14.2. As can be seen, a significant proportion of the sample is reimbursed at least partially for their travel expenses: more than 25 per cent stated that they were reimbursed for at least some of their transport fuel expenses, and 13 per cent for all their fuel costs (paid by the employer); a similar picture is seen for the parking expenses. This is consistent with the widespread phenomenon of company cars in Israel, with the employer providing the employee with a car as part of his or her benefits and in many cases also paying for fuel and parking (Cohen-Blankshtain 2008; Shiftan et al. 2012). It is interesting to note that with regard to the question whether the respondents expected their employer to pay for the potential congestion toll, the proportion who answered affirmatively was similar to that of those who are currently being fully reimbursed for fuel and parking. However, the share of those who said the employer would pay most or only part of the congestion toll was significantly higher than those who said the employer was currently paying most or part of their fuel and parking expenses. This latter result may reflect optimism among those who are not currently fully reimbursed for their car expenses to secure at least part of the congestion toll.

Table 14.2   Response regarding employer's paying for gas and parking expenses

	Choice	Number	Percentage
Employer pays transport fuel costs	All	107	13.4%
	Most of it	37	4.6%
	Part of it	71	8.9%
	No	414	51.8%
	blanks	170	21.3%
Employer pays for parking	All	103	12.9%
	Most of it	29	3.6%
	Part of it	47	5.9%
	No	390	48.8%
	blanks	230	28.8%
Employer may pay the toll	All	99	12.4%
	Most of it	76	9.5%
	Part of it	266	33.3%
	No	188	23.5%
	blanks	170	21.3%

Respondents were asked about their acceptance of and views on the congestion toll. These questions and the results are shown in Table 14.3.

Table 14.3   Respondents' views on congestion toll

	(1 Absolutely Agree, 2 Agree, 3 Neutral, 4 Disagree, 5 Totally Disagree)					
	1	*2*	*3*	*4*	*5*	*Blanks*
I agree with the congestion toll idea	213	118	133	83	82	170
	26.7%	14.8%	16.6%	10.4%	10.3%	21.3%
The congestion toll will reduce traffic congestion in the region	105	96	145	143	140	170
	13.1%	12.0%	18.1%	17.9%	17.5%	21.3%
The congestion toll should be applied only after there is good public transport in the area	44	31	60	100	394	170
	5.5%	3.9%	7.5%	12.5%	49.3%	21.3%
The congestion toll should be applied only if the revenue is used to improve public transport in the area	68	24	66	109	362	170
	8.5%	3.0%	8.3%	13.6%	45.3%	21.3%

The results show that, overall, the public agrees with the toll, with over 40 per cent agreeing or perfectly agreeing with the toll idea, compared to 21 per cent who disagree or totally disagree. This is encouraging. Schuitema et al. (2010) show that acceptance of the congestion charge in Stockholm was higher after the trial period as opposed to its acceptability beforehand. However, the percentage of those who think it will reduce congestion is significantly lower, with only 25 per cent agreeing or perfectly agreeing that it will reduce congestion, compared to 35 per cent who did not agree or totally disagreed with it. Schuitema et al. showed that acceptability is higher when respondents expected the policy to reduce congestion. It is interesting that respondents did not really think that the implementation of congestion pricing should be conditioned on improving public transport, nor did they agree that the toll revenue should be used to improve public transport in the area.

Tour Data

The distribution of the tour main purpose was as follows: 35 per cent for work, 6 per cent for education, 15 per cent for maintenance (various errands and shopping), 23 per cent for discretionary (leisure and social) activities, and the remaining 21 per cent for various other purposes.

After a review of all the daily and tour patterns that appeared in the data, it was decided to group daily activity patterns into four main categories as shown in Table 14.4. Secondary tours are defined as tours that do not include the primary activity; i.e. an additional tour before or after the main tour. Given the small number of observations, only a limited number of daily activity patterns could be defined, compared to other activity-based models. Essentially these patterns distinguished two categories: a very simple pattern of only two trips a day (to and from one's destination) and more complicated patterns involving more trip segments. A set of rules based on a hierarchy of activity purposes and their duration was used to assign each respondent's activity schedule to one of the patterns. As can be seen from Table 14.4, most of the daily activity patterns were simple patterns of one tour and one destination. Only 1 per cent of the respondents had more than one destination in their tour and only 4 per cent had an additional tour during the day.

Table 14.4   Daily tour pattern for respondents

Tour Pattern	Number	Percentage	Description
HPH	621	78	Home-Primary-Home
HPOH	79	10	Home-Primary-Other-Home
HPOOH	66	8	Home-Primary-Other-Other+-Home
HPHSH	14	2	Home-Primary-Home-Secondary-Home
HPOHSH HPOOHSH	13	2	Home-Primary-Other-Home-Secondary-Home Home-Primary-Other-Other+-Home-Secondary-Home
Total	793	100	

Toll Scenario Responses

The toll ranged from NIS 5 (€1 is equal to about NIS 5) to NIS 35; respondents living in the congestion area have a 90 per cent discount. The distribution of the stated responses to the congestion toll over all scenarios and toll levels is shown in Table 14.5.

Table 14.5   Choices made by respondents according to different toll scenarios

Choice	Number	Percentage
Pay the toll	1,851	44.1%
Use public transportation	928	22.1%
Change travel time and travel at a time when there is no toll	830	19.8%
Cancel trip	176	4.2%
Change the destination of the trip	412	9.8%

The response by toll level is shown in Figure 14.1. As expected, the percentage of drivers stating that they would pay the toll decreases as the toll increases. As can be seen from this figure all the other response options increase as the toll increases, with the shift to public transport and time of day being the dominant responses, and also increasing at the highest rate with the increase in toll. This is an important result, since it shows that people will not change their activity because of a toll; at most, they would only adjust their travel behaviour to perform those activities. The relatively small stated responses of changing destination and cancelling the trip indicate that the proposed policy would not affect the vitality of the city centre, which is one of the main reasons for the objection to congestion toll policies, especially among businesses in the urban centre.

The percentages of those who chose to pay the toll, shown according to income level and toll payment is presented in Figure 14.2. As expected, higher income people are more willing to pay the toll before they seek other alternatives.

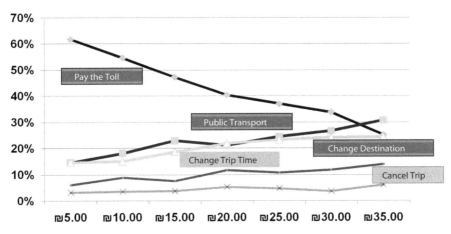

Figure 14.1   Choice behaviour vs the toll

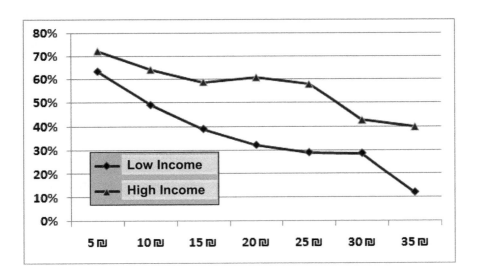

Figure 14.2   Paying toll choice with income level

Table 14.6 shows the distribution of the types of stated response according to tour purpose.

Table 14.6   Types of responses by tour purpose

Purpose	Share of Tour	Pay Toll	Shift to Public Transport	Change Travel Time	Cancel Trip	Change Trip Destination
Work	35%	49%	23%	14%	3%	11%
Education	6%	33%	33%	17%	0%	17%
Maintenance	15%	40%	20%	20%	7%	13%
Discretionary	23%	48%	17%	26%	0%	9%
Other	21%	38%	24%	24%	5%	9%

As expected, too, people who travel to work are willing to pay the toll more than others, perhaps because, in part, as stated above, many of them expect to be reimbursed for this cost. It is interesting to note that a high proportion of people travelling on discretionary tours are also willing to pay the toll, probably reflecting the late hours of leisure trips, when public transport is less frequent or convenient. Students, who are more money conscious than others, are the least likely to pay the toll and the most likely to shift to public transportation. Although 17 per cent of them stated they would change their destination, it does not seem that students really have this flexibility.

All tour purposes have a good proportion of shifting to public transport or changing travel time, which is an encouraging result as explained above. Those making discretionary tours, which are the most flexible type, are most likely to change travel time. Only a few would cancel their trip, and this is mostly for maintenance and other tours. It may be the case that such activities can be rearranged and conducted with less travel. Among some workers, cancelling trips may reflect stopping a habit of going home for the lunch break. A better look at the various factors affecting the choice of response can be obtained from the model estimation results discussed in the next section.

Model Estimation Results

A multinomial logit model was estimated for choosing among the different responses to the congestion toll, with the alternative choices being to pay the toll, shift to public transport, change travel time, change destination, and cancel the trip. The estimated model results are presented in Table 14.7, and the estimated coefficients are briefly discussed in the following sections.

Socio-economic Variables

Employed respondents tend to pay the toll and continue to drive as they used to do more than do unemployed people, and the self-employed are even more willing to pay the toll than employees. Men are less likely to pay the toll and prefer to seek other alternatives. Middle-aged people (from age 25–44) are more likely to stick to their cars and pay the congestion toll although this coefficient was not significant. Orthodox religious people tend to shift to other alternatives rather than paying the toll; this is probably partially due to their low socio-economic status. Finally, single people tend to shift more to public transport, probably because of their greater time flexibility, but this coefficient was not significant.

Tour Variables

People living in the congested area are less likely to pay the congestion toll. Two reasons might account for this: First, people living in central Tel-Aviv might have more options to shift to other means of transportation. Second, the reluctance to pay the toll might indicate some kind of protest against the idea of congestion pricing in the location where they live in. The primary tour purpose, too, has an important role in determining the response to the toll. When the main trip activity is work, people are more likely to pay the toll or shift to public transit, as they have less flexibility to choose the other types of change. When the tour main activity is education, respondents are more likely to shift to public transport, reflecting a lack of flexibility similar to workers but at the same time a tighter budget constraint. When the main tour activity is maintenance, respondents are more likely to cancel their trip as a response to the congestion toll; similarly, when it is discretionary, respondents are more likely to change their destination or to cancel their trip, thus showing more flexibility for these trips. As the tour becomes more complex, the respondents tend to depend more on the car and pay the toll as he or she probably has less flexibility.

Toll Scenario Variables

As expected, as the toll increases, the respondent is less likely to pay it; furthermore, the lower the income, the more sensitivity are these people to the toll rate. The more time that is saved by paying the toll, the more likely that people will pay. These two variables (saving time, paying toll) can be used to calculate the value of time, reflecting how much people are willing to pay in order to save time. The values of time are NIS 13.0 per hour for high-income people, NIS 10.3 for medium-income people, and NIS 9.2 for low-income people. These values are low, given the average hourly wage in Israel: NIS 45 (Israel Central Bureau of Statistics 2009); however, they are reasonable and, therefore, show a low willingness to pay a toll. Finally, as the cost of public transit increases, respondents are less likely to choose this mode.

Table 14.7 Multinomal logit model for choices under different congestion scenarios

Variable	Utility of choice alternative				
	Pay toll	Public transit	Change travel time	Cancel trip	Change destination
Constant	4.5				
[t-test]	[21.2]				
Constant		1.96			
[t-test]		[15.87]			
Constant			1.63		
[t-test]			[16.44]		
Constant					1.1
[t-test]					[9.88]
Socio-economic variables					
Employee dummy (1 if the person is employee)	0.268				
[t-test]	[3.25]				
Self-employed dummy (1 if the person is self-employed)	0.387				
[t-test]	[3.57]				
Male dummy (1 if gender is male)	-0.217				
[t-test]	[-3.22]				
Middle-aged person (1 if person is 25–44 years old)	0.0578				
[t-test]	[1.00]				
Religious dummy (1 if person is an Orthodox religious person)		1.41	1.41	1.41	1.41
[t-test]		[2.00]	[2.00]	[2.00]	[2.00]
Single dummy (1 if status is single)		0.118			
[t-test]		[1.41]			
Tour variables					

Table 14.7 Continued

Live in congestion area dummy (1 if a person lives in congestion-toll area)	-0.307			
[t-test]	[-3.43]			
Main tour activity work dummy (1 if main tour activity is work)	0.128	0.128		
[t-test]	[1.51]	[1.51]		
Main tour activity education dummy (1 if main tour activity is education)		0.447		
[t-test]		[2.73]		
Main tour activity maintenance dummy (1 if main tour activity maintenance)				0.682
[t-test]				[3.64]
Main tour activity discretionary dummy (1 if main tour activity is discretionary)			0.272	0.272
[t-test]			[3.11]	[3.11]
High complexity tour dummy (1 if tour is not simple; i.e., H-P-H, H-P-O-H)	0.139			
[t-test]	[1.5]			
Toll scenario variables				
Toll paid in the scenario for high income [NIS]	-0.0502			
[t-test]	[-9.44]			
Toll paid in the scenario for average income [NIS]	-0.0636			
[t-test]	[-11.36]			
Toll paid in the scenario for low income [NIS]	-0.0714			
[t-test]	[-13.67]			
Saved car travel time when toll is applied [minutes]	0.0109			
[t-test]	[3.15]			
Public transit cost [Shekels]		-0.00559		
[t-test]		[-3.09]		

Conclusions and Recommendations

This chapter tried to explore the response to congestion pricing using an activity-based approach. The analysis reflects the results of a stated-preference survey conducted especially for this purpose and of a multinomial logit model that was developed to estimate the probabilities of the various potential responses to congestion pricing.

Our findings show that daily activity patterns, mainly the tour main activity and its pattern, indeed play an important role in the response to congestion pricing. The tour's main activity reflects travellers' flexibility; thus, people with mandatory tour activities, such as work and education, are less flexible and therefore less likely to change destination or, time or to cancel the trip. Workers are more likely to pay the toll or use public transport, whereas students are more likely to use public transport. Travellers for maintenance activity are more likely to cancel their trip, and those about to conduct discretionary activities are more likely to change their destination or cancel their trip. Travellers with complex tour patterns also have less flexibility and are more likely to pay the toll. Additional results show that people living in the congestion area are less likely to pay the toll and that socio-economic variables are important factors in determining responses to congestion pricing. Finally, the values of the time derived from the toll coefficient and the time saved were somewhat low but reasonable and consistent with income level.

An important result of this study, as shown in Figure 14.1, is that, overall, people are more likely to shift to public transport or change the time of day for the trip than to change destination or cancel the trip. These results show that a congestion-pricing policy can achieve its goal of reducing congestion by causing people to shift mode or time without hampering the vitality of the CBD, which can happen when people choose to go to other destinations or to cancel their trips. Given a willingness to accept congestion pricing, this alternative should constitute an important element in managing any transition toward sustainable transportation.

Although this survey and model provided important insights into travellers' responses to congestion pricing, future work on the subject should be conducted to improve this approach and extend its coverage. One drawback of the survey in the present study is that non-motorized choices, such as walking and biking, were not included in the choice set. These alternatives are becoming more popular, especially in cities like Tel-Aviv, and should be included in future studies of congestion-toll behaviour. Larger sample sizes and further experiments in other regions and countries can assist in confirming the present results. Comparisons can also be made among different geographical regions and cultures, and the effect of additional potential variables identified.

Chapter 15

Evaluation of Transport External Cost Regulation of Atmospheric Pollution: An Investigation Using Global Sensitivity Analysis

Hana Brůhová-Foltýnová and Jan Brůha

Introduction

Analysis of transport regulation has attracted the attention of researchers for a considerable time. One of the most important parts of decision-making processes is modelling, i.e. the use of formal mathematical tools, in which conclusions are logically and transparently related to behavioural and technical assumptions by means of mathematical formulae and algorithms. Mathematical models reflect selected, but important, features of reality. By selecting the relevant features, one hopes that modelling may be used especially for:

- analysing complicated transportation systems;
- forecasting transportation activity;
- planning and allocation;
- presenting reasoned arguments to justify policy actions.

Although mathematical models are not the only available tool for analysing, planning, or forecasting, they play an important role in transportation science.

One of the serious concerns is that model outcomes depend on a number of important, but often unknown, numerical parameters, which must be estimated or calibrated. If the numerical values of these parameters are determined wrongly, model results may be unreliable. Examples of such crucial parameters include, but are not limited to, values of marginal external costs, demand elasticities, subjective values of time, and future costs of motor fuels. There are many sources of uncertainty in the values of estimated or calibrated parameters: statistical sampling errors, noise in data, and ambiguity about the appropriate theory used in the estimation, to name a few.

Methods of sensitivity analysis have been proposed to deal with uncertainty in scientific models. The sensitivity analysis methods can inform model users (policymakers and other stakeholders) about the sensitivity of the modelling results with respect to unknown parameters. Moreover, they can identify parameters whose variation has the most significant impact on the results. The identification of such parameters is important both to researchers (where the effort should be put to make modelling results more reliable) and to policymakers (to indicate a direction for research funding).

Unfortunately, the methods of sensitivity analysis are not always utilized to a satisfactory degree in transportation studies. Some studies report only results for mean values of estimated or calibrated parameters. Such an approach (sometimes called '*certainty equivalence*') is clearly unsatisfactory if a non-linear model is used. Non-linearity implies that the mean value of a model outcome computed by averaging the results for independent draws of model parameters differ from the model outcome computed using mean values of these parameters. Although it is appropriate from the statistical point of view to calculate the expected value of the model outcome by averaging the results of a large number of draws, some studies report results based on the certainty equivalence approach.

There are studies which report model outcomes for several values (usually extreme values) of model parameters. This is definitely a better practice than that of *certainty equivalence*, since such an approach can provide some information about the probable range of the result values and about the sensitivity with respect to individual parameters. Nevertheless, the rigorous application of sensitivity analysis techniques may inform stakeholders (researchers, policymakers, or the public) more completely.

Such applications are still not common in transportation science. For example, the Handbook of Transport Modelling (Hensher and Button 2000), which is otherwise an excellent handbook, does not even include '*sensitivity analysis*' in its subject index. The same comment applies to the textbook Modelling Transport by Ortúzar and Willumsen (2006). We regard this gap as unfortunate, since methods of sensitivity analysis could improve the understanding of transport models and make their outcomes more credible to stakeholders.

This chapter demonstrates how to apply those methods in transportation science. The demonstration is done on a microsimulation model for evaluation of regulation of environmental external costs of transport introduced by Brůha and Brůhová-Foltýnová (2008). The microsimulation model is used to gauge impacts of changes in passenger transport prices on fuel consumption, external effects of air pollution, household welfare and public finance in a transition country and has been applied to the five largest cities in the Czech Republic. In this study, we use this microsimulation model and apply it to Prague: the capital of the Czech Republic.

The rest of the chapter is organized as follows. After this introductory section, the second section briefly describes the microsimulation model. The third section then introduces techniques of sensitivity analysis. The forth section reports on the results of the application of these techniques to the microsimulation model. The last section concludes.

The Model

In this part of the chapter, we describe the model used for the sensitivity analysis exercise. The microsimulation model concentrates on the regulation of external costs of transport related to air pollution. This kind of external costs represents over two-thirds of the total external costs of transport in the Czech Republic[1] (OECD 2001). Indeed, the air pollution caused by transport is identified as one of the most serious environmental problems in the Central European transition countries; see the Ministry of the Environment (2001) for evidence for the Czech Republic. The presented model consists of the following four blocks:

- the demand block;
- the public agency block;
- the external cost block;
- the fiscal block.

These blocks are now described in more detail.

The Demand Block

The goal of this block is to estimate the responses of households to the changes in various transport prices, such as motor fuel and public transport prices. Furthermore, the estimation of the household demand is used to quantify the impact of the price changes on private households' welfare, which is measured by the compensating variation.[2]

Health impacts and the related external costs of motor fuel use differ significantly between urban and rural areas. Thus, to assess the welfare consequences of price changes – no matter whether they are caused by policy interventions or exogenous factors – one has to estimate separate motor-fuel price elasticities for driving in urban and rural areas. The reason is that it would not be plausible to assume that the urban and rural price elasticities are similar: substitution possibilities differ between these areas. To estimate them separately is a difficult task since the databases usually available (such as various kinds of household budget and expenditure surveys) contain data on the total expenditures on motor fuels, but they do not directly provide the information on where the motor fuels are used.

Brůha and Foltýnová (2006) handle the issue by considering an adequate demand system. They consider an extension to the latent separability model by Blundell and Robin (2000). The idea is based on stage budgeting: it is assumed that a household allocates its desired expenditures on transport modes in two stages.

---

1   This situation is probably different than in high-income OECD countries, where congestion costs present the most important problem.

2   'Compensating variation' refers to the amount of additional money an agent would need to reach its initial utility after a change in prices (Mas-Colell et al. 1995).

First, each household allocates its expenditures among expenditures on urban transport, inter-urban transport, and other goods. After deciding on the expenditures on urban transport, rural transport and other goods, the household decides on the modal split of these two broad transport categories. The expenditures on urban transport are divided between urban public transport and motor fuel expenditures on urban travel. Similarly, the expenditures on rural transport are divided between public transport such as bus and rail, and motor fuel expenditures on rural travel. Brůha and Foltýnová (2006) show that if each stage is modelled using an almost ideal demand system (Deaton and Muelbauer 1980), then the model is identified and can be estimated. In this chapter, we use estimates of elasticities reported by Brůha and Foltýnová (2006). The figures are summarized in Table 15.1.

Table 15.1   Benchmark values of demand elasticities

	Price elasticity of		
	Motor fuels used in		*Public urban transport*
	Urban areas	*Rural areas*	
With respect to fuel price	-1.04	-0.40	0.30
With respect to urban public transport price	0.28	0.03	-0.65

Source: Brůha and Foltýnová (2006).

Appendix 15.A explains how we compute the approximation to the compensating variation and new demands based on these elasticities.

The Public Agency Block

The main issue in this block is the calibration of the cost function of public transport operators. To do that, we use the approach suggested by Williams (1979), who proposes a short-run cost function, which relates the logarithm of the average costs to the logarithm of input prices and the logarithm of the total output. The inclusion of the total output in the regression function for average costs measures the possible economies of scale: negative values of the estimated coefficient indicate increasing returns to scale (the total output decreases average costs), while positive values indicate decreasing returns to scale. Brůha and Brůhová-Foltýnová (2008) estimate this equation on a panel of data from urban public transport operators in 19 selected Czech cities for the time period 1997–2005. Table 15.2 summarizes their findings. The economies-of-scale parameter is positive (which suggests decreasing economies of scale) but insignificant.

Table 15.2   Cost function of the public transport operators

Elasticity of the average costs with respect to	Point estimates	Standard errors
Fuel price	0.302	0.088
Wage rate	0.462	0.117
Total output	0.089	0.178

Source: Brůha and Brůhová-Foltýnová (2008).

The External Cost Block

We use external cost estimates given by the ExternE methodology (European Commission 1999, 2003), which are based on the 'impact-pathway' approach and apply a bottom-up analysis of emissions. Therefore, the estimated values depend on a wide range of parameters, such as the location of the emission (population density of the affected area), type of vehicle, vehicle fleet structure, and fuel characteristics. The ExternE results for the Czech Republic are available in the research report on the project for the Ministry of the Environment of the Czech Republic 'Quantification of external costs of energy use in the Czech Republic' (CUEC 2005).

Our model calibrated on data for the five largest Czech cities – Prague, Brno, Ostrava, Pilsen and Olomouc. Their population densities range from 23.6 inhabitants per hectare in Prague to 9.75 inhabitants per hectare in Olomouc. The structure of the vehicle fleet according to the EURO standards and the type of fuel (gasoline/diesel) is taken from the ATEM (2001) study of traffic flows, which was conducted in Prague and Pilsen. To estimate external costs in the other three cities, we assume the same vehicle fleet structure as in Pilsen (we use this assumption since the income levels, the areas and transport performances of these three cities are close to those in Pilsen). Our external cost estimations are static: we do not change the structure of the vehicle fleet during the simulations.

The monetary values of external costs of air pollution are taken from CUEC (2005). The external costs of air pollution consist of the monetary value of the damage to health and the environment caused by vehicle emissions. We evaluate the following emissions: NO_x, SO_2, hydrocarbons, and PM_{10}. The EURO standards do not incorporate CO_2 emission standards so we cannot identify the exact amount of CO_2 produced by different groups of vehicles using the EURO standards as is the case for the other evaluated emissions. For our analysis, we derive the amount of CO_2 emissions produced by cars from the average fuel consumption (7 litres per 100 km).

In our micro-simulation model, we use external costs per litre of fuel consumed. The total value of external costs of air pollution from cars is CZK 20.49 (Euro 0.74) per litre for urban areas of the medium-sized cities (Brno, Ostrava, Pilsen and Olomouc), and CZK 25.57 (Euro 0.88) per litre for Prague (the difference in the values is caused by a higher population density, which more than counterbalances the newer and less polluting car fleet operated in Prague). The external costs for rural areas are CZK 10.24 (Euro 0.37) per litre of fuel for a typical car operated by a medium-sized city inhabitant, and CZK 9.13 (Euro 0.31) for a car owned by an inhabitant of Prague. The estimated external costs of public transport reflect the structure of the public transport vehicle fleet: the electrical traction (including trams, trolleybuses, and metro) is considered 'zero-emission' transport (as if its external costs were already internalized at the electricity producers), and external costs from air pollution are calculated only for buses. The benchmark monetary values used for the external costs of air pollution from public transport are summarized in Table 15.3.

Table 15.3   Benchmark monetary values of external costs of air pollution from public transport in the five largest Czech cities

City	Air pollution external costs	
	CZK, per kilometre	*Euro, per kilometre[1]*
Prague	36.66	1.47
Brno	38.26	1.53
Pilsen	32.89	1.32
Olomouc	62.62	2.50
Ostrava	47.32	1.89

Note: [1] The exchange rate used is CZK 25 = EUR 1.

The Fiscal Block

The fiscal block adds public budget expenses and revenues. The revenue side comprises revenues from the excise tax and value added tax on motor fuels, and public transport fares. The expense side comprises subsidies for public transport providers. We assume that any loss of the public transport providers will be covered by public budgets. To integrate the public budget figures with other model outcomes (private household welfare and external costs), we use the marginal cost of public funds (MCPF). Because of the lack of suitable Czech studies, we use an international 'consensus' figure for the MCPF = 1.2 as a benchmark.

The Aggregation

The social welfare is finally obtained by adding up three welfare measures: the change in public funds (including the change in tax revenues and the change in costs of public transport operators) multiplied by the marginal costs of public funds, the change in external costs of air pollution, and the compensating variation.

These measures are summed into one Kaldor-Hicks type of social welfare measure with equal weights for all changes in the real incomes of individuals.

Methods of Sensitivity Analysis

Techniques of sensitivity analysis can be used to inquire about the influence of model inputs $\{X_1,...,X_n\}$ on model output Y. In general, these techniques can be divided into local and global approaches.

The local approach usually explores local information, i.e. typically the derivative of Y with respect to inputs X_i. Unless the model is linear, local techniques yield only a local picture: the magnitude and even the sign of the derivatives may depend on the point where the differentiation is taken, which is usually at the mode or the mean of possible parameter values. In this way, a lot of useful information may be lost.

Therefore, for non-linear models, global techniques of sensitivity analysis have gained popularity among the research community. The textbook by Saltelli et al. (2004) summarizes the main ideas and selected techniques of global sensitivity analysis. In this chapter, we apply the variance-based approach. There are three basic settings for the variance-based methods:

- **The factor prioritization setting** asks what is the factor that one should fix to achieve the greatest reduction in the uncertainty of the output (Saltelli et al. 2004: 109);
- **The factor fixing setting** identifies non-influential factors;
- **The variance cutting setting** seeks the minimal subset of factors the fixing of which would achieve a prescribed reduction in the model uncertainty.

These settings formalize the quest for the appropriate direction of the effort to increase the reliability of the modelling results. Moreover, these settings use the same mathematical objects.[3]

The variance-based techniques are based on the following decomposition of the variance of the model output $V(Y)$:

$$V(Y) = \sum_i V_i + \sum_{i \neq j} V_j + ... + V_{1...n},$$

---

3   Saltelli et al. (2004) also discuss the factor-mapping setting, which looks for factors mostly responsible for producing realization of the model output in a given region. This setting is, however, not variance-based, and is usually treated with Monte Carlo filtering techniques.

where $V_i = V(E(Y \mid X_i))$ is the variance of the conditional expectation of the model output, given input X_i, and the higher-order terms are defined recursively as follows: $V_{ij} = V(E(Y \mid X_i, X_j)) - V_i - V_j$. Thus the output variance is decomposed into variances of the conditional expectations. To illustrate this, assume that the exact value of the input X_i is almost irrelevant for the model output. Then, the conditional expectation $E(Y|X_i)$ will be close to the unconditional mean $E(Y)$ and hence its variance is (almost) zero. Therefore, when we seek for influential inputs, we seek for high values of $V_i = V(E(Y \mid X_i))$, since high values of this quantity imply that movement in the input X_i is responsible for large movements in the conditional expectation of the model output. The higher-order terms then summarize the additional increase in the explained variance when the model output is jointly conditioned on more inputs.

The decomposition equation is exact if the inputs are orthogonal, which will be the case in the present chapter. It is clear that factors V_i, V_{ij}, and so on represent the knowledge enabling the solution for the three settings outlined above: the factor prioritization setting seeks for the factor with the highest value of V_i, while the factor fixing setting seeks for a factor with $V_i = 0$. The variance cutting setting seeks for a minimal index set $J \in 2^{\{1,\dots,n\}}$ such that $\frac{\sum_{j \in J} V_j}{V(Y)}$ is lower than a prescribed number.

We propose the following computation of the variance $V(E(Y \mid X_i))$. We draw a large sample from the random variable[4] $E(Y \mid X_i)$ and the theoretical variance is then approximated by its sample counterpart:

$$V(E(Y \mid X_i)) \cong \frac{1}{N-1} \sum_{n=1}^{N} \left(y''(x_i) - \left[\frac{1}{N} \sum_{m} y'''(x_i) \right] \right)^2$$

where $y''(x_i)$ are random draws from the random variable $E(Y \mid X_i)$. Obviously, as $N \to \infty$, this expression is consistent for the variance. The hard part is to simulate the draws $y''(x_i)$ from $E(Y \mid X_i)$. This is done as follows: first, we draw a sample from X_i. Then for each draw x_i, we sample a large number of vectors of other inputs x_{-i} conditional on the current draw x_i; denote such vectors as $[x_{-i}^r \mid x_i]$. For these draws, the model outputs are computed and averaged. Formally, if $y(x_i, x_{-i})$ denotes the value of the model output for inputs x_i and x_{-i}, then the random draw $y''(x_i)$ from $E(Y \mid X_i)$ is obtained as follows:

$$y''(x_i) = \frac{1}{R} \sum_{r=1}^{R} y\left(x_i, [x_{-i}^r \mid x_i]\right).$$

---

4   Notice that since the value of X_i is uncertain, the conditional expectation $E(Y \mid X_i)$ is in fact a random variable rather than a fixed number.

Things are computationally somehow easier if the inputs are independent. Then, it is sufficient to draw x_{-i} independently on the current draw x_i and the computational burden of drawing can be reduced; see Saltelli et al. (2004) for details.

Application to the Microsimulation Model

Definition of Scenarios

In this part of the chapter, we apply the variance-based methods of global sensitivity analysis, described in Section 3, to the microsimulation model described in Section 2. We consider three scenarios:

- *Scenario 1* is defined as a 25 per cent increase in the excise duty on fuels, which affects the consumer price of motor fuels. We assume that motor fuels for public transport operators are exempted from the increased tax and that public transport fares remain unchanged.
- *Scenario 2* is similar to Scenario 1. It is defined as a 25 per cent increase in the excise duty on fuels, but without the exemption for public transport operators. This scenario implies a cost increase for the public transport operators. We assume that fares in public transport will change to balance off the cost increase.
- *Scenario 3* evaluates a decrease in public transport fares. This scenario is included since some environmentalists argue for a substantial reduction in public transport prices. This can, on the one hand, induce a shift toward a more environmentally friendly modal split for passenger transport; on the other hand, it may cause a serious budgetary pressure.

Using the variance-based techniques of the global sensitivity analysis, we will seek to identify the influential parameters of the microsimulation model. The following parameters will be considered uncertain, and the sensitivity analysis will be performed with respect to them:

- external costs;
- elasticities of household behaviour;
- elasticities of the cost function of public transport providers;
- the marginal cost of public funds.

We assume that the parameter distributions are mutually independent and we use triangular distributions. The triangular distribution is uniquely characterized by its support (min and max values) and its mode. These characteristics for all investigated parameters are summarized in Table 15.4.

Table 15.4   The distribution of parameters used in the sensitivity analysis

Parameter	Mode	Min	Max
Elasticity of motor fuels used in urban areas with respect to the fuel price ε_F^{FU}	-1.04	-2.00	0.00
Elasticity of motor fuels used in urban areas with respect to the public transport price ε_P^{FU}	0.28	0.00	0.60
Elasticity of motor fuels used in rural areas with respect to the fuel price ε_F^{FR}	-0.30	-0.60	0.00
Elasticity of motor fuels used in urban areas with respect to the public transport price ε_P^{FR}	0.03	0.00	0.20
Elasticity of public transport demand with respect to the fuel price ε_F^{P}	0.30	0.00	0.70
Elasticity of public transport demand with respect to the public transport price ε_P^{P}	-0.65	-1.00	0.00
Elasticity of the cost function with respect to the fuel price c_F	0.30	0.10	0.60
Returns to scale of the cost function c_Q	0.10	0.30	-0.30
Marginal externality of fuel usage (cars, CZK per litre of petrol) in cities ME_U	25.57	19.18	38.35
Marginal externality of fuel usage (cars, CZK per litre of petrol) in rural areas ME_R	9.13	6.85	13.70
Marginal externality (public transport, CZK per litre of diesel) in cities ME_P	36.66	27.50	55.00
Marginal costs of public funds MPCF	1.20	1.00	1.60

We set these values as follows. First, we set modes to be equal to the benchmark values. Then, we consider rather large intervals for all elasticities since their econometric estimation is probably a bigger problem than the estimation of the shape of the cost function of public transport providers. Thus, at the one extreme, we allow for zero elasticities (i.e. no response of the demand to relative prices); at the other extreme, we use a value twice greater than our benchmark estimates. After that, we allow for both increasing and decreasing returns to scale for the cost function of the public transport providers. Additionally, we consider a rather large interval for externalities – the minimum is set at 75 per cent of the benchmark value, the maximum is set to 150 per cent of the benchmark value, and the modes correspond to the benchmark estimates. And finally, we use the international consensus figure of 1.20 as a benchmark for the marginal costs of public funds, and we consider the value of 1.00 to be the minimum (which would correspond to the case of no deadweight loss of taxation), and use a relatively large number of 1.60 as the maximum estimate for the marginal costs of public funds.

There are parameters of the microsimulation model which we leave fixed during the simulations. These parameters are related to tax rates and fuel prices. This choice requires a comment. It could be easily defended if the model were used for an assessment of policy scenarios in a given situation. Then, these figures (taxes and prices) would be available to researchers without any noise and thus it would not make sense to investigate the sensitivity of the model outcome to them. On the other hand, if the model were used for policy assessment under broad circumstances (not for a given year), then it would be sensible to inquire how the results respond to a variation in 'initial conditions' (taxes and prices). In this chapter, we fix these parameters, but this approach can be easily generalized whenever the sensitivity with respect to the initial condition is needed. The summary of these parameters is given in the Table 15.5.

Table 15.5   Parameters fixed during the modelling exercise

Parameter	Value (in CZK)	Value (in Euro)
Excise tax on petrol	CZK 11.84 / litre	Euro 0.47 / litre
Petrol price	CZK 26.73 / litre	Euro 1.07 / litre
Excise tax on diesel	CZK 9.95 / litre	Euro 0.40 / litre
Diesel price (public transport, i.e., without VAT)	CZK 18.68 /litre	Euro 0.75 / litre
VAT on motor fuels	22%	
VAT on public transport fares	5%	

Note: We use the exchange rate of CZK 25 per Euro, which roughly reflects average values in the year 2008.

Results of the Simulation

In this part of the chapter, we report on the simulation results for the Czech capital (Prague) for the three scenarios defined above. The results for the other Czech cities can be obtained from the authors on request.

We report on various kinds of estimates of the social welfare (expressed in millions of CZK). First, we report on the results based on the certainty equivalence approach. Under such an approach, the researcher plugs either the most probable values (mode) or the average values (mean) for unknown parameters and ignores the uncertainty. Then, we report the sampling characteristics for the social welfare, which would be obtained if the researcher used Monte Carlo sampling from the underlying distributions for unknown parameters. We report two percentiles and the mean of the implied distribution for the social welfare.

We use 10,000 samples of the parameters according to the triangular distributions defined above. The samples are obtained as follows. First, we generated 12 samples (sized 10,000 each) from the uniform [0 1] distribution using Halton sequences[5] (obtained by creating a Halton sequence for each

5   Computers cannot generate 'true' random variables. Therefore, either pseudo random numbers (such as generated by linear congruent generators), or quasi random numbers must

dimension with a different prime). From these sequences, we obtained the quasi random samples from the triangular distribution (using the inverse method). Thus, we obtained 10,000 different combinations of the model parameters. Table 15.6 summarizes the results.

Table 15.6   Results for Prague, welfare expressed in millions of CZK

Scenario	The certainty equivalence approach		The approach based on Monte Carlo sampling		
	Mode	Mean	2.5% percentile	Mean	97.5% percentile
Scenario 1	575	710	351	710	1,132
Scenario 2	383	614	150	615	1,178
Scenario 3	436	70	-943	87	1,057

It is apparent that the usage of the mode values under the certainty equivalence approach (i.e. plugging the most likely values for unknown parameters) is unsatisfactory. In fact, it differs significantly from the results obtained under the mean values for the parameters, as well as for the mean of the outcome distribution. This may be surprising, but the explanation is that the triangular distributions are not – in general – symmetric (for example, the mode for the distribution of the marginal cost of public funds is significantly lower than the assumed mean).

Firstly, our results suggest that the introduction of Scenario 1 would be beneficial for the social welfare. Although the dispersion of the computed welfare for various combinations of the model parameters is rather high, the social welfare is positive for almost all. Secondly, even Scenario 2 would increase the social welfare, but somehow less so than the first scenario. Finally, the impact of Scenario 3 is uncertain: there are parameter combinations for which the social welfare is positive, while a non-negligible part of the parameter combinations would imply a decrease in the social welfare.

Figures 15.1, 15.2 and 15.3 demonstrate the sensitivity of the results with respect to the individual parameters. The figures are organized as follows: There are 12 subfigures which show the estimation of the conditional expectation (the solid red line) of the output (social welfare) with respect to the unknown parameters.

---

be used. Contrary to pseudo random numbers, quasi random sequences do not try to mimic exactly the random properties of 'true' independent random variables; they in fact exhibit apparent negative correlations and they are based on number-theoretic considerations. However, research experience shows that quasi random sequences outperform pseudo random sequences in many applications, including integral approximation (see for example Train 2003), which is what is relevant here (the expectation and the variance are integrals *sui generis*).

The conditional expectations are estimated non-parametrically using smoothing splines. The green dots plot the parameter values against the model output for the first 300 samples.[6] Each subfigure refers to one model parameter as described in Table 15.4; the titles of the subfigures contain the abbreviation for the parameters in accordance with Table 15.4. The x-axis refers to the support of the distribution for the relevant parameter, while the y-axis displays the social welfare (in millions of CZK). The titles also contain the normalized variance of the conditional expectation:

$$S_j = \frac{V(E(Y \mid X_i))}{V(Y)},$$

which can be interpreted as the percentage of the variance of the model output explained by the input j.

Figure 15.1 reports the results for Scenario 1 for Prague. There are four most influential parameters:

- The elasticity of the fuel usage in urban areas with respect to the fuel price, which explains about 8 per cent of the welfare variance. Clearly, values of the elasticity close to zero decrease welfare in the first scenario. The explanation is intuitive: low values of the parameter imply a low induced shift from cars (and hence a low decrease in external costs), and a relatively high disutility measured by the compensated variation.

- The elasticity of the public transport demand with respect to the fuel price is another important parameter, which explains about 17 per cent of the welfare variance. High values of this cross-price elasticity make Scenario 1 beneficial since they imply a high shift from cars to public transport (and hence significant falls in external costs) and somehow lower compensated variation (since the high values imply that the agents would not suffer much from the fuel price increase since they would find it easy to substitute cars with public transport).

- The parameter of the external costs from cars in urban areas explains more than 20 per cent of the output variation. The magnitude and the direction of the effect of this parameter are quite intuitive: high estimates of such external costs make Scenario 1 highly desirable. On the contrary, the estimation of the external costs of public transport is of the opposite direction, but the magnitude of the impact of this parameter is much smaller.

- The last of the influential parameters is the marginal costs of public funds. The variation in this parameter explains almost half of the variation in the model output. High values of MCPF increase the social welfare of Scenario 1 because of the additional tax revenues. In fact, under high estimates of MCPF, a revenue-neutral tax reform (which would shift the tax burden to motor fuels) would be highly desirable.

---

6   Obviously, if we included all 10,000 samples, the figures would not be readable.

These four parameters explain about 90 per cent of the variation in the model output for Scenario 1. None of the other parameters (or the higher-order terms) explain more than 5 per cent of the model output variation.

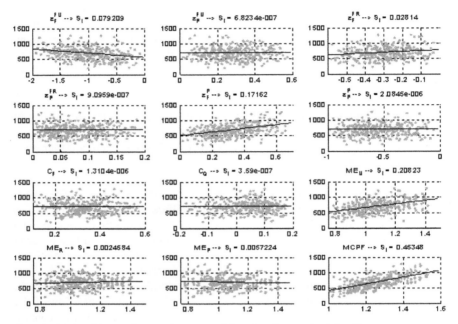

Figure 15.1   The variance decomposition for Scenario 1 for Prague

The sensitivity analysis results for Scenario 2 can be found in Figure 15.2. Compared to Scenario 1, it is worth noticing that the own-price elasticity of public transport becomes important. This can be explained as follows: under Scenario 2, public transport is not exempted from fuel taxation, and the policy intervention is thus transmitted to fare prices. The highly price-elastic public transport demand then implies a small modal shift and therefore a small decrease in external costs.

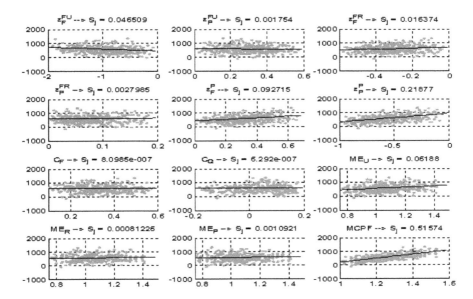

Figure 15.2   The variance decomposition for Scenario 2 for Prague

Lastly, we report the results for Scenario 3; these results are shown in Figure 15.3. In this case, there are four influential parameters:

- Own-price elasticity of public transport, which explains almost half of the output variation.
- The estimation of marginal external costs of individual fuel usage (it explains about 8 per cent). Intuitively, large values of the externality increase the social welfare (since then the change in the modal split brings large social welfare because of decreased externalities).
- The estimation of marginal external costs related to public transport (it explains about 11 per cent) with the obvious direction: large estimates make Scenario 3 undesirable.
- Finally, marginal costs of public funds explain about 22 per cent of the model output. Since Scenario 3 implies budgetary pressures, a large estimate of MCPF implies a decrease in the social welfare: the costs of public funds needed to cover such policy more than counterbalance the fall in externalities.

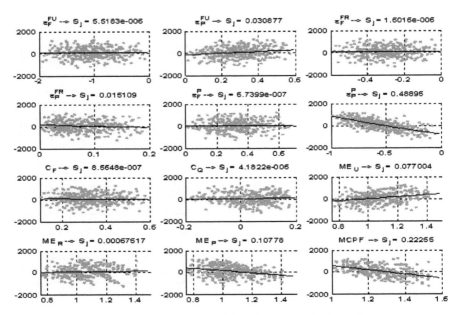

Figure 15.3   The variance decomposition for Scenario 3 for Prague

Therefore, the sensitivity analysis can suggest interesting findings about the desirability of Scenario 3. This scenario would be desirable provided that the own-price elasticity of the public transport is high (in the absolute value), the marginal external costs of cars are significantly higher than those of public transport, and provided that the public budget obtains its funds in a relatively non-distortionary way.

Conclusion

In this chapter, we present methods of global sensitivity analysis and demonstrate how they can be applied to microsimulation models used in transportation science. Our demonstration uses a microsimulation model calibrated to Czech cities and tailored to analyse the welfare consequences of regulation of external costs in Prague.

In particular, we employ the model to analyse three scenarios: (1) a 25 per cent increase in the excise duty on fuels with an exemption for public transport providers, (2) a 25 per cent increase in the excise duty on fuels without an exemption for public transport operators (and with a corresponding fare increase to offset the cost increase), and (3) a decrease in public transport fares covered by public budgets.

Our results suggest that the introduction of Scenario 1 would be beneficial for the social welfare. Although the dispersion of the computed welfare for various combinations of the model parameters is rather high, the social welfare is positive for almost all. It is interesting that 90 per cent of the variation in the output is caused by just four parameters (the elasticity of the fuel usage in urban areas with respect to the fuel price, the elasticity of the public transport demand with respect to the fuel price; the external costs from cars in urban areas; the marginal costs of public funds). Scenario 2 would probably increase the social welfare as well, but somehow less so than the first scenario. An additional parameter (own-price elasticity of public transport) becomes important. Finally, the impact of Scenario 3 is uncertain: there are parameter combinations for which the social welfare is positive, while a non-negligible part of the parameter combinations would imply a decrease in the social welfare. More than 70 per cent of the variation in Scenario 3 outcome is explained by just two parameters (own-price elasticity of public transport and the marginal costs of public funds) and 90 per cent of the variation is explained by four parameters (the marginal external costs of individual fuel usage and the marginal external costs related to public transport in addition to the two above parameters).

We conclude that the global sensitivity analysis techniques can be an important helper to researchers, policymakers and other stakeholders, since they can make modelling results more transparent and therefore more understandable and credible.

Appendix 15.A:
An Elasticity-based Approximation to the Compensating Variation

The compensating variation and changes in demand can be calculated exactly if the complete demand system is specified. However, researchers often find only reported values of elasticities. This appendix explains how to approximate the compensating variation using reported elasticities.

Indeed, use the definition of the compensating variation based on the expenditure function e and expand the function using a second-order Taylor expansion:

$$CV = e(p^0, u^0) - e(p^1, u^0) \cong e(p^0, u^0) - \left[e(p^0, u^0) + \sum_i \frac{\partial e}{\partial p_i}(p_i^1 - p_i^0) + \frac{1}{2} \sum_{ij} \frac{\partial^2 e}{\partial p_i \partial p_j}(p_i^1 - p_i^0)(p_j^1 - p_j^0) \right].$$

Now, the Shepard lemma (Mas-Colell et al. 1995) states that the derivative of the expenditure function with respect to the price is equal to the consumed quantity of the good. Therefore, it is possible to write:

$$CV \cong -\left[\sum_i q_i^0 (p_i^1 - p_i^0) + \frac{1}{2} \sum_j \frac{\partial q_i^0}{\partial p_i}(p_i^1 - p_i^0)(p_j^1 - p_j^0) \right] = -\sum_i q_i^0 (p_i^1 - p_i^0) \left[1 + \frac{1}{2} \sum_j \varepsilon_j^i \Delta p_j \right],$$

where:

$$\varepsilon_j^i = \frac{p_j^0}{q_i^0} \frac{\partial q_i^0}{\partial p_j}$$

is the elasticity of the demand of the good i with respect to the price j, and

$$\Delta p_j = \frac{(p_j^1 - p_j^0)}{p_j^0}$$

is the percentage change in the price j. Now, the equation gives us the approximation to the compensating variation in terms of the old demand, the change in prices, and price elasticities.

Chapter 16

Modelling the Influence of Temporal and Monetary Constraints on Activity Participation, Travel, Consumption of Goods, Residential Location and Work Status: Application in a Land Use Transport Interaction (LUTI) Model

Dick Ettema, Theo Arentze and Harry Timmermans

Introduction

An important objective of LUTI models is to represent the mutual interaction between land use and mobility in evaluations of land use or transportation policies. This interaction goes two ways: the spatial setting of residences, services and facilities impacts individuals' activity and travel patterns, and the resulting traffic (leading to congestion and changes in accessibility) may impact on households' and firms' locational decisions. To account for these interactions, LUTI model systems typically include models of residential (re)location, models of car ownership and work location and models of daily trip making or activity patterns.

In these models, household income and costs of travel and activities are usually included as explanatory variables. That is to say, income and costs are assumed to separately affect different dimensions of spatial behaviour. However, studies in household economics have suggested for several decades that decisions on these dimensions are interrelated through the existence of temporal and monetary budget constraints. Becker (1965) described decisions about how much time to spend on activities as a problem of allocating time and money to activities such that utility is maximized. In this conceptualization, different activities and travel become interrelated by the fact that time and money spent on one activity cannot be spent on another. This basic model has been extended in various ways. One extension has been to include the choice of work hours and commute time in the model (Munizaga et al. 2006; Van Klaveren et al. 2008), suggesting that trade-offs are made between the income earned working against the time needed to earn the money and the remaining leisure time. Likewise, travel mode to the work place has been included into these models, suggesting that people make trade-offs between time gained by choosing a faster mode against the costs of this mode. Another extension concerns the inclusion of longer-term decisions, such as residential location (Jara-Diaz and Martinez 1999). This extension is based on the idea that a trade-off is made between the costs and utility obtained from a dwelling versus the utility that can be realized from activity participation and goods consumption given the remaining monetary budget and the accessibility of locations from the dwelling.

The trade-offs included in these models have also been shown in empirical studies. For instance, Abdel-Ghany and Schwenk (1993) and Moon and Joung (1997) showed that different household types make different trade-offs with respect to the allocation of monetary budgets to travel, activities and goods, such as to fulfil different household needs. Herbst and Barnow (2008) found a relationship between the accessibility of childcare centres and female labour force participation, suggesting that a trade-off is made between money earned working and time involved in driving to a day care centre. Likewise, Van Klaveren et al. (2008) empirically tested the relationship between work hours, the resulting income, the consumption of goods and time spent on household tasks.

These examples illustrate that decisions about daily activities and trips and longer-term decisions about where to live, where and how many hours to work and which vehicles to own, are interrelated through the existence of time and money budgets. Hence, LUTI models, which include decisions on both dimensions, should take these interdependencies into account. Partly, this can be achieved by relying on existing micro-economic models such as Jara-Diaz and Martinez (1999) that are rooted in Becker's (1965) seminal work. Their model allows for trade-offs between activities that cost time and money, consumption of goods costing money and activities that generate money, such as paid work. It is assumed that residential and work locations are chosen such that the utility resulting from the allocation of time and money to activities and consumption of goods is optimized. Hence, various interrelationships between time and money and between short- and longer-term behaviours are accounted for. However, the impact of income constraints goes through a fixed technical relationship between activity duration and costs and between amount of consumption and costs. In this chapter we argue that the relationships between time, money, activity patterns and their resulting utility is becoming increasingly flexible, and is not adequately represented by fixed technical relationships. For instance, Harvey and Mukhopadhyay (2007) found that the degree of time scarcity households experience is related to the monetary resources they can invest to alleviate time shortage by buying more efficient equipment or outsourcing tasks. In essence, this implies that activities can be made more efficient (i.e. producing the same utility in a shorter time) by investing more money. In addition, we argue that due to increasing diversity in the quality of locations and services, the utility of activity participation increasingly depends on the quality of facilities, which is closely related to prices. For instance, eating in a more exclusive restaurant is more expensive but may also produce a higher utility. In general, the availability of a larger budget provides a wider range of options to input goods or facilities in the activity, adding to he quality and hence the utility of the activity. For instance, Ettema et al. (2009) empirically showed that a larger input of money into leisure and task activities indeed increases the utility per time unit. It should be noted, though, that the impact of budget on utility may depend on personal preferences and may therefore vary considerably between individuals and activities. Thus, given that basic needs are fulfilled, the same amount of time can be made more productive (in terms of utility) by investing more money into it. Both ways of investing money (increasing efficiency and quality) are not included in the traditional micro-economic formulations, but are essential for understanding relationships between rising incomes, changing spatial patterns and changing activity patterns (see Susilo and Stead in this volume).

In a micro-simulation approach, Arentze et al. (2010) proposed a modelling framework in which both temporal and monetary budget limitations are taken into account when deciding in which activities to participate and for how long. Although this model is, to the authors' knowledge, the first to combine time and money allocation to a wide range of activities, it cannot be readily implemented in a LUTI framework on the same time scale as the more long-term decisions are made. Therefore, the objective of this chapter is to propose a framework that is able to represent the impact of money inputs on efficiency and quality of activities and the implications this will have on daily and longer-term spatial behaviour in the context of spatial and temporal constraints. To this end, we will outline a formal model of activity frequency and consumption of goods in the context of residential and job location choice. The model is applied in a small scale geographical setting to illustrate its properties and potential. In this respect, we focus on the representation of individual spatial behaviours under different conditions, rather than on the effects on aggregate residential and activity-travel patterns.

The chapter is organized as follows. Section 2 outlines a model of time and money allocation to activities and goods, which creates the base for the model application. Section 3 describes the integration of this model with longer-term decisions of residential location, work location and work hours, and the implementation in the context of the existing PUMA model. Section 4 describes the results of a series of simulations with the model. Section 5, finally draws conclusions about the applicability of the model and addresses avenues for further research.

Time Allocation Model Influenced by Monetary Expenditure

A central element in the proposed model is a time allocation model that is sensitive to money spent on activities in terms of the time allocated to activities and the resulting utility. This time allocation model is outlined in this section. An important consideration when allocating money and time budgets is whether to invest money in activities or in other objectives (goods, dwelling). Obviously, this will depend on the utility derived from spending time and money on activities. The effect of spending time is straightforward in that we assume that spending more time on an activity results in a higher utility, except in cases of fatigue or boredom. The effect of spending money is less straightforward. On the one hand, spending more money may make an activity more attractive, for instance by using better facilities (such as a more expensive restaurant). Ceteris paribus, it is expected that if the activity becomes more attractive, more time is spent on it in the competition with other activities, since this results in a higher utility. On the other hand, spending more money on an activity may increase its efficiency. This can principally occur in two ways. First, one may invest once in equipment that enables one to perform activities (for example, household tasks) in a shorter time. Alternatively, one may spend more money on each occasion (for example, by choosing a faster but more expensive service), such as to decrease the duration of the activity. In this chapter, we will focus on the second type of investment. In this case, one would expect that less time is spent on the activity, creating more time for other activities. The extent to which this effect occurs will however differ between activity types.

To adequately represent time and money allocation to (amongst other things) activities, the following model is proposed, which is capable of representing the impact of expenditures on attractiveness and efficiency as described above. The model presented in this chapter describes allocation of money to activities, goods and the residence, for the time neglecting longer-term decisions such as car ownership. However, the model can be extended to this dimension in a straightforward way. For each activity we assume the following utility function:

$$U_i = \alpha_i F_i \exp(-\gamma_i F_i) \qquad\qquad (1)$$

where:

α_i represents the a priori attractiveness of activity i;

F_i is the frequency at which an activity is performed (e.g. during a month);

γ_i is a parameter representing the diminishing return from another engagement in i;

This formulation is based on earlier work by Becker (1965) and Kitamura (1984), who describe utility as an exponential function of time (i.e. continuously increasing with diminishing marginal returns).The above formulation initially has the same effect for frequency, but adding the term F_i also allows for a decreasing utility after some saturation point has been reached (see Figure 16.1[1]). Thus, given a particular time period (say a month), the frequency of engagement will result in a certain utility. To relate activity engagement to time expenditure, we assume that each activity has a duration d_i which includes travel time. The assumption here is that the optimal duration of an activity is independent of frequency. One may argue that, in contrast, a high frequency of short duration activities is equivalent to a low frequency of long duration activities. However, there does not seem to be a clear correlation between duration and frequency in time-use and activity datasets and, hence, the present assumption may be warranted as an approximation. Thus, the frequency is defined as $F_i = t_i/d_i$, where t_i is the total time spent on activity i. Equation 1 is then rewritten as:

$$U_i = \alpha_i F_i \exp(-\gamma_i F_i) = \frac{\alpha_i t_i}{d_i} \exp(-\frac{\gamma_i t_i}{d_i}) \qquad (2)$$

The above formulation implies that given activity duration d_i, the utility can be expressed as a function of time allocated to the activity. It is noted that in contrast to most time allocation models (for example Becker 1965; Kitamura 1984) we assume that after reaching some saturation point, utility will diminish if more time is spent on the activity.

Based on the above discussion, the model is now extended to account for the effect of spending money on activities. The first effect of expenditure is on the attractiveness of activities. In this respect we assume that attractiveness α_i is determined by a base level α_i^0, which can be adjusted by spending more money on the activity and by the characteristics of the location at which the activity is performed. In equation:

$$\alpha_i = \alpha_i^0 + \beta_i \frac{E_i}{E_i^0} + \sum_j \mu_j X_j \qquad (3)$$

Where:

E_i is the money spent on activity i. Note that both $E_i > E_i^0$ and

$E_i < E_i^0$ may occur;

E_i^0 is the base amount of money to be spent on activity i;

---

1   Comparable functions result from other positive values of α and γ.

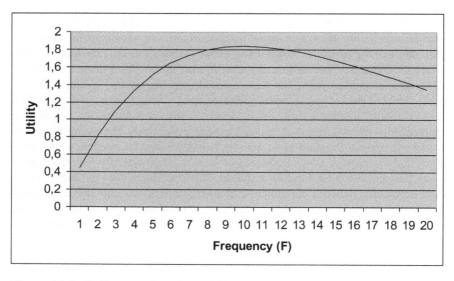

Figure 16.1   Utility as a function of frequency

β_i is a parameter expressing the activities sensitivity to money inputs;

X_j is a characteristic of the individual or the location;

μ_{ij} is a parameter representing the impact of characteristic X_j on the attractiveness α_i;

The expenditures E_i and E_i^0 encompass both travel costs and the costs associated with the activity itself (for example, fees). These expenditures are for the total time period modelled, reflecting the allocation of budget for a longer period (say a month). The allocation of money to activities, E_i, is balanced against the available income. Thus, by spending more money, the attractiveness of the activity is increased. As outlined before, the reasoning is that by investing more money in an activity, more options exist for using goods and facilities that better match the individuals' taste resulting in a higher quality and utility (for example, Ettema et al. 2009). The second impact of money is on duration. In this respect we define duration d_i as:

$$d_i = d_i^0 \left(\frac{E_i^0}{E_i} \right)^{\tau_i} + \rho_i \tag{4}$$

Where :

τ_i is a parameter expressing the activities sensitivity to money inputs;
ρ_i is the travel time to activity i;

This equation suggests that by spending more money in an activity it can be made more efficient to an extent determined by parameter τ_i. Another implication is that we assume that each instance of an activity requires the same amount of travel. It is realized that this is not always the case, since multiple occasions of an activity may take place at different locations or require less travel due to trip chaining. However, the travel time ρ_i can be interpreted as a general measure for longer term decision making. When detailed daily trip patterns are concerned, additional models may be needed to represent more detailed decision making. In sum, equation 2 is extended to:

$$U_i = (\alpha_i^0 + \beta_i \frac{E_i}{E_i^0}) \frac{t_i}{(d_i^0 (E_i^0 / E_i)^{\mathbf{y}_i} + \rho_i)} \exp(-\frac{\gamma_i t_i}{d_i^0 (E_i^0 / E_i)^{\mathbf{y}_i} + \rho_i}) \qquad (5)$$

The impact of this formulation on time allocation is illustrated in the following example, in which time is allocated to two activities, with parameters specified as in Table 16.1.

In this example time is allocated to activities such that $\partial U_1 / \partial t_1 = \partial U_2 / \partial t_2$ using a search procedure. The outcomes in Table 16.1 suggest that with a shorter duration, the time allocated to an activity decreases while the frequency increases. With increasing β, the activity becomes more attractive, leading to more time being allocated and a higher frequency. With increasing τ, the allocated time decreases while the frequency goes up, due to efficiency gains. Hence, the model according to Equation 5 displays the expected behaviour.

However, modelling long- and short-term mobility choices not only encompasses allocation of time, but also allocation of money. Consequently, households/individuals not only decide about the allocation of time to activities, but also about the allocation of budgets to the residence, to consumption of goods etc. To also include this aspect, we assume that money spent on consumption of goods produces a utility:

$$U_g = \sigma_g \ln(E_g) \qquad (6)$$

Where:

E_g is the money spent on good g;

Table 16.1   Illustration of time allocation model

	Activity 1	Activity 2
Base settings		
α	0.5	0.5
γ	0.1	0.1
d^0	100	100
E^0	100	100
E	200	200
β	0.05	0.05
τ	0.05	0.05
T	720	720
F	7.25	7.25
Variant 1		
d^0	90	100
T	691	749
F	7.95	7.75
Variant 2		
β	0.06	0.05
T	723	717
F	7.49	7.42
Variant 3		
τ	0.06	0.05
T	718	722
F	7.49	7.47

The functional form of this utility function is somewhat arbitrary, but is chosen to reflect a situation in which more consumption leads to a higher utility, but with decreasing marginal returns. When allocating time and money to activities, goods (and potentially other purposes). An optimal outcome is obtained if:

$$\partial U_i/\partial t_i = \partial U_j/\partial t_j \quad \forall i,j \tag{7}$$
$$\partial U_g/\partial E_g = \partial U_h/\partial E_h \quad \forall g,h$$
$$\partial U_g/\partial E_g = \partial U_i/\partial E_i \quad \forall g,i$$

Where:

i, j	refer to activities;
g, h	refer to good types.

In other words, the allocation is optimal if no utility can be gained by re-allocating an amount of time from one activity to another or re-allocating an amount of money from one purpose to another. In our model it is explicitly assumed that all budget is spent on activities and goods, since with positive values for parameters σ_g, β_i and τ_i expenditure of the full budget is a prerequisite for an optimal utility. Note that the utility of savings is not included in this stage of development. However, the optimal allocation of time depends on the way in which money is allocated and reverse. Thus, to find the optimal allocation, the following procedure is followed:

1. Given initial time allocation (for example, equal shares), money is reallocated to activities and goods as follows:

   a. Take an equal amount of money away from each spending purpose. The amount of money to be re-allocated depends on the derivatives of the utility functions of various goods and activities to expenditure E_i. In particular, when the differences between the derivatives are smaller, the amount to re-allocate diminishes.

   b. Re-allocate this amount proportionally to the derivative to budget. In other words, a purpose that would increase more due to one unit of extra money, receives more budget than a purpose of which the utility increases less.

2. Given the new money budgets, time is allocated to activities such that utility is maximized as follows:

   a. Take an equal amount of time away from each activity, depending on the derivative of utility to time.

   b. Re-allocate this amount proportionally to the derivative to time. Thus, an activity that would increase more due to one unit of extra time, receives more time than an activity of which the utility increases less.

3. Repeat 1 and 2 until no improvement in utility is obtained.

Table 16.2 Illustration of time allocation model

	Activity 1	Activity 2	Activity 3	Good 1	Good 2
Base settings					
α (activity), σ (good)	0.5	0.5	0.5	0.004	0.006
γ	0.1	0.1	0.1		
d^0	200	200	200		
E^0	200	200	200		
β	0.01	0.01	0.01		
τ	0.05	0.05	0.05		
T	200	200	200		
E	211	211	211	28	41
Variant 1					
d^0	195	200	200		
t	211	195	195		
E	224	204	204	27	41
Variant 2					
β	0.015	0.01	0.01		
t	201	199	199		
E	239	198	198	26	39
Variant 3					
τ	0.07	0.05	0.05		
t	270	165	165		
E	293	171	171	26	38

To illustrate the interaction between temporal and monetary inputs, Table 16.2 displays the outcome of the above optimization procedure for three activities and two goods, when several parameters are varied relative to the base setting. The example shows similar trends as in the previous example, but with the added effect of budget re-allocation. For instance, an increase in β not only leads to more time being allocated due to a higher attractiveness, but also to more money being allocated to the activity, which in turn increases the attractiveness and leads to even more time allocation to the activity. With increasing τ, the duration decreases, but this also leads to the allocation of more money. Due to the effect of money allocation on attractiveness, the net effect is that more time is allocated to the activity, although the duration has become shorter. Thus, the two effects of money allocation can counteract or reinforce each other.

Implementation

The previous section has outlined a model for allocating time to activities and money to activities and goods. This model was applied in a stylized setting that represented the Amsterdam-Almere corridor in the Netherlands (see later for details). When applying this model we model the allocation of time and money to three activity types: (i) in-home; (ii) out-of-home maintenance; and (iii) out-of-home social activities. In addition we assume two types of abstract goods, merely to illustrate the impacts of various scenarios on consumption. Locational characteristics assumed to influence the utility of the out-of-home activities (see equation 3) are the number of jobs in retailing, representing the attractiveness for maintenance activities, and the number of inhabitants, which we assume to be related to attractiveness for social activities. In both cases, this implies that locations in the city centre will be more attractive than locations in suburban areas, implying a trade-off between utility of location and travel distance.

As noted before, incorporating time and money allocation models in a LUTI context requires that these models are embedded in a broader context, that also includes decisions such as residential location, number of work hours, work location, vehicle ownership etc. This section will further elaborate on the relationships that exist between time and money allocation and the longer term decisions mentioned above.

With respect to residential choice, the interaction is primarily that money spent on the residence cannot be spent on activities and travel. As a result activities will be less attractive or take longer time, resulting in a lower utility. Thus, the extra utility derived from a larger housing type (for example, detached versus row house), which is more expensive, needs to be balanced against the loss of utility from less budget being spent on activities and consumption of goods. Based on previous work (Ettema et al. 2007), the utility of the dwelling is defined as:

$$
\begin{aligned}
U_d = \ & size*0.005 + row*0.5 + semi*1.0 + deta*1.5 + prop*1.270 \\
& + old*appa*-1.195 + old*row*-1.144 + kids*appa*1.414 \\
& + semi*kids*1.538 + deta*kids*1.157 + fam*row*1.058 \\
& + fam*deta*1.543 + (popacc > 200{,}000)*1 + (popacc > 100{,}000)*0.5
\end{aligned} \tag{8}
$$

Where:

size	is the size of the dwelling in m2;
row	is a dummy variable indicating a row house;
semi	is a dummy variable indicating a semi-detached house;
deta	is a dummy variable indicating a detached house;
prop	is a dummy variable indicating that the house is owned;
old	is a dummy variable indicating that the households head is older than 55;

kids   is a dummy for the presence of children in the household;
fam   is a dummy for a non-single household;
popacc   is the number of habitants within 30 minutes travel by car.

Note that the utility does not include the costs of housing, since the disutility of housing costs is considered to be the decrease in money budget available for activities and goods.[2] In addition, the residential location, but also the work location, impact on the commute time and the time needed to travel to destinations, and thereby on the time remaining for activities.

The interaction between activities/consumption and work hours is twofold. First, working more hours takes more time (both through the activity itself and through a more frequent commute), so that less time is available for the discretionary activities in our allocation model. However, under the assumption that an individual's education level and experience determine his earning capacity, working more hours also produces more income, thus increasing the monetary budget. In particular, it is assumed that income is proportional to hours worked. The net effect of these two adverse impacts (less time, more money) depends on the allocation model described in the previous section and its parameters.

Car ownership also results in two adverse effects. On the one hand it costs money, which cannot be spent on activities and goods. On the other hand, it allows quicker and more efficient travel (except when only travelling in dens urban areas with high level public transport), saving more time for activities. Again, the net effect depends on the outcome of the above allocation process.

To link the time and money allocation model to longer-term decisions about residential location, car ownership, work hours and work location, we take the following straightforward approach. By regarding the various longer-term dimensions as discrete states (such as, residential locations, work hours, number of cars, work locations), we can generate potential candidate solutions as combinations of these discrete states. Each state produces a time budget (total time minus worked hours) and a monetary budget (worked hours times wage rate for each individual). Then, for each state, the time and money budgets are allocated in an optimal way. That is to say, frequencies of activities will depend on the travel time to these activities, and money and time budgets are affected by expenditures to housing and vehicles and by work hours. In this way, each solution results in a utility defined as:

$$U = U_d + \sum_i \sum_a U_a + \sum_g U_g \qquad (9)$$

where *i* refers to individual *i* in the household and *a* to an activity. Note that the utility obtained from the activity pattern is based on allocation of time to activities

---

2 In the current stage of development of the model, we have ignored the fact that households may transfer part of their budget to/from savings.

during a 20-day period. While the length of this period can be changed without loss of generality, 20 days is believed to adequately represent the longer term impacts of residential and work hour decisions on daily activity patterns. As suggested by longitudinal data (Schlich and Axhausen 2003), many activities appear in weekly cycles, suggesting that a 20-day period suffices to represent repetitive involvement in routine activities. Further work should, however, address this topic in more detail. We assume that residential utility and consumption of goods are defined on the household level, whereas the utility from activities is defined on the individual level. Also we assume that utilities of the household members are simply added up to create a household utility. Accordingly, we assume that money budget constraints apply on the household level, whereas time constraints apply on the individual level. If the utility of the best candidate solution exceeds the current utility by a certain percentage, the solution is adopted, potentially leading to a change in residential location, work location, car ownership and work hours.

The above procedure is applied in the context of the PUMA model (see Ettema et al. 2007 for details). The PUMA model is an agent-based model that simulates demographic transitions, location behaviour and transport in the Dutch Randstad. It has an explicit representation of households, individuals, dwellings and jobs as agents to ensure consistency of for example, housing market developments and to allow for interactions such as competing for jobs or dwellings. PUMA is a dynamic model in the sense that starting from a base year synthetic population, demographic developments (birth, household formation and dissolution and death) and longer term decisions (relocation, work status, work location) are simulated for a consecutive number of years. The rationale for this approach is that in this way interaction between time and money allocation processes and longer-term decisions is achieved in a realistic way. For instance, a low accessibility to services may lead households to move to other regions, thereby affecting the demographic trend in both regions. Within PUMA, demographic processes are modelled stochastically based on age and gender dependent probabilities. Separate models have been developed for education and income depending on age, gender and household type (see Ettema et al. 2007).

The approach taken in this study is that demographic events, and the above procedure in which residential location, work hours and work location are evaluated and possibly adjusted, are applied in random order. That is to say, for each household we simulate which demographic transitions take place and which adjustments in residential location, work location, work hours and car ownership. In addition, the number of activities, the time expenditures and the monetary expenditures for each household and individual are determined for either the existing state or the new residential location/work location/work hours. With respect to destination choice, we take a pragmatic approach in which the best (= yielding the highest utility) location out of a random sample is selected.

Note that at this stage of development, car ownership and mode choice are not explicitly modelled, although they can be incorporated in the framework in a straightforward way. Instead, we assume the existence of one travel mode (car), with travel times between zones being defined on a zone-by-zone basis.

The parameters used in this application are summarized in Table 16.3.

Table 16.3   Parameter settings for simulation

	In-home	**Maintenance**	**Social**	**Good 1**	**Good 2**
α	0.10 (male) 0.11 (female) 0.105 (male+kids) 0.115 (female+kids)	0.05 (male) 0.055 (female)			
σ			0.05	0.004	0.006
γ	0.01	0.01	0.01		
d^0	100	100	100		
E^0	100	100	100		
β	0.0	0.05	0.05		
μ		$0.1*10^{-3}$	$0.1*10^{-5}$		
τ	0.05	0.05	0.05		

Since the objective of the study is to demonstrate the characteristics of the model mainly in terms of the behavioural responses and not with the intention to predict aggregate residential and activity patterns in detail, we have applied it in a somewhat artificial geographical setting. In particular, we modelled part of the population of the municipality of the Almere municipality in the Dutch Randstad (see Figure 16.2). We assume that households only relocate within Almere, however their work locations may also extend to the city of Amsterdam. In that case, workers will balance the extra time and cost of a commute to Amsterdam against potential advantages such as higher wages. In fact we will test how this trade-off is affected by wage differences and travel time differences between Almere and Amsterdam. Likewise, the locations of maintenance and social activities may be in Almere or Amsterdam. Although the restriction of not being allowed to move to Amsterdam is not realistic, this setting allows us to demonstrate some of the properties of the model. In the base year the synthetic population consists of 2,587 individuals in 1,028 households. Almere and Amsterdam consist of 3,410 and 16,870 zones respectively, containing 32,265 and 32,507 jobs respectively.

Figure 16.2   Study area

Thus in this setting competition for jobs will not play a role, and job location is determined by the aforementioned trade-offs. In the base setting, various price and time parameters were set as follows:

> Price per km: 0.4 €
> Travel time per km: 1 minute

To demonstrate the characteristics of the model a series of scenarios were evaluated:

1. BASE: the base scenario, with settings as defined above
2. TT_110 per cent: a scenario in which all travel times are 10 per cent longer as compared to the base
3. TC_150 per cent: a scenario in which travel costs (per km) are 50 per cent higher than in the base scenario
4. INCADAM_120 per cent: a scenario in which only jobs in Amsterdam have a 20 per cent higher income than in the base
5. TCADAM_150 per cent: a scenario in which travel costs to/from Amsterdam are 50 per cent higher due to a toll
6. BETA0.025: a scenario in which β for maintenance and social activities takes the value 0.025 (instead of 0.005) reflecting the potential to increase the utility of an activity by investing more money.

Table 16.4 Simulation results

	BASE	TT_110%	TC_150%	INCADAM_120%	TCADAM_150%	BETA0.025
% working in Amsterdam	50%	49%	46%	56%	49%	52%
Time allocation (hours)						
in home	39.5	38.9	43.4	38.5	41.6	33.2
Maintenance	18.1	18.0	17.1	17.3	17.0	23.7
Social	6.6	6.5	5.5	6.4	5.4	7.9
Travel	6.4	6.4	5.9	6.6	6.1	7.3
Frequencies						
Work	14.3	14.1	14.1	14.3	14.0	14.0
Maintenance	10.8	10.7	10.1	10.2	9.9	14.0
Social	3.9	3.8	3.2	3.7	3.0	4.6
Trip lengths (km)						
Work	13.1	13.9	11.8	14.5	12.3	13.0
Maintenance	14.0	13.1	14.7	13.7	14.8	13.9
Social	12.3	11.4	12.9	12.3	12.6	11.9
Travel distance (km)	384.7	349.1	355.8	396.2	363.2	437.4
Expenditures (Euros)						
in home	119.8	120.9	118.2	137.5	117.1	72.1
Maintenance	137.2	144.6	117.8	172.5	120.8	336.6
Social	78.2	76.9	60.8	94.3	62.0	167.4
Travel	153.9	139.7	213.5	158.5	145.3	175.0
Goods	1,854.1	1,820.3	1,645.1	2,117.9	1,659.4	1,421.1

Simulation Results

For each scenario the model simulates 10 consecutive years, during which demographic events, income development, relocations and activity participation and travel are modelled. Due to demographic events, the population increases in the base case from 2,587 to 2,794 inhabitants, while the number of households hardly changes, thus suggesting larger households. Since we are primarily interested in the impact of time and money allocation on travel behaviour and location decisions, we will focus on time and money expenditures and trip making in the final simulation year (see Table 16.4). The percentage of workers working in Amsterdam is 50 per cent. With the assumed parameter settings, 40 hours of non-working time are spent in home, against 18 and seven for maintenance and social activities out-of-home. In addition, the majority of the budget is spent on goods, and much less on travel and activities. It is noted that these outcomes depend on the parameter settings chosen here. Since the model has not been calibrated, the outcomes are not necessarily representative or realistic. The main objective, however, is to test whether the proposed model structure is capable of realistically representing responses to certain policy scenarios.

In Scenario 2 (TT_110 per cent), where travel speeds are lower, we observe changes in destination choice, leading to shorter trip distances for maintenance and social activities. In the bi-polar setting assumed in this study, this suggests that individuals switch from destinations in Amsterdam to destinations in Almere for maintenance and social trips. Although slightly fewer workers work in Amsterdam, commute distance has increased, but commute frequency is lower. As a net result, average travel distance in the simulation period is reduced by 36 km, although the time spent travelling is the same as in the base scenario. The reduced kilometreage leads to lower expenditures to travel. The overall income is slightly lower (due to lower work frequency), leading to lower expenditures to all purposes except maintenance.

In Scenario 3 (TC_150 per cent), with prices of travel increasing by 50 per cent, we see that the distance of the work trip decreases and that fewer people work in Amsterdam. Further, the model predicts lower frequencies of maintenance and social trips, but with slightly longer distances. Overall, less time but more money is spent on travel.

Since the increased travel costs make out-of-home activities less attractive, less time is spent on them and more on in-home activities. Since travel is more expensive, more money is spent for this purpose, going at the cost of out-of-home activities and consumption of goods.

In Scenario 4 (INCADAM_120 per cent), in which wages in Amsterdam are 120 per cent higher than in Almere, more workers decide to work in Amsterdam, resulting in considerably longer commute distances. The longer commute times are compensated by shorter trip distances for maintenance and lower frequencies of maintenance and social activities. (Note that we assume that all trips are single purpose trips.) As a result of the higher wages earned in Amsterdam, the average budget spent is higher than in the base scenario. The extra budget is equally distributed across activities and goods as well as travel. Thus, the model predicts that many make the trade-off to invest travel time into the possibility of making more money, which increases the utility of their activities and goods.

In Scenario 5 (TCADAM_150 per cent), where trips to Amsterdam are more expensive (+50 per cent), we find that due to the increased travel costs, slightly less workers work in Amsterdam. However, the general increase in costs also affects trips with other purposes, which are less often made to destinations in Amsterdam. This results in lower frequencies of maintenance and social activities although trip distances increase. As a result, more time is spent in home and less on out-of-home purposes. Since travel distance is less and the expensive trips to Amsterdam are diminished, the budget spent on travel is also slightly less.

In Scenario 6 (BETA0.025), in which the impact of money on the utility of maintenance and social activities is stronger, it becomes more attractive to invest money in maintenance and social activities, which is reflected in the expenditures. As a result, the activities become more attractive, resulting in an increased frequency and allocation of time to these activities. Due to the increased frequency of out-of-home activities, total travel time and travel distance increase. The extra investment in out-of-home activities goes at the cost of in-home activities and consumption of goods.

Conclusions

This chapter has proposed a model for simultaneous allocation of temporal and monetary budgets to travel, activities and goods. The model predicts activity and trip frequencies as well as destination choice, time use, monetary expenditures and kilometreage. Since the allocation model is embedded in a framework that includes residential location, work location and work hours, the model can potentially be used to evaluate a wide range of land use and transportation policies. A unique feature of the model is that it evaluates policies also in terms of monetary budget effects, thereby allowing to better assess the impact of income changes and prices on activities, goods and mobility. For instance, in Scenario 6 the effect that spending more budget has on the attractiveness of out-of-home locations reinforces the autonomous trend that out-of-home activities would become more attractive. Although the present applications have focused on pricing and travel time changes, the model is very well capable of assessing impacts of changes in the spatial location of facilities and their characteristics, as well as developments in the housing market.

Having noted the potential advantages of this approach, admittedly much work lies ahead in making the model applicable for policy evaluations. A major issue will be calibration of the behavioural model based on revealed or stated behaviours. At present we are not aware of data sets that include sufficient information on both activity patterns and monetary expenditures, implying that very dedicated data needs to be collected. In addition, application of the model requires that detailed spatial data is available regarding quality and prices of facilities at various locations and that reliable synthetic populations are created which also include income and lifestyle orientation. In this respect, trade-offs will need to be made between the theoretical complexity of the model and data availability. At the same time, it is noted that increasingly detailed data regarding firms and facilities becomes available, as well as parcel level data of dwellings and housing prices. Likewise, procedures for the generation of synthetic populations of household and individuals based on more aggregate demographic data are becoming standard. These developments will increase the options for implementing models as described in this chapter for policy evaluations and strategic forecasts, which account for the trend of increasing specialization of facilities and diversification of preferences, leading individuals to travel to more remote locations.

Chapter 17

The Policy Implementation Process for Road Pricing in the Netherlands

Diana Vonk Noordegraaf, Jan Anne Annema and Odette van de Riet

Introduction

Sustainable mobility is proving a challenge to achieve (Banister 2008). There are negative effects of road use, such as environmental pollution, reduced safety and congestion and a number of policy instruments have been developed to reduce these effects. Road pricing is one such instrument, and from an economic point of view is generally considered to be an effective transport policy (Feitelson and Salomon 2004; McFadden 2007). Given its potential to reduce the need to travel (less trips), to encourage modal shift, to reduce trip lengths and to encourage greater efficiency within the transport system, it may contribute to making the transport system more sustainable (Banister 2008). The EU White Paper aims for a more sustainable transport system and considers road transport pricing to be an effective instrument in achieving this aim (Commission of the European Communities 2001b). In a recent policy update (Commission of the European Communities 2009), pricing policies were again seen as an important step towards more sustainable transportation.

Although there are some examples of successfully implemented road pricing policies in cities such as Singapore, London and Stockholm (Ieromonachou et al. 2007) and nationwide truck tolling schemes in Germany, Austria and Switzerland (McKinnon 2006), in practice implementation is a cumbersome process. It seems very difficult to obtain sufficient public and political support to adopt road pricing and to get it implemented (Ison et al. 2008). In particular the more complex systems such as nationwide distance-based schemes for all road users prove hard to implement. Such is the case with the stalled nationwide road pricing proposal in the United Kingdom (Department for Transport 2004; Milmo 2008) and the halted road pricing policy process for implementing kilometre charging in the Netherlands (Eurlings 2010). Road pricing, and in particular the effects of road pricing, has been studied in detail (e.g. Verhoef et al. 2008). Much progress has been made in recent years in the field of modelling urban road pricing (e.g. De Palma et al. 2006). However, the policy process is one of the remaining challenges (van Wee et al. 2008). The key to a better understanding of why nationwide road pricing initiatives have not yet been implemented is to take a closer look at the policy process and the role of the policy actors. Policy actors are politicians and interest groups that can exert influence on the policy making process. Their role is to decide which policy to implement and to make choices between the available policies. It is not clear why some policy actors are willing to adopt certain policies while other policies reach a deadlock.

One of the countries that has been struggling with the implementation of road pricing is the Netherlands. Since 1988 various road pricing policies have been proposed but to date (2010) none of them have been implemented. Using the Netherlands, and more specifically the attempt to introduce kilometre charging between 2004 and 2010, as a case study, the aim of this chapter is to give an overview of the factors that are important in the implementation of a road pricing policy and to consider the lessons learned, from which other countries may be able to learn. Thus, this chapter aims to contribute to the scarce international literature on road pricing implementation processes by giving insights into the difficult policy processes for implementing road pricing based on the Dutch case of kilometre charging. This chapter complements the work of, amongst others, Ison et al. (2008), Attard and Ison (2010) and Schaller (2010), who investigated road pricing policy implementation in Cambridge, Edinburgh, Valletta and New York. A second aim of this chapter is to develop a conceptual framework that gives a comprehensive overview of the factors that affect the likeliness that a transport policy instrument in general will be implemented. The basis of this framework is the transport innovation literature, the theory of policy learning and the theoretical concept of a policy opportunity. We apply this framework to the Dutch case of kilometre charging to get a first impression of the usefulness of the framework.

The remaining part of this chapter is structured as follows. We begin by discussing the research approach. Next, we present our conceptual framework and then apply our conceptual framework to the Dutch case of kilometre charging. This chapter evaluates the case up until September 2010. The chapter concludes by discussing the lessons learned from the policy implementation process for road pricing in the Netherlands.

Research Approach

The research approach taken consists of three steps: (i) a literature review of the factors that affect the likelihood that a transport policy instrument in general will be implemented, (ii) the integration of these factors into a conceptual framework of the implementation process of a policy by policy actors, and (iii) the application of the conceptual framework to the Dutch case of kilometre charging.

The basis of the conceptual framework developed is the framework of Feitelson and Salomon (2004) on the adoption of transport innovations, in which feasibility is the key concept. Transport innovation is 'new ways to manage transport systems and new technologies' (Feitelson and Salomon 2004). Introducing new policies, including a road pricing policy, can be seen as an example of this. The adoption depends on the actors' appraisal of the feasibility of the transport innovation

(Feitelson and Salomon 2004). Moreover, they identify several feasibility aspects, which they have positioned in a framework.

However, their framework does not give insight into how actors appraise these feasibility aspects and how this appraisal can change over time. We have therefore expanded their framework using the theory of policy learning (Sabatier 1988). Furthermore, we are interested in the implementation of a policy instrument and consider that to be a step further than adoption. We do not consider feasibility to be sufficient to ensure a successful policy implementation and therefore we complement feasibility in our framework with the theoretical concept of a policy opportunity (Kingdon 1984; Koppenjan 1993) and with the factor political decisiveness. A policy opportunity is the moment at which decision-making on a specific policy can take place. Political decisiveness refers to the effort, time and perseverance often needed in a policy implementation process as these processes can be complex, long-lasting and involve many uncertainties (Walker et al. 2001).

The outcome is a conceptual framework that consists of three components: policy actors' appraisal of the feasibility of the policy instrument, the opportunity to put a policy on the policy agenda and the political decisiveness needed for the adoption of a policy instrument.

In the third step, we have applied the conceptual framework to the Dutch case of kilometre charging to give a first impression of the usefulness of the framework. The information for our case study was collected through desk research, and analysing scientific literature and web sources to understand the factors that have affected the policy implementation process for road pricing in the Netherlands.

The Adoption of New Policy Instruments by Policy Actors

When policy actors are faced with a specific problem (e.g. congestion) or an opportunity they can decide to adopt a policy to deal with this. This often implies making choices among the policy instruments available. In this section we describe the conceptual framework that we developed that gives a comprehensive overview of the factors that influence the willingness of a policy actor to adopt a policy instrument. This framework gives more insight into why actors advocate one policy instrument over another. The framework consists of three components, which are discussed below:

a. The feasibility of a policy instrument (A1) and the appraisal of the feasibility of a policy instrument (A2);
b. The need for a policy opportunity;
c. The need for political decisiveness.

The Feasibility of a Policy Instrument (A1)

Feitelson and Salomon (2004) suggest that the adoption of a transport innovation (e.g. a road pricing policy) depends on the economic, technical, social and political feasibility. A policy instrument is *technically feasible* if it can work technically. The positive outcome of a (rudimentary) benefit-cost analysis is a minimal requirement for *economic feasibility*. The *social feasibility* criterion is met if the public (i.e. the majority of voters) support the instrument. Public support is 'a function of the public perception of problems and the perceptions of the effectiveness of the proposed innovation in addressing these problems' (Feitelson and Salomon 2004). Public acceptance depends on the effectiveness and efficiency of the policy.

Furthermore, the policy instrument needs to be fair for the individual and the society as a whole (Banister 2008). The social feasibility is increased if the costs are borne by a large group of voters but are still low enough not to generate opposition. Hence, social feasibility entails issues such as the public's opinion on the need for action (demand for the innovation), equity issues and revenue use. Public perceptions are influenced by the dominant ideologies and what the media and elites see as publicly acceptable, i.e. the 'sanctioned discourse'. The sanctioned discourse also influences the *political feasibility*. If a policy instrument easily suits the sanctioned discourse it is more likely that policy actors will consider the instrument feasible. Moreover, the political feasibility is also increased if there is support from a wide range of specific interest groups. Furthermore, the political feasibility increases if the social feasibility is high. The importance of sufficient public acceptance as a driver for political acceptability is also supported by Banister (2008).

In Feitelson and Salomon's framework (2004) the feasibility components were interrelated with factors that impact these components. We have abstracted this framework and focus only on the four distinguished types of feasibility that are requirements for the adoption of innovations. The relations between the feasibility components are illustrated in Figure 17.1. We follow Feitelson and Salomon (2004), who stated that economic feasibility enables social feasibility which in turn enables political feasibility. The feasibility components together, including technical feasibility, determine the overall feasibility.

In Feitelson and Salomon's framework (2004) the technical and political feasibility are important requisites for the adoption of innovations. We also consider feasibility as a necessary condition for policy implementation. However, we also consider additional aspects to be important for predicting the likelihood that a policy will be implemented. These aspects are discussed in the following subsections (A2, B and C).

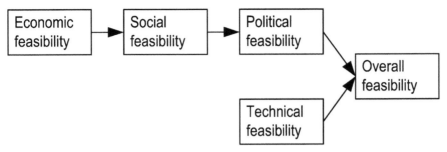

Figure 17.1 Feasibility components

The Appraisal of the Feasibility of a Policy Instrument (A2)

The work of Feitelson and Salomon (2004) does not provide insight into how actors appraise the overall feasibility and how this appraisal can change over time. This appraisal of feasibility components and the overall feasibility is context and actor dependent. Understanding from which perspective a policy instrument is appraised helps to understand the policy actors' willingness to adopt a policy.

Policy instruments are appraised differently by various policy actors. Each policy actor has his own perception of reality based on his beliefs (Deelstra et al. 2003). The adoption of a new policy instrument normally takes place in the context of existing policies or policy plans. A policy actor's preferred policies are important frames of reference in their appraisal of new policy instruments. Hence, to understand the appraisal of the feasibility of new policy instruments, it is necessary to take these preferred public policies into account (Sabatier 1988).

Sabatier (1988) conceptualizes public policies as belief systems. Three types of beliefs are discerned: deep core beliefs, policy core beliefs and secondary aspects. Deep core beliefs contain the basic assumptions of reality such as assumptions about the nature of man, the relative priorities of values such as freedom, security, power, knowledge and the basic criteria of distributive justice (e.g. whose welfare counts). These beliefs apply to all policy areas and are not likely to change. Policy core beliefs are the assumptions of actors about the content of the policy area of interest. Examples are the desirability of participation by various segments of society, basic choices concerning policy instruments (e.g. coercion vs. inducements vs. persuasion) and the proper scope of governmental vs. market activity. Secondary aspects are the components of a policy that are easily modified during the policy process. These are the instrumental decisions and information searches specific to the policy of interest and are customized to support the policy that the policy actors prefer. These aspects are interchangeable and subject to negotiation processes. The adoption of a new policy instrument can imply changes in the policy actors' belief system.

Sabatier's conceptualization helps to explain why policy actors consider certain policy instruments more feasible than others. The policy actors' views on the feasibility of the policy instrument can be influenced by information and experiences and can change their attitudes. This is called policy learning and refers to the 'relatively enduring alterations of thought or behavioural intentions which result from experience and which are concerned with the attainment (or revision) of policy objectives' (Sabatier 1988: 133). Thus, policy learning can imply the change of attitudes of actors and can change the preferred (package of) policy instruments.

However, policy learning can be selective (Sabatier 1988). First, policy actors are more interested in learning about the variables and causal relations that are consistent with the policy core. Thus, their attitude towards a new policy instrument depends on the contribution of the instrument towards the objectives and the resemblance with the preferences of the policy actor. Second, the rationality of the policy actors is limited, i.e. it is not always the best solution that is preferred. Third, policy learning depends on the current policy preferences of policy actors (belief system). In other words, the public policy that policy actors at that moment advocate is taken as a reference to compare the new policy instrument to and hence directs policy learning.

The policy actors' willingness to support a new policy instrument not only depends on if considerable policy learning took place, but also on how radically they have to change their belief system based on new information. Deep core beliefs are not likely to change and also core policy beliefs are rarely modified. Hence, the resistance to change in the attitudes of actors is least when the secondary aspects are concerned (Sabatier 1988). Hence, if no or few changes are required in the policy actor's beliefs, it is more likely that the policy actor will consider the policy instrument feasible. The appraisal of the feasibility of a new policy instrument is thus directed by the perspective of the public policy currently considered feasible by the policy actors.

The Need for a Policy Opportunity (B)

Feitelson and Salomon indicate that the feasibility aspects can be seen as minimal criteria: if these are not met, the innovative policy instrument will not be adopted. We endorse that feasibility is the minimal criterion for a policy actor to implement a new policy instrument. In fact, feasibility and how it is appraised is only the starting point for understanding the implementation of a policy instrument. Even if a policy instrument is considered feasible, whether it has a chance to be put on the policy agenda depends on the context of the policy process.

Feitelson and Salomon (2004) briefly refer to Kingdon's 'policy windows' (Kingdon 1984) to indicate that propitious moments exist when new ideas can be put on the policy agenda. In a 'crisis' situation, different policy solutions (in this chapter we use the term policy instruments) for the perceived problems are competing for the attention of decision makers. Thus, even if a policy instrument is considered feasible, there still has to be an opportunity to get the instrument on the policy agenda.

We use the stream model of Koppenjan (1993), to illustrate the policy-making process (see Figure 17.2). This process consists of solutions (e.g. policy instruments), problems, participants and couplings. The policy process is not a linear, structured, predictable process in which clear phases can be distinguished, but is contingent and unpredictable, being highly dependent on the context in which it takes place. Decisions are taken if there is a (coincidental) coupling between a problem that is urgent for most actors, a solution that can be supported, and participants who are inclined to make a decision. This is called a policy opportunity. All flows are continuously in motion. Therefore, a coupling is a matter of timing and taking temporary chances. This model emphasizes the importance of a receptive policy context and participants for the implementation of a policy instrument. New policy instruments will only be implemented at the moment of decision making when all flows come together and the window of opportunity opens.

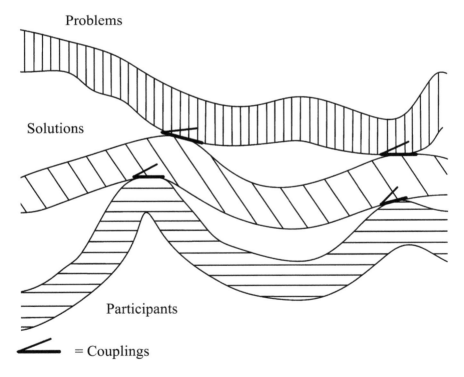

Figure 17.2 The stream model
Source: Koppenjan (1993: 25), reproduced with permission from the publisher.

The Need for Political Decisiveness (C)

Having policy actors consider a policy instrument as feasible and having a policy opportunity are minimum requirements for its implementation, but no guarantee. Another factor that can play a role in the policy actors' willingness to implement a policy instrument is the need for political decisiveness. Overall, policy implementation is more likely when the policy instrument does not require great decisiveness from the policy actor.

The required political decisiveness depends on the nature of the policy instrument (the characteristics of the policy and how it is appraised by the policy actors). Many policy problems are complex and take place in continuously changing and unpredictable systems (Walker et al. 2001). Unpredictability can be caused by uncertainties in the policy context, making policy changes sooner or later almost inevitable. These adjustments may be needed to mitigate vulnerabilities that were previously not noticed or to prevent opportunities being missed. Adjustments can be the result of learning, interactions between stakeholders, changes in stakeholders' behaviour and external changes. These complex problems often require complex policies. As these policies include many assumptions that may be incorrect, the policy itself can also provide reasons why changes in policies take place. Therefore policies should be adaptive to be robust across a range of plausible futures and include explicit provisions for learning (Walker et al. 2001). Complex policies are more difficult to adapt according to new insights when they do not include explicit provisions for learning, and these adaptations are also more costly than for simple policies (the risk of path dependency). Implementing complex policies is therefore more uncertain and challenging for policy actors and requires greater political decisiveness than simple policies.

The required political decisiveness also increases when policies need a longer implementation period (which is often the case with complex policies). This leads to a longer period of time before the policy demonstrates the full results. As long as the policy is not fully implemented the politicians' support is needed which requires decisiveness.

When policy actors appraise a policy the current policy context is also taken into account. Generally, people mistrust proposed changes from their status quo and have the tendency to minimize risk (McFadden 2007). Decision makers also tend to disproportionally stick to the status quo when choosing between alternatives. This status quo bias (resulting from rational and psychological factors) partially accounts for the difficulty in changing public policies (Samuelson and Zeckhauser 1988). It is therefore expected that policy actors will be more willing to implement policies that do not require major changes in the current policies. For example, gradually modifying an existing policy or adding a simple policy measure to a policy package is only a small modification compared to replacing a policy that has been in place for years with a completely different policy.

The required political decisiveness also depends on the nature of the policy making process. The political system, as well as the rules of the game, differ between countries. De Jong (1999: 213) typifies various countries in terms of a 'family of nations' based on institutional and constitutional factors. He argues that whether a policy instrument will land on fertile soil depends on a country's basic structure and culture. Moreover, the implementation of a specific policy instrument might be relatively easy in one country but may be a major challenge in another country. The level of required political decisiveness can differ between various political contexts.

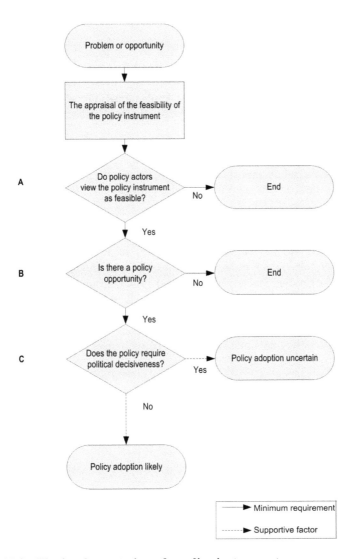

Figure 17.3   The implementation of a policy instrument

Figure 17.3 summarizes the components of our conceptual framework. This framework does not show all the relations between the included components but it shows a likely order of decisions involved in the policy implementation process. It must be noted that this framework is a simplification because policy processes in practice can be messy. Furthermore, the aspects of our conceptual framework that help to explain the likelihood that policy implementation occurs are more important than the order chosen. Policy implementation is most likely when policy actors view the policy instrument as feasible, when there is a policy opportunity and when the policy instrument does not require political decisiveness.

Applying the Conceptual Framework to Road Pricing

In this section we analyse the Dutch implementation process for kilometre charging using our conceptual framework. We will subsequently answer the following questions:

a. Do Dutch policy actors view the road pricing policy as feasible?
b. Is there a policy opportunity for the road pricing policy?
c. Does the road pricing policy require political decisiveness?

We start our analysis with an overview of the Dutch history on the implementation of road pricing. This demonstrates that the implementation process has been long and complicated. Mom and Filarski (2008) found that road pricing was already put forward in 1965 by Dutch transport engineers as a promising policy instrument, inspired by the English Smeed report (Smeed 1964). Around 1970 the government asked two scientific committees to develop future transport policies. Both committees suggested congestion charging or road pricing as possible effective future transport policies. The first notion of pricing incentives in road transport was found in a policy document from 1977 (Structuurschema Verkeer en Vervoer – SVV).

Box 17.1 gives an overview of the different road pricing proposals that have been debated since 1988 and the main reasons why these policy instruments have not been implemented.

Box 17.1   The history of road pricing in the Netherlands

The first concrete proposal for road pricing was introduced in a policy document from 1988 (Tweede Structuurschema Verkeer en Vervoer – SVV2). The proposal to introduce a time and place differentiated cost increase for passenger transport (rekeningrijden) was fiercely debated and not considered socially or politically feasible. In 1990, the cabinet decided, on the basis of the SVV2, to introduce the implementation of a toll charge to enter cities. This proposal was not successful due to the opposition of the provinces, municipalities and political parties. In 1991 fuel tax was increased and a congestion supplement to the vehicle registration taxes was proposed. Although this time an agreement was reached with the four large cities and some pilot projects were executed, the plan failed in 1993 due to the lack of political support. In 1994 growing congestion levels initiated new research into the possibilities of electronic road pricing using toll gates (again referred to as rekeningrijden). However, after years of research no final decision for implementation was taken.

In 1998 the decision to introduce road pricing based on tolling was included in the coalition agreement. In the summer of 1999 fierce opposition suddenly emerged from various interest groups, of which the ANWB* was the most apparent, as well as a national newspaper. The proposal politically 'died' (the official reason claimed was the growing technical opportunities for the implementation of kilometre charging).

After a period of political silence, there was renewed interest in the road pricing expressed in the 2004 policy document (Nota Mobiliteit). Contrary to earlier initiatives, this time the importance of stakeholder support was acknowledged and this resulted in the installation of the Nouwen committee, (named after their chairman). Also called the National Platform for Paying Differently for Mobility (Platform Anders Betalen voor Mobiliteit)), this committee consisted of representatives of governmental organizations, interest groups and societal organizations and was installed to investigate the options for implementing road pricing. In 2005 this committee recommended nationwide kilometre charging (kilometerprijs) for all vehicles to replace the fixed vehicle ownership and registration taxes. This proposal was broadly supported, primarily because the 'pay for usage' principle was considered fair.

Although the new government in 2007 embraced the proposal for kilometre charging they decided to start the implementation preparations to enable a successor cabinet to implement the policy instead of starting the implementation during their period of government (2006–2011). At the end of 2009 the concept kilometre charging act (Ministry of Transport 2009b) was sent to parliament and full implementation was considered feasible around 2018. In addition, several tendering processes for technical systems and for large scale pilot projects (in 2012 with 60,000 volunteers) as preparation for the implementation have been initiated. Amid some political turmoil over the influence of the ANWB on the policy process, the government fell (19 February 2010). The Dutch parliament declared kilometre charging a politically controversial subject and halted the policy process until the formation of the new government (Eurlings, 2010). The new government (installed on 14 October 2010) has decided not to implement kilometre charging (Rijksoverheid 2010).

Note: *The ANWB is the Royal Dutch Tourist Association which aims to represent the interests of their 3.9 million members in the areas of mobility, holiday and leisure (ANWB 2010b).

Source: Van der Sar and Baggen (2005); NOS (2009).

We will focus our analysis on the latest road pricing proposal, kilometre charging, which is considered the most concrete, elaborate and (technically) complex instrument in the history of road pricing in the Netherlands. It must be noted that this evaluation of the policy implementation process for road pricing should be considered as a snapshot of the situation in September 2010 and that, given all the uncertainties included in the implementation process, the picture can change very rapidly.

The main objectives behind kilometre charging were the improvement of accessibility (reduction of congestion on motorways) and environmental quality. Furthermore, replacing the fixed vehicle taxes by a variable usage-based charge is considered fairer. The main characteristics of the concept design of the kilometre charging scheme are (Ministry of Transport 2009a):

- all motor vehicles – trucks, vans and passenger cars, including foreign vehicles – with the exception of motor bikes will be charged;
- road users pay for each kilometre of the Dutch road network that they use (all roads are included);
- the basis consists of a fixed charge per kilometre that is based on the environmental characteristics (CO_2 emissions) of the vehicle type (truck, van, passenger car);
- a peak hour supplement at congested locations is included as a future possibility;
- the current vehicle ownership and registration taxes will be abolished;
- overall no more revenues than the current vehicle taxes will be collected and the revenues from kilometre charging will be earmarked for infrastructure instead of going to the general treasury which is currently the case;
- a GPS-based system for positioning will be used to determine the road use. The vehicles will be equipped with an on-board unit (OBU) that collects information and regularly sends the aggregated data (amount of kilometres driven, classified by different tariff groups) to the collection office to support the billing process.

Do Dutch Policy Actors View the Road Pricing Policy as Feasible?

The road pricing policy is *technically feasible*, according to most technical experts, but there are uncertainties. Kilometre charging will make use of satellite technology for positioning complemented by communication technology. The plan is that the government will provide an on-board unit with minimal functionality. In addition, selected service providers can provide a more sophisticated OBU (e.g. integrated in a navigation system). In addition, the vehicles will be equipped with a trusted element for fraud prevention. However, Cottingham et al. (2007) argue that a complex distance-based nationwide scheme, 'is not technically achievable in the short-term', because the technologies cannot accurately determine the precise location of road use, and because privacy is not adequately protected.

A report by Mapflow (2007) concluded that the technology is sufficiently accurate in determining on which road a vehicle has driven and when. Privacy is protected by aggregating the data in the on-board unit or by the service provider, before sending the data to the collection office. This ensures that the government is not able to track a vehicle or to determine route information. As this scheme is not yet implemented, it is uncertain whether it is technically feasible. However, to explore possible technical problems, the technology was going to be tested in several pilot projects.

Implementing kilometre charging nationwide is *economically feasible*, but again there are uncertainties. Several impact assessment studies have been carried out (for example CPB 2005; Rijkswaterstaat 2005; Geurs and van den Brink 2005). These studies showed that the proposed kilometre charging has a positive impact on reducing congestion and the improvement of environmental quality and demonstrates a positive benefit to cost ratio. Later in the process the uncertainty in these impact estimates was debated scientifically (Geurs et al. 2007). Different Dutch transport scientists argued in a technical workshop that the mobility impacts and the related travel time and environmental gains were overestimated in the impact studies, because of some specific characteristics of the transport model used (Geurs et al. 2007). However, most experts still argue that the benefit to cost ratio would be positive, even if these uncertainties are taken into account (see for example CPB 2008).

The *social feasibility* is uncertain. A very important step in the Dutch policy implementation process was the installation of the Nouwen committee in 2003 (see Box 17.1). The aim of this committee was to create broad support for road pricing, as the Minister of Transport realized that this was vital for the implementation to be successful. The committee included representatives from, amongst others, business representatives, labour unions, the ANWB, some scientists and environmental groups, to give advice on the option of road pricing to reduce congestion. The committee advised the implementation of the kilometre charging nationwide. The core of their advice was to replace the existing fixed vehicle taxes with a variable kilometre charge. The committee was almost unanimous in their advice except for opposition by representatives of environmental organizations who did not agree with the suggestion to start by solving some severe road bottlenecks quickly. However, around 2005 broad public support for road pricing emerged.

In 2009 the kilometre charging act was sent to parliament (see Box 17.1). A brief internet search in February 2010 showed the opinions of some main actors. Environmental groups (SNM 2009), business representatives (RAI-BOVAG 2009; VNO-NCW 2009) and freight transport organizations (Nieuwsblad transport 2009) are all in favour of the concept act. The ANWB had not determined its position on the act and had decided to carry out a web survey to investigate the views (pros and cons) of their members (ANWB 2010).

It was the position of the ANWB in particular that was uncertain. As it represents a large proportion of the Dutch population (at least: motorists), this may explain the reason why the Minister of Transport tried to stay in close contact with them. He told the Dutch press that he would listen very carefully to the result of the web survey of the ANWB. The Dutch parliament was not amused by this because they felt it was up to them and not the ANWB to make a final decision.

Amidst this limited political turmoil and before the survey results were published, the Dutch government fell (19 February 2010). The survey showed that the majority of the respondents (68 per cent of the 400,000 respondents) agreed with the 'pay for usage' principle of road pricing: they think that it is fair that people have to pay for the usage of roads instead of having to pay fixed vehicle ownership taxes (Onkenhout et al. 2010).

Political feasibility concerns the willingness to support the policy in the political arena. In the case of road pricing, the impact of social acceptability on achieving political feasibility as conceptualized by Feitelson and Salomon (see Figure 17.1) seems to be vital. During the elections for the Dutch national parliament in 2006 there was broad political support for road pricing: all major political parties including the VVD (conservative-liberals) and CDA (Christian-Democrats), who now form the new government, favoured road pricing (Annema

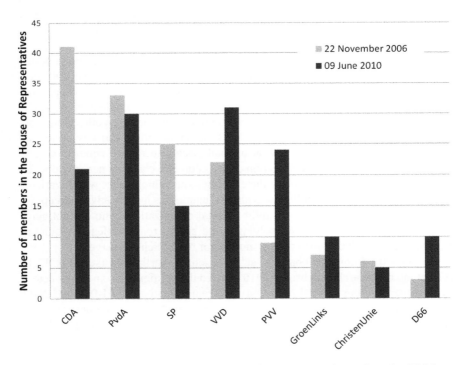

Figure 17.4   Compositions of the House of Representatives after the 2006 and 2010 elections

Source: Kiesraad (2010).

and van Wee 2008). This broad positive attitude in 2006 was, to a considerable extent, the result of the positive advice given by the Nouwen committee in 2004.

After the government fell, the Dutch parliament declared kilometre charging a politically controversial subject and halted the policy process until the new government was formed (Eurlings 2010). The 2010 election changed the political landscape considerably. Figure 17.4 displays the number of members of the House of Representatives of the eight largest political parties (accounting for 146 of the 150 members) in the Netherlands in 2006 and 2010. The new government consists of the VVD and CDA with cooperation from the PVV. They decided not to implement kilometre charging (Rijksoverheid 2010). Hence, initiatives in the field of road pricing are not expected from this government.

The change in political support stems from the position of the PVV (right wing party) and the changed positions of the VVD, CDA and SP (socialists) towards kilometre charging. The PVV, a party that has first entered the parliament in 2006 and made huge gains in the 2010 election, is strongly opposed to road pricing. On their website (PVV 2010b) they denote road pricing simply as 'a disastrous plan just aimed at bamboozling citizens out of their money'. Furthermore, they call the OBU a 'spying device' (PVV 2010a). Although the VVD stated in their election manifesto that road charging would contribute to a more efficient use of roads (VVD 2006), in 2010 on the official VVD website (VVD 2009) road charging is denoted as a 'foolish' idea. The slogan used in 2010 is: 'road pricing: no way!' The VVD opposes the idea because they think that road charging is impossibly expensive, impracticable, results only in a high tax burden and violates privacy (VVD 2009). The CDA also favoured kilometre charging in 2006 (CDA 2006). Although they did not change their position as radically as the VVD, they stated in 2010 that they did not support the proposal for kilometre charging anymore because it had become too complex. They preferred a simpler type of road pricing such as kilometre charging without peak hour supplement or environmental differentiation (CDA 2010b). In their election manifesto they stated that they were in favour of the 'pay for usage' principle if this did not result in the total amount of road taxes raised increasing and they emphasize the importance of support for road pricing (CDA 2010a). The SP (2006) proposed in their election manifesto that a more fair 'pay for road usage' system can be introduced, as long as the revenues were invested in public transport. In 2010 the SP (2010a) opposed the proposed kilometre charging fiercely, because they judged it to be a 'congestion tax' and think it is too expensive, unfair and not effective.

Perhaps these changing attitudes can partially be explained using Sabatier's (1988) theory that the policy actors' willingness to support a new policy instrument depends not only on policy learning but also on how radically they have to change their belief system. It could be that in 2005 and 2006 some policy learning had taken place based on the advice from the Nouwen committee. This, perhaps surprisingly, broad societal consensus enticed parties like the VVD and SP to embrace road pricing. Both VVD and SP have core beliefs that make supporting road pricing less obvious and as time went on they may have realized the political disadvantages more clearly. The VVD is traditionally a party that is suspicious of the societal benefits of raising more taxes. Although the kilometre charging proposal included a change in taxes instead of a tax increase, the VVD was in 2009 not inclined to believe that anymore (VVD 2009). Hence, their perception of kilometre charging conflicted with their core beliefs which could explain their change in position. The SP is traditionally a party for the workers. Given their current concern that if kilometre charging was introduced only prosperous people would be able to afford to drive on sought-after road sections (SP 2010b), it makes sense that they no longer supported kilometre charging. The CDA did not change their policy core beliefs as they still supported the basic 'pay for road usage' principle of road pricing. Their change of position only concerned components of the policy (secondary aspects).

Is There a Policy Opportunity for the Road Pricing Policy?

Around 2006 there seems to have been a policy opportunity. At that time there was broad societal support (platform Nouwen) and almost all the main political parties were in favour. Also congestion was a fast-growing problem in the Netherlands at that time (see Figure 17.5). Figure 17.5 illustrates that the vehicle hours lost in congestion on motorways in the Netherlands has almost tripled between 1985 and 2007; an average growth of 4.8 per cent per year. After the small dip in the Dutch economy around 2001 (when the internet bubble burst), both the economy and congestion grew abundantly between 2004 and 2007. Nevertheless, despite the sense of urgency to reduce congestion and broad support for road pricing that resulted from this growth, the Dutch government had to conclude that implementing the first phase of the system would not be possible before the change of governments. In the coalition agreement, however, this implementation was promised. Therefore they decided to 'carry out a first practicable, meaningful and irreversible step towards road pricing' (Ministry of General Affairs 2007). At that time it was not clear what this step implied but after the installation of the new government it became clear that, despite the effort of the previous government, it was still possible that kilometre charging would not be implemented.

The worldwide financial crisis has affected the Dutch economy considerably – in 2009 the decrease in GNP was 4 per cent (CBS 2010). Congestion levels have also decreased in the past few years (see Figure 17.5), most probably closely related to the financial crisis (Jorritsma et al. 2009a; Jorritsma et al. 2009b). However, it is to be expected that the Dutch economy will recover in the coming years resulting in relatively high congestion levels again. Hence, congestion will remain a problem that is urgent for most policy actors. The proposed solution – kilometre charging – is, although further details have been added, the same as in 2006. Hence, the question of whether there is still a policy opportunity will depend on the policy actors' willingness to make a decision on the implementation of road pricing.

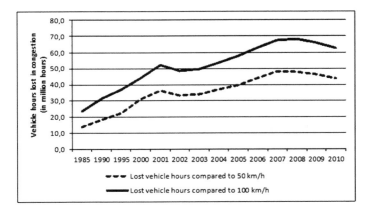

Figure 17.5   Hours in congestion on motorways in the Netherlands (1985–2007). The 2010 estimate is the average number for the period January–July 2010 only

Source: Rijkswaterstaat (2010); Van Mourik et al. (2008).

Does the Road Pricing Policy Require Political Decisiveness?

Road pricing, particularly the proposed kilometre charging, requires political decisiveness. The main factors that determine the required political decisiveness relate to the nature of the policy instrument (the characteristics of the policy and how it is appraised by the policy actors) and policy making process.

The policy instrument, kilometre charging, is complex and cannot be implemented at once. To date, no road pricing policy has been implemented with a comparable spatial scale and scope as the Dutch road pricing proposal. The implementation of kilometre charging therefore consists of many challenges such as the technological system and privacy protection. The technical feasibility of the policy can and would be tested using small-scale experiments. Nonetheless, all road vehicles would have to be equipped with OBUs (requiring investment costs of 4 billion Euros in 2010 prices) that work, all road vehicles would have to be monitored with working GPS technology, all data would have to be correctly sent to the collection office, trustworthy privacy protection agreements would have to be made and so forth. During such an implementation process it is likely that start-up problems would arise which would test the politicians' perseverance.

In addition, the political decisiveness needed to implement complex policies can also be partly understood when the appraisal of policies is considered. Kilometre charging is a significant change in the status quo of the road vehicle taxation which has been in place for decades. Mistrust from the public and interest groups can therefore be expected, making the political process highly complex and again testing politicians' decisiveness. The mistrust in this case can be illustrated easily by the words used by the political opponents (see before), such as: 'foolish plan', 'disastrous plan', 'spy devices', 'congestion taxation'.

Furthermore, the implementation of kilometre charging requires a long transition phase. For example, if the vehicle ownership tax for passenger cars was abolished immediately, it would have a sudden and large effect on car prices (in the Netherlands this tax can amount to 40 per cent of car sales prices without taxes) and, therefore, disturb the car market. To avoid this market disturbance, the concept act proposes phasing out the vehicle ownership tax gradually, and including it in the yearly vehicle registration tax. The yearly vehicle registration tax would then be converted into the base kilometre charge. The whole implementation process is expected to take years (Ministry of Transport 2009). It is likely that over time changes will be required (resulting from the complexity of the design, experiences, and political preferences). This will therefore require a great deal more political decisiveness than policy instruments that can be implemented in a much shorter term.

The implementation of the policy also requires more decisiveness when the policy making process is generally more complex due to the nature of the political system and the culture of policy making. The Netherlands is a parliamentary democracy. Every four years (or sooner if a cabinet falls) Dutch voters choose a new national parliament. The multi-party system requires a coalition to create majority support. This institutional (neo) corporatist system is characterized by social dialogue, negotiation, consensus seeking, compromise and/or joint consultation between a wide range of parties. In the Netherlands this system and the corresponding decision-making culture are referred to as the 'polder model' (Karsten et al. 2008). As the term *polder model* is not internationally widespread, we will use the term bargaining culture to characterize the culture of Dutch policy making processes. Forming a coalition is a complex bargaining process. In the Netherlands it is often said that it is more important for a political party to win this bargaining process than the elections (NIMD and IPP 2008). So, in the Netherlands political decisiveness is related to bargaining, which adds to the complexity of decision-making processes and sometimes makes it relatively unclear and slow. After the 2010 elections, the political power became even more fragmented, resulting in a difficult coalition-forming process. The bargaining culture, combined with an increased fragmentation of political power is expected to make firm majority decisions and holding on to those decisions over time less likely.

Conclusion

We conclude that, although road pricing has been on the political agenda in the Netherlands several times since 1988, to date it has not been implemented. In fact, the latest Dutch government decided in 2010 not to implement the most recent proposal of kilometre charging. Therefore it is unlikely if implementation of road pricing will ever succeed and the Netherlands finds itself in the situation 'policy adoption uncertain' (see Figure 17.3). The first aim of this chapter was to give an overview of the factors that were important for the implementation of the proposed kilometre charging policy between 2004 and 2010. From the analysis of this case we found that the three factors included in our framework have an impact on the policy implementation process for kilometre charging: the feasibility of the policy, the policy opportunity and political decisiveness.

The first aspect that had an impact on the implementation process was the feasibility of the proposed kilometre charging. We conclude that kilometre charging is considered technically, economically and socially feasible by important policy actors. However, these factors are not undisputed and there are uncertainties. The political feasibility has changed from broad consensus on the implementation of kilometre charging in 2006 to insufficient political support in 2010. Part of the explanation is the changing political context. Since 2006 three political parties have revised their position regarding kilometre charging which can be partially explained as a return to their core policy beliefs. The PVV, a party that first entered parliament in 2006 and made huge gains in the 2010 election, denotes kilometre charging simply as a 'disastrous plan'. We particularly feel that psychological aspects (e.g. that the assessment of feasibility aspects is based on beliefs) are important in explaining both why there is insufficient political support and why the policy implementation process failed.

The second aspect, the policy opportunity, exists when a specific problem, a policy instrument that deals with the problem and the support of the actors come together. Due to the lack of actor support, kilometre charging proved politically infeasible in 2010. Hence, there is currently no policy opportunity. However, the other two aspects of a policy opportunity give rise to the expectation that new policy opportunities might occur. First the burden of road transport (e.g. congestion, environmental impact) is severe and expected to increase which increases the sense of urgency among policy actors to implement policies. Second, effective alternatives to reduce congestion and at the same time generate comparable welfare gains are lacking. Therefore, we expect that kilometre charging will remain a potentially attractive policy instrument. In addition, given the long history of political debate on road pricing in the Netherlands, we expect that sooner or later a road pricing policy will be put back on the policy agenda, whether it is kilometre charging or something else.

The third aspect that impacts on policy implementation is political decisiveness. We conclude that, besides political feasibility, the lack of political decisiveness seems to have been the most important barrier in the implementation of kilometre charging in the Netherlands. With the political fragmentation after the 2010 elections and the Dutch bargaining culture political feasibility and decisiveness has become even more difficult. Additional complicating factors include the complex nature of the proposed kilometre charging scheme and the long implementation period necessary before the scheme is fully implemented (and demonstrates its full potential), requiring perseverance by the policy actors.

To summarize, we conclude that a lack of political feasibility and decisiveness are the most important explanatory factors for the failed policy implementation process of kilometre charging in the Netherlands. A second aim of this chapter was to develop a conceptual framework that gives a comprehensive overview of the factors that affect the likeliness that a transport policy instrument in general will be implemented. We conclude that the framework is helpful to systematically describe and analyse the Dutch case of kilometre charging. In addition all factors included in the framework were relevant and contributed to the overall assessment of whether or not kilometre charging will be implemented in the Netherlands. We consider this framework to be generally applicable to assess the likelihood that a transport policy instrument will be implemented, but this is something that needs to be validated.

Chapter 18

Epilogue:
The Role of Instruments,
Individuals and Institutions in
Promoting Sustainable Transport:
Concluding Remarks

Dominic Stead, Harry Geerlings and Yoram Shiftan

Introduction and Reflection

The overall conclusions that are presented in this chapter reflect on all the previous 17 chapters of the book and have been formulated with specific reference to the three issues contained in the subtitle of this book: instruments, individuals and institutions. These three themes were not just chosen for their alliterative qualities: they also neatly reflect the key issues related to transition management and sustainable transport that appear in the previous chapters. The importance of these three issues for sustainable transitions in the transport sector are each considered in turn below. Before turning to these three themes, however, a few general observations are made on the issue of transition management in the context of sustainable transport.

The first observation is that a general awareness appears to exist across many parts of society that a transition to more sustainable forms of transport is essential for a variety of reasons including energy security, environmental quality and resource efficiency. These are all reflected in the contributions to this book. However, although sustainable transitions have occurred over recent decades in a variety of different policy fields (e.g. energy, healthcare and water management), transitions in the transport sector have been more difficult to achieve. Various innovations in the transport sector have proved difficult to implement and/or have not always led to more sustainable outcomes. The authors of contributions in Part I of the book have illustrated that incremental approaches will not be sufficient to achieve significant transitions in the transport sector: this will require a concerted, long-term, multi-dimensional approach to achieve any major steps toward more sustainable patterns of transport use. Achieving significant transitions is also contingent on society being prepared to accept and adapt to broad changes in the way in which transport, infrastructure and fuel is managed.

Second, the contributions have illustrated that there are a wide range of different interpretations of transition management and sustainable transport. This is not peculiar to this book: a review of the literature in the field reveals that many different terms and concepts are currently in use. The variety of interpretations is partly related to the relatively short existence of the discipline and also to the diversity of the aims associated with transition management in the area of sustainable transport. Some of these aims may even appear to be mutually inconsistent. On the one hand, the diversity of definitions, approaches and issues contained in this book provides a richness of subject material on the topic. On the other hand, this diversity makes the identification of overarching conclusions a greater challenge. In this chapter, an attempt has been made to distil common messages and key challenges for all the contributions as a whole.

The third general observation is that the contributions to this book have illustrated that a range of different theoretical and empirical approaches can be used to investigate transition management and sustainable transport, particularly since the topic has a diversity of economic, social and environmental dimensions. The contributions have also illustrated that trade-offs and tensions between actors' aims and objectives are frequently encountered, and that policy assessment methods and techniques often struggle to reconcile these different aims and objectives. The transition management approach has particular value in bringing together a wide range of actors involved in the transport sector and providing a way of identifying commonly agreed priorities and goals. It also offers a way of assessing and reconciling different economic, social and environmental aims, and provides an arena for agreeing actions and timetables amongst many stakeholders.

Fourthly, transitions occur when paradigms change but these can sometimes be slow processes that require substantial time and effort in order to allow niches to emerge and mature. Innovations and transitions need careful management: they often do not manage themselves. The management process is something that can involve both the public and private sector (see below). Moreover, many contributions to the book have illustrated that there are various ways in which these transitions and niches can be promoted and supported by both the public and private sector as well as society more widely. Various contributions have also highlighted the fact that transitions often involve conflicts between old and new patterns of behaviour, consumption or production and that successful transitions to more sustainable forms of transport is not just a matter of tempering these conflicts but also about smoothing the processes associated with transitions.

Instruments

A wide range of policy instruments and strategies can be found in the contributions to this book that might play a role in any transition towards more sustainable forms and uses of transport. These range from the general (e.g. joint visions discussed by Gorris and van den Bosch or land-use planning in the chapter by te Brömmelstroet and Bertolini) through to the specific (e.g. fuel pricing in the chapter by Brůhová-Foltýnová and Brůha, congestion pricing in Shiftan and Zananiri's chapter or road pricing in the chapter by Vonk Noordegraaf et al.). What is clear from all these contributions is that substantial advances towards more sustainable transport require more than single policy levers or initiatives: a range of complementary instruments and strategies are necessary. The contributions to this book have illustrated a range of possible complementary instruments and strategies that may be used, although this is by no means an exhaustive selection.

The role of *backcasting* and *visioning* can be found in contributions by Geerlings, Lohuis and Pel, Gorris and van den Bosch, Hickman et al. and te Brömmelstroet and Bertolini. The chapter by Hickman et al. has provided a detailed account of how backcasting has been used to identify combinations of policies to mitigate transport CO_2 emissions in London. Processes of backcasting and visioning can lend their support to decision-making and policy development where time horizons are relatively long. Moving away from short-term forecasts to longer term visions is already happening in some areas of decision-making but has not yet become firmly established. Developing and implementing plans and policies in the long-term is of course often fraught with political difficulties in contexts where decision-making time horizons frequently do not extend beyond a politician's term of office. Injecting innovation into long-term backcasting and visioning exercises is crucial for their success. The longer the timescale considered, the greater the opportunity there is for developing and implementing novel policies and technologies, and for shaping new attitudes and behaviour. Backcasting and visioning exercises are important tools for illustrating potential transition paths towards more sustainable outcomes. Nevertheless, these types of exercises need to be solidly based on realistic expectations of the future, or they risk being seen as experiments in wild speculation.

Combinations of policies, or *policy packages*, form another common thread between several chapters. The issue of policy packaging occurs, albeit implicitly, in the contribution by Gorris and van den Bosch where they have outlined the Dutch Rush Hour Avoidance experiment, comprising fiscal measures (rewards) in combination with employers' travel schemes. According to the contribution by Hickman et al., policy packaging can provide a way of both improving the acceptability of policy measures and maximizing their effectiveness. The challenge here is to find ways of identifying and evaluating synergies (as well as potential conflicts) between policies, and to develop policy implementation paths that can combine complementary measures while recognizing that there is a limit to which different policy changes (and their implementation) can occur simultaneously.

Various contributions serve as a reminder that policy packaging is not just about identifying complementary policies within a single policy sector: it also entails maximizing synergies between policies across different sectors and/or different institutions. This requires intersectoral and intergovernmental approaches.

The need for *targeted policy*, or developing policies that are specific to certain types of individuals or journeys or times of the day, is apparent from the contributions by Wigan, Susilo and Stead, and Shiftan and Zananiri. Wigan's contribution reminds us of the differential spatial impacts that transport policy decisions can have, where 'winners' and 'losers' are determined by their geographical location or position in society (coinciding with ideas about spatial justice). Susilo and Stead have discussed the need for targeted policy responses to promote transport energy efficiency (based on sociodemographic profiles for example), and Shiftan and Zananiri have highlighted some of the potential policy responses to congestion pricing in high and low income groups. Each of these contributions has helped to illustrate that policies can have differential impacts. Impacts may for example differ greatly between richer and poorer members of society, between young and old or between urban and rural residents. Certain policies aimed at promoting more sustainable transport operation can be regressive (e.g. fuel pricing), which means that the poorest members of society are the most heavily affected by policy change while their contribution to the problem (e.g. emissions) is lower than other sections of society. This has not only illustrated the need for policy packages (see above), it has also highlighted the need for a thorough evaluation of policy impacts on different groups in society in different locations. In addition, it has emphasized the need for a better understanding of travellers' attitudes, behaviour and preferences.

The relationships between *spatial planning* and transport policy have been highlighted in several contributions (e.g. Avelino et al.; Hickman et al. and te Brömmelstroet and Bertolini). Spatial planning is an important complement to transport policies, especially from the point of view of mobility management. Various types of land uses or urban form are thought to influence the demand for transport (e.g. density, diversity and design of the built environment). The challenge here is to identify efficient and attractive combinations of land uses that can significantly reduce the need for transport and which are also sustainable from other perspectives (e.g. emission dispersion or absorption). However, bringing transport and planning policy officials together to develop coherent or integrated policy (see below) is not always easy due to differences in professional cultures, policy priorities and timeframes, which can even occur when these officials belong to the same organization.

Calls for greater *policy integration* have been made in contributions by Geerlings, Lohuis and Shiftan, Hickman et al., and te Brömmelstroet and Bertolini. Te Brömmelstroet and Bertolini, in their contribution on the integration of transport and land-use planning, have argued that the key factors behind the lack of progress on policy integration often concern institutional or procedural discrepancies (e.g. different institutional or financial arrangements) or substantive differences (e.g. knowledge, training, information). In addition to this, the multiplicity of actors and levels of decision-making that are involved in this area of policy-making also add to the complexity and difficulty of achieving policy integration. Whilst a range of factors can help to promote policy integration, there is no single solution. Political will and the allocation of resources are likely to be just as important to policy integration as mechanisms, institutional conditions or practices.

Several chapters have taken up the issue of *knowledge* and *information*, a key element of transition management and one of the substantive differences hindering policy integration to which te Brömmelstroet and Bertolini refer (see above). Wigan for example has examined the role of information in evidence-based policy-making, Huijts et al. has considered the influence of knowledge on policy acceptance in the case of hydrogen-fuelled transport technologies, while te Brömmelstroet and Bertolini have discussed the development of a participatory planning support system for Amsterdam. Wigan has highlighted various new forms of information systems, such as data observatories, data visualization and analysis tools, and has discussed how these might be used to improve decision-making processes. One conclusion here is that information governance needs to be addressed in order to be able to make more sustainable transitions in a timely and effective manner. This requires better access to data (and fewer restrictions on access and use of data). The contributions have also indicated that the enhancement of information systems is also necessary in order to deal with the complexities of policy issues related to transport and spatial planning.

Individuals

Transition management, according to various accounts in the book (see for example the chapters by Geerlings and Lohuis, Gorris and van den Bosch, and Avelino et al.) involves bringing together different individuals or actors ('regimes' according to the transition management literature) in order to develop strategies and actions. It also involves social change (according to the chapter by Avelino et al.). Consequently, transition management necessitates close consideration of individuals, and many of the contributions to the book do exactly this. These include consideration of public engagement, public acceptability issues, behavioural change, opinion-shaping, and time and monetary constraints.

Examples of *public engagement* in strategy-forming and policy-making have been discussed in various chapters. For example, Bressers et al. have argued that fostering learning about system innovations and bringing together different actors (e.g. scientists, academics, government officials, business representatives and citizens) to identify transition strategies are key elements of transition management (in response to sociological criticisms of ecological modernization that it often neglects issues of lifestyles and values and that it places too much emphasis on technological solutions). Niemeier et al. have discussed the engagement of policy and science with communities and citizens on climate change issues. Their opinion is that the way in which the science of climate change is received by local citizens and officials has an important influence on how policies unfold. Future work on transition management needs to identify innovative ways of reconciling the various viewpoints of different actors. It also needs to recognize and address the fact that public engagement on global issues (such as climate change or energy security) is often much more difficult than engagement on local or regional issues (e.g. development of new transport infrastructure or the loss of open space). Individual attitudes and opinions about local or regional issues may be much stronger than for global issues, and may not always be consistent with each other.

The *public acceptability* of policies and strategies is closely related to the previous issue of public engagement. This issue has been considered in chapters by Huijts et al., Wigan, and Susilo and Stead. Focusing on the acceptability of hydrogen technology in transport, Huijts et al. have highlighted some of the relationships between attitudes, intentions and behaviour. Susilo and Stead have illustrated how the support for different transport policy measures can vary significantly across different groups in society and Wigan has discussed how the public acceptability of policies can be influenced through information. Each of these contributions has highlighted the fact that public acceptability is not fixed but is instead open to external influence: various examples can be found that lend their support this idea (e.g. shifts in local public opinion about London's congestion charging scheme before and after its implementation). Consequently, policy decisions do not have to be led by considerations about public acceptability as the latter can change over time. Furthermore, decision-making processes need to carefully distinguish between policy effectiveness and public acceptability: these are not always the same (and may even be inversely related). One of the key challenges for the future is to identify how public acceptability can be modified in favour of more sustainable policies and investments via various channels such as education, marketing and training.

On the issue of *behavioural change*, Hickman et al. have considered a range of policy packages to reduce CO_2 emissions in London including a set of measures that address behavioural change (described under Policy Package 8 in their chapter). Their conclusion is that mechanisms for changing individual behaviour are important for more sustainable transport and robust in most future scenarios of urban development. Meanwhile, Gorris and van den Bosch, in their account of the Rush Hour Avoidance experiment, have illustrated some of the substantial behavioural changes that can be achieved in practice through financial stimuli. Shiftan and Zananiri have presented some of the behavioural changes that might be expected with the introduction of congestion charging in Tel-Aviv, including shifts to public transport, changes to the time that the journey is made, choices in favour of alternative destinations, and decisions not to travel at all. Rocci's contribution has illustrated how individual behaviour or opinions do not necessarily remain fixed: they can be influenced and changed via social interactions and/or changes in an individual's circumstances. In order to enable shifts or transitions in behaviour to occur, the availability of alternatives to support new patterns of behaviour is a prerequisite (e.g. the availability of public transport services to support shifts from car-based travel). Additional stimuli are often also needed to change current habits and deliver shifts in behaviour. These can encompass a wide variety of measures, ranging from economic incentives to avoid travel by car through to the provision of tailored travel information.

Finally, the effect of *time* and *monetary constraints* on individual travel behaviour have been examined in two contributions to the book. Ettema et al. have illustrated how micro-economic modelling might be linked to assumptions about land-use and transport interactions in order to indicate journey frequencies and destination choices under different scenarios of travel costs, employment and wage distribution. Meanwhile, Shiftan and Zananiri have illustrated that personal income can influence individuals' responses to congestion charging. Both contributions have helped to illustrate the point that policies can have quite different impacts on different types of individuals, and that these impacts need to be carefully investigated before policies are implemented in order to avoid unintended social or economic consequences. Adverse effects on specific groups might be avoided by means of policy packaging (see above).

Institutions

The role of institutions, and especially government institutions, in transitions to more sustainable transport systems have featured in all contributions to the book at a diversity of scales, ranging from national through to regional and local. Various contributions have considered several institutional levels and/or several policy sectors at the same institutional level since responsibilities for transport, environmental, energy or innovation policies are often shared: governance is often multisectoral and/or multilevel. These two key dimensions are discussed below.

Various contributions have highlighted the multisectoral nature of governance. Focusing primarily on the national level, Avelino et al. have examined the emergence of transition management in Dutch transport and energy policies, and have described how new institutional structures were developed for this purpose. In the transport sector, a national innovation board on sustainable transport was created which initially comprised civil servants but was later broadened to include representatives of the automotive industry, road users and environmental groups. Several years later, under the national energy transition initiative, an interdepartmental platform for sustainable transport was established (involving six national government ministries) to define transition paths and practical experiments concerning sustainable transport. The composition of the platform for sustainable transport was similar to the earlier national innovation board: as well as involving government officials, it also included representatives from business, an environmental NGO, and the association of road users. In the case of both the national innovation board on sustainable transport and the platform for sustainable transport, the involvement of different stakeholders was considered necessary.

This multi-stakeholder approach has also been reflected in several other contributions to the book, where accounts are given of representatives from different institutions being brought together in order to try to develop strategy (e.g. Gorris and Van den Bosch, Bressers et al. and Hickman et al.). What is apparent from many of the contributions to this book is the wide-ranging nature of institutions and interests that are involved in activities connected to transition management. This is not just a statement of fact: it is also a necessity when a process is multisectoral. This situation means that reaching agreements and decisions can often be both time-consuming and difficult. However, there seems to be little alternative to this position: the challenge lies in skilfully managing such processes and bringing them to successful conclusions.

Other contributions have illustrated the multilevel nature of governance. For example, the contribution by Niemeier et al., focusing on the sub-national level of government policy, has discussed some of the interactions between the state level (in California) and lower levels of government in relation to climate change policy. This contribution has clearly illustrated the variability of interpretation and implementation of state legislation at lower levels of government, which Niemeier et al. have discussed in terms of uncertainty, complexity, discretion, and actor configurations. An additional reason for this variability, the issue of path-dependency, might be added here, to which Geerlings, Lohuis and Shiftan have alluded in their account of paradigm changes and technology trajectories. Their contribution has argued that there is a growing recognition that history matters, and that previous technological advancements influence future developments. By the same token, it can also be argued that previous institutional arrangements and policy regimes influence future forms of governance. As already mentioned (under *Instruments* above), several contributions have contained calls for greater policy integration (see for example the chapters by Geerlings, Lohuis and Shiftan, Hickmanet al., and te Brömmelstroet and Bertolini). The Chapter by te Brömmelstroet and Bertolini for example, focusing mainly on lower levels of government (land-use planning in Amsterdam), has pointed to institutional and procedural discrepancies as key factors behind the lack of progress on policy integration, which means by implication that close attention to institutional conditions is necessary for the development of more integrated policies. Calls for greater policy integration clearly have some important institutional implications, both in terms of multisectoral and multilevel governance. One conclusion here is that policy integration should not be considered as an end in itself but as a way of achieving practical outcomes that simultaneously fulfil the goals of more than one sector or tier of government. What is also vital is that plans and policies result in practical (and integrated) action on the ground. Promoting wider interest in policy integration amongst politicians and the public alike needs to be driven by a sense of need and openness to change, and this frequently requires information, education and training.

Final Conclusions – The Role of Innovation

By way of a final summary to this chapter, attention is briefly turned to the issue of innovation – a fourth I to go alongside the three I's discussed above (instruments, individuals and institutions). For many authors, innovation is central to transition management theory, and might therefore be considered superfluous to any discussion about transition management. However, the main reason for including it here is simply to underline the importance of innovation (in a wide sense) for transitions towards more sustainable transport policies. Substantial innovations are necessary if rapid and/or radical transitions are to occur. To increase their chance of success, innovations not only need support from the public and private sector to help them develop and mature but also need to be able to perform across a wide spectrum of future conditions (e.g. economic, social, environmental, technological and political conditions). This flexibility to a range of future conditions (and robustness to uncertainties) forms a crucial element of transition management.

Many contributions to this book have illustrated that innovation can often have implications or impacts on instruments, individuals and institutions. For example *innovations in information management* might imply new instruments or new institutions. They might in turn lead to new preferences or opinions (of individuals). According to Wigan's chapter, innovations in this area could have significant positive impacts on transitions towards more sustainable transport policies and outcomes. Greater transparency and simplicity in the representation of complex issues presents a great innovation challenge for information management. *Innovation in technology* (discussed in contributions by Geerlings, Lohuis and Shiftan, Huijts et al. and Hickman et al.) can help lead to new policy instruments or change the way of working in existing institutions. It can also affect individual lifestyles. Consequently, consideration of technological innovation should not just be narrowly limited to vehicle technologies: there are many other technologies that influence patterns of work, recreation and consumption and thereby help to shape the demand for transport. Innovation in introducing and adopting technology is also is an important challenge to be addressed. Finally, *innovation in opinion-shaping* might not only have implications for individuals but also for instruments (such as the acceptability that individuals attach to them) as well as institutions (e.g. how governments present policies and strategies). Key challenges here concern the innovative use of information to shape opinions and, more importantly, behaviour. As Hickman et al. recognize, this is a very complex problem and will require huge investment and social change. Shifts in behaviour are essential since any transitions to more sustainable patterns and forms of transport will not be assessed on attitudes or policies but on actions and outcomes. In all, this amounts to some substantial challenges for transition management in the transport sector: there is still so much more to do.

Bibliography

Abbott, J. 2008. Planning for Complex Metropolitan Regions: A Better Future or a More Certain One? *Journal of Planning Education and Research* 28, 503–17.

Abdel-Ghany, M. and Schwenk, F.N. 1993. Differences in Consumption Patterns of Single-parent and Two-parent Families in the United States. *Journal of Family and Economic Issues* 14, 299–315.

Ackoff, R.L. 1989. From Data to Wisdom. *Journal of Applied Systems Analysis* 16, 3–9.

Adams, J. 2005. Hypermobility, a Challenge to Governance, in *New Modes of Governance: Developing an Integrated Policy Approach to Science, Technology, Risk and the Environment*, edited by Lyall, C. and Tait, J. Aldershot: Ashgate.

Adelman, D. and Engel, K. 2008. Adaptive Federalism: The Case Against Reallocating Environmental Regulatory Authority. *Minnesota Law Review* 92(6), 1796–850.

Ajzen, I. 1991. The Theory of Planned Behavior. *Organizational Behavior and Human Decision Processes* 50, 179–211.

Ajzen, I. 2001. Nature and Operation of Attitudes. *Annual Review of Psychology* 52, 27–58.

Albrechts, L. 2003. Planning and Power: Towards an Emancipatory Planning Approach. *Environment and Planning C: Government and Policy* 21, 905–24.

Algemene Wielrijders Bond (ANWB). 2010a. *Dossier kilometerprijs (File kilometre pricing)*. Available from: www.anwb.nl/auto/dossier-kilometerprijs,/overzicht.html [Accessed: 25 February 2010].

Algemene Wielrijders Bond (ANWB). 2010b. *Over ANWB*. Available from: www.anwb.nl/over-anwb/vereniging-en-bedrijf,/Over-ANWB-introductie.html [Accessed: 22 September 2010].

Allemand, S. 2004. Voyages, migrations, mobilité. *Sciences humaines et sociales* 145.

Alter, N. 2002. L'innovation, un processus collectif ambigu, in *Les logiques de l'innovation*, edited by N. Alter. Paris: La Découverte.

Ampt, A., Wundke, J. and Stopher, P. 2006. Households on the Move: New Approach to Voluntary Travel Behavior Change. *Transportation Research Record: Journal of the Transportation Research Board, No.1985*. Transportation Research Board of the National Academies, Washington, D.C., 98–105.

Anable, J., Boardman, B. and Root, A. 1997. *Travel Emission Profiles: A Tool for Strategy Development and Driver Advice*. Environmental Change Unit Research Report No 17. Oxford: University of Oxford Press.

Anable, J., Lane, B. and Kelay, T. 2006. *An Evidence Based Review of Public Attitudes to Climate Change and Transport Behavior*. London: Department for Transport.

Annema, J.A. and Van Wee, G.P. 2008. Transport Policy in Dutch Election Manifestos: Estimating the Environmental Impact. *Transport Policy* 15, 283–90.

Annema, J.A. and Vonk Noordegraaf, D.M. 2009. *De effectiviteit van filebeleid in Nederland, 1970–2008*, Colloquium Vervoersplanologisch Speurwerk, November 2009, Antwerpen.

Arentze, T., Ettema, D. and Timmermans, H. 2010. Incorporating Time and Income Constraints in Dynamic Agent-based Models of Activity Generation and Time Use: Approach and Illustration. *Transportation Research C* 18, 71–83.

Arentze, T. and Timmermans, H. 2001. *A Co-evaluation Approach to Extracting and Predicting Linked Sets of Complex Decision Rules from Activity Diary Data*. Paper presented at the 80th Annual Meeting of the Transportation Research Board. Washington, D.C., January 2001.

Argyris, C. 1999. *On Organizational Learning*. Oxford: Blackwell.

Argyris, C. 2005. Double-Loop Learning in Organizations: A Theory of Action Perspective. In, *Great Minds in Management: The Process of Theory Development*, edited by Smith, K.G. and Hitt, M.A. Oxford: Oxford University Press, Oxford.

Argyris, C., Putnam, R. and McLain Smith, D. 1985. *Action Science: Concept, Methods and Skills for Research and Intervention*. San Fransisco: Jossey-Bass Publisher.

Armitage, C.J. and Connor, M. 2001. Efficacy of the Theory of Planned Behavior: A Meta-analytic Review. *British Journal of Social Psychology* 31, 471–99.

Ashiru, O., Hickman, R. and Banister, D. 2009. *TC-SIM Modelling Specification and Assumptions*. London: Halcrow Group.

Ateliér ekologických modelů (ATEM) 2001. *Zjištění šetření aktuální dynamické skladby vozového parku a jeho emisních parametrů*. Prague: ATEM.

Attard, M. and Ison, S.G. 2010. The Implementation of Road User Charging and the Lessons Learnt: The Case of Valletta, Malta. *Journal of Transport Geography* 18, 14–22.

Avelino, F. 2009. Empowerment and the Challenge of Applying Transition Management to Ongoing Projects. *Policy Sciences* 42(4), 369–90.

Avelino, F. (forthcoming, 2011) *Power in Transition: Empowering Sustainability Governancy. A Case-study of Dutch Transition Management for Sustainable Mobility*. PhD Thesis. Rotterdam: Erasmus University Rotterdam.

Avelino, F. and Kemp, R. 2009. Newspeak or Paradigm Shift? Interpreting Dutch Transition Discourse on Sustainable Mobility, presented at the *International Conference Towards Knowledge Democracy, Consequences for Science, Politics and Media*, August 25–7, 2009, Leiden, the Netherlands and submitted to *Critical Policy Analysis*.

Avelino, F. and Rotmans, J. 2009. Power in Transition: An Interdisciplinary Framework to Study Power in Relation to Structural Change. *European Journal of Social Theory* 12(40), 543–69.

Bain, A. and Van Vorst, W.D. 1999. The Hindenburg Tragedy Revisited: The Fatal Flaw Found. *International Journal of Hydrogen Energy* 24, 399–403.

Ball, M. and Wietschel, M. 2009. The Future of Hydrogen – Opportunities and Challenges. *International Journal of Hydrogen Energy* 34, 615–27.

Banister, D. 2000. Sustainable Urban Development and Transport – A Eurovision for 2020. *Transport Reviews* 20, 113–30.

Banister, D. 2005. *Unsustainable Transport: City Transport in the New Century*. London: Routledge.

Banister, D. 2008. The Sustainable Mobility Paradigm. *Transport Policy* 15(2), 73–80.

Banister, D. and Hickman, R. 2006. How to Design a More Sustainable and Fairer Built Environment: Transport and Communications. *IEEE Proceedings of the Intelligent Transport System* 153(4), 276–91.

Bardach, E. 1998. *Getting Agencies to Work Together: The Practice and Theory of Managerial Craftsmanship*. Washington, D.C.: The Brookings Institute.

Beamish, T.D. 2000. Accumulating Trouble: Complex Organization, a Culture-of-Silence, and a Secret Spill. *Social Problems* 47(4), 473–98.

Beamish, T.D. 2001. Environmental Threat and Institutional Betrayal: Lay Public Perceptions of Risk in the San Luis Obispo County Oil Spill. *Organization and Environment* 14(1), 5–33.

Beamish, T.D. 2002a. *Silent Spill: The Organization of an Industrial Crisis*. Cambridge, MA: MIT Press.

Beamish, T.D. 2002b. Waiting For Crisis: Regulatory Inaction and Ineptitude and the Case of the Guadalupe Dunes Oil Spill. *Social Problems* 49(2), 150–77.

Beamish, T.D. and Luebbers, A. 2009. Alliance-Building Across Social Movements: Bridging Difference in a Peace and Justice Coalition. *Social Problems* 56, 647–76.

Becker, G. 1965. A Theory of the Allocation of Time. *Economic Journal* 75, 493–517.

Berkhout, F., Smith, A. and Stirling, A. 2004. Technological Regimes, Transition Contexts and the Environment. In, *System Innovation and the Transition to Sustainability: Theory, Evidence and Policy*, edited by Elzen, B., Geels, F. and Green, K. Cheltenham, UK: Edward Elgar, 48–75.

Bertolini, L., le Clercq, F. and Kapoen, L. 2005. Sustainable Accessibility: A Conceptual Framework to Integrate Transport and Land Use Plan-making. Two Test-applications in the Netherlands and a Reflection on the Way Forward. *Transport Policy* 2005(12), 207–20.

Bertolini, L., le Clercq, F. and Straatemeier, T. 2008. Urban Transportation Planning in Transition, *Transport Policy* 15, 69–72.

Bishop, I.D. 1998. Planning Support: Hardware, Software in Search of a System. *Computers, Environment and Urban Systems* 22(3), 189–202.

Blundell, R. and Robin, J.M. 2000. Latent Separability: Grouping Goods without Weak Separability. *Econometrica* 68(1), 53–84.

Bonsall, P. 2002. Motivating the Respondent – How Far Should You Go? In, *In Perpetual Motion: Travel Behavior Research Opportunities and Applications Challenges*, edited by Mahmassani, H.S. Oxford: Pergamon, 359–78.

Boy, D. 2007. *Les Représentations sociales de l'effet de serre. 7e vague*. Paris: ADEME.

Boykoff, M. 2008. The Cultural Politics of Climate Change Discourse in UK Tabloids. *Political Geography* 27, 549–69.

Boykoff, M.B. and Boykoff, J. 2004. Balance as Bias: Global Warming and US Prestige Press. *Global Environmental Change* 14, 125–36.

Boykoff, M. and Boykoff, J. 2007. Climate Change and Journalistic Norms: A Case Study of U.S. Mass-media Coverage. *Geoforum* 38(6), 1190–204.

Boykoff, M.T. and Goodman, M.K. 2009. Conspicuous Redemption? Reflections on the Promises and Perils of the 'Celebritization' of Climate Change. *Geoforum* 40, 395–406.

Boykoff, M. and Mansfield, M. 2009. *2004–2009 World Newspaper Coverage of Climate Change or Global Warming*. Oxford: Mediacoverage.

Brand, C. and Boardman, B. 2008. Taming of the Few – The Unequal Distribution of Greenhouse Gas Emissions from Personal Travel in the UK. *Energy Policy* 36(1), 224–38.

Bradley, M., Outwater, M., Jonnalagadda, N. and Ruiter, E. 2002. *Estimation of an Activity-based Micro-simulation Model for San Francisco*. Paper presented at the 81st Annual Meeting of the Transportation Research Board, Washington, D.C. January 2002.

Bradley, M. and Vovsha, P. 2005. A Model for Joint Choice of Daily Activity Pattern Types of Household Members. *Transportation* 32, 545–71.

Bressers, N. and Diepenmaat, H. 2009a. Transumo, *Transitiemonitoring Transumo. Monitoringrapport*, 8 November 2009. Rotterdam: Erasmus University Rotterdam.

Bressers, N. and Diepenmaat, H. 2009b. Leven met Water, *Transitiemonitoring Leven met Water. Monitoringrapport 2*, 18 December 2009. Rotterdam: Erasmus University Rotterdam.

Brewer, G.D. 1973. *Politicians, Bureaucrats, and the Consultant: A Critique of Urban Problem Solving*. New York: Basic Books.

Brög, W. 1998. Individualized Marketing: Implications for Transportation Demand Management. *Transportation Research Record* 1618, 116–21.

Brög, W. and Erl, E. 1996. *Changing Daily Mobility: Less or Differently?* ECMT Round Table Report 102, Paris: OECD.

Brög, W., Erl, E., Funke, S. and James, B. 1999. *Behavior Change Sustainability from Individualized Marketing*. Paper presented at the 23rd Australian Transport Research Forum Conference, Perth, Australia.

Brög, W., Erl, E. and Mense, N. 2002. *Individualised Marketing, Changing Travel Behavior for a Better Environment.* Paper presented at the OECD Workshop: Environmentally sustainable transport, 5–6 December 2002, Berlin.

Brög, W. and Ker, I. 2008. *Myths, (Mis)Perceptions and Reality in Measuring Voluntary Behavior Change.* Resource Paper for the Workshop on Surveys for Behavioral Experiments: 8th International Conference on Survey Methods in Transport, 25–31 May 2008, Annecy.

Brůha, J. and Brůhová-Foltýnová, H. 2008. Assessment of Fiscal Measures on Atmospheric Pollution from Transport in Urban Areas. In, *Critical Issues in Environmental Taxation. International and Comparative Perspectives: Volume V,* edited by Chalifour, N., Milne, J.E., Ashiabor, H., Deketelaere, K. and Kreiser, L. Oxford: Oxford University Press, 335–50.

Brůha, J. and Foltýnová, H. 2006. A Contribution to Predicting the Modal Split in Urban Passenger Transport under Incomplete Data, in *Proceedings from the Extra EURO Conference,* 27–9 September 2006, Bari.

Burby, R.J. and Paterson, R.G. 1993. Improving Compliance with State Environmental Regulations. *Journal of Policy Analysis and Management* 12(4), 753–72.

Burch, S. 2009. In Pursuit of Resilient, Low Carbon Communities: An Examination of Barriers to Action in Three Canadian Cities. *Energy Policy* 38(12), 7575–85.

Burt, R. 1987. Social Contagion and Iinnovation: Cohesion versus Structural Equivalence. *American Journal of Sociology* 92, 1287–335.

Burt, R. 2000. The Network Structure of Social Capital. In, *Research in Organizational Behavior,* edited by Sutton, R.I. and Staw, B.M. *Research in Organizational Behavior.* Greenwich: JAI Press, 345–423.

Cairns, S., Sloman, L., Newson, C., Anable, J., Kirkbride, A. and Goodwin, P. 2004. *Smarter Choices: Changing the Way We Travel.* London: The Stationery Office.

Caniëls, M. and Romijn, H. 2008. Strategic Niche Management: Towards a Policy Tool for Sustainable Development. *Technology Analysis and Strategic Management* 20(2), 245–66.

Carson, R.T., Flores, N.E. and Meade, N.F. 2001. Contingent Valuation: Controversies and Evidence. *Environmental and Resource Economics* 19, 173–210.

Centraal Bureau voor Statistiek (CBS) 2010. *Voortgaande economische groei in tweede kwartaal (Continious economic growth in the second quarter)* [Online]. Available from: www.cbs.nl/nl-NL/menu/themas/macro-economie/ publicaties/dne/economische-groei/archief/2010/2010-12-02-01-ne-e.htm [Accessed: 22 September 2010].

Centraal Planbureau (CPB) 2005. *Economische analyse van verschillende vormen van prijsbeleid voor het wegverkeer* (Economic analysis of different road pricing schemes). Document 87. Den Haag: Centraal Planbureau.

Centraal Planbureau (CPB) 2008. *Economische analyses van Anders Betalen voor Mobiliteit (ABvM), Verslag ten behoeve van de hoorzitting van de vaste kamercommissie verkeer en vervoer van de Tweede Kamer* (Economic analysis of nationwide road pricing schemes. Report to the transport committee of Dutch parliament). CPB-notitie. Den Haag: Centraal Planbureau.

Cervero, R. 1998. *The Transit Metropolis: A Global Inquiry*. Washington, D.C.: Island Press.

Charles University Environment Centre (CUEC) 2005. Final Report from the Project of the R&D of the Czech Ministry of the Environment 'Quantification of External Costs from Energy Use in the Czech Republic' No. VaV/320/1/03. Prague: Charles University Environment Centre.

Checkland, P. 2001. Soft Systems Methodology. In, *Rational Analysis for a Problematic World Revisited: Problem Structuring Methods for Complexity, Uncertainty and Conflict*, edited by Rosenhead, J. and Mingers, J. New York: John Wiley and Sons, 61–90.

Checkland, P. and Holwell, S. 1998. *Information, Systems and Information Systems: Making Sense of the Field*. Chicester: John Wiley and Sons.

Checkland, P. and Scholes, J. 1990. *Soft Systems Methodology in Action*. Chicester: John Wiley and Sons.

Chilvers, J. and Evans, J. 2009. Understanding Networks at the Science-policy Interface. *Geoforum* 40(3), 355–62.

Chinn, S. 2000. *Technology and the Logic of American Racism*. London: Continuum.

Christen-Democratisch Appèl (CDA) 2006. Vertrouwen in Nederland. Vertrouwen in elkaar. Verkiezingsprogramma 2006–2011 (Trust in the Netherlands. Trust in each other. Election manifesto 2006–2011). Available from: www.verkiezingsprogramma.info/component/option,com_weblinks/catid,19/Itemid,38/ [Accessed: 9 November 2010].

Christen-Democratisch Appèl (CDA) 2010a. Slagvaardig en Samen. Verkiezingsprogramma 2010–2015 (Sharp and Jointly. Election manifesto 2010–2015). Available from: www.verkiezingsprogramma.info/component/option,com_weblinks/catid,50/Itemid,72/ [Accessed: 9 November 2010].

Christen-Democratisch Appèl (CDA) 2010b. *Standpunt: Kilometerheffing (Position: Kilometre charging)*. Available from: www.cda.nl/Waar_staan_we_voor/Standpunten/Kilometerheffing.aspx [Accessed: 9 November 2010].

Cilliers, P. 2005. Complexity, Deconstruction and Relativism. *Theory, Culture and Society* 22(5), 255–67.

Cohen, M.J. 2006. A Social Problems Framework for the Critical Appraisal of Automobility and Sustainable Systems Innovation. *Mobilities* 1(1), 23–38.

Cohen-Blankshtain, G. 2008. Institutional Constraints on Transport Policymaking: The Case of Company Cars in Israel. *Transportation* 35, 411–24.

Commission of the European Communities (CEC). 2001a. *European Governance: A White Paper*, COM(2001)428. Luxembourg: Office for Official Publications of the European Communities.

Commission of the European Communities (CEC). 2001b. *European Transport Policy for 2010: Time to Decide*. Commission for the European Communities, COM(2001)370. Brussels: Office for Official Publications of the European Communities.

Commission of the European Communities (CEC). 2006. *Keep Europe Moving: Sustainable Mobility for Our Continent*. Mid-term Review of the European Commission's 2001 Transport White Paper. Commission for the European Communities, COM(2006)214. Luxembourg: Office for Official Publications of the European Communities.

Commission of the European Communities (CEC). 2007. *Towards a New Culture for Urban Mobility* COM(2007)551, Luxembourg: Office for Official Publications of the European Communities.

Commission of the European Communities (CEC). 2009. *A Sustainable Future for Transport. Towards an Integrated, Technology-led and User-friendly System* COM(2009)279. Luxembourg: Publications Office of the European Union.

Commission for Integrated Transport (UK) 2007. *Transport and Climate Change*. London: Commission for Integrated Transport.

Committee on Climate Change (UK). 2009. *Meeting the UK Aviation Target. Options for Reducing Emissions to 2050*. London: Committee on Climate Change.

Committee on Human Dimensions of Global Change. 2009. *Informing Decisions in a Changing Climate. Panel on Strategies and Methods for Climate-related Decision Support*. Washington, D.C.: National Academy of Science, National Research Council.

Corburn, J. 2005. *Street Science: Community Knowledge and Environmental Health Justice*. Cambridge, MA: MIT Press.

Cottingham, D.N., Beresford, A.R. and Harle, R.K. 2007. Survey of Technologies for the Implementation of National-scale Road User Charging. *Transport Reviews* 27, 499–523.

Couclelis, H. 2005. Where Has the Future Gone? Rethinking the Role of Integrated Land-use Models in Spatial Planning. *Environment and Planning A*, 37, 1353–71.

Crano, W.D. and Prislin, P. 2006. Attitudes and Persuasion. *Annual Review of Psychology* 57, 345–74.

Crossley, D.J. 1983. Identifying Barriers to the Success of Consumer Energy Conservation Strategies. *Energy* 8(7), 533–46.

Cvetkovich, G., Siegrist, M., Murray, R. and Tragesser, S. 2002. New Information and Social Trust: Asymmetry and Perseverance of Attributions about Hazard Managers. *Risk Analysis* 22, 359–67.

Daamen, D., De Best-Waldhoer, M., Damen, K. and Faaij, A. 2006. Pseudo-opinions on CCS Technologies. *Paper presented at GHGT-8*. Trondheim.

Danielson, M. 1979. *The Politics of Exclusion*. New York: Columbia University Press.

Danziger, J.N. 1977. Computers, Local Government, and the Litany to EDP. *Public Administration Review* 37, 28–37.

Davidson, W., Donnelly, R., Vovsha, P., Freedman, J., Ruegg, S., Hick, J., Castiglione, J. and Picado, R. 2007. Synthesis of First Practices and Operational Research Approaches in Activity-based Travel Demand Modeling. *Transportation Research A* 41(5), 464–88.

Deaton, A.S. and Muellbauer, J. 1980. An Almost Ideal Demand System. *The American Economic Review* 70(3), 312–36.

De Jong, W.M. 1999. *Institutional Transplantation: How to Adopt Good Transport Infrastructure Decision-making Ideas from Other Countries?* Delft: Eburon.

De la Peña, C. 2007. Risky Food, Risky Lives: The 1977 Saccharin Rebellion. *Gastromica: The Journal of Food and Culture* 7(2), 100–105.

De Palma, A., Lindsey, R. and Proost, S. 2006. Research Challenges in Modelling Urban Road Pricing: An Overview. *Transport Policy* 13, 97–105.

Deelstra, Y., Nooteboom, S.G., Kohlmann, H.R., Van Den Berg, J. and Innanen, S. 2003. Using Knowledge for Decision-making Purposes in the Context of Large Projects in The Netherlands. *Environmental Impact Assessment Review* 23, 517–41.

Degenne, A. and Forsé, M. 1994. *Les réseaux sociaux: une analyse structurale en sociologie*. Paris: Armand Colin.

Department for Communities and Local Government (UK). 2010. *Policy Options for Geographic Information from Ordnance Survey: Consultation*. London: Department for Communities and Local Government, Available from: www.communities.gov.uk/publications/corporate/ordnancesurveyconsultation [Accessed: 10 August 2010].

Department for Transport (UK). 2004. *Feasibility Study of Road Pricing in the UK*. London: Department for Transport.

Department for Transport (UK). 2006. *Transport Statistics for Great Britain: 2006 Edition*. London: The Stationery Office.

Department for Transport (UK). 2008. *Attitudes to Climate Change and the Impact of Transport (2006, 2007, 2008)*. London: Department for Transport.

Deyle, R.E. and Smith, R.A. 1998. Local Government Compliance with State Planning Mandates: The Effects of State Implementation in Florida. *Journal of the American Planning Association* 64(4), 457–69.

Dirven, J., Rotmans, J. and Verkaik, A.P. 2002, Samenleving in transitie, een vernieuwend gezichtspunt (*Society in Transition: An Innovative Viewpoint*), Essay voor het Ministerie van Landbouw, Natuurbeheer en Voedselkwaliteit (LNV), Den Haag, Available from: www.innovatienetwerk.org/nl/bibliotheek [Accessed: 10 August 2010].

Diver, C. 1980. A Theory of Regulatory Enforcement. *Public Policy* 28, 259–99.

Dodson, J.E. 1995. International Conferences Address GIS in Coastal Zone Management. *GIS World* 8(5), 42–4.

Dosi, G. 1988. Sources, Procedures and Microeconomic Effects of Innovation. *Journal of Economic Literature* 26, 1120–71.

Duineveld, M., Beunen, R., Ark, R.G.H. van, Assche, K.A.M. van and During, R. 2007. *The Difference between Knowing the Path and Walking the Path: een essay over het terugkerend maakbaarheidsdenken in beleidsonderzoek.* Working paper. Wageningen: Socio-spatial Analysis Group, Wageningen University.

Dumit, J. 2005. *Picturing Personhood: Brain Scans and Biomedical Identity.* Princeton: Princeton University Press.

Dupuy, G. 1999. From the 'Magic Circle' to 'Automobile Dependence': Measurements and Political Implications. *Transport Policy* 6, 1–17.

Duurzame Technologische Ontwikkeling (DTO) 1992. *Een uitdaging aan de technologie! Interdepartementaal onderzoeksprogramma duurzame technologische ontwikkeling.* Leidschendam/Delft: Duurzame Technologische Ontwikkeling.

Eagly, A. and Chaiken, S. 1996. Attitude Structure and Function. In, *The Handbook of Social Psychology*, edited by Gilbert, D., Fiske, S. and Lindzey, G. New York: McGraw-Hill.

Economic and Social Data Service (ESDS). 2007. *Economic and Social Data Service Website: National Travel Survey* (http://www.esds.ac.uk/government/nts).

Edelman, L.B., Uggen, C. and Erlanger, H.S. 1999. The Endogeneity of Legal Regulation: Grievance Procedures as Rational Myths. *American Journal of Sociology* 105, 406–54.

Edgar, A., Rockliffe, N. and Wigan, M.R. 1996. *Pricing Principles for Digital Geographic Data—Manual for the Ramsey Model.* FDF Management Report MP9603/2 to the Office of Geographic Coordination, Victorian Treasury, Melbourne. Available from: www.mwigan.com/mrw/Downloadable_Publications.html [Accessed: 10 August 2010].

Edwards, P.P., Kutznetzov, V.L., David, W.I.F. and Brandon, N.P. 2008. Hydrogen and Fuel Cells: Towards a Sustainable Energy Future. *Energy Policy* 36, 4356–62.

Ehrmann, J., and Stinson, B. 1999. Joint Fact-finding and the Use of Technical Experts. In, *The Consensus Building Handbook*, edited by Susskind, L., McKearnan, S. and Thomas-Larmer, J. Thousand Oaks: Sage.

Ellis, G., Barry, J. and Robinson, C. 2007. Many Ways to Say 'No', Different Ways to Say 'Yes': Applying Q-methodology to Understand Public Acceptance of Wind Farm Proposals. *Journal of Environmental Planning and Management* 50, 517–51.

Elzen, B., Geels, F. and Green, K. (eds). 2004. *System Innovation and the Transition to Sustainability: Theory, Evidence and Policy.* Cheltenham: Edward Elgar.

Emberger, G. and Ibesich, N. 2006. *Mars in Asia; How a Model Can Help and Influence Decision Makers.* Proceedings of the CORP 2006 Congress, Vienna, 193–200.

Emmert, S., Van den Bosch, S., Van de Lindt, M. and Van Sandick, E. 2006. *Achtergronddocument TNO-Transitioneringsmethode, modules voor het opschalen van experimenten.* Delft/Rotterdam: TNO/DRIFT.

Engel, K. 2006. Harnessing the Benefits of Dynamic Federalism in Environmental Law. *Emory Law Journal* 56(1), 159–88.

Ettema, D., Arentze, T. and Timmermans, H. 2009. *Money Talks: Developing Activity Generation Models based on Time and Money Allocation.* Paper presented at the International Choice Modelling Conference, Harrogate (UK).

Ettema, D., De Jong, K., Timmermans, H. and Bakema, A. 2007. PUMA: Multi-agent Modelling of Urban Systems. In, *Land Use Modeling,* edited by Koomen, E., Bakema, A., Stillwell, J. and Scholten, H. Heidelberg: Spinger Verlag, 237–58.

Etzkowitz, H. 2003. Innovation in Innovation: The Triple Helix of University-Industry-Government Relations, *Social Science Information* 42, 293–337.

Eurlings, C. 2010. *Anders Betalen voor Mobiliteit [Paying differently for mobility].* Den Haag: Ministerie van Verkeer en Waterstaat.

European Commission (EC). 1999. ExternE: Externalities of Energy. Vol. 7: Methodology 1998 Update (EUR 19083); Vol. 8: Global Warming (EUR 18836); Vol. 9: Fuel Cycles for Emerging and End-Use Technologies, Transport and Waste (EUR 18887); Vol. 10: National Implementation (EUR 18528). Brussels: Office for Official Publications of the European Communities, L-2920 Luxembourg: Office for Official Publications of the European Communities.

European Commission (EC). 2003. *External Costs: Research Results on Socio-environmental Damages due to Electricity and Transport.* Brussels: European Commission, Directorate-General for Transport and Energy.

European Commission (EC). 2006. *Introducing Hydrogen as an Energy Carrier.* Brussels: European Commission, Directorate-General for Research.

European Commission (CEC) 2007a. *Commission Proposes an Integrated Energy and Climate Change Package to Cut Emissions for the 21st Century.* European Commission Press Release IP/07/29 (10/01/2007). Brussels: European Commission.

European Commission (CEC) 2007b. *Attitudes on Issues Related to EU Transport Policy.* Analytical report. Flash Eurobarometer 206b. Brussels: European Commission.

European Commission (CEC) 2008. *EU Energy and Transport in Figures.* Statistical Pocketbook 2007/2008. Brussels: European Commission, Directorate-General for Energy and Transport.

European Conference of Ministers of Transport (ECMT). 2002. *Implementing Sustainable Urban Travel Policies.* Final Report. Paris: European Conference of Ministers of Transport.

European Environment Agency (EEA). 2007. *Annual European Community Greenhouse Gas Inventory 1990–2005 and Inventory Report 2007.* Technical report No. 7/2007. Copenhagen: European Environment Agency.

EUROSTAT. 2007. *Panorama of Transport – 2007 Edition.* Office for Official Publications of the European Communities, Brussels.

Fargione, J., Hill, J., Tilman, D., Polasky, S. and Hawthorne, P. 2008. Land Clearing and the Biofuel Carbon Debt. *Science* 319, 1235–8.

Feitelson, E. and Salomon, I. 2004. The Political Economy of Transport Innovations. In, *Transport Developments and Innovations in an Evolving World*, edited by Beuthe, M., Himanen, V., Reggiani, A. and Zamparini, L. Heidelberg: Springer Verlag, 11–26.

Flood, R.L. 1999. *Rethinking the Fifth Discipline; Learning within the Unknowable*. London: Routledge.

Forester, J. 1999. *The Deliberative Practitioner: Encouraging Participatory Planning Processes*. Cambridge: MIT Press.

Fouche, R. 2003. *Black Inventors in the Age of Segregation: Granville T. Woods, Lewis H. Latimer, and Shelby J. Davidson*. Baltimore: Johns Hopkins Press.

Fransson, N. and Gärling, T. 1999. Environmental Concern: Conceptual Definitions, Measurement Methods and Research Findings. *Journal of Environmental Psychology* 19(4) 369–82.

Freudenburg, W. and Pastor, S. 1992. NIMBYs and LULUs: Stalking the Syndromes. *Journal of Social Issues* 48(4), 39–61.

Friedmann, J. 1987. *Planning in the Public Domain: From Knowledge to Action*. Princeton: Princeton University Press.

Fuglestvedt, J., Bersten, T.J., Godal, O., Sausen, R., Shine, K.P. and Skodvin, T. 2003. Metrics of Climate Change: Assessing Radiative Forcing and Emission Indices. *Climatic Change* 58(3), 267–331.

Galle, B. and Leahy, J. 2009. Laboratories of Democracy? Policy Innovation in Decentralized Governments. *Emory Law Journal* 58(6), 1333–99.

Geels, F.W. 2002. Technological Transitions as Evolutionary Reconfiguration Processes: A Multi-level Perspective and a Case-study, *Research Policy* 31(8/9), 1257–74.

Geels, F.W. 2004. Een lange termijn analyse van het Nederlandse rijkswegenbeleid (1950–2000): Belemmeringen en mogelijkheden voor toekomstige systeeminnovaties, *Tijdschrift Vervoerswetenschap* 40(3), 2–9.

Geels, F.W. 2005. *Technological Transitions and System Innovations, A Co-evolutionary and Socio-technical Analysis*. Cheltenham: Edgar Elgar.

Geels, F.W. 2007. 'Transformations of Large Technical Systems: A Multi-level Analysis of the Dutch Highway System (1950–2000)', *Science Technology and Human Values* 32(2), 123–49.

Geels, F.W., Kemp, R., Dudley, G. and Lyons, G. (eds) 2012. *Automobility in Transition? A Sociotechnical Analysis of Sustainable Transport*. New York: Routledge (in press).

Geels, F.W. and Schot, J. 2007. Typology of Socio-technical Transition Pathways. *Research Policy* 36, 399–417.

Geerlings, H. 1999. *Meeting the Challenge of Sustainable Mobility; The Role of Technological Innovations*. Heidelberg: Springer Verlag.

Geerlings, H., Lohuis, J., Wiegmans, B. and Willemsen, A. 2009. A Renaissance in Understanding Technology Dynamics? The Emerging Concept of Transition Management. *Transportation Planning and Technology* 32(5), 401–22.

Geerlings, H. and Stead, D. 2003. The Integration of Land Use Planning, Transport and Environment in European Policy and Research. In, *Transport Policy* 10, 79–196.

Geertman, S. 2006. Potentials for Planning Support: A Planning-Conceptual Approach. *Environment and Planning B : Planning and Design* 33(6), 863–80.

Geurs, K.T., Annema, J.A. and Van Mourik, H. 2007. *Analyse van onzekerheden in de verkeerskundige en wagenparkeffecten van de eerste stap Anders Betalen voor Mobiliteit* [Uncertainty analysis of transport and enviromental impact assessments of nationwide road pricing]. Bilthoven/Den Haag: Planbureau voor de Leefomgeving/Kennisinstituut voor Mobiliteitsbeleid.

Geurs, K.T. and Van den Brink, R.M.M. 2005. *Milieu-effecten van Anders Betalen voor Mobiliteit (Environmental impacts of road pricing schemes).* Rapport 773002029/2005. Bilthoven: Milieu- en Natuur Planbureau.

Geurs, K.T. and Van Wee, G.P. 2004. Accessibility Evaluation of Land-use and Transport Strategies: Review and Research Directions. *Journal of Transport Geography* 12(2), 127–40.

Geurs, K.T. and Van Wee, G.P. 2010. De kwaliteit van prognoses van de verkeerskundige effecten van de kilometerprijs (The quality of prognosis of traffic effects of kilometre pricing). *Tijdschrift Vervoerwetenschap.* Delft: Stichting Vervoerwetenschap.

Giuliano, G. 2004. Land Use Impacts of Transportation Investments. In, *The Geography of Urban Transportation*, edited by Hanson, S. and Giuliano, G. New York and London: The Guilford Press, 237–73.

Golovtchenko, N. and Zelem, M.C. 2003. La place des usagers dans les politiques de réduction des gaz à effet de serre. Le cas de la pollution automobile, in *Développement durable et participation publique. De la contestation écologiste aux défis de la gouvernance*, edited by Gendron, C. and Vaillancourt, J.G. Montréal: Presses Universitaires de Montréal, 173–205.

Gorris, T. and Pommer, J. 2008. *Transition to Sustainable Mobility; Theory Put into Practice.* Paper presented at the Second European Transport Research Arena, 21–24 April 2008, Ljubljana.

Goulias, K., Brög, W., James, B. and Graham, C. 2002. Travel Behavior Analysis of South Perth: Individualised Marketing Intervention. *Transportation Research Record: Journal of the Transportation Research Board 1807*, 77–86.

Grattet, R. and Jenness, V. 2005. The Reconstitution of Law in Local Settings: Agency Discretion, Ambiguity, and a Surplus of Law in the Policing of Hate Crime. *Law and Society Review* 39(4), 893–941.

Grattet, R. and Jenness, V. 2008. Transforming Symbolic Law into Organizational Action: Hate Crime Policy and Law Enforcement Practice. *Social Forces* 87(1), 1–28.

Greater London Authority (GLA). 2007. *Climate Change Action Plan.* London: Greater London Authority.

Greater London Authority (GLA). 2009. *The London Plan [Draft Replacement].* London: Greater London Authority.

Green, V. 2001. *Race on the Line*. Durham: Duke University Press.

Greening, L.A. 2004. Effects of Human Behaviour on Aggregate Carbon Intensity of Personal Transportation: Comparison of 10 OECD Countries for the Period 1970–1993. *Energy Economics* 26(1), 1–30.

Greening, L.A., Schipper, L., Davis, R.E. and Bell, S.R. 1997. Prediction of Household Levels of Greenhouse-gas Emissions from Personal Automotive Transportation. *Energy* 22(5), 449–60.

Greenwood, D.J. and Levin, M. 1998. *Introduction to Action Research. Social Research for Social Change*. London: Sage Publications.

Grin, J. 2006. Reflexive Modernization as a Governance Issue – Or: Designing and Shaping Re-Structuration. In, *Reflexive Governance for Sustainable Development*, edited by Voß, J.-P., Bauknecht, D. and Kemp, R. Cheltenham: Edward Elgar: 57–81.

Grin, J., Rotmans, J. and Schot, J. 2010. *Transitions to Sustainable Development; New Directions in their Long Term Transformative Change*. New York: Routledge.

Guba, E.G. and Lincoln, Y.S. 1989. *Fourth Generation Evaluation*. Newbury Park/London/New Delhi: Sage.

Hanson, S. and Giuliano, G. 2004. *The Geography of Urban Transportation*. New York and London: Guilford Press.

Haraldssom, K., Folkesson, A., Saxe, M. and Alvfors, P. 2006. A First Report on the Attitude towards Hydrogen Fuel Cell Buses in Stockholm. *International Journal of Hydrogen Energy* 31, 317–25.

Harding, D. 2008. *FuelWatch Evidence Runs on Empty*. The Age, Melbourne 2 July. Available from: http://business.theage.com.au/fuelwatch-evidence-runs-on-empty-20080701-3045.html?page=1 [Accessed: 2 July 2008].

Harvey, A.S. and Mukhopadhyay, H.K. 2007. When Twenty-four Hours is Not Enough: Time Poverty of Working Parents. *Social Indicators Research* 82, 57–77.

Hawkins, K. 1984. *Environmental Enforcement: Regulation and the Social Definition of Pollution*. New York: Oxford University Press.

Healey, P. 1997. *Collaborative Planning; Shaping Places in Fragmented Societies*. Hampshire/New York: Palgrave.

Healey, P. 2007. *Urban Complexity and Spatial Strategies: Towards a Relational Planning for Our Times*. London: Taylor and Francis.

Heinz, B. and Erdmann, G. 2008. Dynamic Effects on the Acceptance of Hydrogen Technologies – An International Comparison. *International Journal of Hydrogen Energy* 33, 3004–8.

Hendriks, C. 2009. Making Democratic Sense of Transition Management, *Policy Sciences* 42, 341–68.

Hensher, D.A. and Button, K.J. 2000. *Handbook of Transport Modelling 1*. London: Elsevier.

Hensher, D.A., Rose, J.M. and Greene, W.H. 2005. *Applied Choice Analysis: A Primer*. New York: Cambridge University Press.

Herbst, C.M. and Barnow, B.S. 2008. Close to Home: A Simultaneous Equations Model of the Relationship between Child Care Accessibility and Female Labor Force Participation. *Journal of Family and Economic Issues* 29, 128–51.

Hibino, A. and Nagata, M. 2008. Meaning of 'Don't Know' Response in the Questionnaire Survey on Public Perception of Biotechnology in Japan and Europe. *Paper Presented at the Annual Meeting of the Society for Social Studies of Science and the European Association for the Study of Science and Technology*, 20–23 August 2008, Rotterdam.

Hickman, R., Ashiru, O. and Banister, D. 2009a. *Visioning and Backcasting for Transport in London. Stage Reports 1, 2 and 3 and Executive Summary.* London: Halcrow Group. Available from: www.vibat.org [Accessed: 20 July 2010].

Hickman, R., Ashiru, O. and Banister, D. 2009b. Achieving Carbon Efficient Transport: Backcasting from London. *Transportation Research Record* 2139, 172–82.

Hickman, R. and Banister, D. 2007. Looking Over the Horizon: Transport and Reduced CO2 Emissions in the UK by 2030. *Transport Policy* 14(5), 377–87.

Hickman, R., Seaborn, C., Headicar, P. and Banister, D. 2009. *Planning for Sustainable Travel. Summary Guide.* London: Halcrow and Commission for Integrated Transport.

Hickson, A., Phillips, A. and Morales, G. 2007. Public Perception Related to a Hydrogen Hybrid Internal Combustion Engine Transit Bus Demonstration and Hydrogen Fuel. *Energy Policy* 35, 2249–55.

Hilgartner, S. and Bosk, C.L. 1988. The Rise and Fall of Social Problems: A Public Arenas Model. *American Journal of Sociology* 94(1), 53–78.

Hine, J. 2000. Integration, Integration, Integration: Planning for Sustainable and Integrated Transport Systems in the New Millennium, *Transport Policy* 7, 175–77.

Hoogma, R., Kemp, R., Schot., J. and Truffer, B. 2002. *Experimenting for Sustainable Transport Futures. The Approach of Strategic Niche Management.* London: E. and F.N. Spon.

Houghton, J. 2004. *Global Warming: The Complete Briefing.* 3rd Edition. Cambridge: Cambridge University Press.

House, L., Lusk, J., Jaegers, S., Traill, W.B., Moore, M., Valli, C., Morrow, B. and Yee, W.M.S. 2004. Objective and Subjective Knowledge: Impacts on Consumer Demand for Genetically Modified Foods in the United States and the European Union. *AgBioForum* 7, 113–23.

Howarth, C., Waterson, B. and McDonald, M. 2009. *Public Understanding of Climate Change and the Gaps between Knowledge, Attitude and Travel Behavior.* Paper to the Transport Research Board, 88th Annual Meeting, 11–15 January 2009, Washington, D.C.

Hull, A. 2005. Integrated Transport Planning in the UK: From Concept to Reality. *Journal of Transport Geography* 13(4), 318–28.

Hull, A. 2008. Policy Integration: What Will it Take to Achieve More Sustainable Transport Solutions in Cities? *Transport Policy* 15, 94–103.

Hull, A. and Tricker, R. 2006. *Findings of the 'Phase 1' Survey on the Barriers to the Delivery of Sustainable Transport Solutions*. Bristol: Faculty of the Built Environment, University of the West of England.

Hutter, B. 1989. Variation in Regulatory Styles of Enforcement. *Law and Policy* 11, 153–74.

Iermonachou, P., Potter, S. and Waren, J.P. 2007. A Strategic Niche Analysis of Urban Road Pricing in the UK and Norway. *European Journal of Transport and Infrastructure Research* 7, 15–38.

Immers, L. and Van der Knaap, R. 2007. *Xpert Roadmap towards Sustainable Traffic Management*. Colloquium Vervoersplanologisch Speurwerk. Antwerpen 2007.

Innes, J.E. 1995. Planning Theory's Emerging Paradigm: Communicative Action and Interactive Practice. *Journal of Planning Education and Research* 14(3), 183–9.

Innes, J. and Booher, D. 2004. Reframing Public Participation: Strategies for the 21st Century. *Planning Theory and Practice* 5, 419–36.

Intergovernmental Panel on Climate Change. 2007. *Climate Change 2007: The Physical Science Basis*.

International Energy Agency (IEA). 2004. *Energy Technologies for a Sustainable Future*. Paris: International Energy Agency.

International Energy Agency (IEA). 2007. *World Energy Outlook 2007*. Paris: International Energy Agency.

International Energy Agency (IEA). 2009. *Transport Energy and CO_2*. Paris: International Energy Agency.

Ison, S., Hughes, G. and Tuckwell, R. 2008. Cambridge's Experience of Road User Charging: Lessons Learned. *Transport Proceedings of the Institution of Civil Engineers* 161, 135–41.

James, B. 1998. *Changing Travel Behavior through Individualised Marketing: Application and Lessons from South Perth*. Paper presented at the 23rd Australasian Transport Research Forum, 30 September–2 October 1998, Sydney.

Janis, A. (ed.) 1983. *Simultaneity and Conventionality. Physics, Philosophy and Psychoanalysis*. Dordrecht/Boston: Reidel.

Jara-Diaz, S.R. and Martinez, F.J. 1999. On the Specification of Indirect Utility and Willingness to Pay for Discrete Residential Location Models. *Journal of Regional Science* 39, 675–88.

Jenness, V. and Grattet, R. 2005. The Law in Between: The Effects of Organizational Perviousness on the Policing of Hate Crime. *Social Problems* 52(3), 337–59.

Jones, P. and Lucas, K. 2000. Integrating Transport into 'Joined-up' Policy Appraisal. *Transport Policy* 7, 185–93.

Jones, P. and Lucas, K. 2005. *Option Generation: Literature Review*. London: Department of Civil Engineering, University College London.

Jones, P. and Sloman, L. 2003. *Encouraging Behavioral Change through Marketing and Management: What Can be Achieved?* Resource paper for the 10th International Conference on Travel Behavior Research, Lucerne, August 10–15.

Jonnalagadda, N., Freedman, J., Davidson, W. and Hunt, J. 2001. Development of a Micro-simulation Activity-based Model for San Francisco – Destination and Mode Choice Models. *Transportation Research Record* 1777, 25–30.

Jorritsma, P., Derriks, H.M., Francke, J.M., Gordijn, H., Groot, W., Harms, L., Van de Loop, H., Peer, S., Savelberg, F. and Wouters, P. 2009a. *Mobiliteitsbalans 2009* (Mobility Balance 2009). Den Haag: Kennisinstituut voor Mobiliteitsbeleid.

Jorritsma, P., Francke, J.M., Gordijn, H., Groot, W. and Koopmans, C. 2009b. *Slow Motion. Economische Crisis en Mobiliteit* (Slow Motion. Economic Crisis and Mobility). Den Haag: Kennisinstituut voor Mobiliteitsbeleid (KiM).

Karsten, L., Van Veen, K. and Van Wulfften Palthe, A. 2008. What Happened to the Popularity of the Polder Model? Emergence and Disappearance of a Political Fashion. *International Sociology* 23, 35–65.

Kaswan, A. 2009. Climate Change, Consumption and Cities. *Fordham Urban Law Journal* XXXVI(2), 253–312.

Kaufmann, V. 2001. Mobilité et vie quotidienne; synthèse et questions de recherche. *2001 Plus* 48.

Kaufmann, V. 2002. *Rethinking Mobility.* Aldershot: Ashgate.

Kaufmann, V. 2006. Motilité, latence de mobilité et modes de vie urbains, in La ville aux limites de la mobilité, edited by Bonnet, M. and Aubertel, P. Paris: PUF.

Kemp, R. 2009. Eco-innovation and Transitions. *Economia delle fonti di energia e dell'ambiente* 0(1), 103–24.

Kemp, R. and Loorbach, D. 2005. Dutch Policies to Manage the transition to Sustainable Energy, *Jahrbuch Ökologische Ökonomik 4 Innovationen und Nachhaltigkeit*, Amrburg: Metropolis Verlag, 123–50.

Kemp, R. and Loorbach, D. 2006. Transition Management: A Reflexive Governance Approach. In, J.-P. Voss, Bauknecht, D. and Kemp, R. (eds) *Reflexive Governance for Sustainable Development.* Cheltenham, Edward Elgar, 103–30.

Kemp, R., Loorbach, D. and Rotmans, J. 2007a. Transition Management as a Model for Managing Processes of Co-evolution. *The International Journal of Sustainable Development and World Ecology* (special issue on (co)-evolutionary approach to sustainable development) 14, 78–91.

Kemp, R., Loorbach, D. and Rotmans, J. 2007b. Assessing the Dutch Energy Transition Policy: How Does it Deal with Dilemmas of Managing Transitions? *Journal of Environmental Policy and Planning* 9, 315–31.

Kemp, R. and Rotmans, J. 2004. Managing the Transition to Sustainable Mobility. In, *System Innovation and the Transition to Sustainability: Theory, Evidence and Policy*, edited by Elzen, B., Geels, F. and Green, K. Cheltenham: Edward Elgar, 137–67.

Kemp, R. and Rotmans, J. 2009. Transitioning Policy: Co-production of a New Strategic Framework for Energy Innovation Policy in the Netherlands, *Policy Sciences* 42, 303–22.

Kemp, R., Schot, J. and Hoogma, R. 1998. Regime Shifts to Sustainability through Processes of Niche Formation. The Approach of Strategic Niche Management, *Technology Analysis and Strategic Management* 10(2), 175–95.

Kemp, R. and Soete, L. 1999. The Greening of Technological Progress: An Evolutionary Perspective, *Futures* 24(5), 437–45.

Kempton, W. 1993. Will Public Environmental Concern Lead to Action on Global Warming. *Annual Review Energy Environment* 18, 217–45.

Kendall, A., Chang, B. et al. 2009. Accounting for Time-dependent Effects in Biofuel Life Cycle Greenhouse Gas Emissions Calculations. *Environmental Science and Technology* 43(18), 7142–7.

Kennis en Technologische Innovaties (KETI) 2000. *Van saneren naar innoveren. De rol van kennis en technologische innovaties bij het realiseren van de beleidsopgaven van NMP4.* Den Haag: Kennis en technologische innovaties.

Ker, I. and James, B. 1999. *Evaluating Behavioral Change in Transport. A Case Study of Individualised Marketing in South Perth, Western Australia.* Paper presented at the 23rd Australasian Transport Research Forum, 30 September–2 October 1999, Perth.

Kern, F. and Howlett, M. 2009. Implementing Transition Management as Policy Reforms: A Case Study of the Dutch Energy Sector. *Policy Sciences* 42(4), 391–408.

Khare, M. and Sharma, P. 2003. Fuel Options. In, Hensher, D.A. and Button, K.J., *Handbook of Transport and the Environment.* London: Elsevier, 159–83.

Kiesraad 2010. *Nederlandse verkiezingsuitslagen 1918-nu. (Dutch election results 1918-now)* Available from: http://www.verkiezingsuitslagen.nl/Na1918/Verkiezingsuitslagen.aspx?VerkiezingsTypeId=1 [Accessed: 25 February 2010].

Kingdon, J. 1984. *Agendas, Alternatives and Public Policie.* Boston: Little, Brown & Co.

Kitamura, R. 1984. A Model of Daily Time Allocation to Discretionary Out-Of-Home Activities and Trips. *Transportation Research B* 18, 255–66.

Kitamura, R. 1997. *Applications of Models of Activity Behavior for Activity-based Demand Forecasting. Activity-based Travel Forecasting Conference Proceedings, 2–5 June 1996: Summary, Recommendations and Compendium of Papers.* Arlington TX: Texas Transportation Institute.

Klosterman, R.E. 1997. Planning Support Systems: A New Perspective on Computer-Aided Planning. *Journal of Planning Education and Research* 17(1), 45–54.

Klosterman, R.E. 2001. Planning Support Systems: A New Perspective on Computer-Aided Planning. In, *Planning Support Systems: Integrating Geographical Information Systems, Models and Visualization Tools,* edited by Brai, R.K.L. and Klosterman, R.E. New Brunswick: ESRI, 1–23.

Klosterman, R.E. 2007. Deliberating About the Future. In, *Engaging the Future: Forecasts, Scenarios, Plans and Projects*, edited by Hopkins, L.D. and Zapata, M.A. Cambridge: Lincoln Institute of Land Policy, 199–219.

Knockaert, J., Bliemer, M., Ettema, D., Joksimovic, D., Mulder, A., Rouwendal, J. and van Amelsfoort, D. 2007. *Experimental Design and Modelling Spitsmijden*. Utrecht: Consortium Spitsmijden.

Kolb, D.A. 1984. *Experiential Learning: Experience as the Source of Learning and Development*. New Jersey: Prentice Hall.

Kondriatieff, N.D. 1926. Die Langen Wellen der Konjunktur. In, *Archiv für Sozialwissenschaft und Sozialpolitik* 56(3) 573–609.

Koppenjan, J.F.M. 1993. *Management van de beleidsvorming. Een studie naar de totstandkoming van het beleid op het terrein van het binnenlandse bestuur (Managing the policy-making process. A study of public policy formation in the field of Home Administration)*. PhD thesis. Erasmus University Rotterdam, Den Haag: VUGA.

Kroll-Smith, J. and Couch, S. 1990. *The Real Disaster is Above Ground: A Mine Fire and Social Conflict*. Louisville: University Press of Kentucky.

Krosnick, J., Holbrook, A.L., Lowe, L. and Visser, P.S. 2006. Policy Agendas: A Study of Popular Concern about Global Warming. *Climatic Change* 77(1/2), 7–43.

Kuipers, B., Van Rooijen, M. and Vonk Noordegraaf, D.M. 2008. *Deliverable 15 Uitwerking Maatregelenpakket 2: "Duurzaam, Dynamisch en geDurfd"*. Delft: TNO.

Langendorf, R. 1985. Computers and Decision Making. *Journal of the American Planning Association* 51, 422–33.

Lawrence, D., Slater, A. et al. 2008. Accelerated Artic Land Warming and Permafrost Degradation during Rapid Sea Ice Loss. *Geophysical Research Letters* 35, L11506.

Lee, D.B. 1973. Requiem for Large-scale Models. *Journal of the American Planning Association* 39, 163–78.

Lee, D.B. 1994. Retrospective on Large-Scale Urban Models. *Journal of the American Planning Association* 60(1), 35–40.

Levine, A. 1982. *Love Canal: Science Politics, and People*. Lexington MA: Lexington Books.

Liévanos, R., London, J. et al. in press. Uneven Transformations and Environmental Justice: Regulatory Science, Street Science, and Pesticide Regulation in California. In, *Engineers, Scientists, and Environmental Justice: Transforming Expert Cultures through Grassroots Engagement*, edited by Ottinger, G. and Cohen, B. Cambridge: MIT Press.

Lindblom, C.E. 1959. The Science of Muddling Through. *Public Administration Review* 19, 79–99.

Lohuis, J., Bouma I., Avelino, F., Bressers, N., Vonk Noordegraaf, D.M., Soeterbroek, F. and Geerlings, H. 2008. *Deliverable 16 Uitkomsten van de innovatie-impuls*. Rotterdam: Erasmus University Rotterdam.

London, J., Starrs, P. and Fortmann, L. 2005. Power Plants and Forest Plans: Two Decades of Mobilization in a Mountain Forest Community. In, *Communities and Forests: Where People Meet the Land*, edited by Lee, R. and Field, D. Corvallis, OR: Oregon State University Press, 116–37.

Loorbach, D. 2007. *Transition Management: New Mode of Governance for Sustainable Development*. Utrecht: International Books.

Loorbach, D. and Rotmans, J. 2006. Managing Transitions for Sustainable Development. In, *Industrial Transformation – Disciplinary Approaches Towards Transformation Research*, edited by Olsthoorn, X. and Wieczorek, A.J. Dordrecht: Springer, 187–206.

Loorbach, D. and Rotmans, J. 2010. Towards a Better Understanding of Transitions and their Governance: A Systemic and Reflexive Approach. In, Grin, J., Rotmans, J. and Schot, J. (eds), *Transitions to Sustainable Development; New Directions in the Study of Long Term Transformative Change*. New York: Routledge.

Luhmann, N. 1989. *Ecological Communication*. Cambridge: Polity.

Luhmann, N. 1990. *Essays on Self-reference*. New York: Columbia University Press.

Luhmann, N. 1995. *Social Systems*. Stanford, CA: Stanford University Press.

Luhmann, N. 2000. *Organisation und Entscheidung*. Wiesbaden: Westdeutscher Verlag.

Lutsky, N. and Sperling, D. 2008. America's Bottom-up Climate Change Mitigation Policy. *Energy Policy* 38, 673–85.

Manheim, M.L. 1974. *Fundamentals of Transportation Systems Analysis; Volume 1: Basic Concepts*. Cambridge: MIT Press.

Mapflow 2007. *Analysis of TFL GPS OBU Data – Final Report for the Dutch Ministry of Transport*. Available from: http://www.rijksoverheid.nl/bestanden/documenten-en-publicaties/rapporten/2007/04/02/analyse-van-tfl-gps-obu-data-door-mapflow/17-analyse-van-tfl-gps-obu-data-door-mapflow-april-2007.pdf [Accessed: 20 September 2010].

March, J.G. and Olsen, J.P. 1995. *Democratic Governance*. New York: The Free Press.

Marsden, G. and King, S. 2009. *Using Deliberative Methods to Understand Travel Choices in the Context of Climate Change*. Paper presented at the Transport Research Board, 88th Annual Meeting, 11–15 January 2009, Washington, D.C.

Marsh, K.L. and Wallace, H.M. 2005. The Influence of Attitudes on Beliefs: Formation and Change. In, *The Handbook of Attitudes*, edited by Albarracin, D., Johnson, B.T. and Zanna, M.P. London: Lawrence Erlbaum Associates.

Marvin, C. 1990. *When Old Technologies were New: Thinking about Electric Communication in the Late Nineteenth Century*. New York: Oxford University Press.

Mas-Colell, A., Whinston, M. and Green, J.R. 1995. *Microeconomic Theory*. Oxford: Oxford University Press.

Matlin, M.W. and Foley, H.J. 1997. *Sensation and Perception*. Needham Heights, Allyn and Bacon.

Mauss, A.L. 1975. *Social Problems as Social Movements*. New York: Lippincott.

May, A., Kelly, C. and Shepherd, S. 2006. The Principles of Integration in Urban Transport Strategies. *Transport Policy* 13, 319–27.

May, P.J. and Burby, R.J. 1998. Making Sense Out of Regulatory Enforcement. *Law and Policy* 20(2), 157–81.

McCarthy, L. 2003. The Good of the Many Outweighs the Good of One: Regional Cooperation Instead of Individual Competition in the US and Western Europe? *Journal of Planning Education and Research* 23, 140–52.

McDonough, W. and Braungart, M. 2002. *Cradle to Cradle: Remaking the Way We Make Things*. San Francisco: North Point Press.

McDowell, W. and Eames, M. 2006. Forecasts, Scenarios, Visions, Backcasts and Roadmaps to the Hydrogen Economy: A Review of the Hydrogen Futures Literature. *Energy Policy* 34, 1236–50.

McFadden, D. 2007. The Behavioral Science of Transportation. *Transport Policy* 14, 269–74.

McKinnon, A.C. 2006. Government Plans for Lorry Road-user Charging in the UK: A Critique and an Alternative. *Transport Policy* 13, 204–16.

McKinnon, A. 2007. CO_2 *Emissions from Freight Transport in the UK. Background Report*. London: Commission for Integrated Transport.

Meadowcroft, J. 2005. Environmental Political Economy, Technological Transitions and the State. *New Political Economy* 10, 479–98.

Meadowcroft, J. 2007. *Steering or Muddling Through? Transition Management and the Politics of Socio-technical Transformation*. Paper presented at the International Workshop 'Politics and Governance in Sustainable Socio-Technical Transitions', 19–21 September 2001, Berlin: Blankensee.

Meadowcroft, M. 2009. What about the Politics? Sustainable Development, Transition Management, and Long Term Energy Transitions', *Policy Sciences* 42(4), 323–40.

Meadows, D.H. and Robinsons, J.M. 2002. The Electronic Oracle: Computer Models and Social Decisions. *System Dynamics Review* 18(2), 271–308.

Mendras, H. and Forsé, M. 1983. *Le changement social*. Paris: Armand Colin.

Merriam-Webster 1997. *Merriam Webster's Collegiate Dictionary*. Springfield, MA: Merriam-Webster,

Metz, D. 2008a. The Myth of Travel Time Saving. *Transport Reviews* 28(3), 321–36.

Metz, D. 2008b. Response to the Responses. *Transport Reviews* 28(6), 713–15.

Meurs, H. 2002. *Land Use and Mobility*. Utrecht: NOVEM.

Meyer, M.D. and Miller, E.J. 2001. *Urban Transportation Planning: A Decision-oriented Approach*. New York: McGraw-Hill.

Meyer, J.W. and Rowan, B. 1977. Institutional Organizations: Formal Structure as Myth and Ceremony. *American Journal of Sociology* 83, 340–63.

Midden, C.J.H. and Huijts, N.M.A. 2009. The Role of Trust in the Affective Evaluation of Novel Risks: The Case of CO_2 Storage. *Risk Analysis* 29, 743–51.

Milmo, D. 2008. Road Pricing Scheme Stalled. Tuesday 4 March 2008. Available from: www.guardian.co.uk/politics/2008/mar/04/transport.transport1 [Accessed: 20 November 2010].

Ministerie van Algemene Zaken (NL). 2007. *Samen werken samen leven, Beleidsprogramma Kabinet Balkenende IV, 2007–2011 (Working together, Living together, Policy Programme of the Balkenende IV Cabinet, 2007–2011).* Den Haag: Koninklijke De Swart.

Ministerie van Economische Zaken (NL). 2001. De Reis. *Transitie naar een duurzame energiehuishouding (The Journey. Transition to a Sustainable Energy System).* Den Haag: Ministerie van Economische Zaken.

Ministerie van Economische Zaken (NL). 2003a. Plan van aanpak. Project Implementatie Energietransitie fase 2 (Action plan. Project implementation of energy transition phase 2). Den Haag: Ministerie van Economische Zaken.

Ministerie van Economische Zaken (NL). 2003b. Steering Towards the South. (Reinvigorating Government Policy for the Energy Transition). Advies van het PIT-deelproject Beleidsvernieuwing, Den Haag: Ministerie van Economische Zaken.

Ministerie van Economische Zaken (NL). 2004. *Innovatie in het Energiebeleid. Energietransitie stand van zaken en vervolg (Innovation in Energy Policy. State of Affairs in the Energy Transition and Follow-up Action).* Den Haag: Ministerie van Economische Zaken.

Ministerie van Verkeer en Waterstaat (NL). 2004. *Nota Mobiliteit I.* Den Haag: Ministerie van Verkeer en Waterstaat/Ministerie van Volkshuisvesting, Ruimtelijke Ordening en Milieu.

Ministerie van Verkeer en Waterstaat (NL). 2005a. *Nota Mobiliteit III, Kabinetsstandpunt.* Den Haag: Ministerie van Verkeer en Waterstaat/Ministerie van Volkshuisvesting, Ruimtelijke Ordening en Milieubeheer.

Ministerie van Verkeer en Waterstaat (NL). 2005b. *Nota Mobiliteit III, Uitvoeringsagenda; van Nota naar Mobiliteit.* Den Haag: Ministerie van Verkeer en Waterstaat/Ministerie van Volkshuisvesting, Ruimtelijke Ordening en Milieubeheer.

Ministerie van Verkeer en Waterstaat (NL). 2006. *Nota Mobiliteit IV, Na parlementaire behandeling vastgestelde PKB.* Den Haag: Ministerie van Verkeer en Waterstaat/Ministerie van Volkshuisvesting, Ruimtelijke Ordening en Milieubeheer.

Ministerie van Verkeer en Waterstaat (NL). 2007. *Beleidskader benutten.* Den Haag: Ministerie van Verkeer en Waterstaat.

Ministerie van Verkeer en Waterstaat (NL). 2009a. *Memorie van Toelichting Wet Kilometerprijs (concept) (Explanatory memorandum Kilometre Pricing Act).* Den Haag: Ministerie van Verkeer en Waterstaat.

Ministerie van Verkeer en Waterstaat (NL). 2009b. *Wet Kilometerprijs (Concept) (Kilometre Pricing Act (concept)).* Den Haag: Ministerie van Verkeer en Waterstaat.

Ministerie van Volkshuisvesting, Ruimtelijke Ordening en Milieubeheet (NL). 2001. *Vierde Nederlandse nationale milieubeleidsplan: Een wereld en een wil. Werken aan duurzaamheid. (A World and a Will. Working towards Sustainability)*. Den Haag: Ministerie van Volkshuisvesting, Ruimtelijke Ordening en Milieu.

Ministry of the Environment (CZ). 2001. *Czech Environmental Policy*. Prague: Ministry of Environment.

Mitchell, R.B. and Rapkin, C. 1954. *Urban Traffic. A Function of Land Use*. New York: Columbia University Press.

Mitchell, R.C. and Carson, R.T. 1989. *Using Surveys to Value Public Goods*. Washington, D.C.: Resources for the Future.

Molin, E. 2005. *A Causal Analysis of Hydrogen Acceptance*. Transportation Research Record, 1941, 115–21.

Molin, E., Aouden, F. and Van Wee, G.P. 2007. *Car Drivers' stated Choices for Hydrogen Cars: Evidence from a Small-scale Experiment*. Transportation Research Board 86th Annual Meeting Compendium of Papers. Washington, D.C.: Transportation Research Board.

Mom, G.P.A. and Filarski, R. 2008. *Van transport naar mobiliteit. De mobiliteitsexplosie [1895–2005] (From Transport to Mobility: The Mobility Explosion, 1895–2005)*. Zutphen: Uitgeversmaatschappij Walburg Pers.

Montroll, E.W. 1978. *Social Dynamics and the Quantifying of Social Forces*. Proceedings of the National Academy of Sciences, LXXV, 4633–7.

Moon, S.J. and Joung, S.H. 1997. Expenditure Patterns of Divorced Single-mother Families and Two-parent Families in South Korea. *Journal of Family and Economic Issues* 18, 147–62.

Mourato, S., Saynor, B. and Hart, D. 2004. Greening London's Black Cabs: A Study of Driver's Preferences for Fuel Cell Taxis. *Energy Policy* 32, 685–95.

Munizaga, M.A., Jara-Diaz, S. and Greeven, P. 2006. *Joint Modelling of Time Assignment and Mode Choice for the Chilean TASTI sample*. Paper presented at the 11th IATBR Conference, Kyoto, Japan.

Nederlandse Omroep Stichting (NOS). 2009. *Van rekeningrijden naar kilometerheffing*. Available from: http://nos.nl/artikel/97963-van-rekeningrijden-naar-kilometerheffing.html [Accessed: 22 September 2010].

Nelson, R.R. and Winter, S.G. 1977. In Search for a Useful Theory of Innovation. *Research Policy* 6, 36–76.

Netherlands Institute for Multiparty Democracy (NIMD) and Instituut voor Publiek en Politiek (IPP) 2008. *The Dutch Political System in a Nutshell*. Den Haag/Amsterdam: Netherlands Institute for Multiparty Democracy/Instituut voor Publiek en Politiek.

Newman, J. 2001. *Understanding Governance*. Bristol: Policy Press.

Newman, P. and Kenworthy, J.R. 1999. *Sustainability and Cities: Overcoming Automobile Dependence*. Washington, D.C.: Island.

NICHES Consortium 2007. *Guide to Innovative Urban Transport Strategies*. Available from: www.niches-transport.org [Accessed: 20 November 2010].

Nieuwsblad Transport 2009. *Kabinet achter plannen kilometerheffing (Cabinet supports plans kilometre charging).* Available from: www.nieuwsbladtransport. nl/nieuws/id27905-Kabinet_achter_plannen_kilometerheffing.html [Accessed: February 2010].

Noland, R. and Lem, L. 2002. A Review of the Evidence for Induced Travel and Changes in Transportation and Environmental Policy in the US and the UK. *Transportation Research D* 7, 1–26.

Nonaka, I. 1994. A Dynamic Theory of Organizational Knowledge Creation. *Organization Science* 5(1), 14–37.

Nonaka, I. and Konno, N. 1998. The Concept of 'Ba': Building a Foundation for Knowledge Creation. *California Management Review* 40(3), 40–54.

Nonaka, I. and Takeuchi, H. 1995. *The Knowledge-creating Company: How Japanese Companies Create the Dynamics of Innovation.* New York: Oxford University Press.

Nooteboom, S.G. 2006. *Adaptive Networks. The Governance for Sustainable Development*, PhD thesis. Rotterdam: Erasmus University Rotterdam.

Ntziachristos, L. and Samaras, Z. 2000. *COPERT III – Computer Programme to Calculate Emissions from Road Transport.* Methodology and Emission Factors. EEA Technical Report No 49. Copenhagen: European Environment Agency.

O'Garra, T. and Mourato, S. 2007. Public Preferences for Hydrogen Buses: Comparing Interval Data, OLS and Quantile Regression Approaches. *Environmental and Resource Economics* 36, 389–411.

O'Garra, T., Mourato, S., Garrity, L., Sshmidt, P., Beerenwinkel, A., Altmann, M., Hart, D., Graesel, C. and Whitehouse, S. 2007. Is the Public Willing to Pay for Hydrogen Buses? A Comparative Study of Preferences in Four Cities. *Energy Policy* 35, 3630–42.

O'Garra, T., Mourato, S. and Pearson, P. 2005. Analysing Awareness and Acceptability of Hydrogen Vehicles: A London Case Study. *International Journal of Hydrogen Energy* 30, 649–59.

O'Garra, T., Mourato, S. and Pearson, P. 2008. Investigating Attitudes to Hydrogen Refuelling Facilities and the Social Cost to Local Residents. *Energy Policy* 36, 2074–85.

O'Hare, M. et al. 2009. Proper Accounting for Time Increases Crop-Based Biofuels' GHG Deficit versus Petroleum. *Environmental Research Letters* 4, 024001, 1–7.

Onkenhout, H., Massen, K., Ruigrok, M. and Vlek, O. 2010. *Ledenpeiling Kilometerprijs Rapportage.* Amsterdam: Ruigrok | NetPanel / Synthetron.

Organisation of Economic Cooperation and Development (OECD) 1996. *Building Policy Coherence: Tools and Tensions.* Paris: OECD.

Organisation of Economic Cooperation and Development (OECD) 2001a. *Policies to Enhance Sustainable Development.* Paris: OECD.

Organisation of Economic Cooperation and Development (OECD) 2001b. *Sustainable Development: Critical Issues.* Paris: OECD.

Organisation of Economic Cooperation and Development (OECD) 2001c. *Governance in the 21st Century*. Paris: OECD.

Organisation of Economic Cooperation and Development (OECD) 2001d. *External Costs of Transport in Central and Eastern Europe*. Report ENV/EPOC/WPNEP/T(2002)5. Paris: OECD.

Organisation of Economic Cooperation and Development (OECD) 2010. *Key Transport Statistics*. Paris, OECD.

Ortúzar, J. and Willumsen, L.G. 2006. *Modelling Transport*. New York: John Wiley and Sons.

Ostrom, E. 1990. *Governing the Commons. The Evolution of Institutions for Collective Action*. Cambridge: Cambridge University Press.

O'Toole, L.R. 2004. The Theory-Practice Issue in Policy Implementation Research. *Public Administration* 82(2), 309–29.

Ottens, H. 1990. The Application of Geographical Information Systems in Urban and Regional Planning. *Geographical Information Systems for Urban and Regional Planning*, edited by Scholten, H.J. and Stillwell, J. Dordrecht: Kluwer, 15–22.

Pacala, S. and Socolow, R. 2004. Stabilisation Wedges: Solving the Climate Problem for the Next 50 Years with Current Technologies. *Science* 305, 968–72.

Panel on Strategies and Methods for Climate-Related Decision Support (PSMCRDS) 2009. *Informing Decisions in a Changing Climate*. Washington, D.C.: National Research Council, National Academies Press.

Partij van de Vrijheid (PVV) 2010a. *AO Anders Betalen voor Mobilitieit (kilometerheffing) (AO Paying Differently for Mobility (Kilometre charging))*. Available from: www.pvv.nl/index.php/component/content/article/12-spreekteksten/2468-ao-anders-betalenv-oor-mobilitieit-kilometerheffing.html [Accessed: 22 September 2010].

Partij van de Vrijheid (PVV) 2010b. *PVV opent meldpunt tegen kilometerheffing (PVV opens service desk against kilometre charging)*. Available from: www.pvv.nl/index.php/component/content/article/55-edities/2618-pvv-opent-meldpunt-tegen-kilometerheffing.html [Accessed: 22 September 2010].

Pawson, R. and Tilley, N. 1997. *Realistic Evaluation*. London: Sage.

Payne, J.W., Bettman, J.R. and Johnson, E.J. 1993. *The Adaptive Decision Maker*. New York: Cambridge University Press.

Pel, B. and Boons, F. 2010. Transition through Subsystem Innovation? The Case of Traffic Management. *Technological Forecasting and Social Change* 77, 1249–59.

Pel, B. and Teisman, G. 2009. *Governance of Transitions as Selective Connectivity*. Paper presented at the International Research Society for Public Management (IRSPM) conference, 6–8 April 2009, Copenhagen.

Pendall, R. 2001. Municipal Plans, State Mandates and Property Rights: Lessons from Maine. *Journal of Planning Education and Research* 21, 154–65.

Penner, J.E., Lister, D., Griggs, D.J., Dokken, D.J. and McFarland, M. 1999. *Aviation and the Global Atmosphere.* IPCC Special Report. Cambridge: Cambridge University Press.

Perritt, H.H.J. 1995. Should Local Governments Sell Local Spatial Databases through State Monopolies? *Jurimetrics* 35, 449–69.

Peterse, E. and Slovic, P. 1996. The Role of Affect and Worldviews as Orienting Dispositions in the Perception and Acceptance of Nuclear Power. *Journal of Applied Social Psychology* 16, 1427–53.

Petersen, R. 2008. Land Use Planning and Urban Transport. In, *Transport and Climate Change Module 5e. Sustainable Transport: A Sourcebook for Policymakers in Developing Cities*, edited by Dalkmann, H. and Brannigan, C. Eschborn: GTZ, 6–38.

Polanyi, M. 1967. *The Tacit Dimension.* New York: Doubleday.

Poortinga, W., Steg, L. and Vlek, C. 2004. Values, Environmental Concern and Environmental Behavior: A Study into a Household Energy Use. *Environment and Behavior* 36(1), 70–93.

Porter, M.E. 1980. *Competitive Strategy.* New York: Free Press.

Potter, S., Enoch, M. and Fergusson, M. 2001. *Fuel Taxes and Beyond: UK Transport and Climate Change.* Godalming: World Wildlife Fund.

Potter, S. and Skinner, M. 2000. On Transport Integration: A Contribution to Better Understanding. *Futures* 32, 275–87.

Pressman, J. and Wildavsky, A. 1979. *Implementation: How Great Expectations in Washington are Dashed in Oakland.* Berkeley: University of California Press.

RAI-BOVAG. 2009. *Eerlijker betalen voor gebruik auto met kilometerprijs (Fairer payment with kilometre pricing for car usage).* Available from: www. raivereniging.nl/actueel/nieuwsberichten/2009_4/20091113-eerlijker-betalen-voor-gebruik-auto-met-kilometerprijs.aspx [Accessed: 25 February 2010].

Raven, R., Van den Bosch, S. and Weterings, R. 2008. Transitions and Strategic Niche Management: Towards a Competence Kit for Practitioners. *International Journal of Technology Management* 51(1), 57–74.

Reagans, R. and McEvily, B. 2003. Network Structure and Knowledge Transfer: The Effects of Cohesion and Range. *Administrative Science Quarterly* 48, 240–67.

Recker, W.W. and Parimi, A. 1999. Development of a Microscopic Activity-based Framework for Analyzing the Potential Impacts of Transportation Control Measures on Vehicle Emissions. *Transportation Research D* 357–78.

Renewable Fuels Agency (RFA). 2008. *The Gallagher Review of the Indirect Effects of Biofuels Production.* St Leonards-on-Sea, Renewable Fuels Agency. Available from: www.renewablefuelsagency.gov.uk [Accessed: 25 November 2010].

Ricci, M., Bellaby, P. and Flynn, R. 2008. What do We Know about Public Perceptions and Acceptance of Hydrogen? A Critical Review and New Case Study Evidence. *International Journal of Hydrogen Energy* 33, 5868–80.

Richardson, T. 1996. Foucauldian Discourse: Power and Truth in Urban and Regional Policy Making. *European Planning Studies* 4(3), 279–93.

Rignot, E., Bamber, J. et al. 2008. Recent Antarctic Ice Mass Loss from Radar Interferometry and Regional Climate Modeling. *Nature Geoscience* 1, 106–10.

Rijksoverheid. 2010. *Regeerakkoord VVD-CDA 'Vrijheid en verantwoordelijkheid' [Coalition Agreement VVD-CDA 'Freedom and Responsibility']*. Available from: www.rijksoverheid.nl/documenten-en-publicaties/rapporten/2010/09/30/regeerakkoord-vvd-cda.html [Accessed: 9 November 2010].

Rijkswaterstaat. 2005. *Verkeerskundige effecten varianten 'Anders betalen voor Mobiliteit' (Transport Effects of Different Road Pricing Schemes).* Commissioned by het Ministerie van Verkeer en Waterstaat. Den Haag: Rijkswaterstaat -Adviesdienst Verkeer en Vervoer.

Rijkswaterstaat. 2007. *Verkeersmanagement 2020; de verkeersmanagement ambitie van ijkswaterstaat voor Hoofdwegen.* Den Haag: Ministerie van Verkeer en Waterstaat.

Rijkswaterstaat. 2010. *Kwartaalmonitor bereikbaarheidsontwikkeling Hoofdwegennet 2e kwartaal 2010 1 April – 30 Juni 2010 (Quarterly Monitoring Accessibility Development Main Road Network).* Den Haag: Ministerie van Verkeer en Waterstaat.

Rittel, H.W.J. and Webber, M.M. 1973. Dilemmas in a General Theory of Planning. *Policy Sciences* 4(2), 155–69.

Rocci, A. 2007. *De l'automobilité à la multimodalité? Analyse sociologique des freins et leviers au changement de comportements vers une réduction de l'usage individuel de la voiture. Le cas de la région parisienne et perspective internationale.* PhD Thesis. Paris: University of Paris V René Descartes.

Rocci, A. 2008a. Communication, information, formation: quels impacts sur les comportements de mobilité? Entre conscience environnementale et pratiques innovantes. Final research report, INRETS-DEST for the French Ministry of Ecology.

Rocci, A. 2008b. Comprendre les freins et leviers du changement de comportement de mobilité à travers la notion de capital mobility. In, *Automobilités et altermobilités. Quels changements?* edited by F. Clochard, A. Rocci, and S. Vincent. Paris: L'Harmattan, 157–70.

Rocci, A. 2009a. Changer les comportements de mobilité. Exploration d'outils de management de la mobilité: les programmes d'incitation au changement de comportements volontaire. Final research report, INRETS-DEST for the French Ministry of Ecology.

Rocci, A. 2009b. The Use of the Semi-directive Interview Method to Analyze Behavioral Changes. *Transportation Research Record: Journal of the Transportation Research Board, No. 1912.* Transportation Research Board of the National Academies, 37–43.

Rogers, E. 1962. *Diffusion of Innovations.* New York: Free Press.

Rogers, E. and Storey, J.D. 1987. Communication Campaigns, in *Handbook of Communication Science.* Thousand Oaks: Sage.

Roorda, M.J., Miller, E. and Khandker, M.N.H. 2008. Validation of TASHA: A 24-h Activity Scheduling Microsimulation Model. *Transportation Research A* 42(2), 360–75.

Rose, G. and Ampt, E. 2003. Travel Behavior Change through Individual Engagement, in *Handbook of Transport and the Environment*, edited by Hensher, D. and Button, K. London: Elsevier, 739–55.

Rosenberg, N. 1971. *The Economics of Technological Change*. Hammondsworth: Penguin.

Rosenberg, N. 1982. *Inside the Black Box*. Cambridge: Cambridge University Press.

Rothengatter, W. 2009. *European Transport in a Competitive Market*. Expert Workshop on 'Getting into the Right Lane for 2050'. Den Haag: Rijksinstituut voor Volksgezondheid en Milieubekeer (RIVM).

Rotmans, J. 2003. *Transitiemanagement: sleutel voor een duurzame samenleving*. Assen: Van Gorcum.

Rotmans, J. 2005. *Societal Innovation: Between Dream and Reality Lies Complexity*. Inaugural Address. Rotterdam: Erasmus Research Institute of Management, Erasmus University Rotterdam.

Rotmans, J. and Kemp, R. 2008. Detour Ahead: A Response to Shove and Walker about the Perilous Road of Transition Management', *Environment and Planning A* 40, 1006–11.

Rotmans, J., Kemp, R. and Asselt, M. 2001. More Evolution than Revolution: Transition Management in Public Policy Foresight. *The Journal of Futures Studies, Strategic Thinking and Policy* 3(1), 15–31.

Rotmans, J., Kemp, R., van Asselt, M., Geels, F., Verbong, G. and Molendijk, K. 2000. *Transitions and Transition Management: The Case of an Emission-poor Energy Supply*. ICIS/MERIT Report. Maastricht: International Centre for Integrative Studies (ICIS) and Maastricht Economic Research Institute on Innovation and Technology (MERIT).

Rotmans, J. and Loorbach, D. 2006. Transition Management: Reflexive Steering of Societal Complexity through Searching, Learning and Experimenting. In, *The Transition to Renewable Energy: Theory and Practice*, edited by J.C.J.M. van den Bergh and F.R. Bruinsma. Cheltenham: Edward Elgar, 15–46.

Rotmans, J. and Loorbach, D. 2009. Complexity and Transition Management. *Journal of Industrial Ecology* 13, 184–96.

Rouwette, E.A.J.A., Vennix, J.A.M. and Van Mullekom, T. 2002. Group Model Building Effectiveness: A Review of Assessment Studies. *System Dynamics Review* 18(1), 5–45.

Ruttan, V.W. 1959. Usher and Schumpeter on Invention, Innovation and Technological Change. *Quarterly Journal of Economics* 73, 596–606.

Rye, T., Gaunt, M. and Ison, S. 2008. Edinburgh's Congestion Charging Plans: An Analysis of Reasons for Non-implementation. *Transportation Planning and Technology* 31, 641–61.

Sabatier, P.A. 1988. An Advocacy Coalition Framework of Policy Change and the Role of Policy-oriented Learning therein. *Policy Sciences* 21, 129–68.

Saltelli, A., Tarantola, S., Campolongo, F. and Ratto, M. 2004. *Sensitivity Analysis in Practice: A Guide to Assessing Scientific Models*. New York: John Wiley and Sons.

Sammer, G., Gruber, C. and Röschel, G. 2006. *Quality of Information and Knowledge about Mode Attributes in Mode Choice*. Paper presented at the 11th International Conference on Travel Behavior Research, 16–20 August 2006, Kyoto.

Samuelson, W. and Zeckhauser, R. 1988. Status Quo Bias in Decision Making. *Journal of Risk and Uncertainty* 1, 7–59.

Sanderson, I. 2000. Evaluation in Complex Policy Systems, *Evaluation* 6(4), 433–54.

Saxe, M., Folkesson, A. and Alvfors, P. 2007. A Follow-up and Conclusive Report on the Attitude towards Hydrogen Fuel Cell Busses in the CUTE Project – From Passengers in Stockholm to Bus Operators in Europe. *International Journal of Hydrogen Energy* 32(17), 4295–305.

Schade, J. and Schlag, B. 2003. Acceptability of Urban Transport Pricing Strategies. *Transportation Research F* 9, 45–61.

Schäfer, A., Heywood, J.B., Jacoby, H.D. and Waitz, I.A. 2009. *Transportation in a Climate Constrained World*. Cambridge USA: MIT Press.

Schaller, B. 2010. New York City's Congestion Pricing Experience and Implications for Road Pricing Acceptance in the United States. *Transport Policy* 17, 266–73.

Schlich, R. and Axhausen, K.W. 2003. Habitual Travel Behaviour: Evidence from a Six-week Travel Diary. *Transportation* 30, 13–36.

Scholten, H.J. and Stillwell, J. 1990. *Geographical Information Systems for Urban and Regional Planning*. Dordrecht: Kluwer.

Schuitema, G., Steg, L. and Forward, S. 2010. Explaining Differences in Acceptability Before and Acceptance After the Implementation of a Congestion Charge in Stockholm. *Transportation Research A* 44(2), 99–109.

Schuitema, G., Steg, L. and Rothengatter, J.A. 2010. The Acceptability, Personal Outcome Expectations, and Expected Effects of Transport Pricing Policies. *Journal of Environmental Psychology* 30(4), 587–59.

Schultz, P.W. 2001. The Structure of Environmental Concern: Concern for Self, Other People, and the Biosphere. *Journal of Environmental Psychology* 21(4), 327–39.

Schumpeter, J.A. 1939. *Business Cycles. A Theoretical, Historical and Statistical Analysis of the Capitalist Process*. McGraw-Hill, New York-London.

Seiffert, U. and Walzer, P. 1989. *Automobiltechnik der Zukunft*. Düsseldorf: VDI-Verlag.

Senge, P. 1999. *The Fifth Discipline. The Art and Practice of the Learning Organization*. New York: Doubleday.

Sevdalis, N. and Harvey, N. 2006. Determinants of Willingness to Pay in Separate and Joint Evaluations of Options: Context Matters. *Journal of Economic Psychology* 27, 377–85.

Shiftan, Y., Albert, G. and Keinan, T. 2012. The Impact of Company-Car Taxation Policy on Travel Behavior, *Transport Policy* 19, 139–46.

Shiftan, Y. and Suhrbier, J. 2002. The Analysis of Travel and Emission Impacts of Travel Demand Management Strategies Using Activity-based Models. *Transportation* 29(2), 145–68.

Shove, E. 2004. Sustainability, System Innovation and the Laundry. In, *System Innovation and the Transition to Sustainability: Theory, Evidence and Policy*, edited by Elzen, B., Geels, F. and Green, K. Cheltenham, UK: Edward Elgar, 76–94.

Shove, E. and Walker, G. 2007. CAUTION! Transitions Ahead: Politics, Practice, and Sustainable Transition Management. *Environment and Planning* A 39, 763–70.

Shove, E. and Walker, G. 2008. Transition Management and the Politics of Shape Shifting, *Environment and Planning A* 40, 1012–14.

Siegrist, M. 1999. A Causal Model Explaining the Perception and Acceptance of Gene Technology. *Journal of Applied Social Psychology* 10, 2093–106.

Siegrist, M. and Cvertkovich, G. 2000. Perception of Hazards: The Role of Social Trust and Knowledge. *Risk Analysis* 20, 713–19.

Sloman, L., Cairns, S., Newson, C., Anable, J., Pridmore, A. and Goodwin, P. 2010. *The Effects of Smarter Choice Programmes in the Sustainable Travel Towns: Summary Report*. London: Department for Transport (UK).

Smeed, R.J. 1964. *Road Pricing – The Economic and Technical Possibilities*. Report of a Commission chaired by Her Majesty's Stationary Service. London: HMSO.

Smith, A. and Kern, F. 2007. The Transitions Discourse in Dutch Energy Policy: Reinvigorating Ecological Modernisation? *Keynote Paper Presented at the 7th International Summer Academy on Technology Studies*, 27–31 August 2007, Deutschlandsberg, Austria.

Smith, A. and Stirling, A. 2008. *Social-ecological Resilience and Socio-technical Transitions: Critical Issues for Sustainability Governance*. STEPS Working Paper 8, Brighton: STEPS Centre. Available from: www.steps-centre.org/ourresearch/resilience.html [Accessed: 26 September 2010].

Smith, E.R. and Decoster, J. 2000. Dual-process Models in Social and Cognitive Psychology: Conceptual Integration and Links to Underlying Memory Systems. *Personality and Social Psychology Review* 4, 108–31.

Socialistische Partij (SP) 2006. *Een beter Nederland, voor hetzelfde geld. Verkiezingsprogramma 2006–2010 (The Netherlands improved, for the same budget. Election manifesto 2006–2010)* [Online]. Available from: www.sp.nl/2006/programma [Accessed: 26 September 2010].

Socialistische Partij (SP) 2010a. *Dossier kilometerheffing (File kilometre charging)*. Available from: www.sp.nl/geld/dossier/65/kilometerheffing.html [Accessed: 26 September 2010].

Socialistische Partij (SP) 2010b. *Standpunt kilometerheffing (Position kilometre charging)*. Available from: www.sp.nl/standpunten/cd_198/standpunt_over_kilometerheffing.html [Accessed: 9 November 2010].

Socolow, R., Pacala, S. and Greenblatt, J. 2004. *Wedges: Early Mitigation with Familiar Technology.* Proceedings of the 7th International Conference on Greenhouse Gas Control Technology (GHGT-7), 5–9 September 2004, Vancouver.

Sondeijker, S. 2009. *Imagining Sustainability: Methodological Building Blocks for Transition Scenarios*. PhD thesis. Rotterdam: Erasmus University Rotterdam.

Sondeijker, S., Geurts, J., Rotmans, J. and Tukker, A. 2006. Imagining Sustainability: The Added Value of Transition Scenarios in Transition Management. *Foresight* 8(5), 15–30.

Spaargaren, G. 2003. Sustainable Consumption: A Theoretical and Environmental Policy Perspective. *Society and Natural Resources* 16, 687–701.

Spitsmijden. 2007a. *The Effects of Rewards in Spitsmijden 2. Summary.* Available from: http://www.spitsmijden.nl [Accessed: 9 August 2010].

Spitsmijden. 2007b. *Leerervaringen Spitsmijden.* Available from: http://www.spitsmijden.nl [Accessed: 9 August 2010].

Stapleton, J. and Constable, P. 1997. *DSDM: A Framework for Business Centered Development.* Boston: Addison-Wesley.

Statistics Netherlands. 2008. *StatLine – Online Database of Statistics Netherlands* (www.statline.nl).

Stead, D. and Geerlings, H. 2005. Integrating Transport, Land Use Planning and Environment Policy in Denmark, Germany and England: From Theory to Practice. *Innovation* 18(4), 443–53.

Stead, D., Geerlings, H. and Meijers, E. 2004. *Integrating Transport, Land Use Planning and Environment Policy in Denmark, Germany and England: From Theory to Practice.* Delft University Press.

Steg, L., Geurs, K. and Ras, M. 2001. Motives in Transport Models: Can they be Ignored? In, *Travel Behavior Research. The Leading Edge*, edited by Hensher, D. Oxford: Pergamon.

Stern, N. 2006. *Stern Review on the Economics of Climate Change. Executive Summary.* Cambridge: Cambridge University Press.

Stern, P.C., Aronson, E., Darley, J.M., Kempton, W., Hill, D.H., Hirst, E. and Wilbanks, T.J. 1987. Answering Behavioral Questions about Energy Efficiency in Buildings. *Energy* 12(5), 339–53.

Stichting Natuur en Milieu (SNM). 2009. *Kilometerprijs: je betaalt wat je rijdt* (Kilometre pricing: you pay for how far you drive) Available from: www.natuurenmilieu.nl/page.php?pageID=80&itemID=5179&themaID=3 [Accessed: 26 September 2010].

Stillwell, J., Geertman, S. and Openshaw, S. 1999. *Geographical Information and Planning*. Heidelberg: Springer Verlag.

Strahan, D. 2008. *The Last Oil Shock*. London: John Murray.

Strang, D. and Meyer, J.W. 1993. Institutional Conditions for Diffusion. *Theory and Society* 22(4), 487–511.

Struben, J. and Sterrman, J.D. 2008. Transition Challenges for Alternative Fuel Vehicle and Transportation Systems. *Environment and Planning B: Planning and Design* 35(6) 1070–97.

Sturup, S. and Low, N.P. 2008. *OMEGA Project Methodology, Comparative Research and the Hypothesis Led Questions*. OMEGA Working Paper 3. Melbourne: GAMUT, University of Melbourne.

Susilo, Y.O. and Maat, K. 2007. The Influence of Built Environment to the Trends in Commuting Journeys in the Netherlands. *Transportation* 34(5), 589–609.

Susilo, Y.O. and Stead, D. 2007. Urban Form, Vehicle Emissions and Energy Use of Commuters in the Netherlands. *Proceedings of the eceee Summer Study, 4–9 June 2007*. European Council for an Energy Efficient Economy (eceee), Stockholm.

Susilo, Y.O. and Stead, D. 2008. Urban Form and the Trends of Transport Emissions and Energy Consumption in the Netherlands. *Transportation Research Record* 2139, 142–52.

Te Brömmelstroet, M. 2010. Equip the Warrior Instead of Manning the Equipment: Land Use and Transport Planning Support in the Netherlands. *Journal of Transport and Land Use* 3, 25–41.

Te Brömmelstroet, M. and Schrijnen, P.M. 2010. From Planning Support Systems to Mediated Planning Support: A Structured Dialogue to Overcome the Implementation Gap. *Environment and Planning B: Planning and Design* 37, 3–20.

Teisman, G.R. 2005. *Publiek Management op de grens van Orde en Chaos*. Den Haag: SDU.

Teisman, G., Van Buuren, A. and Gerrits, L (eds). 2009. *Managing Complex Governance Systems; Dynamics, Self-organization and Coevolution in Public Investments*. London: Routledge.

Ter Huurne, E.F.J. 2008. *Information Seeking in a Risky World*. PhD Thesis. Enschede: Universiteit Twente.

Tertoolen, G. 1998. Psychological Resistance Against Attempts to Reduce Private Car Use. *Transport Research* 32(3).

Topp, H.H. 1995. A Critical Review of Current Illusions in Traffic Management and Control. *Transport Policy* 2(1), 33–42.

Train, K. 2003. *Discrete Choice Methods with Simulation*. Cambridge University Press.

Transport Direct 2008. *Carbon Emission Assumptions*. Transport Direct. Available from: http://www.transportdirect.info/Downloads/TransportDirectCO2Data.pdf [Accessed: 30 January 2010].

Transport for London (TfL) 2006. *Transport 2025: Transport Vision for a Growing World City*. London: Transport for London.

Transport for London (TfL) 2007a. *Congestion Charging Fifth Annual Monitoring Report*. London: Transport for London.

Transport for London (TfL) 2007b. *Annual Monitoring Report*. London: Transport for London.

Transport for London (TfL) 2009. *The Mayor's Transport Strategy*. London: Transport for London.

Transportation Research Board (TRB) 1997. *A Guidebook for Forecasting Freight Transport Demand*. NCHRP Report 388. Washington, D.C.: Transportation Research Board.

Transportation Research Board (TRB) 2004. *A New Vision for Mobility: Guidance to Foster Collaborative Multimodal Decision Making*. Washington, D.C.: Transportation Research Board.

Transportation Research Board (TRB) 2008. *Sustainable Transportation Indicators: A Recommended Research Program for Developing Sustainable Transportation Indicators and Data Report ADD40[1]*. Washington, D.C.: Transportation Research Board.

Transportation Research Board (TRB) 2010. *Report of the TRB Innovations in Freight Modelling Task Force*. Washington, D.C.: Transportation Research Board.

TransportMistra. 2007. Impact – IMplementation Paths for ACTion towards sustainable mobility. Available from: www.Mistra.Org/Program/Mobility/Impact/Home.4.58b55df710900f8463c800022822.Html [Accessed: 25 November 2009].

Tukker, A., Charter, M., Vezzoli, C., Stø, I. and Andersen. M.M. 2009. *System Innovation for Sustainability 1*. Sheffield: Greenleaf Publishing.

Ulrich, W. 1983. *Critical Heuristics of Social Planning. A New Approach to Practical Philosophy*. Bern: Haupt.

Ulrich, W. 2003. Beyond Methodology Choice: Critical Systems Thinking as Critically Systemic Discourse. *Journal of the Operational Research Society* 54, 325–42.

United Nations Commission on Environment and Development (UNCED) 1980. *World Conservation Strategy*. UNCED, New York.

United Nations Commission on Environment and Development (UNCED) 1992. *The Declaration of Rio: Agenda 21*. UNCED, New York.

Uran, O. and Janssen, R. 2003. Why are Spatial Decision Support Systems Not Used? Some Experiences from the Netherlands. *Computers, Environment and Urban Systems* 27, 511–26.

Urry, J. 2000. *Sociology Beyond Societies*. London: Routledge.

Urry, J. 2004. The 'System' of Automobility. *Theory, Culture and Society* 21(4/5), 25–39.

Urry, J. 2007. *Mobilities*. Cambridge: Polity Press.

Valente, T.W. 1995. *Networks Models of the Diffusion of Innovations*. Cresskill: Hampton Press.

Valente, T.W. 1996. Social Network Thresholds in the Diffusion of Innovations. *Social Networks* 18, 69–89.

Van Aken, J.E. 2004. Management Research Based on the Paradigm of the Design Sciences: The Quest for Field-tested and Grounded Technological Rules. *Journal of Management Studies* 41(2), 219–46.

Van Aken, J.E. 2005. Management Research as a Design Science: Articulating the Research Products of Mode 2 Knowledge Production in Management. *British Journal of Management* 16(1), 19–36.

Van de Lindt, M. and Van den Bosch, S. 2007. *Raamwerk Transitioneren. Bijlage bij werksessie transitioneren Europese Netwerken*, 21 November 2007, Nijmegen. Internal document. Delft/Rotterdam: TNO/DRIFT.

Van den Belt, M. 2004. *Mediated Modeling: A System Dynamics Approach to Environmental Consensus Building*. Washington, D.C.: Island Press.

Van den Bosch, S. 2010. *Transition Experiments: Exploring Societal Changes towards Sustainability*, PhD Thesis. Rotterdam: Erasmus University Rotterdam.

Van den Bosch, S. and Rotmans, J. 2008. *Deepening, Broadening and Scaling up: A Framework for Steering Transition Experiments*. Essay 02. Delft/Rotterdam: Knowledge Centre for Sustainable System Innovations and Transitions (KCT). Available from: http://repub.eur.nl/resource/pub_15812/index.html [Accessed: 23 November 2010].

Van den Bosch, S. and Taanman, M. 2006. *How Innovation Impacts Society. Patterns and Mechanisms through which Innovation Projects Contribute to Transitions*. Paper presented at the International ProAct conference 'Innovation pressure – Rethinking Competitiveness, Policy and the Society in a Globalised Economy', 15–17 March 2006, Tampere.

Van den Brink, R. and Van Wee, G.P. 1997. *Energiegebruik en emissies per vervoerwijze. (Energy Use and Emissions by Transport Mode)*. RIVM Report 773002007. Bilthoven: National Institute for Public Health and the Environment (RIVM).

Van der Bijl, R. and Witsen, P.P. 2000. *Probleemoplossers Versus Toekomstdenkers. Blauwe Kamer* 4, 28–36.

Van der Sar, J. and Baggen, J. 2005. *Prijsbeleid op de weg in Nederland, een histrorisch overzicht (Pricing on roads in the Netherlands, and historical overview)*. Colloquium Vervoersplanologisch Speurwerk. Antwerpen: CVS.

Van Evert, H., Brog, W. and Erl, E. 2006. Survey Design: The Past, the Present and the Future. In, *Travel Survey Methods – Quality and Future Directions*, edited by Stopher, P. and Stecher, C. London: Elsevier, 75–93.

Van Klaveren, C., Van Praag, B. and Maassen van den Brink, H. 2008. A Public Good Version of the Collective Household Model: An Empirical Approach with an Application to British Household Data. *Review of Economics of the Household* 6, 169–91.

Van Mourik, H., Annema, J.A., Derriks, H.M., Francke, J.M. and Groot, W. 2008. *Verkenning autoverkeer 2012 (Investigating car traffic 2012).* Den Haag: Kennisinstituut voor Mobiliteitsbeleid.

Van Wee, G.P., Bliemer, M., Steg, L. and Verhoef, E. 2008. Conclusions and Directions of Further Research. In, *Pricing in Road Transport. A Multi-disciplinary Perspective,* edited by Verhoef, E., Bliemer, M., Steg, L. and Van Wee, G.P. Cheltenham: Edward Elgar.

Vennix, J., Andersen, D. and Richardson, G. 1997. Group Model Building: Adding More Science to the Craft. *System Dynamics Review* 13(2), 187–201.

Verhoef, E., Bliemer, M., Steg, L. and Van Wee, G.P. (eds) 2008. *Pricing in Road Transport. A Multi-disciplinary Perspective.* Cheltenham: Edward Elgar.

Verweij, S. and Gerrits, L. 2010. *Spannend publieksgericht netwerkmanagement,* work in progress Victoria, Australia: Department of Infrastructure. 2002. *Melbourne 2030: Planning for Sustainable Growth.* Available from: http://www.dse.vic.gov.au/melbourne2030online/downloads/2030_complete.pdf [Accessed: 10 August 2010].

Visschers, V.H.M., Meertens, R.M., Passchier, W.F. and De Vries, N.K. 2007. How Does the General Public Evaluate Risk Information? The Impact of Associations with Other Risks. *Risk Analysis* 27, 715–27.

VNO-NCW 2009. *Commentaar VNO-NCW kilometerprijs (Comment VNO-NCW kilometre pricing).* Available from: www.vnoncw.nl/publicaties/Brieven_en_commentaren/Pages/Commentaar_VNONCW_kilometerprijs_840.aspx [Accessed: 20 September 2010].

Volkspartij voor Vrijheid en Democratie (VVD). 2006. *Voor een samenleving met ambitie. Verkiezingsprogramma VVD 2006 (For an ambitious society. Election manifesto VVD 2006)* Available from: www.verkiezingsprogramma.info/component/option,com_weblinks/catid,19/Itemid,38/ [Accessed: 26 September 2010].

Volkspartij voor Vrijheid en Democratie (VVD). 2009. *Kilometerheffing, no way! (Kilometre Charging, No Way!)* Available from: www.vvd.nl/detail/538 [Accessed: 26 September 2010].

Vonk, G. 2006. *Improving Planning Support; The Use of Planning Support Systems for Spatial Planning.* Utrecht: Nederlandse Geografische Studies.

Vonk, G., Geertman, S. and Schot, P. 2005. Bottlenecks Blocking Widespread Usage of Planning Support Systems. *Environment and Planning A* 37, 909–24.

Voss, J.-P. and Kemp, R. 2006. Sustainability and Reflexive Governance: Introduction. In, J.-P. Voss, Bauknecht, D. and Kemp, R. (eds), *Reflexive Governance for Sustainable Development.* Cheltenham: Edward Elgar, 3–28.

Voss, J.-P., Smith, A. and Grin, J. (eds) 2009. Designing Long-term Policy: Rethinking Transition Management. *Policy Sciences* 42(4), 275–302.

Wachs, M. 1985. When Planners Lie with Numbers. *Journal of the American Planning Association* 55, 476–9.

Waddell, P. 2002. Urbanism: Modeling Urban Development for Land Use, Transportation and Environmental Planning. *Journal of the American Planning Association* 68(3), 297–314.

Walker, W.E.W., Rahman, S.A. and Cave, J. 2001. Adaptive Policies, Policy Analysis, and Policy-making. *European Journal of Operational Research* 128, 282–9.

Wallack, L.M. 1981. Mass Media Campaigns: The Odds Against Finding Behavior Change. *Health Education Quarterly* 8(3), 209–60.

Wegener, M. and Fürst, F. 1999. Land-use Transport Interaction: State of the Art. Deliverable 2a of the TRANSLAND project, Berichte aus dem Institut für Raumplanung, 46. Dortmund: Institut für Raumplanung, Fakultät Raumplanung, Universität Dortmund. Available from: http://129.3.20.41/eps/urb/papers/0409/0409005.pdf [Accessed: 12 September 2010].

Weterings, R., Kuijper, J., Smeets, E., Annokkée, G.J. and Minne, B. 1997. 81 mogelijkheden: Technologie voor duurzame ontwikkeling (81 possibilities: Technology for sustainable development). Delft: TNO report for the Ministerie van Volksgezondheid, Ruimtelijke Ordening en Milieuhygiëne (VROM).

Wiess, P. 2002. Borders in Cyberspace: Conflicting Public Information Policies and their Economic Impacts. US Department of Commerce National Oceanic and Atmospheric Administration, National Weather Service. Available from: http://www.primet.org/documents/weiss%20-%20borders%20in%20cyberspace.htm [Accessed: 2 January 2009].

Wigan, M.R. 1999. Costing and Pricing Transport Data. In, GIS *Technologies for the Transportation Industry*, edited by Perkins, H. Park Ridge IL: The Urban and Regional Information Systems Association, 20–33.

Wigan, M.R. 2005. *What's Wrong with Freight Models?* Proceedings of the AET European Transport Conference, 3–5 September 2005, Strasbourg. Available from: http://www.etcproceedings.org/paper/what-s-wrong-with-freight-models [Accessed: 10 August 2010].

Wigan, M.R. 2006. *Data Observatories and Metadata: Linked Issues in Operation.* Proceedings of the Transportation Research Board 85th Annual General Meeting, 22–6 January 2006, Washington, D.C.

Wigan, M.R. 2008. *Governance and Evidence Based Policy under a National Security Framework*, Proceedings of the Third RSNA Workshop on the Social Implications of National Security, 23–4 July 2008, Canberra.

Wigan, M.R. 2010. Owning Identity – One or Many – Do We Have a Choice? *IEEE Technology and Society Magazine* 29(2) 33–8.

Wigan, M.R. and Grashoff, P. 2010. *Cooperative Web Based Bicycle Routing Database for Trip Planning, Including Dynamic Weather Integration.* Standing International Road Weather Commission (SIRWEC) Conference, 5–7 February 2010, Quebec. Available from: www.sirwec.org/conferences/Quebec/full_paper/23_sirwec_2010_paper_wigan.pdf [Accessed: 10 August 2010].

Wigan, M.R., Kukla, R., Benjamins, M. and Grashoff, P. 2007. *RKB: A Knowledge Base to Support Research Documentation, Data, GIS, and Communications for a Major Rail Freight Project*. AET European Transport Conference, 17–19 October 2007, Leeuwenhorst. Available from: www.etcproceedings.org/paper/download/1852 [Accessed: 10 August 2010].

Wigan, M.R., Rockliffe, N. and Edgar A. 1996. *Pricing Principles for Digital Geographic Data*. FDF Management Report MP9603, Office of Geographic Coordination, Victorian Treasury, Melbourne. Available from: www.mwigan.com/mrw/Downloadable_Publications.html [Accessed: 10 August 2010].

Williams, M. 1979. Firm Size and Operating Costs in Urban Bus Transportation. *The Journal of Industrial Economics* 28(2), 209–18.

Willson, R. 2001. Assessing Communicative Rationality as a Transportation Planning Paradigm. *Transportation* 28, 1–31.

Wolfe, A.K., Bjornstad, D.J., Russell, M. and Kerchner, N.D. 2002. A Framework for Analyzing Dialogues Over the Acceptability of Controversial Technologies. *Science, Technology and Human Values* 27, 134–59.

World Bank. 1996. *Sustainable Development in a Dynamic World*. Washington, D.C.: World Bank.

World Bank. 1999. *Gender and Transport: A Rationale for Action*. The World Bank PremNotes No. 14. Washington, D.C.: World Bank.

World Bank. 2002. *Cities on the Move: A World Bank Urban Transport Strategy Review*. Washington, D.C.: World Bank.

World Business Council for Sustainable Development (WBCSD). 2001. *Mobility 2001 – World Mobility at the End of the Twentieth Century and Its Sustainability*. Geneva: World Business Council for Sustainable Development (Prepared by MIT and Charles River Associates).

World Business Council for Sustainable Development (WBCSD). 2004. *Mobility 2030: Meeting the Challenges to Sustainability*. Geneva: World Business Council for Sustainable Development.

World Commission on Environment and Development (WCED). 1987. *Our Common Future*. Oxford: Oxford University Press.

Wustenhagen, R., Wolsink, M. and Burer, M.J. 2007. Social Acceptance of Renewable Energy Innovation: An Introduction to the Concept. *Energy Policy* 35, 2683–91.

Yetano Roche, M., Mourato, S., Fischedick, M., Pietzner, K. and Viebahn, P. 2010. Public Attitudes towards and Demand for Hydrogen and Fuel Cell Vehicles: A Review of the Evidence and Methodological Implications. *Energy Policy* 38, 5301–10.

Young, R. 1993. Changing Behavior and Making it Stick: The Conceptualization and Management of Conservation Behavior. *Environment and Behavior* 25(4), 485–505.

Young, Y. 2000. New Ways to Promote Pro-environmental Behavior: Expending and Evaluating Motives for Environmentally Responsible Behavior. *Journal of Social Issues* 56(3), 509–26.

Zachariah-Wolff, J.L. and Hemmes, K. 2006. Public Acceptance of Hydrogen in the Netherlands: Two Surveys that Demystify Public Views on a Hydrogen Economy. *Bulletin of Science, Technology and Society* 26, 339–45.

Zapatha, M.A. and Hopkins, L.D. 2007. *Engaging the Future: Forecasts, Scenarios, Plans and Projects*. Cambridge MA: Lincoln Institute of Land Policy.

Index

Page numbers in bold (**183**) refer to a figure or table. Page numbers followed by 'n' (318 n) refer to a note at the bottom of the page

For Product Safety Concerns and Information please contact our EU
representative GPSR@taylorandfrancis.com
Taylor & Francis Verlag GmbH, Kaufingerstraße 24, 80331 München, Germany